Sociology of Religion

Selected Readings

Edited by Roland Robertson

Penguin Books

Penguin Books Inc, 7110 Ambassador Road,
Baltimore, Md 21207, USA
Penguin Books Australia Ltd, Ringwood,
Victoria, Australia

First published 1969
Reprinted 1971, 1972
This selection copyright © Roland Robertson, 1969
Introduction and notes copyright © Roland Robertson, 1969

Made and printed in Great Britain by
Richard Clay (The Chaucer Press) Ltd,
Bungay, Suffolk
Set in Monotype Times

Penguin Education

Sociology of Religion

Edited by Roland Robertson

Penguin Modern Sociology Readings

General Editor

Tom Burns

Advisory Board

Fredrik Barth
Michel Crozier
Ralf Dahrendorf
Erving Goffman
Alvin Gouldner
Eric Hobsbawm
Edmund Leach
David Lockwood
Gianfranco Poggi
Hans Peter Widmaier
Peter Worsley

Contents

Editor's Acknowledgements

I wish to thank Joseph Seldin and Bryan Wilson for their very helpful comments on my efforts to compile this volume of readings. I am particularly indebted to Jenny Robertson for her tireless efforts in such matters as translating and checking.

Introduction

One of the most intriguing intellectual phenomena of the mid-twentieth century is the widespread interest in religion at a time when there is also extensive agreement that religious belief, as traditionally understood, has markedly declined in its *intrinsic* significance for most members of modern societies. This is readily understandable in so far as much public interest in religious matters relates precisely to the efforts of religious people to modify and adapt religious beliefs and institutions in the light of changes occurring in modern societies. The controversies surrounding the publication of Bishop John Robinson's *Honest to God* (1963) and, on an almost global scale, the Papal Encyclical on birth control (1968) fall into this category. More fundamentally, however, intellectual interest in religious beliefs and institutions appears to be part of a generalized concern with problems of meaning and purpose in social life, the foundations of ethics, morals and values, and so on. For the sociologist religion tends to assume great importance precisely in terms of the relationship between these more general aspects of human culture and the apparent decline in religious orthodoxy.

Anthropologists and sociologists of the mid- and late-nineteenth century tended to write of religion principally in terms of its alleged inappropriateness to industrial societies: religion was regarded as a phenomenon whose significance diminished as societies evolved to a more advanced condition. This form of evolutionary thinking was strongly rejected by a number of major sociologists writing from the turn of the 1920s.[1] The most significant figures in this respect were Max Weber and Emile Durkheim, who, although different in their specific interests and in many of their conclusions, had a common desire to comprehend and expose the dominant social and cultural characteristics of industrial societies. Both of these sociologists, although not denying the decline of traditional forms of religion, were highly

1. For a good discussion of the development of positive sociological interest in religion, see R. A. Nisbet (1966).

suspicious of the optimism with which this decline had been treated by the evolutionists. Weber and Durkheim were very much preoccupied with the question of how societies would manage without religion. In Weber's emphasis upon the importance of bureaucratic organizations and rational–legal authority relationships, and the decline in significance of charismatic leadership, in his discussions of the notion of salvation and, most clearly, in his observations on the 'disenchantment' of the modern world we can see parallels with Durkheim's concern with such themes as the major processes of social, economic and political specialization relating to the division of labour; his distinction between the sacred and profane aspects of human societies; his search for modern equivalents of the sacred beliefs and symbols of primitive and pre-industrial societies; and his interest in the problems of group cohesion, individual identity and suicide. These preoccupations which Weber and Durkheim had in common, and which were also the concerns of many of their contemporaries, were closely linked to their specific studies of religion – although Weber wrote very much more than Durkheim on this topic.

During the past ten years or so a number of sociologists have revived this kind of interest in religious phenomena. Although there are again critical differences in perspectives and conclusions, we may see in the work of such sociologists as Peter Berger, Thomas Luckmann, Guy Swanson and Robert Bellah an interest in religious phenomena in the same broad context as that considered by Weber and Durkheim. Each of these sociologists is represented in the pages which follow. It should be noted, however, that the sociology of religion in many respects lay dormant for some thirty or more years following the death of Weber in 1920. During this period sociologists either tended to neglect religious phenomena or to deal with them on a narrow, descriptive basis. There were, of course, exceptions to this; but on the whole the period from the early 1920s to the late 1950s was one in which the sociology of religion languished for want of theoretical sophistication and the pinpointing of challenging themes. In England very little study of religion in modern societies was accomplished; in some other societies, such as France and America, numerous studies were made on the basis of a religious, pastoral interest in understanding the social and cultural circumstances which promoted or inhibited religious commitment and the success of religious organizations. The best developed such interest was the French Catholic one. On the whole, however, these religiously inspired studies have contributed very little to the more genuinely sociological analysis of religion; starting as they did from specific religious assumptions and being relatively uninterested in problems of more general and, to the sociologist, profounder significance. The sociologist as such is *usually* committed to a distinctive and wide-ranging perspective deriving from within his own discipline and to this extent is able to ask questions which relate to all religions on a comparative basis or to distil the main social features of one (or a small group) of religious beliefs and the social processes by and through which the beliefs are maintained and expressed. Similarly the sociologist of religion, as opposed to the *religious sociologist*, is able to illuminate more adequately the relationships between religion and other spheres of society, such as economics, politics and science. The sociologist of religion typically has no over-riding commitment – at least not in his professional publications – to the view that religious commitment of any kind *ought* to influence economic or political behaviour, whereas the person grounding his analysis in a religious perspective obviously does (by definition) have some such view. However, in recent years, studies of the social and cultural significance of religion deriving from religious contexts have become less parochial and more adequate *sociologically* in their procedures. In addition some religious intellectuals both in Western Europe and in the United States have begun to engage with sociologists on themes of common interest.[2] The work of Berger and Bellah reflects this coalescence of interest.[3]

In contrast to sociology, social anthropology did not undergo decline in the quality of studies of religious phenomena. The 1920s and 1930s were, in many ways, the years in which the foundations of modern social anthropology were established. Since then many important studies of religion and associated

2. For an interesting report on the East European Communist situation, see N. Birnbaum (1968).

3. For an extensive discussion see R. Robertson (1970).

phenomena in primitive societies have been undertaken. In the early part of this period such names as Malinowski and Radcliffe-Brown tended to predominate, while in more recent years excellent studies of primitive religion have been undertaken by anthropologists such as Evans-Pritchard, Lienhardt and Worsley. Samples of the work of each of these latter three are presented in this book. During the last few years there has rapidly developed an anthropological perspective owing much to Claude Lévi-Strauss which is principally interested in the structure and meaning of primitive belief systems – in terms of the symbolic significance of primitive beliefs. (See Lévi-Strauss, 1965.)

The importance of religion in generating and/or 'storing' beliefs and values relating to human meaning and human significance, as observed in different ways by the classical sociologists, is currently being revived in the modern period. But given the problematic status of religious belief and religious institutions in the modern world – in the sense of an apparent decline in their social and cultural importance in many societies – sociologists are tending to see the study of religion as but part of a more general sociology of culture and knowledge. Opinions differ as to whether the study of religion should be centred on beliefs in supernatural entities and forces, and the social conditions which are associated with and which facilitate such beliefs; or whether 'religion' should be interpreted in a very wide sense to refer to all basic, fundamental beliefs which have to do with the ultimate problems of human existence – in which case we would have to regard religion as a central and permanent anthropological feature of social life. In this book of readings I have not included very much material on this kind of debate; but I have taken as a point of departure the theme of religion as a major, and historically *the* major, provider of meaning in human societies. The *extent* to which religion is declining in significance in this respect is touched upon at a number of points in this book and is precisely the kind of question which it is hoped will be followed up by the reader.

The compilation of this book has been guided by the following considerations:

(a) the analyses presented should be as up to date as possible, except where older contributions to the field remain influential in the mainstream of the sociology of religion;

(b) the book should try to establish a pattern of concerns which appear to be central to the field as a sociological discipline. Thus I have not tried to maximize coverage of numerous and varied types of focus simply for the sake of giving full representation to what goes on under the heading of the sociology of religion. Rather, I have in the main made selections in terms of my own conception of what constitutes the mainstream, with a special eye on growth-points in the field;

(c) I have taken it as axiomatic that the book should both indicate analytic issues and provide some empirical grounding for the student. In the first case I have considered it necessary to deal with general perspectives in the sociology of religion, as well as more detailed and specific problems of analysis. In respect of providing empirical information I have considered it best to indicate the *range* of empirical phenomena, sometimes in the form of rather wide-ranging interpretive essays, as opposed to minutely descriptive pieces full of facts and figures. In some branches of the sociology of religion such equipment is very necessary. But the intention of this book is to stimulate interest in an inter-related set of problems, not to provide clusters of information on a piecemeal basis;

(d) I *have* tried to attain a wide coverage in respect of the variety of religions and types of society. There are two aspects to this coverage: historical and spatial. There is, then, an emphasis upon sociological comparison of religion in different social and cultural settings. I have tried to get away from the tendency to deal mainly with Western industrial societies and have included rather more anthropological material than is usual in readers on the sociology of religion – which ties in with the effort to stake out a set of central issues, regardless of the types of society involved. Clearly, no relatively short book of readings could adequately cover all major religious forms; but in some way or other most varieties of religion are attended to in this book.

The aim, in sum, has been to provide a core beginning to study in the field of the sociology of religion. The pattern of such a book should ideally, perhaps, represent a definite theoretical

15

scheme of exposition. But in elaborating such a scheme editors tend often to discover that, while they feel confidence in the scheme itself, the material available in the field does not fit very satisfactorily into it. Thus I have compromised in this respect. The book begins with a presentation of some major general perspectives in the field. Then, in Part Two, the reader is confronted with readings which range across a number of societal circumstances in which religion has been or is located. The third part sees a return to theoretical issues – but there the emphasis is more on specific problems, rather than upon general styles of analysis. Finally, in Part Four, there are detailed discussions of particular aspects of the sociology of religion – religion and politics, religion and social class, the analysis of religious movements and the nature of religious authority.

References

BIRNBAUM, N. (1968), 'Eastern Europe and the death of God', in D. R. Cutler, ed., *The Religious Situation: 1968*, Beacon Press, pp. 917–30.

LÉVI-STRAUSS, C. (1965), *The Savage Mind*, Weidenfeld and Nicolson, and the University of Chicago Press.

NISBET, R. A. (1966), *The Sociological Tradition*, Basic Books, pp. 221–63.

PAPAL ENCYCLICAL ON BIRTH CONTROL (1968), *Humanae Vitae*, Catholic Truth Society.

ROBERTSON, R. (1970), *The Sociological Interpretation of Religion*, Blackwell, and Schocken Books.

ROBINSON, J. (1963), *Honest to God*, S.C.M. Press.

Part One General Approaches and Perspectives

The selections in this part indicate the main general perspectives which either have dominated or continue to dominate the sociology of religion. We have noted in the introduction the long-standing and pervasive influence of Weber and Durkheim. The outstanding differences between them were: firstly, Weber was primarily interested in the ways in which different types of social experience, such as those attendant upon social class and social stratum distinctions, were related to different modes of religious expression and belief, whereas Durkheim concentrated upon the *general* social significance of religious expression and belief; secondly, Weber adopted a distinctively historical and dynamic approach to religious beliefs, being above all concerned with the *rationalization* of religious belief systems – the process whereby consistency and rationality were achieved in relation to the contingencies and problems of social life. Durkheim concerned himself very little with historical or evolutionary aspects of this problem; and the manifest importance of his work lies in the ways in which he sees religious belief as synchronized with, indeed for Durkheim *founded upon*, the network of social relations obtaining in a given society. The fact that Durkheim mainly spoke in reference to primitive societies precludes easy comparison of his theories with those of Weber. The relatively undifferentiated nature of social life in a primitive society, which Durkheim deliberately chose in order to elaborate his theory, probably gives an exaggerated mark of divergence to the more sociological, as opposed to the historical, interests of Weber and Durkheim. As Parsons' contribution suggests, Weber and Durkheim were at least interested in the same general kind of sociological problem. Basically this has to do with the problem which social individuals face in respect of the *meaning* of social life. In another sense both were concerned with the problem of how individuals and groups identify themselves in the world – in relation to each other and to the social, cultural and natural conditions of their existence.[1]

Such themes are highlighted and further developed by Berger and Luckmann, mainly in reference to changes in religious culture and religious institutions occurring at the present time. They argue that the sociology of religion has been too preoccupied with religion in the institutional context of churches and denominations. The focus of the sociology of religion should be broad enough, they suggest, to encompass new forms of belief and commitment which serve to maintain the sense of reality and consistency necessary for the continuation of everyday social life.[2] The kind of sociology of religion which they envisage is more ambitious theoretically and philosophically than much of what is currently undertaken by those working in this field. One of their major theses, therefore, is that the sociology of religion should join hands with the sociology of knowledge in exploring a large area of beliefs which have to do with the conditions of man's social existence.

1. A number of the themes mentioned here are codified and elaborated in Bellah's contribution (Reading 16).

2. The most elaborate and satisfying discussion of these problems is contained in Peter Berger, *The Sacred Canopy*, Doubleday, 1967. In Reading 9 Luckmann discusses religious commitment in modern societies in the general context of the views expressed jointly with Berger in Reading 4.

1 M. Weber

Major Features of World Religions

Excerpt from chapter 11 of H. H. Gerth and C. Wright Mills (eds.), *From Max Weber*, Oxford University Press, 1946, pp. 267–87. (First published 1915.)

By 'world religions', we understand the five religions or religiously determined systems of life regulation which have known how to gather multitudes of confessors around them. The term is used here in a completely value-neutral sense. The Confucian, Hinduist, Buddhist, Christian and Islamist religious ethics all belong to the category of world religion. A sixth religion, Judaism, will also be dealt with. It is included because it contains historical preconditions decisive for understanding Christianity and Islamism, and because of its historic and autonomous significance for the development of the modern economic ethic of the Occident – a significance, partly real and partly alleged, which has been discussed several times recently. References to other religions will be made only when they are indispensable for historical connexions.[1]

What is meant by the 'economic ethic' of a religion will become increasingly clear during the course of our presentation. This term does not bring into focus the ethical theories of theological compendia; for however important such compendia may be under certain circumstances, they merely serve as tools of knowledge. The term 'economic ethic' points to the practical impulses for action which are founded in the psychological and

1. 'Die Wirtschaftsethik der Weltreligionen', *Gesammelte Aufsätze zur Religionssoziologie*, vol. 1 (1922–3), pp. 237–68. This is a translation of the Introduction to a series of studies which Weber published as articles in the *Archiv für Sozialforschung* under the title 'Die Wirtschaftsethik der Weltreligionen' (The Economic Ethic of the World Religions). The Introduction and the first parts on Confucianism and Taoism were written in 1913. They were not published until September 1915, in the 41st volume of the *Archiv*.

pragmatic contexts of religions. The following presentation may be sketchy, but it will make obvious how complicated the structures and how many-sided the conditions of a concrete economic ethic usually are. Furthermore, it will show that externally similar forms of economic organization may agree with very different economic ethics and, according to the unique character of their economic ethics, how such forms of economic organization may produce very different historical results. An economic ethic is not a simple 'function' of a form of economic organization; and just as little does the reverse hold, namely, that economic ethics unambiguously stamp the form of the economic organization.

No economic ethic has ever been determined solely by religion. In the face of man's attitudes towards the world – as determined by religious or other (in our sense) 'inner' factors – an economic ethic has, of course, a high measure of autonomy. Given factors of economic geography and history determine this measure of autonomy in the highest degree. The religious determination of life conduct, however, is also one – note this – only one, of the determinants of the economic ethic. Of course, the religiously determined way of life is itself profoundly influenced by economic and political factors operating within given geographical, political, social and national boundaries. We should lose ourselves in these discussions if we tried to demonstrate these dependencies in all their singularities. Here we can only attempt to peel off the directive elements in the life conduct of those social *strata* which have most strongly influenced the practical ethic of their respective religions. These elements have stamped the most characteristic features upon practical ethics, the features that distinguish one ethic from others; *and*, at the same time, they have been important for the respective economic ethics.

By no means must we focus upon only one stratum. Those strata which are decisive in stamping the characteristic features of an economic ethic may change in the course of history. And the influence of a single stratum is never an exclusive one. Nevertheless, as a rule one may determine the strata whose styles of life have been at least predominantly decisive for certain religions. Here are some examples, if one may anticipate:

20

Confucianism was the status ethic of prebendaries, of men with literary educations who were characterized by a secular rationalism. If one did not belong to this *cultured* stratum he did not count. The religious (or if one wishes, irreligious) status ethic of this stratum has determined the Chinese way of life far beyond the stratum itself.

Earlier Hinduism was borne by a hereditary caste of cultured literati, who, being remote from any office, functioned as a kind of ritualist and spiritual advisers for individuals and communities. They formed a stable centre for the orientation of the status stratification, and they placed their stamp upon the social order. Only Brahmans, *educated* in the Veda, formed, as bearers of tradition, the fully recognized religious status group. And only later a non-Brahman status group of ascetics emerged by the side of the Brahmans and competed with them. Still later, during the Indian Middle Ages, Hinduism entered the plain. It represented the ardent sacramental religiosity of the saviour, and was borne by the lower strata with their plebeian mystagogues.

Buddhism was propagated by strictly contemplative, mendicant monks, who rejected the world and, having no homes, migrated. Only these were full members of the religious community; all others remained religious laymen of inferior value: objects, not subjects, of religiosity.

During its first period, Islamism was a religion of world-conquering warriors, a knight order of disciplined crusaders. They lacked only the sexual asceticism of their Christian copies of the age of the Crusades. But during the Islamic Middle Ages, contemplative and mystical Sufism attained at least an equal standing under the leadership of plebeian technicians of orgiastics. The brotherhoods of the petty bourgeoisie grew out of Sufism in a manner similar to the Christian Tertiarians, except they were far more universally developed.

Since the Exile, Judaism has been the religion of a civic 'pariah people'. We shall in time become acquainted with the precise meaning of the term. During the Middle Ages Judaism fell under the leadership of a stratum of intellectuals who were trained in literature and ritual, a peculiarity of Judaism. This stratum has represented an increasingly quasi-proletarian and rationalist petty bourgeois intelligentsia.

Christianity, finally, began its course as a doctrine of itinerant artisan journeymen. During all periods of its mighty external and internal development it has been a quite specifically urban, and above all a civic, religion. This was true during Antiquity, during the Middle Ages and in Puritanism. The city of the Occident, unique among all other cities of the world – and citizenship, in the sense in which it has emerged only in the Occident – has been the major theatre for Christianity. This holds for the pneumatic piety of the ancient religious community, for the mendicant monk orders of the high Middle Ages, and for the (Protestant) sects of the reformation up to pietism and methodism.

It is not our thesis that the specific nature of a religion is a simple 'function' of the social situation of the stratum which appears as its characteristic bearer, or that it represents the stratum's 'ideology', or that it is a 'reflection' of a stratum's material or ideal interest situation. On the contrary, a more basic misunderstanding of the standpoint of these discussions would hardly be possible.

However incisive the social influences, economically and politically determined, may have been upon a religious ethic in a particular case, it receives its stamp primarily from religious sources, and, first of all, from the content of its annunciation and its promise. Frequently the very next generation reinterprets these annunciations and promises in a fundamental fashion. Such reinterpretations adjust the revelations to the needs of the religious community. If this occurs, then it is at least usual that religious doctrines are adjusted to *religious needs*. Other spheres of interest could have only a secondary influence; often, however, such influence is very obvious and sometimes it is decisive.

For every religion we shall find that a change in the socially decisive strata has usually been of profound importance. On the other hand, the type of a religion, once stamped, has usually exerted a rather far-reaching influence upon the life conduct of very heterogeneous strata. In various ways people have sought to interpret the connexion between religious ethics and interest situations in such a way that the former appear as mere 'functions' of the latter. Such interpretation occurs in so-called historical materialism – which we shall not here discuss – as well as in a purely psychological sense.

A quite general and abstract class determination of religious ethics might be deduced from the theory of 'resentment', known since Friedrich Nietzsche's brilliant essay and since then spiritedly treated by psychologists. As is known, this theory regards the moral glorification of mercy and brotherliness as a 'slave revolt in morals' among those who are disadvantaged, either in their natural endowments or in their opportunities as determined by life fate. The ethic of 'duty' is thus considered a product of 'repressed' sentiments for vengeance on the part of banausic men who 'displace' their sentiments because they are powerless, and condemned to work and to money making. They resent the way of life of the lordly stratum who live free of duties. A very simple solution of the most important problems in the typology of religious ethics would obviously result if this were the case. However fortunate and fruitful the disclosure of the psychological significance of resentment as such has been, great caution is necessary in estimating its bearing for social ethics.

Later we shall have to discuss the motives that have determined the different forms of ethical 'rationalization' of life conduct, *per se*. In the main, these have had nothing whatsoever to do with resentment. But that the evaluation of *suffering* in religious ethics has been subject to a typical change is beyond doubt. If properly understood, this change carries a certain justification for the theory first worked out by Nietzsche. The primeval attitude towards suffering has been thrown into relief most drastically during the religious festivities of the community, especially in the treatment of those haunted by disease or other cases of obstinate misfortune. Men, permanently suffering, mourning, diseased or otherwise unfortunate, were, according to the nature of their suffering, believed either to be possessed by a demon or burdened with the wrath of a god whom they had insulted. To tolerate such men in the midst of the cultic community could result in disadvantages for it. In any case, they were not allowed to participate in cultic feasts and sacrifices, for the gods did not enjoy the sight of them and could be incited to wrath by it. The sacrificial feasts were occasions for rejoicing – even in Jerusalem during times of siege.

In treating suffering as a symptom of odiousness in the eyes of the gods and as a sign of secret guilt, religion has psychologically met a very general need. The fortunate is seldom satisfied with the fact of being fortunate. Beyond this, he needs to know that he has a *right* to his good fortune. He wants to be convinced that he 'deserves' it, and above all, that he deserves it in comparison with others. He wishes to be allowed the belief that the less fortunate also merely experience his due. Good fortune thus wants to be 'legitimate' fortune.

If the general term 'fortune' covers all the 'good' of honour, power, possession and pleasure, it is the most general formula for the service of legitimation, which religion has had to accomplish for the external and the inner interests of all ruling men, the propertied, the victorious and the healthy. In short, religion provides the theodicy of good fortune for those who are fortunate. This theodicy is anchored in highly robust ('pharisaical') needs of man and is therefore easily understood, even if sufficient attention is often not paid to its effects.

In contrast, the way in which this negative evaluation of suffering has led to its religious glorification is more complicated. Numerous forms of chastisement and of abstinences from normal diet and sleep, as well as from sexual intercourse, awaken, or at least facilitate, the charisma of ecstatic, visionary, hysterical, in short, of all extraordinary states that are evaluated as 'holy'. Their production therefore forms the object of magical asceticism. The prestige of these chastisements has resulted from the notion that certain kinds of suffering and abnormal states provoked through chastisement are avenues to the attainment of superhuman, that is magical, powers. The ancient prescriptions of taboo and abstinences in the interest of cultic purity, which follow from a belief in demons, have worked in the same direction. The development of cults of 'redemption' has been added to these prescriptions, abstinences and interests. In principle, these cults have occupied an independent and new position in the face of individual suffering. The primeval cult, and above all, the cult of the political associations, have left all individual interests out of consideration. The tribal and local god, the gods of the city and of the empire, have taken care only of interests that have concerned the collectivity as a whole. They have been concerned with rain and with sunshine, with the booty of the hunt and with victory over enemies. Thus, in the community cult, the collectivity as such turned to its god. The individual, in order to avoid or remove evils that concerned himself – above all, sickness – has not turned to the cult of the community, but as an individual he has approached the sorcerer as the oldest personal and 'spiritual adviser'. The prestige of particular magicians, and of those spirits or divinities in whose names they have performed their miracles, has brought them patronage, irrespective of local or of tribal affiliation. Under favourable conditions this has led to the formation of a religious 'community', which has been independent of ethnic associations. Some, though not all, 'mysteries' have taken this course. They have promised the salvation of individuals *qua* individuals from sickness, poverty, and from all sorts of distress and danger. Thus the magician has transformed himself into the mystagogue; that is, hereditary dynasties of mystagogues or organizations of trained personnel under a head determined in accordance with some sort of rules have developed. This head has either been recognized as the incarnation of a superhuman being or merely as a prophet, that is, as the mouthpiece and agent of his god. Collective religious arrangements for individual 'suffering' *per se*, and for 'salvation' from it, have originated in this fashion.

The annunciation and the promise of religion have naturally been addressed to the masses of those who were in need of salvation. They and their interests have moved into the centre of the professional organization for the 'cure of the soul', which, indeed, only therewith originated. The typical service of magicians and priests becomes the determination of the factors to be blamed for suffering, that is, the confession of 'sins'. At first, these sins were offences against ritual commandments. The magician and priest also give counsel for behaviour fit to remove the suffering. The material and ideal interests of magicians and priests could thereby actually and increasingly enter the service of specifically *plebeian* motives. A further step along this course was signified when, under the pressure of typical and ever-recurrent distress, the religiosity of a 'redeemer' evolved. This religiosity presupposed the myth of a saviour, hence (at least relatively) of a *rational* view of the world. Again, suffering became the most important topic. The primitive mythology of nature frequently offered a point of departure for this religiosity. The spirits who governed the coming and going of vegetation and the paths of celestial bodies important for the seasons of the year became the preferred carriers of the myths of the suffering, dying and resurrecting god to needful men. The resurrected god guaranteed the return of good fortune in this world or the security of happiness in the world beyond. Or, a popularized figure from heroic sagas – like Krishna in India – is embellished with the myths of childhood, love and struggle; and such figures became the object of an ardent cult of the saviour. Among people under political pressure, like the Israelites, the title of 'saviour' (Moshuach name) was originally attached to the saviours from political distress, as transmitted by hero sagas (Gideon, Jephthah). The 'Messianic' promises were determined by these sagas. With this people, and in this clear-cut fashion only among them and under other very particular conditions, the suffering of a people's *community*, rather than the suffering of an individual, became the object of hope for religious salvation. The rule was that the saviour bore an individual and universal character at the same time that he was ready to guarantee salvation for the *individual* and to every individual who would turn to him.

The figure of the saviour has been of varying stamp. In the late form of Zoroastrianism with its numerous abstractions, a purely constructed figure assumed the role of the mediator and saviour in the economy of salvation. The reverse has also occurred: a historical person, legitimized through miracles and visionary reappearances, ascends to the rank of saviour. Purely historical factors have been decisive for the realization of these very different possibilities. Almost always, however, some kind of theodicy of suffering has originated from the hope for salvation.

The promises of the religions of salvation at first remained tied to ritualist rather than to ethical preconditions. Thus, for instance, both the worldly and the other worldly advantages of the Eleusinian mysteries were tied to ritual purity and to attendance at the Eleusinian mass. When law gained in significance, these special deities played an increasing role, and the task of protecting the traditional order, of punishing the unjust and rewarding the righteous, was transferred to them as guardians of juridical procedure.

Where religious development was decisively influenced by a prophecy, naturally 'sin' was no longer a mere magical offence. Above all, it was a sign of disbelief in the prophet and in his commandments. Sin figured as the basic cause of all sorts of misfortunes.

The prophet has not regularly been a descendant or a representative of depressed classes. The reverse, as we shall see, has almost always been the rule. Neither has the content of the prophet's doctrine been derived preponderantly from the intellectual horizon of the depressed classes. As a rule, however, the oppressed, or at least those threatened by distress, were in need of a redeemer and prophet; the fortunate, the propertied, the ruling strata were not in such need. Therefore, in the great majority of cases, a prophetically announced religion of redemption has had its permanent locus among the less-favoured social strata. Among these, such religiosity has either been a substitute for, or a rational supplement to, magic.

Wherever the promises of the prophet or the redeemer have not sufficiently met the needs of the socially less-favoured strata, a secondary salvation religion of the masses has regularly developed beneath the official doctrine. The rational conception of the world is contained in germ within the myth of the redeemer. A rational theodicy of misfortune has, therefore, as a rule, been a development of this conception of the world. At the same time, this rational view of the world has often furnished suffering as such with a 'plus' sign, which was originally quite foreign to it.

Suffering, voluntarily created through mortification, changed its meaning with the development of ethical divinities who punish and reward. Originally, the magical coercion of spirits by the formula of prayer was increased through mortification as a source of charismatic states. Such coercion was preserved in mortification by prayer as well as in cultic prescriptions of abstinence. This has remained the case, even after the magical formula for coercing spirits became a supplication to be heard by a deity. Penances were added as a means of cooling the wrath of deities by repentance, and of avoiding through self-punishment the sanctions that have been incurred. The numerous abstinences were originally attached to the mourning for the dead (with special clarity in China) in order to turn away their jealousy and wrath. These abstinences were easily transferred to relations with the appropriate divinities; they made self-mortification, and finally, unintentional deprivation as such, appear more pleasing to the gods than the naïve enjoyment of the goods of this earth. Such enjoyment, indeed, made the pleasure-seeking man less accessible to the influence of the prophet or the priest.

The force of all these individual factors was tremendously enhanced under certain conditions.

The need for an ethical interpretation of the 'meaning' of the distribution of fortunes among men increased with the growing rationality of conceptions of the world. As the religious and ethical reflections upon the world were increasingly rationalized, and primitive and magical notions were eliminated, the theodicy of suffering encountered increasing difficulties. Individually 'undeserved' woe was all too frequent; not 'good' but 'bad' men succeeded – even when 'good' and 'bad' were measured by the yardstick of the master stratum and not by that of a 'slave morality'.

One can explain suffering and injustice by referring to individual sin committed in a former life (the migration of souls), to the guilt of ancestors, which is avenged down to the third and fourth generation, or – the most principled – to the wickedness of all creatures *per se*. As compensatory promises, one can refer to hopes of the individual for a better life in the future in this world (transmigration of souls) or to hopes for the successors (Messianic realm), or to a better life in the hereafter (paradise).

The metaphysical conception of God and of the world, which the ineradicable demand for a theodicy called forth, could produce only a few systems of ideas on the whole – as we shall see, only three. These three gave rationally satisfactory answers to the questioning for the basis of the incongruity between destiny and merit: the Indian doctrine of Karma, Zoroastrian dualism and the predestination decree of the *deus absconditus*. These solutions are rationally closed; in pure form, they are found only as exceptions.

The rational need for a theodicy of suffering and of dying has had extremely strong effects. As a matter of fact, this need has moulded important traits of such religions as Hinduism, Zoro-astrism and Judaism, and, to a certain extent, Paulinian and later Christianity. Even as late as 1906, a mere minority among a rather considerable number of proletarians gave as reasons for their disbelief in Christianity conclusions derived from modern theories of natural sciences. The majority, however, referred to the 'injustice' of the order of this world – to be sure, essentially because they believed in a revolutionary compensation in this world.

The theodicy of suffering can be coloured by resentment. But the need of compensation for the insufficiency of one's fate in this world has not, as a rule, had resentment as a basic and decisive colour. Certainly, the need for vengeance has had a special affinity with the belief that the unjust are well off in this world only because hell is reserved for them later. Eternal bliss is reserved for the pious; occasional sins, which, after all, the pious also commit, ought therefore to be expiated in this world. Yet one can readily be convinced that even this way of thinking, which occasionally appears, is not always determined by resentment, and that it is by no means always the product of socially oppressed strata. We shall see that there have been only a few examples of religion to which resentment contributed essential features. Among these examples only one is a fully developed case. All that can be said is that resentment *could* be, and often and everywhere has been, significant as one factor, among others, in influencing the religiously determined rationalism of socially disadvantaged strata. It has gained such significance, in highly diverse and often minute degrees, in accordance with the nature of the promises held out by different religions.

In any case, it would be quite wrong to attempt to deduce 'ascetism' in general from these sources. The distrust of wealth and power, which as a rule exists in genuine religions of salvation, has had its natural basis primarily in the experience of redeemers, prophets and priests. They understood that those strata which were 'satiated' and favoured in this world had only a small urge to be saved, regardless of the kind of salvation offered. Hence, these master strata have been less 'devout' in the sense of salvation religions. The development of a rational religious ethic has had positive and primary roots in the inner conditions of those social strata which were less socially valued.

Strata in solid possession of social honour and power usually tend to fashion their status legend in such a way as to claim a special and intrinsic quality of their own, usually a quality of blood; their sense of dignity feeds on their actual or alleged being. The sense of dignity of socially repressed strata or of strata whose status is negatively (or at least not positively) valued is nourished most easily on the belief that a special 'mission' is entrusted to them; their worth is guaranteed or constituted by an *ethical imperative* or by their own functional *achievement*. Their value is thus moved into something beyond themselves, into a 'task' placed before them by God. One source of the ideal power of ethical prophecies among socially disadvantaged strata lies in this fact. Resentment has not been required as a leverage; the rational interest in material and ideal compensations as such has been perfectly sufficient.

There can be no doubt that prophets and priests through intentional or unintentional propaganda have taken the resentment of the masses into their service. But this is by no means always the case. This essentially negative force of resentment, so far as is known, has never been the source of those essentially metaphysical conceptions which have lent uniqueness to every salvation religion. Moreover, in general, the nature of a religious promise has by no means necessarily or even predominantly been the mere mouthpiece of a class interest, either of an external or internal nature.

By themselves, the masses, as we shall see, have everywhere remained engulfed in the massive and archaic growth of magic – unless a prophecy that holds out specific promises has swept them into a religious movement of an ethical character. For the rest, the specific nature of the great religious and ethical systems has been determined by social conditions of a far more particular nature than by the mere contrast of ruling and ruled strata.

In order to avoid repetition, some further comments about these relationships may be stated in advance. For the empirical student, the sacred values, differing among themselves, are by no means only, nor even preferably, to be interpreted as 'other-worldly'. This is so quite apart from the fact that not every religion, nor every world religion, knows of a 'beyond' as a locus of definite promises. At first the sacred values of primitive as well as of cultured, prophetic or non-prophetic, religions were quite solid goods of this world. With only the partial exception of Christianity and a few other specifically ascetic creeds, they have consisted of health, a long life and wealth. These were offered by the promises of the Chinese, Vedic, Zoroastrian, ancient Hebrew and Islamite religions; and in the same manner by the Phoenician, Egyptian, Babylonian and ancient Germanic religions, as well as by the promises of Hinduism and Buddhism for the devout laymen. Only the religious virtuoso, the ascetic, the monk, the Sufi, the Dervish strove for sacred values, which were 'other-worldly' as compared with such solid goods of this world, as health, wealth and long life. And these other-wordly sacred values were by no means only values of the *beyond*. This was not the case even where it was understood to be so by the participants. Psychologically considered, man in quest of salvation has been primarily preoccupied by attitudes of the here and now. The puritan *certitudo salutis*, the permanent state of grace that rests in the feeling of 'having proved oneself', was psychologically the only concrete object among the sacred values of this ascetic religion. The Buddhist monk, certain to enter Nirvana, seeks the sentiment of a cosmic love; the devout Hindu seeks either Bhakti (fervent love in the possession of God) or apathetic ecstasy. The Chlyst with his radjeny, as well as the dancing Dervish, strives for orgiastic ecstasy. Others seek to be possessed by God and to possess God, to be a bridegroom of the Virgin Mary, or to be the bride of the Saviour. The Jesuit's cult of the heart of Jesus, quietistic edification, the pietists' tender love for the child Jesus and its 'running sore', the sexual and semi-sexual orgies at the wooing of Krishna, the sophisticated cultic dinners of the Valla-bhacharis, the gnostic onanist cult activities, the various forms of the *unio mystica* and the contemplative submersion in the All-one – these states undoubtedly have been sought, first of all, for the sake of such emotional value as they directly offered the devout. In this respect, they have in fact been absolutely equal to the religious and alcoholic intoxication of the Dionysian or the soma cult; to totemic meat-orgies, the cannibalistic feasts, the ancient and religiously consecrated use of hashish, opium and nicotine; and, in general, to all sorts of magical intoxication. They have been considered specifically consecrated and divine

31

because of their psychic extraordinariness and because of the intrinsic value of the respective states conditioned by them. Even the most primitive orgy has not entirely lacked a meaningful interpretation, although only the rationalized religions have imputed a metaphysical meaning into such specifically religious actions, in addition to the direct appropriation of sacred values. Rationalized religions have thus sublimated the orgy into the 'sacrament'. The orgy, however, has had a pure animist and magical character; it has contained only small or, indeed, no beginnings of the universalist, cosmic pragmatism of the holy. And such pragmatism is peculiar to all religious rationalism.

Yet even after such a sublimation of orgy into sacrament has occurred, the fact remains, of course, that for the devout the sacred value, first and above all, has been a psychological state in the *here and now*. Primarily this state consists in the emotional attitude *per se*, which was directly called forth by the specifically religious (or magical) act, by methodical asceticism or by contemplation.

As extraordinary attitudes, religious states can be only transient in character and in external appearance. Originally, this of course, was everywhere the case. The only way of distinguishing between 'religious' and 'profane' states is by referring to the extraordinary character of the religious states. A special state, attained by religious means, can be striven for as a 'holy state' which is meant to take possession of the entire man and of his lasting fate. The transition from a passing to a permanent holy state has been fluid.

The two highest conceptions of sublimated religious doctrines of salvation are 'rebirth' and 'redemption'. Rebirth, a primeval magical value, has meant the acquisition of a new soul by means of an orgiastic act or through methodically planned asceticism. Man transitorily acquired a new soul in ecstasy; but by means of magical asceticism, he could seek to gain it permanently. The youth who wished to enter the community of warriors as a hero, or to participate in its magical dances or orgies, or who wished to commune with the divinities in cultic feasts, had to have a new soul. The heroic and magical asceticism, the initiation rites of youths and the sacramental customs of rebirth at important phases of private and collective life are thus quite ancient. The means used in these activities varied, as did their ends: that is, the answers to the question, 'For what should I be reborn?'

The various religious or magical states that have given their psychological stamp to religions may be systematized according to very different points of view. Here we shall not attempt such a systematization. In connexion with what we have said, we merely wish to indicate quite generally the following.

The kind of empirical state of bliss or experience of rebirth that is sought after as the supreme value by a religion has obviously and necessarily varied according to the character of the stratum which was foremost in adopting it. The chivalrous warrior class, peasants, business classes and intellectuals with literary education have naturally pursued different religious tendencies. As will become evident, these tendencies have not by themselves determined the psychological character of religion; they have, however, exerted a very lasting influence upon it. The contrast between warrior and peasant classes, and intellectual and business classes, is of special importance. Of these groups, the intellectuals have always been the exponents of a rationalism which in their case has been relatively theoretical. The business classes (merchants and artisans) have been at least possible exponents of rationalism of a more practical sort. Rationalism of either kind has borne very different stamps, but has always exerted a great influence upon the religious attitude.

Above all, the peculiarity of the intellectual strata in this matter has been in the past of the greatest importance for religion. At the present time, it matters little in the development of a religion whether or not modern intellectuals feel the need of enjoying a 'religious' state as an 'experience', in addition to all sorts of other sensations, in order to decorate their internal and stylish furnishings with paraphernalia guaranteed to be genuine and old. A religious revival has never sprung from such a source. In the past, it was the work of the intellectuals to sublimate the possession of sacred values into a belief in 'redemption'. The conception of the idea of redemption, as such, is very old, if one understands by it a liberation from distress, hunger, drought, sickness and ultimately from suffering and death. Yet redemption attained a specific significance only where it expressed a systematic and rationalized 'image of the world' and represented a stand in the face of the world. For the meaning as well as the intended and actual psychological quality of redemption has depended upon such a world image and such a stand. Not ideas, but material and ideal interests, directly govern men's conduct. Yet very frequently the 'world images' that have been created by 'ideas' have, like switchmen, determined the tracks along which action has been pushed by the dynamic of interest. 'From what' and 'for what' one wished to be redeemed and, let us not forget, 'could be' redeemed, depended upon one's image of the world.

There have been very different possibilities in this connexion: one could wish to be saved from political and social servitude and lifted into a Messianic realm in the future of this world; or one could wish to be saved from being defiled by ritual impurity and hope for the pure beauty of psychic and bodily existence. One could wish to escape being incarcerated in an impure body and hope for a purely spiritual existence. One could wish to be saved from the eternal and senseless play of human passions and desires and hope for the quietude of the pure beholding of the divine. One could wish to be saved from radical evil and the servitude of sin and hope for the eternal and free benevolence in the lap of a fatherly god. One could wish to be saved from peonage under the astrologically conceived determination of stellar constellations and long for the dignity of freedom and partaking of the substance of the hidden deity. One could wish to be redeemed from the barriers to the finite, which express themselves in suffering, misery and death, and the threatening punishment of hell, and hope for an eternal bliss in an earthly or paradisical future existence. One could wish to be saved from the cycle of rebirths with their inexorable compensations for the deeds of the times past and hope for eternal rest. One could wish to be saved from senseless brooding and events and long for the dreamless sleep. Many more varieties of belief have, of course, existed. Behind them always lies a stand towards something in the actual world which is experienced as specifically 'senseless'. Thus, the demand has been implied: that the world order in its totality is, could, and should somehow be a meaningful 'cosmos'. This quest, the core of genuine religious rationalism, has been borne precisely by strata of intellectuals. The avenues, the results, and the efficacy of this metaphysical need for a meaningful cosmos have varied widely. Nevertheless, some general comments may be made.

The general result of the modern form of thoroughly rationalizing the conception of the world and of the way of life, theoretically and practically, in a purposive manner, has been that religion has been shifted into the realm of the irrational. This has been the more the case the further the purposive type of rationalization has progressed, if one takes the standpoint of an intellectual articulation of an image of the world. This shift of religion into the irrational realm has occurred for several reasons. On the one hand, the calculation of consistent rationalism has not easily come out even with nothing left over. In music, the Pythagorean 'comma' resisted complete rationalization oriented to tonal physics. The various great systems of music of all peoples and ages have differed in the manner in which they have either covered up or by-passed this inescapable irrationality or, on the other hand, put irrationality into the service of the richness of tonalities. The same has seemed to happen to the theoretical conception of the world, only far more so; and above all, it has seemed to happen to the rationalization of practical life. The various great ways of leading a rational and methodical life have been characterized by irrational presuppositions, which have been accepted simply as 'given' and which have been incorporated into such ways of life. What these presuppositions have been is historically and socially determined, at least to a very large extent, through the peculiarity of those strata that have been the carriers of the ways of life during its formative and decisive period. The *interest* situation of these strata, as determined socially and psychologically, has made for their peculiarity, as we here understand it.

Furthermore, the irrational elements in the rationalization of reality have been the *loci* to which the irrepressible quest of intellectualism for the possession of supernatural values has been compelled to retreat. That is the more so the more denuded of irrationality the world appears to be. The unity of the primitive image of the world, in which everything was concrete magic, has tended to split into rational cognition and mastery of nature, on the one hand, and into 'mystic' experiences, on the other. The inexpressible contents of such experiences remain the only possible 'beyond', added to the mechanism of a world robbed of gods. In fact, the beyond remains an incorporeal and meta-physical realm in which individuals intimately possess the holy. Where this conclusion has been drawn without any residue, the individual can pursue his quest for salvation only as an individual. This phenomenon appears in some form, with progressive intellectualist rationalism, wherever men have ventured to rationalize the image of the world as being a cosmos governed by impersonal rules. Naturally it has occurred most strongly among religions and religious ethics which have been quite strongly determined by genteel strata of intellectuals devoted to the purely cognitive comprehension of the world and of its 'meaning'. This was the case with Asiatic and, above all, Indian world religions. For all of them, contemplation became the supreme and ultimate religious value accessible to man. Contemplation offered them entrance into the profound and blissful tranquillity and immobility of the All-one. All other forms of religious states, however, have been at best considered a relatively valuable *Ersatz* for contemplation. This has had far-reaching consequences for the relation of religion to life, including economic life, as we shall repeatedly see. Such consequences flow from the general character of 'mystic' experiences, in the contemplative sense, and from the psychological preconditions of the search for them.

The situation in which strata decisive for the development of a religion were active in practical life has been entirely different. Where they were chivalrous warrior heroes, political officials, economically acquisitive classes or, finally, where an organized hierocracy dominated religion, the results were different than where genteel intellectuals were decisive.

The rationalism of hierocracy grew out of the professional preoccupation with cult and myth or – to a far higher degree – out of the cure of souls, that is, the confession of sin and counsel to sinners. Everywhere hierocracy has sought to monopolize the administration of religious values. They have also sought to bring and to temper the bestowal of religious goods into the form of 'sacramental' or 'corporate grace', which could be ritually bestowed only by the priesthood and could not be attained by the individual. The individual's quest for salvation or the quest of free communities by means of contemplation, orgies or asceticism, has been considered highly suspect and has had to be regulated ritually and, above all, controlled hierocratically. From the standpoint of the interests of the priesthood in power, this is only natural.

Every body of *political* officials, on the other hand, has been suspicious of all sorts of individual pursuits of salvation and of the free formation of communities as sources of emancipation from domestication at the hands of the institution of the state. Political officials have distrusted the competing priestly corporation of grace and, above all, at bottom they have despised the very quest for these impractical values lying beyond utilitarian and worldly ends. For all political bureaucracies, religious duties have ultimately been simply official or social obligations of the citizenry and of status groups. Ritual has corresponded to rules and regulations, and, therefore, wherever a bureaucracy has determined its nature, religion has assumed a ritualist character.

It is also usual for a stratum of *chivalrous* warriors to pursue absolutely worldly interests and to be remote from all 'mysticism'. Such strata, however, have lacked – and this is characteristic of heroism in general – the desire as well as the capacity for a rational mastery of reality. The irrationality of 'fate' and, under certain conditions, the idea of a vague and deterministically conceived 'destiny' (the Homeric *Moira*) has stood above and behind the divinities and demons who were conceived of as passionate and strong heroes, measuring out assistance and hostility, glory and booty, or death to the human heroes.

Peasants have been inclined towards magic. Their whole economic existence has been specifically bound to nature and has made them dependent upon elemental forces. They readily believe in a compelling sorcery directed against spirits who rule over or through natural forces, or they believe in simply buying divine benevolence. Only tremendous transformations of life orientation have succeeded in tearing them away from this universal and primeval form of religiosity. Such transformations have been derived either from other strata or from mighty prophets, who, through the power of miracles, legitimize themselves as sorcerers. Orgiastic and ecstatic states of 'possession', produced by means of toxics or by the dance, are strange to the status honour of knights because they are considered undignified.

Among the peasants, however, such states have taken the place that 'mysticism' holds among the intellectuals.

Finally, we may consider the strata that in the Western European sense are called 'civic', as well as those which elsewhere correspond to them: artisans, traders, enterprisers engaged in cottage industry and their derivatives existing only in the modern Occident. Apparently these strata have been the most ambiguous with regard to the religious stands open to them. And this is especially important to us.

Among these 'civic' strata the following religious phenomena have had especially strong roots: the institutional and sacramental grace of the Roman church in the medieval cities – the pillars of the Popes; the mystagogic and sacramental grace in the ancient cities and in India; the orgiastic and contemplative Sufi, and Dervish religion of the Middle Eastern Orient; the Taoist magic; the Buddhist contemplation; the ritualist appropriation of grace under the direction of souls by mystagogues in Asia; all the forms of love for a saviour; the beliefs in redemption the world over, from the cult of Krishna to the cult of Christ; the rational ritualism of the law and the sermon of the synagogue denuded of all magic among Jewry; the pneumatic and ancient as well as the ascetist medieval sects; the grace of predestination and the ethical regeneration of the Puritan and the Methodist; as well as all sorts of individual pursuits of salvation. All of these have been more firmly rooted among 'civic' strata than among any other.

Of course, the religions of all strata are certainly far from being unambiguously dependent upon the character of the strata we have presented as having special affinities with them. Yet, at first sight, civic strata appear, in this respect and on the whole, to lend themselves to a more varied determination. Yet it is precisely among these strata that elective affinities for special types of religion stand out. The tendency towards a *practical* rationalism in conduct is common to all civic strata; it is conditioned by the nature of their way of life, which is greatly detached from economic bonds to nature. Their whole existence has been based upon technological or economic calculations and upon the mastery of nature and of man, however primitive the means at their disposal. The technique of living handed down among them may, of course, be frozen in traditionalism, as has occurred repeatedly and everywhere. But precisely for these, there has always existed the possibility – even though in greatly varying measure – of letting an *ethical* and rational regulation of life arise. This may occur by the linkage of such an ethic to the tendency of technological and economic rationalism. Such regulation has not always been able to make headway against traditions which, in the main, were magically stereotyped. But where prophecy has provided a religious basis, this basis could be one of two fundamental types of prophecy: 'exemplary' prophecy and 'emissary' prophecy.

Exemplary prophecy points out the path to salvation by exemplary living, usually by a contemplative and apathetic–ecstatic life. The emissary type of prophecy addresses its *demands* to the world in the name of a god. Naturally these demands are ethical; and they are often of an active ascetic character.

It is quite understandable that the more weighty the civic strata as such have been, and the more they have been torn from bonds of taboo and from divisions into sibs and castes, the more favourable has been the soil for religions that call for action in this world. Under these conditions, the preferred religious attitude could become the attitude of active asceticism, of God-willed *action* nourished by the sentiment of being God's 'tool', rather than the possession of the deity or the inward and contemplative surrender to God, which has appeared as the supreme value to religions influenced by strata of genteel intellectuals. In the Occident the attitude of active ascetism has repeatedly retained supremacy over contemplative mysticism and orgiastic or apathetic ecstasy, even though these latter types have been well known in the Occident. Active asceticism, however, has not been confined to civic strata. Such an unambiguous social determination has not in any way existed. The prophecy of Zoroaster was directed at the nobility and the peasantry; the prophecy of Islam was directed to warriors. These prophecies, like the Israelite and the early Christian prophecy and preaching, have had an active character, which stands in contrast with the propaganda of Buddhism, Taoism, Neo-Pythagorism, Gnosticism and Sufism. Certain specific conclusions of emissary prophecies, however, have been drawn precisely on 'civic' grounds.

In the missionary prophecy the devout have not experienced

themselves as vessels of the divine but rather as instruments of a god. This emissary prophecy has had a profound elective affinity to a special conception of God: the conception of a supra-mundane, personal, wrathful, forgiving, loving, demanding, punishing Lord of Creation. Such a conception stands in contrast to the supreme being of exemplary prophecy. As a rule, though by no means without exception, the supreme being of an exemplary prophecy is an impersonal being because, as a static state, he is accessible only by means of contemplation. The conception of an active God, held by emissary prophecy, has dominated the Iranian and Mid-Eastern religions and those Occidental religions which are derived from them. The conception of a supreme and static being, held by exemplary prophecy, has come to dominate Indian and Chinese religiosity.

These differences are not primitive in nature. On the contrary, they have come into existence only by means of a far-reaching sublimation of primitive conceptions of animist spirits and of heroic deities which are everywhere similar in nature. Certainly the connexion of conceptions of God with religious states, which are evaluated and desired as sacred values, have also been strongly influential in this process of sublimation. These religious states have simply been interpreted in the direction of a different conception of God, according to whether the holy states, evaluated as supreme, were contemplative mystic experiences or apathetic ecstasy, or whether they were the orgiastic possession of god, or visionary inspirations and 'commands'.

At the present time, it is widely held that one should consider emotional content as primary, with thoughts being merely its secondary expression. Of course, this point of view is to a great extent justified. From such a standpoint one might be inclined to consider the primacy of 'psychological' as over against 'rational' connexions as the only decisive causal nexus, hence to view these rational connexions as *mere* interpretations of the psychological ones. This, however, would be going much too far, according to factual evidence. A whole series of purely historical motives have determined the development towards the supra-mundane or the immanent conception of God. These conceptions, in turn, have decisively influenced the way in which experiences of salvation have been articulated. This definitely holds for the conception of the supra-mundane God, as we shall see again and again. If even Meister Eckhart occasionally and expressly placed Martha above Mary, he did so ultimately because he could not realize the pantheist experience of God, which is peculiar to the mystic, without entirely sacrificing all the decisive elements of Occidental belief in God and creation.

The rational elements of a religion, its 'doctrine', also have an autonomy: for instance, the Indian doctrine of Karma, the Calvinist belief in predestination, the Lutheran justification through faith and the Catholic doctrine of sacrament. The rational religious pragmatism of salvation, flowing from the nature of the images of God and of the world, have under certain conditions had far-reaching results for the fashioning of a practical way of life.

These comments presuppose that the nature of the desired sacred values has been strongly influenced by the nature of the external interest situation and the corresponding way of life of the ruling strata and thus by the social stratification itself. But the reverse also holds: wherever the direction of the whole way of life has been methodically rationalized, it has been profoundly determined by the ultimate values towards which this rationalization has been directed. These values and positions were thus *religiously* determined. Certainly they have not always, or exclusively, been decisive; however, they have been decisive in so far as an *ethical* rationalization held sway, at least so far as its influence reached. As a rule, these religious values have been also, and frequently absolutely, decisive.

2 E. Durkheim

The Social Foundations of Religion

Excerpts from E. Durkheim, *The Elementary Forms of the Religious Life*, trans. J. Swain, Free Press of Glencoe, 1961, pp. 52–6, 62–3 and 464–72. (First published 1912.)
[The footnotes in these excerpts have been abridged by the editor. The reader will also find that information on literary references is not always complete due to the early date of the work.]

All known religious beliefs, whether simple or complex, present one common characteristic: they presuppose a classification of all the things, real and ideal, of which men think, into two classes or opposed groups, generally designated by two distinct terms which are translated well enough by the words *profane* and *sacred* (*profane, sacré*). This division of the world into two domains, the one containing all that is sacred, the other all that is profane, is the distinctive trait of religious thought; the beliefs, myths, dogmas and legends are either representations or systems of representations which express the nature of sacred things, the virtues and powers which are attributed to them, or their relations with each other and with profane things. But by sacred things one must not understand simply those personal beings which are called gods or spirits; a rock, a tree, a spring, a pebble, a piece of wood, a house, in a word, anything can be sacred. A rite can have this character; in fact, the rite does not exist which does not have it to a certain degree. There are words, expressions and formulae which can be pronounced only by the mouths of consecrated persons; there are gestures and movements which everybody cannot perform. If the Vedic sacrifice has had such an efficacy that, according to mythology, it was the creator of the gods, and not merely a means of winning their favor, it is because it possessed a virtue comparable to that of the most sacred beings. The circle of sacred objects cannot be determined, then, once for all. Its extent varies infinitely, according to the different religions. That is how Buddhism is a religion: in default of gods, it admits the existence of sacred things, namely, the four noble truths and the practices derived from them.

Up to the present we have confined ourselves to enumerating a certain number of sacred things as examples: we must now show by what general characteristics they are to be distinguished from profane things.

One might be tempted, first of all, to define them by the place they are generally assigned in the hierarchy of things. They are naturally considered superior in dignity and power to profane things, and particularly to man, when he is only a man and has nothing sacred about him. One thinks of himself as occupying an inferior and dependent position in relation to them; and surely this conception is not without some truth. Only there is nothing in it which is really characteristic of the sacred. It is not enough that one thing be subordinated to another for the second to be sacred in regard to the first. Slaves are inferior to their masters, subjects to their king, soldiers to their leaders, the miser to his gold, the man ambitious for power to the hands which keep it from him; but if it is sometimes said of a man that he makes a religion of those beings or things whose eminent value and superiority to himself he thus recognizes, it is clear that in any case the word is taken in a metaphorical sense, and that there is nothing in these relations which is really religious.

On the other hand, it must not be lost to view that there are sacred things of every degree, and that there are some in relation to which a man feels himself relatively at his ease. An amulet has a sacred character, yet the respect which it inspires is nothing exceptional. Even before his gods, a man is not always in such a marked state of inferiority; for it very frequently happens that he exercises a veritable physical constraint upon them to obtain what he desires. He beats the fetish with which he is not contented, but only to reconcile himself with it again, if in the end it shows itself more docile to the wishes of its adorer. To have rain, he throws stones into the spring or sacred lake where the god of rain is thought to reside; he believes that by this means he forces him to come out and show himself. Moreover, if it is true that man depends upon his gods, this dependence is reciprocal. The gods also have need of man; without offerings and sacrifices they would die. We shall even have occasion to show that this dependence of the gods upon their worshippers is maintained even in the most idealistic religions.

But if a purely hierarchic distinction is a criterion at once too general and too imprecise, there is nothing left with which to characterize the sacred in its relation to the profane except their heterogeneity. However, this heterogeneity is sufficient to characterize this classification of things and to distinguish it from all others, because it is very particular: *it is absolute.* In all the history of human thought there exists no other example of two categories of things so profoundly differentiated or so radically opposed to one another. The traditional opposition of good and bad is nothing beside this; for the good and the bad are only two opposed species of the same class, namely morals, just as sickness and health are two different aspects of the same order of facts, life, while the sacred and the profane have always and everywhere been conceived by the human mind as two distinct classes, as two worlds between which there is nothing in common. The forces which play in one are not simply those which are met with in the other, but a little stronger; they are of a different sort. In different religions, this opposition has been conceived in different ways. Here, to separate these two sorts of things, it has seemed sufficient to localize them in different parts of the physical universe; there, the first have been put into an ideal and transcendental world, while the material world is left in full possession of the others. But howsoever much the forms of the contrast may vary,[1] the fact of the contrast is universal.

This is not equivalent to saying that a being can never pass from one of these worlds into the other: but the manner in which this passage is effected, when it does take place, puts into relief the essential duality of the two kingdoms. In fact, it implies a veritable metamorphosis. This is notably demonstrated by the initiation rites, such as they are practised by a multitude of peoples. This initiation is a long series of ceremonies with the object of introducing the young man into the religious life: for the first time, he leaves the purely profane world where he passed his first infancy, and enters into the world of sacred things. Now this change of state is thought of, not as a simple and regular

1. The conception according to which the profane is opposed to the sacred, just as the irrational is to the rational, or the intelligible is to the mysterious, is only one of the forms under which this opposition is expressed. Science being once constituted, it has taken a profane character, especially in the eyes of the Christian religions; from that it appears as though it could not be applied to sacred things.

development of pre-existent germs, but as a transformation *totius substantiae* – of the whole being. It is said that at this moment the young man dies, that the person that he was ceases to exist, and that another is instantly substituted for it. He is reborn under a new form. Appropriate ceremonies are felt to bring about this death and rebirth, which are not understood in a merely symbolic sense, but are taken literally.[2] Does this not prove that between the profane being which he was and the religious being which he becomes, there is a break of continuity?

This heterogeneity is even so complete that it frequently degenerates into a veritable antagonism. The two worlds are not only conceived of as separate, but as even hostile and jealous rivals of each other. Since men cannot fully belong to one except on condition of leaving the other completely, they are exhorted to withdraw themselves completely from the profane world, in order to lead an exclusively religious life. Hence comes the monasticism which is artificially organized outside of and apart from the natural environment in which the ordinary man leads the life of this world, in a different one, closed to the first, and nearly its contrary. Hence comes the mystic asceticism whose object is to root out from man all the attachment for the profane world that remains in him. From that come all the forms of religious suicide, the logical working-out of this asceticism; for the only manner of fully escaping the profane life is, after all, to forsake all life.

The opposition of these two classes manifests itself outwardly with a visible sign by which we can easily recognize this very special classification, wherever it exists. Since the idea of the sacred is always and everywhere separated from the idea of the profane in the thought of men, and since we picture a sort of logical chasm between the two, the mind irresistibly refuses to allow the two corresponding things to be confounded, or even

2. See Frazer, 'On some ceremonies of the Central Australian tribes' in *Australian Association for the Advancement of Science*, 1901, pp. 313 ff. This conception is also of an extreme generality. In India, the simple participation in the sacrificial act has the same effects; the sacrificer, by the mere act of entering within the circle of sacred things, changes his personality. (See, Hubert and Mauss, 'Essai sur la nature et la fonction du sacrifice' in the *Année Sociologique*, vol. 2, 1899, p. 101.)

to be merely put in contact with each other; for such a promiscuity, or even too direct a contiguity, would contradict too violently the dissociation of these ideas in the mind. The sacred thing is *par excellence* that which the profane should not touch, and cannot touch with impunity. To be sure, this interdiction cannot go so far as to make all communication between the two worlds impossible; for if the profane could in no way enter into relations with the sacred, this latter could be good for nothing. But, in addition to the fact that this establishment of relations is always a delicate operation in itself, demanding great precautions and a more or less complicated initiation, it is quite impossible, unless the profane is to lose its specific characteristics and become sacred after a fashion and to a certain degree itself. The two classes cannot even approach each other and keep their own nature at the same time.

Thus we arrive at the first criterion of religious beliefs. Undoubtedly there are secondary species within these two fundamental classes which, in their turn, are more or less incompatible with each other. But the real characteristic of religious phenomena is that they always suppose a bipartite division of the whole universe, known and knowable, into two classes which embrace all that exists, but which radically exclude each other. Sacred things are those which the interdictions protect and isolate; profane things, those to which these interdictions are applied and which must remain at a distance from the first. Religious beliefs are the representations which express the nature of sacred things and the relations which they sustain, either with each other or with profane things. Finally, rites are the rules of conduct which prescribe how a man should comport himself in the presence of these sacred objects.

[. . .] We arrive at the following definition: *a religion is a unified system of beliefs and practices relative to sacred things, that is to say, things set apart and forbidden – beliefs and practices which unite into one single moral community called a Church, all those who adhere to them*. The second element which finds a place in our definition is no less essential than the first; for by showing that the idea of religion is inseparable from that of the Church, it makes it clear that religion should be an eminently collective thing. [. . .]

Our entire study rests upon the postulate that the unanimous sentiment of the believers of all times cannot be purely illusory.[3] Together with an apologist of the faith[4] we admit that these religious beliefs rest upon a specific experience whose demonstrative value is, in one sense, not one bit inferior to that of scientific experiments, though different from them. We, too, think that 'a tree is known by its fruits',[5] and that fertility is the best proof of 'what the roots are worth', But from the fact that a 'religious experience', if we choose to call it this, does exist and that it has a certain foundation – and, by the way, is there any experience which has none? – it does not follow that the reality which is its foundation conforms objectively to the idea which believers have of it. The very fact that the fashion in which it has been conceived has varied infinitely in different times is enough to prove that none of these conceptions express it adequately. If a scientist states it as an axiom that the sensations of heat and light which we feel correspond to some objective cause, he does not conclude that this is what it appears to the senses to be. Likewise, even if the impressions which the faithful feel are not imaginary, still they are in no way privileged intuitions; there is no reason for believing that they inform us better upon the nature of their object than do ordinary sensations upon the nature of bodies and their properties. In order to discover what this object consists of, we must submit them to an examination and elaboration analogous to that which has substituted for the sensuous idea of the world another which is scientific and conceptual.

This is precisely what we have tried to do, and we have seen that this reality, which mythologies have represented under so many different forms, but which is the universal and eternal objective cause of these sensations *sui generis* out of which religious experience is made, is society. We have shown what moral forces it develops and how it awakens this sentiment of a refuge, of a shield and of a guardian support which attaches the believer to his cult. It is that which raises him outside himself; it is even that which made him. For that which makes a man is the totality

3. Durkheim refers here and subsequently to the details of his analysis of aboriginal religion in Australia – *Ed*.
4. William James, *The Varieties of Religious Experience*.
5. Quoted by James, op. cit., p. 20.

of the intellectual property which constitutes civilization, and civilization is the work of society. This is explained by the preponderating role of the cult in all religions, whichever they may be. This is because society cannot make its influence felt unless it is in action, and it is not in action unless the individuals who compose it are assembled together and act in common. It is by common action that it takes consciousness of itself and realizes its position; it is before all else an active cooperation. The collective ideas and sentiments are even possible only owing to these exterior movements which symbolize them, as we have established. Then it is action which dominates the religious life, because of the mere fact that it is society which is its source.

In addition to all the reasons which have been given to justify this conception, a final one may be added here, which is the result of our whole work. As we have progressed, we have established the fact that the fundamental categories of thought, and consequently of science, are of religious origin. We have seen that the same is true for magic and consequently for the different processes which have issued from it. On the other hand, it has long been known that up until a relatively advanced moment of evolution, moral and legal rules have been indistinguishable from ritual prescriptions. In summing up, then, it may be said that nearly all the great social institutions have been born in religion. Now in order that these principal aspects of the collective life may have commenced by being only varied aspects of the religious life, it is obviously necessary that the religious life be the eminent form and, as it were, the concentrated expression of the whole collective life. If religion has given birth to all that is essential in society, it is because the idea of society is the soul of religion.

Religious forces are therefore human forces, moral forces. It is true that since collective sentiments can become conscious of themselves only by fixing themselves upon external objects, they have not been able to take form without adopting some of their characteristics from other things: they have thus acquired a sort of physical nature; in this way they have come to mix themselves with the life of the material world, and then have considered themselves capable of explaining what passes there. But when they are considered only from this point of view and in this role, only their most superficial aspect is seen. In reality, the essential elements of which these collective sentiments are made have been borrowed by the understanding. It ordinarily seems that they should have a human character only when they are conceived under human forms;[6] but even the most impersonal and the most anonymous are nothing else than objectified sentiments.

It is only by regarding religion from this angle that it is possible to see its real significance. If we stick closely to appearances, rites often give the effect of purely manual operations: they are anointings, washings, meals. To consecrate something, it is put in contact with a source of religious energy, just as today a body is put in contact with a source of heat or electricity to warm or electrize it; the two processes employed are not essentially different. Thus understood, religious technique seems to be a sort of mystic mechanics. But these material maneuvers are only the external envelope under which the mental operations are hidden. Finally, there is no question of exercising a physical constraint upon blind and, incidentally, imaginary forces, but rather of reaching individual consciousnesses of giving them a direction and of disciplining them. It is sometimes said that inferior religions are materialistic. Such an expression is inexact. All religions, even the crudest, are in a sense spiritualistic: for the powers they put in play are before all spiritual, and also their principal object is to act upon the moral life. Thus it is seen that whatever has been done in the name of religion cannot have been done in vain: for it is necessarily the society that did it, and it is humanity that has reaped the fruits.

But, it is said, what society is it that has thus made the basis of religion? Is it the real society, such as it is and acts before our very eyes, with the legal and moral organization which it has laboriously fashioned during the course of history? This is full of defects and imperfections. In it, evil goes beside the good, injustice often reigns supreme, and the truth is often obscured by error. How could anything so crudely organized inspire the sentiments of love, the ardent enthusiasm and the spirit of

6. It is for this reason that Frazer and even Preuss set impersonal religious forces outside of, or at least on the threshold of religion, to attach them to magic.

abnegation which all religions claim of their followers? These perfect beings which are gods could not have taken their traits from so mediocre, and sometimes even so base a reality.

But, on the other hand, does someone think of a perfect society, where justice and truth would be sovereign, and from which evil in all its forms would be banished for ever? No one would deny that this is in close relations with the religious sentiment; for, they would say, it is towards the realization of this that all religions strive. But that society is not an empirical fact, definite and observable; it is a fancy, a dream with which men have lightened their sufferings, but in which they have never really lived. It is merely an idea which comes to express our more or less obscure aspirations towards the good, the beautiful and the ideal. Now these aspirations have their roots in us; they come from the very depths of our being; then there is nothing outside of us which can account for them. Moreover, they are already religious in themselves; thus it would seem that the ideal society presupposes religion, far from being able to explain it.

But, in the first place, things are arbitrarily simplified when religion is seen only on its idealistic side: in its way, it is realistic. There is no physical or moral ugliness, there are no vices or evils which do not have a special divinity. There are gods of theft and trickery, of lust and war, of sickness and of death. Christianity itself, howsoever high the idea which it has made of the divinity may be, has been obliged to give the spirit of evil a place in its mythology. Satan is an essential piece of the Christian system; even if he is an impure being, he is not a profane one. The anti-god is a god, inferior and subordinated, it is true, but nevertheless endowed with extended powers; he is even the object of rites, at least of negative ones. Thus religion, far from ignoring the real society and making abstraction of it, is in its image; it reflects all its aspects, even the most vulgar and the most repulsive. All is to be found there, and if in the majority of cases we see the good victorious over evil, life over death, the powers of light over the powers of darkness, it is because reality is not otherwise. If the relation between these two contrary forces were reversed, life would be impossible; but, as a matter of fact, it maintains itself and even tends to develop.

But if, in the midst of these mythologies and theologies we

see reality clearly appearing, it is none the less true that it is found there only in an enlarged, transformed and idealized form. In this respect, the most primitive religions do not differ from the most recent and the most refined. For example, we have seen how the Arunta place at the beginning of time a mythical society whose organization exactly reproduces that which still exists today; it includes the same clans and phratries, it is under the same matrimonial rules and it practises the same rites. But the personages who compose it are ideal beings, gifted with powers and virtues to which common mortals cannot pretend. Their nature is not only higher, but it is different, since it is at once animal and human. The evil powers there undergo a similar metamorphosis: evil itself is, as it were, made sublime and idealized. The question now raises itself of whence this idealization comes.

Some reply that men have a natural faculty for idealizing, that is to say, of substituting for the real world another different one, to which they transport themselves by thought. But that is merely changing the terms of the problem; it is not resolving it or even advancing it. This systematic idealization is an essential characteristic of religions. Explaining them by an innate power of idealization is simply replacing one word by another which is the equivalent of the first; it is as if they said that men have made religions because they have a religious nature. Animals know only one world, the one which they perceive by experience, internal as well as external. Men alone have the faculty of conceiving the ideal, of adding something to the real. Now where does this singular privilege come from? Before making it an initial fact or a mysterious virtue which escapes science, we must be sure that it does not depend upon empirically determinable conditions.

The explanation of religion which we have proposed has precisely this advantage, that it gives an answer to this question. For our definition of the sacred is that it is something added to and above the real; now the ideal answers to this same definition; we cannot explain one without explaining the other. In fact, we have seen that if collective life awakens religious thought on reaching a certain degree of intensity, it is because it brings about a state of effervescence which changes the conditions of psychic activity. Vital energies are over-excited, passions more active, sensations stronger; there are even some which are produced only at this moment. A man does not recognize himself; he feels himself transformed and consequently he transforms the environment which surrounds him. In order to account for the very particular impressions which he receives, he attributes to the things with which he is in most direct contact properties which they have not, exceptional powers and virtues which the objects of everyday experience do not possess. In a word, above the real world where his profane life passes he has placed another which, in one sense, does not exist except in thought, but to which he attributes a higher sort of dignity than to the first. Thus, from a double point of view it is an ideal world.

The formation of the ideal world is therefore not an irreducible fact which escapes science; it depends upon conditions which observation can touch; it is a natural product of social life. For a society to become conscious of itself and maintain at the necessary degree of intensity the sentiments which it thus attains, it must assemble and concentrate itself. Now this concentration brings about an exaltation of the mental life which takes form in a group of ideal conceptions where is portrayed the new life thus awakened; they correspond to this new set of psychical forces which is added to those which we have at our disposition for the daily tasks of existence. A society can neither create itself nor recreate itself without at the same time creating an ideal. This creation is not a sort of work of supererogation for it, by which it would complete itself, being already formed; it is the act by which it is periodically made and remade. Therefore when some oppose the ideal society to the real society, like two antagonists which would lead us in opposite directions, they materialize and oppose abstractions. The ideal society is not outside of the real society; it is a part of it. Far from being divided between them as between two poles which mutually repel each other, we cannot hold to one without holding to the other. For a society is not made up merely of the mass of individuals who compose it, the ground which they occupy, the things which they use and the movements which they perform, but above all is the idea which it forms of itself. It is undoubtedly true that it hesitates over the manner in which it ought to conceive itself; it feels itself drawn in divergent directions. But these conflicts which break forth are not between the ideal and reality, but between two different ideals, that of yesterday and that of today, that which has the authority of tradition and that which has the hope of the future. There is surely a place for investigating whence these ideals evolve; but whatever solution may be given to this problem, it still remains that all passes in the world of the ideal.

Thus the collective ideal which religion expresses is far from being due to a vague innate power of the individual, but it is rather at the school of collective life that the individual has learned to idealize. It is in assimilating the ideals elaborated by society that he has become capable of conceiving the ideal. It is society which, by leading him within its sphere of action, has made him acquire the need of raising himself above the world of experience and has at the same time furnished him with the means of conceiving another. For society has constructed this new world in constructing itself, since it is society which this expresses. Thus both with the individual and in the group, the faculty of idealizing has nothing mysterious about it. It is not a sort of luxury which a man could get along without, but a condition of his very existence. He could not be a social being, that is to say, he could not be a man, if he had not acquired it. It is true that in incarnating themselves in individuals, collective ideals tend to individualize themselves. Each understands them after his own fashion and marks them with his own stamp; he suppresses certain elements and adds others. Thus the personal ideal disengages itself from the social ideal in proportion as the individual personality develops itself and becomes an autonomous source of action. But if we wish to understand this aptitude, so singular in appearance, of living outside of reality, it is enough to connect it with the social conditions upon which it depends.

Therefore it is necessary to avoid seeing in this theory of religion a simple restatement of historical materialism: that would be misunderstanding our thought to an extreme degree. In showing that religion is something essentially social, we do not mean to say that it confines itself to translating into another language the material forms of society and its immediate vital necessities. It is true that we take it as evident that social life depends upon its material foundation and bears its mark, just as the mental life of an individual depends upon his nervous system and in fact his whole organism. But collective consciousness is something more than a mere epiphenomenon of its morphological basis, just as individual consciousness is something more than a simple efflorescence of the nervous system. In order that the former may appear, a synthesis *sui generis* of particular consciousnesses is required. Now this synthesis has the effect of disengaging a whole world of sentiments, ideas and images which, once born, obey laws all their own. They attract each other, repel each other, unite, divide themselves and multiply, though these combinations are not commanded and necessitated by the condition of the underlying reality. The life thus brought into being even enjoys so great an independence that it sometimes indulges in manifestations with no purpose or utility of any sort, for the mere pleasure of affirming itself. We have shown that this is often precisely the case with ritual activity and mythological thought.

3 T. Parsons

Religion and the Problem of Meaning

Excerpt from T. Parsons, *Essays in Sociological Theory*, Free Press of Glencoe, 1954, pp. 204–10. (First published 1944.)

Malinowski shows quite clearly that neither ritual practices, magical or religious, nor the beliefs about supernatural forces and entities integrated with them can be treated simply as a primitive and inadequate form of rational techniques or scientific knowledge; they are qualitatively distinct and have quite different functional significance in the system of action (see Malinowski, 1926). Durkheim (1915; see also Parsons, 1937, ch. 11), however, went farther than Malinowski in working out the specific character of this difference, as well as in bringing out certain further aspects of the functional problem. Whereas Malinowski tended to focus attention on functions in relation to action in a situation, Durkheim became particularly interested in the problem of the specific attitudes exhibited towards supernatural entities and ritual objects and actions. The results of this study he summed up in the fundamental distinction between the sacred and the profane. Directly contrasting the attitudes appropriate in a ritual context with those towards objects of utilitarian significance and their use in fields of rational technique, he found one fundamental feature of the sacred to be its radical dissociation from any utilitarian context. The sacred is to be treated with a certain specific attitude of respect, which Durkheim identified with the appropriate attitude towards moral obligations and authority. If the effect of the prominence which Durkheim gives to the conception of the sacred is strongly to reinforce the significance of Malinowski's observation that the two systems are not confused but are in fact treated as essentially separate, it also brings out even more sharply than did Malinowski the inadequacy of the older approach to this range of problems which treated them entirely as the outcome of intellectual processes in ways indistinguishable from the solution of empirical problems. Such treatment could not but obscure the fundamental distinction upon which Durkheim insisted.

The central significance of the sacred in religion, however, served to raise in a peculiarly acute form the question of the source of the attitude of respect. Spencer, for instance, had derived it from the belief that the souls of the dead reappear to the living, and from ideas about the probable dangers of association with them. Max Müller and the naturalist school, on the other hand, had attempted to derive all sacred things in the last analysis from personification of certain phenomena of nature which were respected and feared because of their intrinsically imposing or terrifying character. Durkheim opened up an entirely new line of thought by suggesting that it was hopeless to look for a solution of the problem on this level at all. There was in fact no common intrinsic quality of things treated as sacred which could account for the attitude of respect. In fact, almost everything from the sublime to the ridiculous has in some society been treated as sacred. Hence the source of sacredness is not intrinsic; the problem is of a different character. Sacred objects and entities are symbols. The problem then becomes one of identifying the referents of such symbols. It is that which is symbolized and not the intrinsic quality of the symbol which becomes crucial.

At this point Durkheim became aware of the fundamental significance of his previous insight that the attitude of respect for sacred things was essentially identical with the attitude of respect for moral authority. If sacred things are symbols, the essential quality of that which they symbolize is that it is an entity which would command moral respect. It was by this path that Durkheim arrived at the famous proposition that society is always the real object of religious veneration. In this form the proposition is certainly unacceptable, but there is no doubt of the fundamental importance of Durkheim's insight into the exceedingly close integration of the system of religious symbols of a society and the patterns sanctioned by the common moral sentiments of the members of the community. In his earlier work (see also Parsons, 1937, chs. 8 and 10) Durkheim had progressed far in understanding the functional significance of an integrated system of morally sanctioned norms. Against this background the integration he demonstrated suggested a most important aspect of the functional significance of religion. For the problem arises, if moral norms and the sentiments supporting them are of such primary importance, what are the mechanisms by which they are maintained other than external processes of enforcement? It was Durkheim's view that religious ritual was of primary significance as a mechanism for expressing and reinforcing the sentiments most essential to the institutional integration of the society. It can readily be seen that this is closely linked to Malinowski's view of the significance of funeral ceremonies as a mechanism for reasserting the solidarity of the group on the occasion of severe emotional strain. Thus Durkheim worked out certain aspects of the specific relations between religion and social structure more sharply than did Malinowski, and in addition put the problem in a different functional perspective in that he applied it to the society as a whole in abstraction from particular situations of tension and strain for the individual.

One of the most notable features of the development under consideration lay in the fact that the cognitive patterns associated with religion were no longer, as in the older positivism, treated as essentially given points of reference, but were rather brought into functional relationship with a variety of other elements of social system of action. Pareto in rather general terms showed their interdependence with the sentiments. Malinowski contributed the exceedingly important relation to particular types of human situation, such as those of uncertainty and death. He in no way contradicted the emphasis placed by Pareto on emotional factors or sentiments. These, however, acquire their significance for specifically structured patterns of action only through their relation to specific situations. Malinowski was well aware in turn of the relation of both these factors to the solidarity of the social group, but this aspect formed the center of Durkheim's analytical attention. Clearly, religious ideas could only be treated sociologically in terms of their interdependence with all four types of factors.

There were, however, still certain serious problems left unsolved. In particular, neither Malinowski nor Durkheim raised the problem of the relation of these factors to the variability of social structure from one society to another. Both were primarily concerned with analysis of the functioning of a given social system without either comparative or dynamic references. Furthermore, Durkheim's important insight into the role of symbolism in religious ideas might, without further analysis, suggest that the specific patterns, hence their variations, were of only secondary importance. Indeed, there is clearly discernible in Durkheim's thinking in this field a tendency to circular reasoning in that he tends to treat religious patterns as a symbolic manifestation of 'society', but at the same time to define the most fundamental aspect of society as a set of patterns of moral and religious sentiment.

Max Weber (1930) approached the whole field in very different terms. In his study of the relation between Protestantism and capitalism, his primary concern was with those features of the institutional system of modern Western society which were most distinctive in differentiating it from the other great civilizations. Having established what he felt to be an adequate relation of congruence between the cognitive patterns of Calvinism and some of the principal institutionalized attitudes towards secular roles of our own society, he set about systematically to place this material in the broadest possible comparative perspective through studying especially the religion and social structure of China, India and ancient Judea (Weber, 1921; see also Parsons, 1937, chs. 14, 15 and 17). As a generalized result of these studies, he found it was not possible to reduce the striking variations of pattern on the level of religious ideas in these cases to any features of an independently existent social structure or economic situation, though he continually insisted on the very great importance of situational factors in a number of different connexions.[1] These factors, however, served only to pose the problems with which great movements of religious thought have been concerned. But the distinctive cognitive patterns were only understandable as a result of a cumulative tradition of intellectual effort in grappling with the problems thus presented and formulated.

1. See especially his treatment of the role of the balance of social power in the establishment of the ascendancy of the Brahmans in India, and of the international position of the people of Israel in the definition of religious problems for the prophetic movement.

For present purposes, even more important than Weber's views about the independent causal significance of religious ideas is his clarification of their functional relation to the system of action. Following up the same general line of analysis which provides one of the major themes of Pareto's and Malinowski's work, Weber made clear above all that there is a fundamental distinction between the significance for human action of problems of empirical causation and what, on the other hand, he called the 'problem of meaning'. In such cases as premature death through accident, the problem of *how* it happened in the sense of an adequate explanation of empirical causes can readily be solved to the satisfaction of most minds and yet leave a sense not merely of emotional but of cognitive frustration with respect to the problem of *why* such things must happen. Correlative with the functional need for emotional adjustment to such experiences as death is a cognitive need for understanding, for trying to have it 'make sense'. Weber attempted to show that problems of this nature, concerning the discrepancy between normal human interest and expectations in any situation or society and what actually happens are inherent in the nature of human existence. They always pose problems of the order which on the most generalized line have come to be known as the problem of evil, of the meaning of suffering, and the like. In terms of his comparative material, however, Weber shows there are different directions of definition of human situations in which rationally integrated solutions of these problems may be sought. It is differentiation with respect to the treatment of precisely such problems which constitute the primary modes of variation between the great systems of religious thought.

Such differences as, for instance, that between the Hindu philosophy of Karma and transmigration and the Christian doctrine of Grace with their philosophical backgrounds are not of merely speculative significance. Weber is able to show, in ways which correlate directly with the work of Malinowski and Durkheim, how intimately such differences in doctrine are bound up with practical attitudes towards the most various aspects of everyday life. For if we can speak of a need to understand ultimate frustrations in order for them to 'make sense', it is equally urgent that the values and goals of everyday life should also 'make sense'. A tendency to integration of these two levels seems to be inherent in human action. Perhaps the most striking feature of Weber's analysis is the demonstration of the extent to which precisely the variations in socially sanctioned values and goals in secular life correspond to the variations in the dominant religious philosophy of the great civilizations.

It can be shown with little difficulty that those results of Weber's comparative and dynamic study integrate directly with the conceptual scheme developed as a result of the work of the other writers. Thus Weber's theory of the positive significance of religious ideas is in no way to be confused with the earlier naïvely rationalistic positivism. The influence of religious doctrine is not exerted through the actor's coming to a conviction and then acting upon it in a rational sense. It is rather, on the individual level, a matter of introducing a determinate structure at certain points in the system of action where, in relation to the situation men have to face, other elements, such as their emotional needs, do not suffice to determine specific orientations of behavior. In the theories of Malinowski and Durkheim, certain kinds of sentiments and emotional reactions were shown to be essential to a functioning social system. These cannot stand alone, however, but are necessarily integrated with cognitive patterns; for without them there could be no coordination of action in a coherently structured social system. This is because functional analysis of the structure of action shows that situations must be subjectively defined, and the goals and values to which action is oriented must be congruent with these definitions, must that is, have 'meaning'.

References
DURKHEIM, E. (1915) *The Elementary Forms of the Religious Life* (trans. J. Swain), Allen and Unwin, and Macmillan.
DURKHEIM, E. (1933), *The Division of Labor in Society* (trans. G. Simpson), Macmillan.
MALINOWSKI, B. (1926), '*Magic, science, and religion*', in J. Needham, ed. *Science, Religion and Reality*, Macmillan, pp. 19–84
PARSONS, T. (1937), *The Structure of Social Action*, Free Press of Glencoe.
WEBER, M. (1921), *Gesammelte Aufsätze zur Religionssoziologie*, Mohr.
WEBER, M. (1930), *The Protestant Ethic and the Spirit of Capitalism*, Allen and Unwin.

4 P. Berger and T. Luckmann

Sociology of Religion and Sociology of Knowledge

P. Berger and T. Luckmann, 'Sociology of religion and sociology of knowledge', *Sociology and Social Research*, vol. 47 (1963), pp. 417–27.

Religion is both an important and an ambivalent phenomenon in contemporary Western society. This is true on both sides of the Atlantic, despite significant differences between America and Europe with regard to the social situation of religion. In America, religion continues to occupy an important position in public life and, on a quite voluntary basis, continues to enlist the formal allegiance of well over *half* the population in its organized bodies. In Europe, despite the survival of various degrees of legal establishment in various countries, popular participation in organized religion lags considerably behind the conspicuous piety of the cis-Atlantic masses. This lag, however, is compensated by the political prominence of organized religion as best exemplified by the political parties identified with one or both of the two major Christian confessions. In both Europe and America religion plays an important part in the over-all ideological posture *vis-à-vis* the Communist world. Moreover, again in both sectors of the emerging North Atlantic civilization, there is widespread popular interest in religion, strongly reflected by the mass media but also visible on more intellectually sophisticated levels. Both Protestantism and Catholicism have given birth to intellectual movements strong enough to be called a theological revival. Interestingly enough, it is precisely among the theologians that there are to be heard severe criticisms of the sort of religion that is prominent in the society and doubts as to whether this prominence may not be profoundly deceptive. Among some theologians there has been blunt mention of a 'post-Christian era' only thinly veiled by the continuing busy-work of the religious organizations. The ambivalence of the religious phenomenon is thus present in the consciousness of the religious world itself, prior to any sociological imputation from without.

The ecclesiastical authorities of the two major confessions have commonly stopped short of these extreme diagnoses. Nevertheless it is a commonplace even in the inner circles of the religious bureaucracies that things are not what they ought to be and that there is something not quite real about the Christian rhetoric of public life. Minimally this ecclesiastical uneasiness can be seen in an awareness of certain obvious trouble spots on the religious scene, such as the persistent alienation of much of the working class in Europe or the problem of racial segregation within the churches of America. One of the rather surprising consequences of this uneasiness has been a turning towards sociology on the part of the churches.

In the period since the Second World War there has been a remarkable development of sociologically oriented research carried on under ecclesiastical auspices, to the point where today a sizeable body of literature has been produced by this enterprise.[1] In this country, Protestant agencies have been engaging in this sort of research since the 1920s, largely in connexion with the strategic planning of denominational and inter-denominational offices, but the over-all research enterprise has greatly expanded and also become more formalized in the wake of the postwar 'religious revival'. Catholic agencies in America have been influenced by this Protestant research happiness as well as by the booming Catholic 'religious sociology' in Europe, while Jewish organizations have been engaging in widespread research activities of their own. The most spectacular inroad of sociological techniques, however, has occurred in European Catholicism. It began in France, but today has spread to every country with a sizeable Catholic population. Under various headings ('religious sociology', 'parish sociology', 'pastoral sociology' and others) a considerable number of research institutes, brought together in an international federation, is carrying on investigations under the direct sponsorship of the Catholic authorities.[2] European

1. Cf. the extensive international bibliography in Goldschmidt and Matthes (1962).

2. Cf. the principal international periodical published under these Catholic auspices, *Social Compass*, Brussels and The Hague.

Protestants have not quite caught up with this development, but strenuous efforts are well under way to emulate the Catholic example (cf. Anon, 1959). This is not the place to evaluate these research enterprises, some of which have unquestionably yielded valuable data for the sociology of religion in contemporary society. However, a few comments ought to be made about the general character of this sociological activity.

This character is determined by the economic base of the enterprises in question. Generally speaking, the latter constitute a religious variety of market research. They are financed by ecclesiastical organizations facing pragmatic problems and seeking pragmatic solutions to these problems. It should not surprise anyone that this research is employer oriented in its motivations. What is more important to see is that its conceptual framework is also determined by this employer orientation. The focus of interest is church-affiliated religiosity, its presence or absence constituting respectively a 'good' or a 'bad' situation from the management point of view. Needless to say, research carried on under ecclesiastical auspices shares this problem with the activities of sociologists employed by other types of bureaucratic management, for example in industry or government. It should also not be too surprising, consequently, that this ecclesiastically based research has borrowed its methodology from other branches of bureaucratically functional sociology. This methodology is narrowly sociographic, a fact which is both technically and ideologically functional. It avoids questions that go beyond the immediate pragmatic concerns of the employer (since such questions are not amenable to treatment by the methods utilized) and it legitimates the 'scientific' respectability of the enterprise (since these methods are acceptable precisely to the most rabidly positivistic scientism outside the churches).

There is something precious in this unexpected liaison between archbishops and pollsters. What concerns us here, however, is the enormous discrepancy between this latter-day sociology of religion and the place that religion occupied in classical sociological theory. It is hardly necessary in this context to amplify this statement in terms of the theoretical systems of Weber, Durkheim or Pareto, only to mention three crucial ones. One might recall, however, that none of the theorists just mentioned were personally 'religious'. They were concerned with religion for sociological reasons. Religion was perceived by them as a central phenomenon of social reality, therefore necessarily central for sociological understanding in general. Weber's recognition of religion as a prime factor in the historical process, Durkheim's insistence on the ultimately religious character of all human solidarity and Pareto's analysis of the place of religion in the perennial human pastime of self-deception – whatever one may want to do with these positions in one's own theorizing, it is clear that they are a long way, as starting points of sociological research, from the headaches of ecclesiastical bureaucrats.

This is not to say that, at any rate in American sociology, there is not some continuity with these classical sociological approaches to religion. Thus one can find strong Weberian undertones in the works on religion of Howard Becker and Gerhard Lenski, or a definite Durkheimian flavour in those of Lloyd Warner and Milton Yinger. The influence of both Weber and Durkheim on Talcott Parsons' treatment of religion is evident. It remains true that the sociology of religion is marginal in terms of the sociological enterprise proper (as distinguished from the ecclesiastical research enterprise discussed before), both in terms of its practice and in terms of its thought. Whatever may be the historical reasons for this segregation of the sociology of religion into a somewhat eccentric preserve, the implication is quite clear: religion is not a central concern for sociological theory or for the sociological analysis of contemporary society. Religion can, therefore, be left in the main to the social historians, to the ethnologists or to those few sociologists with an antiquarian interest in 'the classics' – and, of course, to that fairly alienated group of colleagues employed by religious institutions.

Is this implication defensible? We would say that it is – but *only* if the field of the sociology of religion is defined in ecclesiastical terms, that is, if its focus is to be church-affiliated religiosity and its various degrees of presence or absence. The obvious next question is whether this definition makes sense from the standpoint of sociological theory. Our answer here is resoundingly negative. The reason for this answer is based on our understanding of the nature of the sociological enterprise.

We would say, first of all, that the sociologist who operates exclusively with an ecclesiastically oriented definition of religion has an altogether too narrow and, as it were, juridical concept of institution.[3] The latter must, of course, be taken into account by the sociologist, but it does not exhaust the pertinent social reality of this or any other phenomenon. The juridical or other 'official' versions of society invariably distort sociological perspective if taken at face value. The sociologist who so takes them simply adopts the viewpoint of 'management' on the matter at hand. He is well on the way from that point on towards becoming a conservative ideologist, as is best illustrated by the positivistic school of jurisprudence which became precisely that with respect to the institution of law. What happens in this case is that the 'official' or 'management' viewpoint comes to delimit the area of sociological relevance. Or, speaking empirically, it is not the sociologist but his employers (be they archbishops or admirals, welfare officials or business executives) who define the proper objects of his investigations. Whatever does not fall within his definition of what is relevant is either relegated to an allegedly 'subjective' and 'scientifically inaccessible' domain or is courteously conceded to some other academic discipline. The former solution is that of the positivists, the latter of those sociologists who are anxious not to infringe on the territory of the psychologists. A pragmatic solution somewhere between the positivistic and the psychologistic alternatives is the one that would leave these institutionally undefined phenomena to such research on 'opinions' or 'attitudes' as dwells in the antechambers of the temple of sociology. We would contend that none of these options is viable for a sociologist who understands and respects his own universe of discourse.

Sociology must be concerned with everything which, already on the common-sense level, is taken as social reality, even if it does not fit into the 'official' definition of what the institutions of society are.[4] There is a wide range of human phenomena that are socially objectivated but not institutionalized in the narrow sense of the word. Not only is it methodologically inadmissible

3. We would like to see a broader concept, but will not argue the point here. For a very suggestive development of the sociological concept of institution, see Gehlen (1956).

4. This understanding of the scope of sociology has been strongly influenced by the sociological theories of Schutz (1962).

to exclude these phenomena from the perspective of sociology, but any concept of institution hangs theoretically in mid-air if it is not grounded in a sociological understanding of objectivation as such. The basic form of social objectivation is language. Language analyses, recombines and 'fixes' biologically based subjective consciousness and forms it into intersubjective, typical and communicable experiences. The metaphorical and analogical potential of language facilitates the crystallization of social values and norms by which experience is interpreted. It is this edifice of semantic fields, categories and norms which structures the subjective perceptions of reality into a meaningful, cohesive and 'objective' universe. This universe, 'reality as seen' in a culture, is taken for granted in any particular society or collectivity. For the members of a society or collectivity it constitutes the 'natural' way of interpreting, remembering and communicating individual experience. In this sense it is internal to the individual, as his way of experiencing the world. At the same time it is external to him as that universe in which he *and* his fellow-men exist and act.[5]

Such a universe is fundamentally legitimated by the fact that it is there, confronting the individual from the beginning of his biography as the self-evident external reality which exercises unremitting constraint upon his individual experiences and actions. Nevertheless, this universe *as* a coherent configuration of meaning requires reiterated and explicitly formulated legitimation. The individual already learns in his primary socialization the fundamental formulae of this legitimation. Socialization, however, is never totally successful and never completed. The legitimating formulae must be reiterated in the ongoing life of the adult, especially in the great crises of this life (as in rites of passage). One can put this a little differently by saying that all universes, as meaning structures, are precarious. The individual's 'knowledge' of the world is socially derived and must be socially sustained. Using Alfred Schutz's expression, the individual's world-taken-for-granted must be legitimated over and over

5. In addition to Schutz we would point here to the classic formulations of the character of this *conscience collective* in the works of Durkheim and Maurice Halbwachs. For more recent interpretations, cf. Voegelin (1951), Redfield (1953) and Lévi-Strauss (1962).

gain.[6] Normally this legitimation will occur in specific institutional forms. Yet one must be careful not to confound 'knowledge' (i.e. the meaning configuration of the universe) with the formal institutions of learning or legitimation (i.e. the explicit – and symbolic – 'explanation' of the coherence of that universe) with institutionally organized ideologies. This theoretical distinction is especially important in terms of the religious dimension of this socially constituted universe.

Throughout human history religion has played a decisive part in the construction and maintenance of universes.[7] This statement does not necessarily imply an extreme Durkheimian position that religion has done nothing else or is nothing else apart from this social function, but it does imply that this function is sociologically central. In any case, while this function of religion can be discovered crossculturally, the institutionally specialized location of religion in churches or similar bodies is relatively rare in history. It is, of course, characteristic of the development of Christianity. But it is generally absent in ancient civilizations and is almost totally unknown in primitive societies. *Ergo*, for the purposes of a general sociology of religion, this institutional specialization cannot be used as the defining criterion of religion. The ecclesiastically oriented definition of the field of the sociology of religion betrays then, at the very least, a marked historical and cultural parochialism.

There is, indeed, a sociological problem in the relationship of institutionalized religion, where it exists, with the more general religious business of universe building. But this is not the only problem. The recent history of secularization in Western and westernizing societies indicates, on the contrary, that the part of institutionally specialized religion in the fundamental processes of legitimation is on the wane. This development is of great sociological importance in itself and there already exist various theories seeking to explain it (cf. Schelsky, 1957; Parsons, 1960

6. For the phenomenological analysis of the 'natural' way of looking at the world and its social relativity, cf. Scheler (1960).

7. The classic sociological formulation of this is, of course, to be found in the works of Durkheim and his school. For important corroboration from the fields of phenomenology and history of religion, cf. the works of Eliade (1959) and Voegelin (1956–7). For a recent sociological interpretation, cf. W. Lloyd Warner (1959).

pp. 295–321; Acquaviva, 1961; Goldschmidt and Matthes, 1962, pp. 65–77). Another interesting problem lies in what has been described as the 'emigration' and subsequent 'privatization' of even traditionally Christian religiosity from the churches, a phenomenon especially significant in Europe (cf. Stammler, 1960). Yet another sociological problem is posed by the transformation of the traditional religious meanings within the churches themselves, something to be observed very clearly in America but also present in varying degrees in Europe (cf. Schneider and Dornbusch, 1958; Goldsen, 1960, pp. 153–95; Berger, 1961; Woelber, 1959). From our viewpoint, however, another problem is sociologically the crucial one: what are the characteristics of the legitimating processes actually operative in contemporary society?

No human society can exist without legitimation in one form or another. If it is correct to speak of contemporary society as increasingly secularized (and we think that this is correct), one is thereby saying that the sociologically crucial legitimations are to be found outside the area of institutionally specialized religion. To say this, however, is only the beginning of the sociological analysis that must now take place. One must now ask what forms these legitimations take, to what extent they are institutionalized and where they are so institutionalized (since there is no longer any reason to fixate one's attention on the traditional religious institutions). At this point, needless to say, one has arrived at some of the central questions of a sociological understanding of modern society.

Before we venture on some statements concerning the implications of this for the sociology of religion in this modern society we would return for a moment to more general theoretical considerations. Legitimation cannot be discussed apart from the universe that is being legitimated. Such a universe, as we have briefly tried to indicate, is a socially constituted reality, which the individual member of society learns to take for granted as 'objective' knowledge about the world. This 'objectivity' (what Durkheim called the 'thing-like' character of social reality) is determined by the fact that socialization is not simply individual learning of cultural items but also social constraint in the formation of the most fundamental categories of experience, memory, thinking and communication. This means that knowledge, in the broadest sense, is socially derived. The task of the sociology of knowledge is the analysis of the social forms of knowledge, of the processes by which individuals acquire this knowledge and, finally, of the institutional organization and social distribution of knowledge. It will be clear that we are here giving to the sociology of knowledge a considerably broader meaning than has hitherto been given to it. We conceive the sociology of knowledge as being properly concerned with the whole area of the relationship of social structure and consciousness.[8] The sociology of knowledge thus understood ceases to be an idiosyncratic activity of sociologists with a penchant for the history of ideas and is placed squarely at the very center of sociological theory.[9]

The consequence for the sociology of religion as a discipline is clear: – the sociology of religion is an integral and even central part of the sociology of knowledge. Its most important task is to analyse the cognitive and normative apparatus by which a socially constituted universe (that is, 'knowledge' about it) is legitimated. Quite naturally, this task will include the analysis of both the institutionalized and the non-institutionalized aspects of this apparatus. This will involve the sociology of religion in the study of religion in the sense in which this term is commonly understood in Western civilization (that is, as a Christian or Jewish interpretation of the world and of human destiny). But the sociology of religion will also have to deal with other legitimating systems, whether one wishes to call these religious or pseudo-religious, that are increasingly important in a secularized society

8. The authors of this article, in cooperation with several colleagues in sociology and philosophy, are currently engaged in the preparation of a systematic treatise in the sociology of knowledge that will seek to integrate with what is now known as the sociology of knowledge three other streams of sociological thought hitherto largely left outside this discipline – the phenomenological analysis of the life world (especially in the opus of Alfred Schutz), the Durkheimian approaches to the sociology of knowledge and those of American social psychology as derived from the work of G. H. Mead.

9. The problem of ideology in its relationship to social strata and their onflicts, the original impetus and subject matter of the sociology of knowledge, remains an important area within such a broader definition of the discipline. In addition to the well-known works of Karl Mannheim, cf. Merton (1957), Stark (1958) and Wolff (1959).

(such as scientism, psychologism, Communism and so forth). Indeed, only if the latter is also done will it be possible to obtain an adequate sociological understanding of the phenomena that persist within the traditional religious systems and their institutional manifestations.

What results can be expected from this reinterpretation of the task of the sociology of religion for empirical research? First of all, such a reinterpretation leads to a detachment of the sociologist (*qua* sociologist, that is) from the ideological interests of all, not only of the traditional religious legitimating systems. This includes an emancipation from the 'management' point of view within the churches, and also from any scientist ideology that may exist within the field of sociology itself. In terms of research practice, there will be an obvious broadening in scope of the sociology of religion. This broader scope is especially important in a modern pluralistic society in which different legitimating systems compete for the patronage of potential consumers of *Weltanschauungen*. Indeed, we strongly believe that this market character of legitimating systems is in itself an important characteristic deserving of sociological analysis. The sociology of religion here finds itself in close proximity to the problems already investigated by the sociology of mass culture and mass communications.

This leads to further important problems. We think that the relative freedom of the consumer *vis-à-vis* the various legitimating systems influences personality structure (cf. Riesman, 1950; Gehlen, 1957; Luckmann, 1963). Compared with the obligatory and unambiguous internalization of any one legitimating system in traditional societies, the consumer status of the individual *vis-à-vis* competing legitimating systems in modern society provides, if nothing else, at least the illusion of freedom. We think that the collision of the private 'freedom' with the strict controls of functionally rational and bureaucratic institutions over the public conduct of the individual represents one of the central problems of the social psychology of modern society. There is a significant sociological problem involved in the loss of monopoly status incurred by the major legitimating systems of Western civilization. We believe that this process is one of the social causes of the 'privatization' of belief, that is, of the withdrawal of religious commitments from their traditionally designated locations in society into that curious area which German sociologists (not too happily) have called the 'sphere of the intimate'. The same global processes may well be related to the legitimating functions of psychoanalysis and other forms of psychologism in modern society, functions that can be said to be paradigmatic in terms of 'privatization'. The sociological analysis of contemporary sexuality, its myths and its rituals, would belong in the same area.

The market character of legitimation (a central aspect of what one likes to call pluralistic society) is very likely to have important consequences for the content of legitimating systems. It is one thing to preside in the role of Brahman over the metaphysical cravings of an isolated and fairly homogeneous peasant population which has no choice in the matter. It is quite another matter to try and market one legitimating system (even if it is Vedanta!) to an affluent and sophisticated clientele of suburbanites, Midwestern housewives, metropolitan secretaries, etc. A certain similarity between these social types may remain in the domains of emotion, sex, consumption, etc. – in short, in the 'intimate sphere' which is relatively less dependent on class and institutional factors. The social as well as economic imperative of appealing immediately to the changeable taste of the largest possible number of 'privatized' consumers may account for the importance of psychoanalysis, a legitimating system tailored to the 'intimate sphere' *par excellence*. This, of course, does not preclude the success of Zen Buddhism or political chauvinism in narrower special segments of the mass market. It must not be overlooked that Presbyterianism and Reform Judaism are not exempt either from the mechanism of marginal differentiation called into play in this situation.

These considerations probably point to a comprehensive analysis of legitimation in modern society on the basis of a non-monopolistic market model. Special attention must be given here to the function of the mass media in the socialization of these consumer attitudes. The mass media are further significant in the direct, anonymous and, as it were, non-institutionalized transmission of a synthetic universe with its appropriate pre-fabricated legitimations. Another important area of investigation in this connexion is the place of the family, the consuming entity *par excellence* with reference to all marketable commodities from television sets to 'peace of mind'. The ideological constellation of 'familism', with its broad institutional base in contemporary society ranging from child-centered church programs to the 'kiddy-korners' of the suburban shopping centers, is to be analysed as another aspect of the over-all process of 'privatization'.

Some of these problems have been investigated by sociologists in various subdisciplines of the field. The reinterpretation of the sociology of religion here undertaken thus in no way pretends that the task indicated above must begin from some sort of *tabula rasa* as far as empirical data are concerned. There is already existent a wealth of data both within and without the area of research more narrowly called the sociology of religion. However, we would contend that the conception of the sociology of religion here formulated would place these data in a more comprehensive theoretical frame of reference. Beyond that it can bring into focus as yet unexplored avenues of empirical research.

References

ANON (1959), 'Report on the European colloquium on the Sociology of Protestantism, 1959', *Arch. Sociol. Relig.*, vol. 8, pp. 3–157.

ACQUAVIVA, S. (1961), *L'Eclissi del Sacro nella Civiltà Industriale*, Communità, Milan.

BERGER, P. (1961), *The Noise of Solemn Assemblies*, Doubleday.

ELIADE, M. (1959), *Cosmos and History*, Harper.

GEHLEN, A. (1956), *Urmensch und Spaetkultur*, Athenaeum, Bonn.

GEHLEN, A. (1957), *Die Seele in technischen Zeitalter*, Rowohlt, Hamburg.

GOLDSCHMIDT, D., and MATTHES, J. (1962), *Probleme der Religionssoziologie*, Westdeutscher Verlag, Cologne.

GOLDSEN, R. (1960), *What College Students Think*, Van Nostrand.

LÉVI-STRAUSS, C. (1962), *La Pensée Sauvage*, Plon, Paris.

LUCKMANN, T. (1963), *Zum Problem der Religion in der Moderner Gesellschaft*, Rombach, Freiburg.

MERTON, R. (1957), *Social Theory and Social Structure*, Free Press of Glencoe.

PARSONS, T. (1960), *Structure and Process in Modern Societies*, Free Press of Glencoe.

REDFIELD, R. (1953), *The Primitive World and its Transformations*, Cornell University Press.

RIESMAN, D. (1950), *The Lonely Crowd*, Yale University Press.

SCHELER, M. (1960), *Die Wissensformen und die Gesellschaft*, Francke, Bern.

SCHELSKY, H. (1957), 'Ist die Dauerreflektion institutionalisierbar?', *Zeitschr. evangel. Ethik.*, vol. 4, pp. 153–74.

SCHNEIDER, L., and DORNBUSCH, S. M. (1958), *Popular Religion*, University of Chicago Press.

SCHUTZ, A. (1962), *Collected Papers, I – The Problem of Social Reality*, Nijhoff, The Hague.

STAMMLER, E. (1960), *Protestanten ohne Kirche*, Kreuz, Stuttgart.

STARK, W. (1958), *The Sociology of Knowledge*, Free Press of Glencoe.

VOEGELIN, E. (1951), *The New Science of Politics*, University of Chicago Press.

VOEGELIN, E. (1956–7), *Order and History*, vols. 1–3, Louisiana State University Press.

WARNER, W. L. (1959), *The Living and the Dead*, Yale University Press.

WOELBER, H.-O. (1959), *Religion ohne Entscheidurg*, Vandenhoeck a Ruprecht, Goettingen.

WOLFF, K. (ed.) (1959), 'The sociology of knowledge', *Transactions of the Fourth World Congress of Sociology*, vol. 4, International Sociological Association, Louvain.

Part Two **Major Patterns of Religion**

The second part of the book is subdivided into four sections:
(I) religion in primitive societies; (II) historical aspects of religion;
(III) religion in modern societies; and (IV) mixed forms of religion
in the contemporary world. The choice of items has, of necessity,
been highly selective. The main aim has been to cover a wide range
of relationships between, on the one hand, religious beliefs and
activities, and, on the other hand, the wider social and cultural
context in which such beliefs and activities are located. A brief
commentary introduces each section.

I. Aspects of Primitive Religion

Primitive societies are characterized by the relative absence of social and cultural differentiation. That is, such societies tend not to possess clearly specialized groups and collectivities geared to distinct tasks, problems and preoccupations; nor do they tend to have distinct sets of beliefs relating to the various aspects of social and natural life, or to physical phenomena. Claims as to the pre-logical mentality of primitive peoples are now extensively discredited and current anthropological interest tends to focus on the ways in which individuals in primitive societies cope with the problems of meaning, identity, misfortune, sickness and so on in terms appropriate to the study of any kind of society – for these are problems which in some form or other all human societies face. Primitiveness thus resides basically in the undifferentiated nature of the society – as is excellently brought out by Mary Douglas in Reading 5. The contributions of Douglas and Evans-Pritchard (Reading 6) are both good examples of social-anthropological analyses of the meaning and significance of primitive beliefs and symbols; Douglas's approach being more general and theoretical than Evans-Pritchard's exploration of the religious symbolism of one particular society, that of the Nuer.

5 M. Douglas

Primitive Thought-Worlds

Excerpts from M. Douglas, *Purity and Danger*, Routledge and Kegan Paul, 1966, pp. 74–93.

We feel there is something discourteous in the term 'primitive' and so we avoid it and the whole subject too. Why else should Professor Herskovits have renamed the second edition of *Primitive Economics* to *Economic Anthropology* if his sophisticated West African friends had not expressed dislike of being lumped together with naked Fuegians and Aborigines under this general sign? Perhaps it is partly also in healthy reaction to early anthropology: 'perhaps nothing so sharply differentiates the savage from the civilized man as the circumstance that the former observes taboos, the latter does not' (Rose, 1926, p. 111). No one can be blamed for wincing at a passage such as the following, though I do not know who would take it seriously:

We know that the primitive man of today has mental equipment very different from that of the civilized man. It is much more fragmented, much more discontinuous, more 'Gestalt-free'. Professor Jung once told me how, in his travels in the African bush, he had noticed the quivering eye-balls of his native guides: not the steady gaze of the European, but a darting restlessness of vision, due perhaps to the constant expectation of danger. Such eye movements must be co-ordinated with a mental alertness and a swiftly changing imagery that allows little opportunity for discursive reasoning, for contemplation and comparison (H. Read, 1955).

If this were written by a professor of psychology it might be significant, but it is not. I suspect that our professional delicacy in avoiding the term 'primitive' is the product of secret convictions of superiority. The physical anthropologists have a similar problem. While they attempt to substitute 'ethnic group' for the word 'race' (see *Current Anthropology*, 1964), their terminological problems do not inhibit them from their task of distinguishing and classifying forms of human variation. But social anthropologists, to the extent that they avoid reflecting on the grand distinctions between human cultures, seriously impede their own work. So it is worth asking why the term 'primitive' should imply any denigration.

Part of our difficulty in England is that Lévy-Bruhl, who first posed all the important questions about primitive cultures and their distinctiveness as a class, wrote in deliberate criticism of the English of his day, particularly of Frazer. Furthermore, Lévy-Bruhl laid himself open to powerful counter-attack. Most textbooks on comparative religion are emphatic about the mistakes he made, and say nothing about the value of the questions he asked. (For example see Bartlett, 1923, pp. 283–4, and Radin, 1956, pp. 230–31.) In my view he has not deserved such neglect.

Lévy-Bruhl was concerned to document and to explain a peculiar mode of thought. He started (1922) with the problem set by an apparent paradox. On the one hand there were convincing reports of the high level of intelligence of Eskimo or Bushmen (or of other such hunters and gatherers, or primitive cultivators or herdsmen), and on the other hand reports of peculiar leaps made in their reasoning and interpretation of events which suggested that their thought followed very different paths from our own. He insisted that their alleged dislike of discursive reasoning is not due to intellectual incapacity but to highly selective standards of relevance which produce in them an 'insuperable indifference to matters bearing no apparent relation to those which interest them'. The problem then was to discover the principles of selection and of association which made the primitive culture favour explanation in terms of remote, invisible mystic agencies and to lack curiosity about the intermediate links in a chain of events. Sometimes Lévy-Bruhl seems to be putting his problem in terms of individual psychology, but it is clear that he saw it as a problem of the comparison of cultures first and as a psychological one only in so far as individual psychology is affected by cultural environment. He was interested in analysing 'collective representations', that is standardized assumptions and categories, rather than in individual aptitudes. It is precisely on this score that he criticized Tylor and Frazer, who tried to explain primitive beliefs in terms of individual psychology, whereas he followed Durkheim in seeing collective representations as social phenomena, as common patterns of thought which are related to social institutions. In this he was undoubtedly right, but as his strength lay more in massive documentation than in analysis he was unable to apply his own precepts.

What Lévy-Bruhl should have done, Evans-Pritchard has said, was to examine the variations in social structure and relate them to concomitant variations in the patterns of thought. Instead he contented himself with saying that all primitive people present uniform patterns of thought when contrasted with ourselves, and laid himself open to further criticism by seeming to make primitive cultures more mystical than they are and making civilized thought more rational than it is (Evans-Pritchard, 1934). It seems that Evans-Pritchard himself was the first person to listen sympathetically to Lévy-Bruhl and to direct his research to carrying Lévy-Bruhl's problems into the more fruitful field which Lévy-Bruhl himself missed. For his analysis of Azande witchcraft beliefs was exactly an exercise of this sort. It was the first study to describe a particular set of collective representations and to relate them intelligibly to social institutions (1937). Many studies have now ploughed lines parallel to this first furrow, so that from England and America a large body of sociological analysis of religions has vindicated Durkheim's insight. I say Durkheim's insight and not Lévy-Bruhl's advisedly, for in so far as he contributed his own original slant to the matter, so Lévy-Bruhl earned the just criticism of his reviewers. It was his idea to contrast primitive mentality with rational thought instead of sticking to the problem adumbrated by the master. If he had stayed with Durkheim's view of the problem he would not have been led into the confusing contrast of mystical with a scientific thought, but would have compared primitive social organization with complex modern social organization and perhaps have done something useful towards elucidating the difference between organic and mechanical solidarity, between two types of social organization which Durkheim saw to underlie differences in beliefs.

Since Lévy-Bruhl the general tendency in England has been to treat each culture studied as wholly *sui generis*, a unique and more or less successful adaptation to a particular environment (see Beattie, 1960, p. 83, 1964, p. 272). Evans-Pritchard's criticism that Lévy-Bruhl treated primitive cultures as if they were more uniform than they really are has stuck. But it is vital now to take up this matter again. We cannot understand sacred contagion unless we can distinguish a class of cultures in which pollution ideas flourish from another class of cultures, including our own, in which they do not. Old Testament scholars do not hesitate to enliven their interpretations of Israelite culture by comparison with primitive cultures. Psychoanalysts since Freud, and metaphysicians since Cassirer are not backward in drawing general comparisons between our present civilization and others very different. Nor can anthropologists do without such general distinctions.

The right basis for comparison is to insist on the unity of human experience and at the same time to insist on its variety, on the differences which make comparison worth while. The only way to do this is to recognize the nature of historical progress and the nature of primitive and of modern society. Progress means differentiation. Thus primitive means undifferentiated; modern means differentiated. [. . .]

It seems unlikely that institutions should diversify and proliferate without a comparable movement in the realm of ideas. Indeed we know that it does not happen. Great steps separate the historical development of the Hadza in Tanganyikan forests, who still never have occasion to count beyond four, from that of West Africans who for centuries have reckoned fines and taxes in thousands of cowries. Those of us who have not mastered modern techniques of communication such as the language of mathematics or of computers can put ourselves in the Hadza class compared with the ones who have become articulate in these media. We know only too well the educational burden our own civilization carries in the form of specialized compartments of learning. Obviously the demand for special expertise and the education for providing it create cultural environments in which certain kinds of thinking can flourish and others cannot. Differentiation in thought patterns goes along with differentiated social conditions.

From this basis it ought to be straightforward to say that in the realm of ideas there are differentiated thought systems which contrast with undifferentiated ones, and leave it at that. But the trap is just here. What could be more complex, diversified and elaborate than the Dogon cosmology? Or the Australian Murinbata cosmology, or the cosmology of Samoa, or of Western Pueblo Hopi for that matter? The criterion we are looking for is not in elaborateness and sheer complication of ideas.

There is only one kind of differentiation in thought that is relevant, and that provides a criterion that we can apply equally to different cultures and to the history of our own scientific ideas. That criterion is based on the Kantian principle that thought can only advance by freeing itself from the shackles of its own subjective conditions. The first Copernican revolution, the discovery that only man's subjective viewpoint made the sun seem to revolve round the earth, is continually renewed. In our own culture mathematics first and later logic, now history, now language and now thought processes themselves and even knowledge of the self and of society, are fields of knowledge progressively freed from the subjective limitations of the mind. To the extent to which sociology, anthropology and psychology are possible in it, our own type of culture needs to be distinguished from others which lack this self-awareness and conscious reaching for objectivity.

Radin interprets the Trickster myth of the Winnebago Indians on lines which serve to illustrate this point. Here is a primitive parallel to Teilhard de Chardin's theme that the movement of evolution has been towards ever-increasing complexification and self-awareness.

These Indians lived technically, economically and politically in the most simple undifferentiated conditions. Their myth contains their profound reflections on the whole subject of differentiation. The Trickster starts as an unselfconscious, amorphous being. As the story unfolds he gradually discovers his own identity, gradually recognizes and controls his own anatomical parts; he oscillates between female and male, but eventually fixes his own male sexual role; and finally learns to assess his environment for what it is. Radin (1956) says in his preface:

He wills nothing consciously. At all times he is constrained to behave as he does from impulses over which he has no control . . . he is at the mercy of his passions and appetites ... possesses no defined and well-fixed form ... primarily an inchoate being of indeterminate proportions, a figure foreshadowing the shape of man. In this version he possesses intestines wrapped around his body and an equally long penis, likewise wrapped round his body with his scrotum on top of it.

Two examples of his strange adventures will illustrate this theme. Trickster kills a buffalo and is butchering it with a knife in his right hand:

In the midst of all these operations suddenly his left arm grabbed the buffalo. 'Give that back to me, it is mine! Stop that or I will use my knife on you!' So spoke the right arm. 'I will cut you to pieces, that is what I will do to you,' continued the right arm. Thereupon the left arm released its hold. But shortly after, the left arm again grabbed hold of the right arm ... again and again this was repeated. In this manner did Trickster make both his arms quarrel. That quarrel soon turned into a vicious fight and the left arm was badly cut up ...

In another story Trickster treats his own anus as if it could act as an independent agent and ally. He had killed some ducks and before going to sleep he tells his anus to keep guard over the meat. While he is asleep some foxes draw near:

When they came close, much to their surprise however, gas was expelled from somewhere. 'Pooh' was the sound made. 'Be careful! He must be awake,' so they ran back. After a while one of them said 'Well, I guess he is asleep now.' That was only a bluff. He is always up to some tricks. So again they approached the fire. Again gas was expelled and again they ran back. Three times this happened ... Then louder, still louder, was the sound of gas expelled. 'Pooh! Pooh! Pooh!' Yet they did not run away. On the contrary they now began to eat the roasted pieces of duck ...

When Trickster woke up and saw the duck gone:

... 'Oh, you too, you despicable object, what about your behaviour? Did I not tell you to watch this fire? You shall remember this! As a punishment for your remissness, I will burn your mouth so that you will not be able to use it!' So he took a piece of burning wood and burned the mouth of his anus ... and cried out of pain he was inflicting on himself.

Trickster begins, isolated, amoral and unselfconscious, clumsy, ineffectual, an animal-like buffoon. Various episodes prune down and place more correctly his bodily organs so that he ends by looking like a man. At the same time he begins to have a more consistent set of social relations and to learn hard lessons about his physical environment. In one important episode he mistakes a tree for a man and responds to it as he would to a person until eventually he discovers it is a mere inanimate thing. So gradually he learns the functions and limits of his being.

I take this myth as a fine poetic statement of the process that leads from the early stages of culture to contemporary civilization, differentiated in so many ways. The first type of culture is not pre-logical, as Lévy-Bruhl unfortunately dubbed it, but pre-Copernican. Its world revolves round the observer who is trying to interpret his experiences. Gradually he separates himself from his environment and perceives his real limitations and powers. Above all this pre-Copernican world is personal. Trickster speaks to creatures, things and parts of things without discrimination as if they were animate, intelligent beings. This personal universe is the kind of universe that Lévy-Bruhl describes. It is also the primitive culture of Tylor and the animist culture of Marett, and the mythological thought of Cassirer.

In the next few pages I am going to press as hard as I can the analogy between primitive cultures and the early episodes of the Trickster myth. I will try to present the characteristic areas of non-differentiation which define the primitive world view. I shall develop the impression that the primitive world view is subjective and personal, that different modes of existence are confused, that the limitations of man's being are not known. This is the view of primitive culture which was accepted by Tylor and Frazer and which posed the problems of primitive mentality. I shall then try to show how this approach distorts the truth.

First, this world view is man-centered in the sense that explanations of events are couched in notions of good and bad fortune, which are implicitly subjective notions ego-centered in reference. In such a universe the elemental forces are seen as linked so closely to individual human beings that we can hardly speak of an external, physical environment. Each individual carries within himself such close links with the universe that he is like the centre of a magnetic field of force. Events can be explained in terms of his being what he is and doing what he has done. In this world it makes good sense for Thurber's fairy tale king to complain that falling meteors are being hurled at himself, and for Jonah to come forward and confess that he is the cause of a storm. The distinctive point here is not whether the working of the universe is thought to be governed by spiritual beings or by impersonal powers. That is hardly relevant. Even powers which are taken to be thoroughly impersonal are held to be reacting directly to the behaviour of individual humans.

A good example of belief in anthropocentric powers is the !Kung Bushmen belief in *N!ow*, a force thought to be responsible for meteorological conditions at least in the Nyae-Nyae area of Bechuanaland. *N!ow* is an impersonal, amoral force, definitely a thing and not a person. It is released when a hunter who has one kind of physical make-up kills an animal which has the corresponding element in its own make-up. The actual weather at any time is theoretically accounted for by the complex interaction of different hunters with different animals (Marshall, 1957). This hypothesis is attractive and one feels it must be intellectually satisfying since it is a view which is theoretically capable of being verified and yet no serious testing would ever be practical.

To illustrate further the man-centered universe I quote from what Father Tempels says of Luba philosophy. He has been criticized for implying that what he says so authoritatively from his intimate knowledge of Luba thought applies to all the Bantu. But I suspect that in its broad lines his view on Bantu ideas of vital force applies not merely to all the Bantu, but much more widely. It probably applies to the whole range of thought which I am seeking to contrast with modern differentiated thought in European and American cultures.

For the Luba, he says, the created universe is centered on man. The three laws of vital causality are:

(1) That a human (living or dead) can directly reinforce or diminish the being (or force) of another human.
(2) That the vital force of a human can directly influence inferior force-beings (animal, vegetable or mineral).
(3) That a rational being (spirit, dead or living human) can act indirectly on another by communicating his vital influence to an intermediary inferior force.

Of course there are very many different forms which the idea of a man-centered universe may take. Inevitably ideas of how men affect other men must reflect political realities. So ultimately we shall find that these beliefs in man-centered control of the environment vary according to the prevailing tendencies in the political system. But in general we can distinguish beliefs which hold that all men are equally involved with the universe from beliefs in the special cosmic powers of selected individuals. There are beliefs about destiny which are thought to apply universally to all men. In the culture of Homeric literature it was not certain outstanding individuals whose destiny was the concern of the gods, but all and each whose personal fate was spun on the knees of the gods and woven for good or ill with the fates of others. Just to take one contemporary example, Hinduism today teaches, as it has for centuries, that for each individual the precise conjunction of the planets at the time he was born signifies much for his personal good or ill-fortune. Horoscopes are for everybody. In both these instances, though the individual can be warned by diviners about what is in store for him, he cannot change it radically, only soften a little the hard blows, defer or abandon hopeless desires, be alert to the opportunities that will lie in his path.

Other ideas about the way in which the individual's fortune is bound up with the cosmos may be more pliable. In many parts of West Africa today, the individual is held to have a complex personality whose component parts act like separate persons. One part of the personality speaks the life course of the individual before he is born. After birth, if the individual strives for success in a sphere which has been spoken against, his efforts will always be in vain. A diviner can diagnose this spoken destiny as cause of his failures and can then exorcise his pre-natal choice. The nature of his pre-destined failure which a man has to take account of varies from one West African society to another. Among the Tallensi in the Ghana hinterland the conscious personality is thought to be amiable and uncompetitive. His unconscious element which spoke his destiny before birth is liable to be diagnosed as over-aggressive and rivalrous, and so makes him a misfit in a system of controlled statuses. By contrast the Ijo of the Niger Delta, whose social organization is fluid and competitive, take the conscious component of the self to be full of aggression, desire to compete and to excel. In this case it is the unconscious self which may be pre-destined to failure because it chose obscurity and peace. Divination can discover the discrepancy of aims within the person, and ritual can put it right (Fortes, 1959; Horton, 1961).

These examples point to another lack of differentiation in the personal world view. We saw above that the physical environment is not clearly thought of in separate terms, but only with reference to the fortunes of human selves. Now we see that the self is not clearly separated as an agent. The extent and limits of its autonomy are not defined. So the universe is part of the self in a complementary sense, seen from the angle of the individual's idea, not this time of nature, but of himself.

The Tallensi and Ijo ideas about the multiple warring personalities in the self seem to be more differentiated than the Homeric Greek idea. In these West African cultures the binding words of destiny are spoken by part of the individual himself. Once he knows what he has done he can repudiate his earlier choice. In Ancient Greece the self was seen as a passive victim of external agents:

In Homer one is struck by the fact that his heroes with all their magnificent vitality and activity feel themselves at every turn not free agents but passive instruments or victims of other powers . . . a man felt that he could not help his own emotions. An idea, an emotion, an impulse came to him; he acted and presently rejoiced or lamented. Some god had inspired him or blinded him. He prospered, then was poor, perhaps enslaved; he wasted away with disease, or died in battle. It was divinely ordained, his portion apportioned long before. The prophet or diviner might discover it in advance; the plain man knew a little about omens and merely seeing his shaft hit its mark or the enemy prevailing, concluded that Zeus had assigned defeat to himself and his comrades. He did not wait to fight further but fled (Onians, 1951, p. 302).

The pastoral Dinka living in the Sudan similarly are said not to distinguish the self as an independent source of action and of reaction. They do not reflect on the fact that they themselves react with feelings of guilt and anxiety and that these feelings initiate other states of mind. The self acted upon by emotions they portray by external powers, spiritual beings who cause misfortune of various kinds. So in an effort to do justice to the complex reality of the self's interaction within itself the Dinka universe is peopled with dangerous personal extensions to the self. This is almost exactly how Jung described the primitive world view when he said:

An unlimited amount of what we now consider an integral part of our own psychic being disports itself merrily for the primitive in projections reaching far and wide.

I give one more example of a world in which all individuals are seen as personally linked with the cosmos to show how varied these linkages can be. Chinese culture is dominated by the idea of harmony in the universe. If an individual can place himself to ensure the most harmonious relationship possible, he can hope for good fortune. Misfortune may be attributed to lack of just such a happy alignment. The influence of the waters and the airs, called Feng Shwe, will bring him good fortune if his house and his ancestors' graves are well placed. Professional geomancers can divine the causes of his misfortune and he can then rearrange his home or his parental graves to better effect. Dr Freedman in his forthcoming book holds that geomancy has an important place in Chinese beliefs alongside ancestor worship. The fortune which a man can manipulate thus by geomantic skills has no moral implications; but ultimately it must be brought to terms with the reward of merit which in the same set of beliefs is meted out by heaven. Finally then, the whole universe is interpreted as tied in its detailed working to the lives of human persons. Some individuals are more successful in dealing with Feng Shwe than others, just as some Greeks have a more splendid fate decreed for them and some West Africans a spoken destiny more committed to success.

Sometimes it is only marked individuals and not all humans who are significant. Such marked individuals draw lesser men in their wake, whether their endowment is for good or evil fortune. For the ordinary man in the street, not endowed himself, the practical problem is to study his fellow-men and discover whom among them he ought to avoid or follow.

In all the cosmologies we have mentioned so far, the lot of individual humans is thought to be affected by power inhering in themselves or in other humans. The cosmos is turned in, as it were, on man. Its transforming energy is threaded on to the lives of individuals so that nothing happens in the way of storms, sickness, blights or droughts except in virtue of these personal links. So the universe is man-centered in the sense that it must be interpreted by reference to humans.

But there is a quite other sense in which the primitive undifferentiated world view may be described as personal. Persons are essentially not things. They have wills and intelligence. With their wills they love, hate and respond emotionally. With their intelligence they interpret signs. But in the kind of universe I am contrasting with our own world view, things are not clearly distinct from persons. Certain kinds of behaviour characterize person-to-person relations. First, persons communicate with one another by symbols in speech, gesture, rite, gift and so on. Second, they react to moral situations. However impersonally the cosmic forces may be defined, if they seem to respond to a person-to-person style of address their quality of thing is not fully differentiated from their personality. They may not be persons but nor are they entirely things.

Here there is a trap to avoid. Some ways of talking about things might seem to the naïve observer to imply personality. Nothing can necessarily be inferred about beliefs from purely linguistic distinctions or confusions. For instance a Martian anthropologist might come to the wrong conclusion on overhearing an English plumber asking his mate for the male and female parts of plugs. To avoid falling into linguistic pitfalls, I confine my interests to the kind of behaviour which is supposed to produce a response from allegedly impersonal forces.

It may not be at all relevant here that the Nyae-Nyae Bush men attribute male and female character to clouds, any more than it is relevant that we use 'she' for cars and boats. But it may be relevant that the pygmies of the Ituri forest, when misfortune befalls, say that the forest is in a bad mood and go to the trouble of singing to it all night to cheer it up, and that they then expect their affairs to prosper (Turnbull, 1961). No European mechanic in his senses would hope to cure engine trouble by serenade or curse.

So here is another way in which the primitive, undifferentiated universe is personal. It is expected to behave as if it was intelligent, responsive to signs, symbols, gestures, gifts, and as if it could discern between social relationships.

The most obvious example of impersonal powers being thought responsive to symbolic communication is the belief in sorcery. The sorcerer is the magician who tries to transform the path of events by symbolic enactment. He may use gestures or plain words in spells or incantations. Now words are the proper mode of communication between persons. If there is an idea that words correctly said are essential to the efficacy of an action, then, although the thing spoken to cannot answer back, there is a belief in a limited kind of one-way verbal communication. And this belief obscures the clear thing status of the thing being addressed. A good example is the poison used for the oracular detection of witches in Zandeland (Evans-Pritchard, 1937). The Azande themselves brew their poison from bark. It is not said to be a person but a thing. They do not suppose there is a little man inside which works the oracle. Yet for the oracle to work the poison must be addressed aloud, the address must convey the question unequivocally and, to eliminate error of interpretation, the same question must be put in reverse form in the second round of consultation. In this case not only does the poison hear and understand the words, but it has limited powers of reply. Either it kills the chicken or it does not. It can only give yes and no answers. It cannot initiate a conversation or conduct an unstructured interview. Yet this limited response to questioning radically modifies its thing status in the Azande universe. It is not an ordinary poison, but more like a captive interviewee filling in a survey questionnaire with crosses and ticks.

Frazer's Golden Bough is full of examples of belief in an impersonal universe which, nevertheless, listens to speech and responds to it one way or another. So are modern field-workers' reports. Stanner says: 'Most of the choir and furniture of heaven and earth are regarded by the Aborigines as a vast sign system. Anyone who understandingly has moved in the Australian bush with aborigine associates becomes aware of the fact. He moves, not in a landscape but in a humanised realm saturated with significations.'

Finally there are the beliefs which imply that the impersonal universe has discernment. It may discern between fine nuances in social relations, such as whether the partners in sexual intercourse are related within prohibited degrees, or between less fine ones such as whether a murder has been committed on a fellow-tribesman or on a stranger, or whether a woman is married or not. Or it may discern secret emotions hidden in men's breasts. There are many examples of implied discernment of social status. The hunting Cheyenne thought that the buffaloes who provide their main livelihood were affected by the rotten smell of a man who had murdered a fellow-tribesman and they moved away, thus endangering the survival of the tribe. The buffalo were not supposed to react to the smell of murder of a foreigner. The Australian Aborigines of Arnhemland conclude their fertility and initiation ceremonies with ceremonial copulation, believing that the rite is more efficacious if sexual intercourse takes place between persons who are at other times strictly prohibited (Berndt, p. 49). The Lele believe that a diviner who has had sexual intercourse with the wife of his patient, or whose patient has had sexual intercourse with his wife, cannot heal him, because the medicine intended to heal would kill. This result is not dependent on any intention or knowledge on the part of the doctor. The medicine itself is thought to react in this discriminating way. Furthermore, the Lele believe that if a cure is effected and the patient omits to pay his healer promptly for his services, early relapse or even a more fatal complication of the illness will result. So Lele medicine, by implication, is credited with discerning debt as well as secret adultery. Even more intelligent is the vengeance magic bought by the Azande which detects unerringly the witch responsible for a given death, and does capital justice on him. So impersonal elements in the universe are credited with discrimination which enables them to intervene in human affairs and uphold the moral code.

In this sense the universe is apparently able to make judgements on the moral value of human relations and to act accordingly. *Malweza*, among the Plateau Tonga in Northern Rhodesia, is a misfortune which afflicts those who commit certain specific offences against the moral code. Those offences are in general of a kind against which ordinary punitive sanctions cannot be applied. For example, homicide within the group of matrilineal kinsmen cannot be avenged because the group is organized to avenge the murder of its members by outsiders. *Malweza* punishes offences which are inaccessible to ordinary sanctions.

To sum up, a primitive world view looks out on a universe which is personal in several different senses. Physical forces are thought of as interwoven with the lives of persons. Things are not completely distinguished from persons and persons are not completely distinguished from their external environment. The universe responds to speech and mime. It discerns the social order and intervenes to uphold it.

I have done my best to draw from accounts of primitive cultures a list of beliefs which imply lack of differentiation. The materials I have used are based on modern fieldwork. Yet the general picture closely accords with that accepted by Tylor or Marett in their discussions of primitive animism. They are the kind of beliefs from which Frazer inferred that the primitive mind confused its subjective and objective experiences. They are the same beliefs which provoked Lévy-Bruhl to reflect on the way that collective representations impose a selective principle on interpretation. The whole discussion of these beliefs has been haunted by obscure psychological implications.

If these beliefs are presented as the result of so many failures to discriminate correctly they evoke to a startling degree the fumbling efforts of children to master their environment. Whether we follow Klein or Piaget, the theme is the same; confusion of internal and external, of thing and person, self and environment, sign and instrument, speech and action. Such confusions may be necessary and universal stages in the passage of the individual from the chaotic, undifferentiated experience of infancy to intellectual and moral maturity.

So it is important to point out again, as has often been said before, that these connexions between persons and events which characterize the primitive culture do not derive from failure to differentiate. They do not even necessarily express the thoughts of individuals. It is quite possible that individual members of such cultures hold very divergent views on cosmology. Vansina recalls affectionately three very independent thinkers he encountered among the Bushong, who liked to expound their personal philosophies to him. One old man had come to the conclusion that there was no reality, that all experience is a shifting illusion.

The second had developed a numerological type of metaphysics, and the last had evolved a cosmological scheme of great complexity which no one understood but himself (Vansina, 1964). It is misleading to think of ideas such as destiny, witchcraft, *mana*, magic as part of philosophies, or as systematically thought out at all. They are not just linked to institutions, as Evans-Pritchard put it, but they are institutions – every bit as much as habeas corpus or Hallow-e'en. They are all compounded part of belief and part of practice. They would not have been recorded in the ethnography if there were no practices attached to them. Like other institutions they are both resistant to change and sensitive to strong pressure. Individuals can change them by neglect or by taking an interest.

If we remember that it is a practical interest in living and not an academic interest in metaphysics which has produced these beliefs, their whole significance alters. To ask an Azande whether the poison oracle is a person or a thing is to ask a kind of nonsensical question which he would never pause to ask himself. The fact that he addresses the poison oracle in words does not imply any confusion whatever in his mind between things and persons. It merely means that he is not striving for intellectual consistency and that in this field symbolic action seems appropriate. He can express the situation as he sees it by speech and mime, and these ritual elements have become incorporated into a technique which, to many intents and purposes is like programming a problem through a computer. I think that this is something argued by Radin in 1927 and by Gellner (1962) when he points to the social function of incoherences in doctrines and concepts.

Robertson Smith first tried to draw attention away from beliefs considered as such, to the practices associated with them. And much other testimony has piled up since on the strictly practical limitation on the curiosity of individuals. This is not a peculiarity of primitive culture. It is true of 'us' as much as of 'them', in so far as 'we' are not professional philosophers. As businessman, farmer, housewife no one of us has time or inclination to work out a systematic metaphysics. Our view of the world is arrived at piecemeal, in response to particular practical problems.

In discussing Azande ideas about witchcraft Evans-Pritchard insists on this concentration of curiosity on the singularity of an individual event. If an old and rotten granary falls down and kills someone sitting in its shadow, the event is ascribed to witchcraft. Azande freely admit that it is in the nature of old and rotten granaries to collapse, and they admit that if a person sits for several hours under its shadow, day after day, he may be crushed when it falls. The general rule is obvious and not an interesting field for speculation. The question that interests them is the emergence of a unique event out of the meeting point of two separate sequences. There were many hours when no one was sitting under that granary and when it might have collapsed harmlessly, killing no one. There were many hours when other people were seated by it, who might have been victims when it fell, but who happened not to be there. The fascinating problem is why it should have fallen just when it did, just when so-and-so and no one else was sitting there. The general regularities of nature are observed accurately and finely enough for the technical requirements of Azande culture. But when technical information has been exhausted, curiosity turns instead to focus on the involvement of a particular person with the universe. Why did it have to happen to him? What can he do to prevent misfortune? Is it anyone's fault? This applies, of course, to a theistic world view. As with witchcraft only certain questions are answered by reference to spirits. The regular procession of the seasons, the relation of cloud to rain and rain to harvest, of drought to epidemic and so on, is recognized. They are taken for granted as the back-drop against which more personal and pressing problems can be solved. The vital questions in any theistic world view are the same as for the Azande: why did this farmer's crops fail and not his neighbour's? Why did this man get gored by a wild buffalo and not another of his hunting party? Why did this man's children or cows die? Why me? Why today? What can be done about it? These insistent demands for explanation are focused on an individual's concern for himself and his community. We now know what Durkheim knew, and what Frazer, Tylor and Marett did not. These questions are not phrased primarily to satisfy man's curiosity about the seasons and the rest of the natural environment. They are phrased to satisfy a dominant social concern, the problem of how to organize together in society. They can only be answered, it is true, in terms of man's place in nature. But the metaphysic is a by-product, as it were, of the urgent practical concern. The anthropologist who draws out the whole scheme of the cosmos which is implied in these practices does the primitive culture great violence if he seems to present the cosmology as a systematic philosophy subscribed to consciously by individuals. We can study our own cosmology – in a specialized department of astronomy. But primitive cosmologies cannot rightly be pinned out for display like exotic lepidoptera, without distortion to the nature of a primitive culture. In a primitive culture the technical problems have been more or less settled for generations past. The live issue is how to organize other people and oneself in relation to them; how to control turbulent youth, how to soothe disgruntled neighbours, how to gain one's rights, how to prevent usurpation of authority, or how to justify it. To serve these practical social ends all kinds of beliefs in the omniscience and omnipotence of the environment are called into play. If social life in a particular community has settled down into any sort of constant form, social problems tend to crop up in the same areas of tension or strife. And so as part of the machinery for resolving them, these beliefs about automatic punishment, destiny, ghostly vengeance and witchcraft crystallize in the institutions. So the primitive world view which I have defined above is rarely itself an object of contemplation and speculation in the primitive culture. It has evolved as the appanage of other social institutions. To this extent it is produced indirectly, and to this extent the primitive culture must be taken to be unaware of itself, unconscious of its own conditions.

In the course of social evolution institutions proliferate and specialize. The movement is a double one in which increased social control makes possible greater technical developments and the latter opens the way to increased social control again. Finally we find ourselves in the modern world where economic interdependence is carried to the highest pitch reached by mankind so far. One inevitable by-product of social differentiation is social awareness, self-consciousness about the processes of communal life. And with differentiation go special forms of social coercion, special monetary incentives to conform, special types of punitive sanctions, specialized police and overseers and progress men scanning our performance, and so on, a whole paraphernalia of social control which would never be conceivable in small-scale undifferentiated economic conditions. This is the experience of organic solidarity which makes it so hard for us to interpret the efforts of men in primitive society to overcome the weakness of their social organization. Without forms filled in triplicate, without licences and passports and radio-police cars they must somehow create a society and commit men and women to its norms. I hope I have now shown why Lévy-Bruhl was mistaken in comparing one type of thought with another instead of comparing social institutions.

We can also see why Christian believers, Moslems and Jews are not to be classed as primitive on account of their beliefs. Nor necessarily Hindus, Buddhists or Mormons, for that matter. It is true that their beliefs are developed to answer the questions 'Why did it happen to me: Why now?' and the rest. It is true that their universe is man-centered and personal. Perhaps in entertaining metaphysical questions at all these religions may be counted anomalous institutions in the modern world. For unbelievers may leave such problems aside. But this in itself does not make of believers promontories of primitive culture sticking out strangely in a modern world. For their beliefs have been phrased and rephrased with each century and their intermeshing with social life cut loose. The European history of ecclesiastical withdrawal from secular politics and from secular intellectual problems to specialized religious spheres is the history of this whole movement from primitive to modern.

Finally we should revive the question of whether the word 'primitive' should be abandoned. I hope not. It has a defined and respected sense in art. It can be given a valid meaning for technology and possibly for economics. What is the objection to saying that a personal, anthropocentric, undifferentiated world view characterizes a primitive culture? The only source of objection could be from the notion that it has a pejorative sense in relation to religious beliefs which it does not carry in technology and art. There may be something in this for a certain section of the English-speaking world.

The idea of a primitive economy is slightly romantic. It is true that we are materially and technically incomparably better equipped, but no one would frankly base a cultural distinction on purely materialist grounds. The facts of relative poverty and wealth are not in question. But the idea of the primitive economy is one which handles goods and services without the intervention of money. So the primitives have the advantage over us in that they encounter economic reality direct, while we are always being deflected from our course by the complicated, unpredictable and independent behaviour of money. But on this basis, when it comes to the spiritual economy, we seem to have the advantage. For their relation to their external environment is mediated by demons and ghosts whose behaviour is complicated and unpredictable, while we encounter our environment more simply and directly. This latter advantage we owe to our wealth and material progress which has enabled other developments to take place. So, on this reckoning, the primitive is ultimately at a disadvantage both in the economic and spiritual field. Those who feel this double superiority are naturally inhibited from flaunting it and this is presumably why they prefer not to distinguish primitive culture at all.

Continentals seem to have no such squeamishness. '*Le primitif*' enjoys honour in the pages of Leenhard, Lévi-Strauss, Ricoeur and Eliade. The only conclusion that I can draw is that they are not secretly convinced of superiority, and are intensely appreciative of forms of culture other than their own.

References
BARTLETT, F. C. (1923), *Psychology and the Primitive Culture*, Cambridge University Press.
BARTLETT, F. C. (1932), *Remembering: A Study in Experimental and Social Psychology*, Cambridge University Press.
BEATTIE, J. (1960), *Bunyoro, An African Kingdom*, Holt.
BEATTIE, J. (1964), *Other Cultures*, Free Press.
BERNDT, R. (1951), *Kunapipi, A Study of an Australian Aboriginal Religious Cult*, Cheshire, Melbourne.
EVANS-PRITCHARD, E. E. (1934), 'Lévy-Bruhl's theory of primitive mentality', *Bulletin of the Faculty of Arts*, vol. 2, part 1, Imprimerie de l'Institut Français d'Archéologie Orientale, Cairo.
EVANS-PRITCHARD, E. E. (1937), *Witchcraft, Oracles and Magic among the Azande*, Oxford University Press.
FORTES, M. (1959), *Oedipus and Job in West African Religion*, Cambridge University Press.
GELLNER, E. (1962), Concepts and society, *Transactions of the Fifth World Congress of Sociology*, vol. 1, International Sociological Association.

HORTON, R. (1961), 'Destiny and the unconscious in West Africa', *Africa*, vol. 2.

LÉVY-BRUHL, L. (1922), *La Mentalité Primitive*, Paris. [*Primitive Mentality*, Beacon, 1966.]

LÉVY-BRUHL, L. (1936), *Primitives and the Supernatural*, London.

MARSHALL, L. (1957), 'N!ow', *Africa*, vol. 27.

ONIANS, R. B. (1951), *Origins of European Thought about the Body, the Mind, etc.*, Cambridge University Press.

RADIN, P. (1927), *Primitive Man as Philosopher*, Dover.

RADIN, P. (1956), *The Trickster, A Study in American Indian Mythology*, London.

READ, H. (1955), *Icon and Idea, The Function of Art in the Development of Human Consciousness*, Harvard University Press.

ROBERTSON SMITH, W. (1889), *The Religion of the Semites*.

ROSE, H. J. (1926), *Primitive Culture in Italy*, Methuen.

TURNBULL, C. (1961), *The Forest People*, Doubleday.

TYLOR, E. B. (1873), *Primitive Culture*, Brentano's (7th edn. 1924).

VANSINA, J. (1955), 'Initiation rituals of the Bushong', *Africa*, vol. 25, pp. 138–52.

VANSINA, J. (1964), 'Le royaume Luba', *Annales Sciences Humaines*, no. 49, Musée Royal de l'Afrique Centrale.

6 E. E. Evans-Pritchard

Nuer Symbolism

Excerpt from chapter 5 of E. E. Evans-Pritchard, *Nuer Religion*, Clarendon Press, 1956, pp. 123–35.

In Nuer religion God is, properly speaking, not figured in any material representations, nor are almost all the spirits of the above, though both God and his supra-terrestrial refractions may reveal themselves in signs. But the spirits of the below are represented in creatures and things. Our problem chiefly concerns these spirits of the below. It can be simply stated by the question: What meaning are we to attach to Nuer statements that such-and-such a thing is *kwoth*, spirit? The answer is not so simple.

There are several ways in which what we would render as 'is' is indicated in the Nuer language. The one which concerns us here is the particle *e*. It is used to tell the listener that something belongs to a certain class or category and hence about some character or quality it has, as '*e dit*', 'it is a bird', '*gat nath e car*', 'the Nuer is black', and '*Duob e ram me goagh*', 'Duob is a good man.' The question we are asking is what meaning or meanings it has for Nuer when they say of something '*e kwoth*', 'it is Spirit' (in the sense either of God or of a divine refraction).

Nuer do not claim to see God, nor do they think that anyone can know what he is like in himself. When they speak about his nature they do so by adjectives which refer to attributes, such as 'great' and 'good', or in metaphors taken from the world around them, likening his invisibility and ubiquity to wind and air, his greatness to the universe he has created, and his grandeur to an ox with widespread horns. They are no more than metaphors for Nuer, who do not say that any of these things is God, but only that he is like (*cere*) them. They express in these poetic images as best they can what they think must be some of his attributes.

Nevertheless, certain things are said, or may be said, 'to be' God – rain, lightning and various other natural (in the Nuer way of speech, created) things which are of common interest. There is here an ambiguity, or an obscurity, to be elucidated, for Nuer are not now saying that God or Spirit is like this or that, but that this or that 'is' God or Spirit. Elucidation here does not, however, present great difficulties.

God being conceived of as in the sky, those celestial phenomena which are of particular significance for Nuer, rain and lightning, are said, in a sense we have to determine, to be him. There is no noun denoting either phenomenon and they can only be spoken of by verbs indicating a function of the sky as '*ce nhial deam*', 'the sky rained', and '*ce nhial mar*', 'the sky thundered'. Also pestilences, murrains, death and indeed almost any natural phenomenon significant for men are commonly regarded by Nuer as manifestations from above, activities of divine being. Even the earthly totems are conceived of as a relationship deriving from some singular intervention of Spirit from above in human affairs. It is chiefly by these signs that Nuer have knowledge of God. It might be held, therefore, that the Nuer conception of God is a conceptualization of events which, on account of their strangeness or variability as well as on account of their potentiality for fortune or misfortune, are said to be his activities or his activities in one or other of his hypostases or refractions. Support for such a view might be found in the way Nuer sometimes speak of one or other of these effects. They may say of rain or lightning or pestilence '*e kwoth*', 'it is God', and in storms they pray to God to come to earth gently and not in fury – to come gently, it will be noted, not to make the rain come gently.

I do not discuss this ontological question here beyond saying that were we to suppose that such phenomena are in themselves regarded as God we would misunderstand and misrepresent Nuer religious thought, which is pre-eminently dualistic. It is true that for them there is no abstract duality of natural and supernatural, but there is such a duality between *kwoth*, Spirit, which is immaterial rather than supernatural, and *cak*, creation, the material world known to the senses. Rain and lightning and pestilences and murrains belong to this created world and are referred to by Nuer as *nyin kwoth*, instruments of God.

Nevertheless, they and other effects of significance for men are διοσημία, signs or manifestations of divine activity; and since

Nuer apprehend divine activity in these signs, in God's revelation of himself to them in material forms, the signs are, in a lower medium, what they signify, so that Nuer may say of them '*e kwoth*', 'it is God'. Rain and pestilence come from God and are therefore manifestations of him, and in this sense rain and pestilence are God, in the sense that he reveals himself in their falling. But though one can say of rain or pestilence that it is God one cannot say of God that he is rain or pestilence. This would make no sense for a number of reasons. In the first place, the situation could scarcely arise, God not being an observable object, in which Nuer would require or desire to say about him that he is anything. In the second place, the word *kwoth* does not here refer to a particular refraction of Spirit, a spirit, but to Spirit in its oneness, God, and he could not be in any way identified with any one of his manifestations to the exclusion of all the others. A third, and the most cogent, reason is that rain is water which falls from the sky and pestilence is a bodily condition and they are therefore in their nature material things and not Spirit. Indeed, as a rule, rain is only thought of in connexion with Spirit, and is therefore only said to be Spirit, when it does not fall in due season or falls too much or too violently with storm and lightning – when, that is, the rain has some special significance for human affairs. This gives us a clue to what is meant when Nuer say of something that it is God or that it is a spirit of the air, as thunder may be said to be the spirit *wiu* or a prophet of the spirit *deng* may be said to be *deng* – especially as Nuer readily expand such statements by adding that thunder, rain and pestilence are all instruments (*nyin*) of God or that they are sent by (*jak*) God, and that the spirit *deng* has filled (*gwang*) the prophet through whom it speaks. In the statement here that something is Spirit or a spirit the particle *e*, which we translate 'is', cannot therefore have the meaning of identity in a substantial sense. Indeed, it is because Spirit is conceived of in itself, as the creator and the one, and quite apart from any of its material manifestations, that phenomena can be said to be sent by it or to be its instruments. When Nuer say of rain or lightning that it is God they are making an elliptical statement. What is understood is not that the thing in itself is Spirit but that it is what we would call a medium or manifestation or sign of divine activity in relation to men and of significance for them.

What precisely is posited by the hearer of any such elliptical statement depends on the nature of the situation by reference to which it is made. A vulture is not thought of as being in itself Spirit; it is a bird. But if it perches on the crown of a byre or hut Nuer may say '*e kwoth*', 'it is Spirit', meaning that its doing so is a spiritual signal presaging disaster. A lion is not thought of as being in itself Spirit; it is a beast. But it may, on account of some event which brings it into a peculiar relation to man, such as being born, as Nuer think sometimes happens, as twin to a human child, be regarded as a revelation of Spirit for a particular family and lineage. Likewise, diseases, or rather their symptoms, are not thought of as being in themselves Spirit, but their appearance in individuals may be regarded as manifestations of Spirit for those individuals. Spirit acts, and thereby reveals itself, through these creatures. This distinction between the nature of a thing and what it may signify in certain situations or for certain persons is very evident in totemic relationships. A crocodile is Spirit for certain persons, but it is not thought to be in its nature Spirit, for others kill and eat it. It is because Nuer separate, and quite explicitly when questioned about the matter, spiritual conceptions from such material things as may nevertheless be said 'to be' the conceptions, that they are able to maintain the unity and autonomy of Spirit in spite of a great diversity of accidents and are able to speak of Spirit without reference to any of its material manifestations.

So far I have been mostly speaking of the conception of God and of those of his refractions which belong to the category of the sky or of the above. With two possible exceptions, we cannot say that the things said 'to be' these spirits are material symbols or representations of them; at any rate not in the same sense as we can speak of things being symbols of those lesser refractions of Spirit Nuer call spirits of the earth or of the below, in which God stands in a special relationship to lineages and individuals – such diverse things as beasts, birds, reptiles, trees, phosphorescent objects and pieces of wood. These lesser refractions of Spirit, regarded as distinct spirits in relation to each other, cannot, unlike the spirits of the air, easily be thought of except in relation to the things by reference to which they derive their individuality, and which are said 'to be' them.

When, therefore, Nuer say that the pied crow is the spirit *buk* or that a snake is Spirit, the word 'is' has a different sense from what it has in the statement that rain is Spirit. The difference does not merely lie in the fact that *kwoth* has here a more restricted connotation, being spoken of in reference to a particular and exclusive refraction – a spirit – rather than comprehensively as God or Spirit in its oneness. It lies also in the relation understood in the statement between its subject (snake or crow) and its predicate (Spirit or a spirit). The snake in itself is not divine activity whereas rain and lightning are. The story accounting for a totemic relationship may present it as arising from a revelation of divine activity, but once it has become an established relationship between a lineage and a natural species, the species is a representation or symbol of Spirit to the lineage. What then is here meant when it is said that the pied crow 'is' *buk* or that a snake 'is' Spirit: that the symbol 'is' what it symbolizes? Clearly Nuer do not mean that the crow is the same as *buk*, for *buk* is also conceived of as being in the sky and also in rivers, which the pied crow certainly is not; nor that a snake is the same as some spiritual refraction, for they say that the snake just crawls on the earth while the spirit it is said to be is in the sky. What then is being predicated about the crow or snake in the statement that either is Spirit or a spirit?

It will be simpler to discuss this question in the first place in relation to a totemic relationship. When a Nuer says of a creature '*e nyang*', 'it is a crocodile', he is saying that it is a crocodile and not some other creature, but when he says, to explain why a person behaves in an unusual manner towards crocodiles '*e kwothdien*', 'it (the crocodile) is their spirit', he is obviously making a different sort of statement. He is not saying what kind of creature it is (for it is understood that he is referring to the crocodile) but that what he refers to is Spirit for certain people. But he is also not saying that the crocodile is Spirit – it is not so for him – but that certain people so regard it. Therefore a Nuer would not make a general statement that '*nyang e kwoth*', 'crocodile is Spirit', but would only say, in referring to the crocodile, '*e kwoth*', 'it is Spirit', the distinction between the two statements being that the first would mean that the crocodile is Spirit for everyone whereas the second, being made in a special context of situation, means that it is Spirit for certain persons who are being discussed, or are understood in that context. Likewise, whilst it can be said of the crocodile that it is Spirit, it cannot be said of Spirit that it is the crocodile, or rather, if a statement is framed in this form it can only be made when the word *kwoth* has a pronominal suffix which gives it the meaning of 'his spirit', 'their spirit' and so forth; in other words, where the statement makes it clear that what is being spoken of is Spirit conceived of in relation to particular persons only. We still have to ask, however, in what sense the crocodile is Spirit for these persons.

Since it is difficult to discuss a statement that something which can be observed, crocodile, is something more than what it appears to be when this something more, Spirit, cannot be observed, it is helpful first to consider two examples of Nuer statements that things are something more than they appear to be when both the subject term and the predicate term refer to observable phenomena.

When a cucumber is used as a sacrificial victim Nuer speak of it as an ox. In doing so they are asserting something rather more than that it takes the place of an ox. They do not, of course, say that cucumbers are oxen, and in speaking of a particular cucumber as an ox in a sacrificial situation they are only indicating that it may be thought of as an ox in that particular situation; and they act accordingly by performing the sacrificial rites as closely as possible to what happens when the victim is an ox. The resemblance is conceptual, not perceptual. The 'is' rests on qualitative analogy. And the expression is asymmetrical, a cucumber is an ox, but an ox is not a cucumber.

A rather different example of this way of speaking is the Nuer assertion that twins are one person and that they are birds. When they say 'twins are not two persons, they are one person' they are not saying that they are one individual but that they have a single personality. It is significant that in speaking of the unity of twins they only use the word *ran*, which, like our word 'person', leaves sex, age and other distinguishing qualities of individuals undefined. They would not say that twins of the same sex were one *dhol*, boy, or one *nyal*, girl, but they do say, whether they are of the same sex or not, that they are one *ran*, person. Their single social personality is something over and above their physical

105

duality, a duality which is evident to the senses and is indicated by the plural form used when speaking of twins and by their treatment in all respects in ordinary social life as two quite distinct individuals. It is only in certain ritual situations, and symbolically, that the unity of twins is expressed, particularly in ceremonies connected with marriage and death, in which the personality undergoes a change. Thus, when the senior of male twins marries, the junior acts with him in the ritual acts he has to perform; female twins ought to be married on the same day; and no mortuary ceremonies are held for twins because, for one reason, one of them cannot be cut off from the living without the other. A woman whose twin brother had died some time before said to Miss Soule, to whom I am indebted for the information, 'Is not his soul still living? I am alive, and we are really children of God.'

There is no mortuary ceremony even when the second twin dies, and I was told that twins do not attend the mortuary ceremonies held for their dead kinsfolk, nor mourn them, because a twin is a *ran nhial*, a person of the sky or of the above. He is also spoken of as *gat kwoth*, a child of God. These dioscuric descriptions of twins are common to many peoples, but the Nuer are peculiar in holding also that they are birds. They say 'a twin is not a person (*ran*), he is a bird (*dit*)', although, as we have just seen, they assert, in another sense, that twins are one person (*ran*). Here they are using the word *ran* in the sense of a human being as distinct from any other creature. The dogma is expressed in various ways. Very often a twin is given the proper name *Dit*, bird, *Gwong*, guineafowl, or *Ngec*, francolin. All Nuer consider it shameful, at any rate for adults, to eat any sort of bird or its eggs, but were a twin to do this it would be much more than shameful. It would be *nueer*, a grave sin, for twins respect (*thek*) birds, because, Nuer say, birds are also twins, and they avoid any sort of contact with them. The equivalence of twins and birds is expressed particularly in connexion with death. When an infant twin dies people say '*ce par*', 'he has flown away', using the word denoting the flight of birds. Infant twins who die, as so often happens, are not buried, as other infants are, but are covered in a reed basket or winnowing-tray and placed in the fork of a tree, because birds rest in trees. I was told that birds which feed on carrion would not molest the bodies but would look at their dead kinsmen – twins and birds are also said to be kin, though the usage may be regarded as metaphorical – and fly away again. When I asked a Nuer whether adult twins would be buried like other people he replied 'no, of course not, they are birds and their souls go up into the air'. A platform, not used in the normal mode of burial, is erected in the grave and a hide placed over it. The body is laid on this hide and covered with a second hide. Earth is then carefully patted over the upper hide instead of being shovelled in quickly, as in the burial of an ordinary person. I was told that the corpse is covered with earth lest a hyena eat it and afterwards drink at a pool, for men might drink at the same pool and die from contamination (*nueer*).

It is understandable that Nuer draw an analogy between the multiple hatching of eggs and the dual birth of twins. The analogy is explicit, and, through an extension of it, the flesh of crocodiles and turtles is also forbidden to twins on the ground that these creatures too, like birds, lay eggs. Miss Soule once had a girl twin in her household who refused fish for the same reason – the only case of its kind known to either of us. But the analogy between multiple births in birds and men does not adequately explain why it is with birds that human twins are equated when there are many other creatures which habitually bear several young at the same time and in a manner more closely resembling human parturition. It cannot be just multiple birth which leads Nuer to say that twins are birds, for these other creatures are not respected by twins on that account. The prohibition on eating eggs is clearly secondary, and it is extended to include crocodiles and turtles – and by Miss Soule's girl fish also – not because they lay eggs but because their laying eggs makes them like birds. Moreover, it is difficult to understand why a resemblance of the kind should in any case be made so much of. The multiple hatching of chicks is doubtless a resemblance which greatly strengthens the idea of twins being birds, but it is only part of a more complex analogical representation which requires to be explained in more general terms of Nuer religious thought. A twin, on account of his peculiar manner of conception is, though not Spirit himself, a special creation, and, therefore, manifestation of Spirit; and when he dies his soul goes into the air, to which things associated with Spirit belong. He is a *ran nhial*, a person of the above, whereas an ordinary person is a *ran piny*, a person of the below. A bird, though also not in itself Spirit, belongs by nature to the above and is also what Nuer call, using 'person' metaphorically, a *ran nhial*, a person of the above, and being such is therefore also associated with Spirit. It cannot, of course, be determined for certain whether a twin is said to be a person of the above because he is a bird or whether he is said to be a bird because he is a person of the above, but the connexion in thought between twins and birds is certainly not simply derived from the multiple birth similitude but also, and in my view primarily, from both birds and twins being classed by Nuer as *gaat kowth*, children of God. Birds are children of God on account of their being in the air, and twins belong to the air on account of their being children of God by the manner of their conception and birth.

It seems odd, if not absurd, to a European when he is told that a twin is a bird as though it were an obvious fact, for Nuer are not saying that a twin is like a bird but that he is a bird. There seems to be a complete contradiction in the statement; and it was precisely on statements of this kind recorded by observers of primitive peoples that Lévy-Bruhl based his theory of the prelogical mentality of these peoples, its chief characteristic being, in his view, that it permits such evident contradictions – that a thing can be what it is and at the same time something altogether different. But, in fact, no contradiction is involved in the statement, which, on the contrary, appears quite sensible, and even true, to one who presents the idea to himself in the Nuer language and within their system of religious thought. He does not then take their statements about twins any more literally than they make and understand them themselves. They are not saying that a twin has a beak, feathers, and so forth. Nor in their everyday relations with twins do Nuer speak of them as birds or act towards them as though they were birds. They treat them as what they are, men and women. But in addition to being men and women they are of a twin-birth, and a twin-birth is a special revelation of Spirit; and Nuer express this special character of twins in the 'twins are birds' formula because twins and birds, though for different reasons, are both associated with Spirit and this makes twins, like birds, 'people of the above' and 'children of God', and hence a bird a suitable symbol in which to express the special relationship in which a twin stands to God. When, therefore, Nuer say that a twin is a bird they are not speaking of either as it appears in the flesh. They are speaking of the *anima* of the twin, what they call his *tie*, a concept which includes both what we call the personality and the soul; and they are speaking of the association birds have with Spirit through their ability to enter the realm to which Spirit is likened in metaphor and where Nuer think it chiefly is, or may be. The formula does not express a dyadic relationship between twins and birds but a triadic relationship between twins, birds and God. In respect to God, twins and birds have a similar character.

It is because Nuer do not make, or take, the statement that twins are birds in any ordinary sense that they are fully aware that in ritual relating to twins the actions are a kind of miming. This is shown in their treatment of the corpse of a twin, for, according to what they themselves say, what is a bird, the *tie* or *anima*, has gone up into the air and what is left and treated – in the case of adults platform burial being a convenient alternative to disposal in trees – as though it might be a bird is only the *ring*, the flesh. It is shown also in the convention that should one of a pair of twins die, the child who comes after them takes his place, counting as one of them in the various ceremonies twins have to perform and respecting birds as rigorously as if he were himself a twin, which he is not. The ceremonies have to be performed for the benefit of the living twin and their structure and purpose are such that there have to be two persons to perform them, so a brother or sister acts in the place of the dead.

This discussion of what is meant by the statement that a twin is a bird is not so far away from the subject of totemism as it might seem to be, for the stock explanation among the Nuer of a totemic relationship is that the ancestor of a lineage and a member of a natural species were born twins. The relationship of lineage to species is thereby made to derive not only from the closest of all possible relationships but also from a special act of divine revelation; and since the link between a lineage and its totem is the tutelary spirit of the lineage associated with the totem it is appropriate that the relationship should be thought of as having come about by an event which is a direct manifestation of Spirit.

However, an examination of the Nuer dogma that twins are

birds was made not on account of totemic relationships commonly being explained in terms of twinship but because it was hoped that it would be easier to understand, in the light of any conclusions reached about what is meant by the statement that a twin is a bird, what Nuer mean when they say that some totemic creature, such as the crocodile, is Spirit. Certainly there is here neither the sort of metaphor nor the sort of ellipsis we found in earlier statements. Nor can Nuer be understood to mean that the creature is identical with Spirit, or even with a spirit, Spirit conceived of in a particular totemic refraction. They say quite definitely themselves that it is not; and it is also evident, for Nuer as well as for us, that a material symbol of Spirit cannot, by its very nature, be that which it symbolizes. Nevertheless, though crocodile and Spirit are quite different and unconnected ideas, when the crocodile is for a certain lineage a symbol of their special relationship to God, then in the context of that relationship symbol and what it symbolizes are fused. As in the case of the 'twins are birds' formula, the relation is a triadic one, between a lineage and a natural species and God.

There are obvious and significant differences between the creature–Spirit expression and the cucumber–ox and bird–twin expressions. Cucumber, ox, man and bird are all things which can be known by the senses; but where Spirit is experienced other than in thought it is only in its effects or through material representations of it. We can, therefore, easily see how Nuer regard it as being in, or behind, the crocodile. The subject and predicate terms of the statement that something is Spirit are here no longer held apart by two sets of visible properties. Consequently, while Nuer say that totemic spirits and totems are not the same they sometimes not only speak of, but act towards, a totem as if the spirit were in it. Thus they give some meat of a sacrifice to the lion-spirit to lions, and when they sacrifice to the durra-bird-spirit they address also the birds themselves and tell them that the victim is for them. Nevertheless, they make it clear in talking about their totems that what respect they show for them is on account of their representing the spirits associated with them and not for their own sake.

Another difference is that whereas in the cases of the cucumber–ox and twin–bird expressions the equivalence rests on analogies which are quite obvious even to us once they are pointed out – the cucumber being treated in the ritual of sacrifice as an ox is, and twins and birds both being 'children of God' and also multiple births – analogy is lacking in the creature–Spirit expression. There is no resemblance between the idea of Spirit and that of crocodile. There is nothing in the nature of crocodiles which evokes the idea of Spirit for Nuer, and even for those who respect crocodiles the idea of Spirit is evoked by these creatures because the crocodile is a representation of Spirit in relation to their lineage and not because there is anything crocodile-like about Spirit or Spirit-like about crocodiles. We have passed from observation of resemblances to thought by means of symbols in the sort of way that the crocodile is used as a symbol for Spirit.

We are here faced with the same problem we have been considering earlier, but in what, in the absence of analogical guidance to help us, is a more difficult form. The difficulty is increased by Nuer symbols being taken from an environment unfamiliar to us and one which, even when we familiarize ourselves with it, we experience and evaluate differently. We find it hard to think in terms of crocodiles, snakes and fig-trees. But reflection shows us that this problem is common to all religious thought, including our own; that a religious symbol has always an intimate association with what it represents, that which brings to the mind with what it brings to the mind. Nuer know that what they see is a crocodile, but since it represents Spirit to some of them it is for those people, when thought of in that way, also what it stands for. The relationship of members of a Nuer lineage to Spirit is represented by a material symbol by which it can be thought of concretely, and therefore as a relationship distinct from the relationships of other lineages to Spirit. What the symbols stand for is the same thing. It is they, and not what they stand for, which differentiate the relationships. There results, when what acts as a symbol is regarded in this way, a fusion between Spirit, as so represented, and its material representation. I would say that then Nuer regard Spirit as being in some way in, or behind, the creature in which in a sense it is beholden.

The problem is even more difficult and complex than I have stated it, because we might say that what are fused are not so much the idea of Spirit and its material representation as the idea of Spirit and the idea of its material representation. It is rather the idea of crocodile than the saurian creatures themselves which stands for Spirit to a lineage. If a Nuer cannot see Spirit he likewise in some cases seldom, if ever, sees his totem; so that it is no longer a question of a material object symbolizing an idea but of one idea symbolizing another. I doubt whether those who respect monorchid bulls or waterbuck often see a member of the class or species, and children in these and other cases must often be told about their totemic attachments before they have seen their totems. There must also be Nuer who respect dom palms who live in parts of Nuerland to the east of the Nile where this tree does not grow. Indeed, I feel confident that one totem, the *lou* serpent, a kind of Loch Ness monster, does not exist, and if this is so, a totem can be purely imaginary. As this point has some theoretical importance for a study of totemism I draw attention to a further significant fact. Nuer do not speak of the spirit of crocodiles, lions, tamarind-trees and so on, but always of the spirit of crocodile, lion and tamarind-tree, and they would never say that crocodiles, lions and tamarind-trees were somebody's spirit but always that crocodile, lion and tamarind-tree was his spirit. The difference in meaning between the plural and singular usage is not, perhaps, very obvious in English but it is both clear and vital in Nuer. It is the difference between crocodiles thought of as they are seen in rivers and crocodiles thought of as crocodile or as the crocodile, as a type of creature, crocodile as a conception.

II. Religion in Historical Perspective

Judaism, Christianity and Islam are generally acknowledged as
having been the most dynamic of the major religious
traditions. Each of them has manifested a definite sense of
historical development and destiny. Troeltsch (Reading 7) and
Gellner (Reading 8) point to the problems encountered
respectively by Christianity and Islam in trying to maintain or
promote religious hegemony.[1] Troeltsch's contribution deals
very specifically with Catholicism in the medieval period;
while Gellner's essay is more general, discussing the dynamics
of Islam and its relationship to 'the world' in comparison
with Christianity. In contrast with primitive religion we see
in the case of these two religions, Christianity and Islam, a
very much greater degree of differentiation of religious ideals;
and particularly in the case of Christianity, a highly
specialized set of institutions in which religious ideas are
maintained and produced. Both Troeltsch and Gellner
emphasize the importance of urban-rural variation in the
respective religious developments of Christianity and Islam.

1. Willems (Reading 12) outlines the attempts by Portugal and Spain
to achieve Catholic hegemony in Latin America. In Reading 17, Eisenstadt
deals with the political and economic consequences of the rise of Protestantism in Europe.

7 E. Troeltsch

Medieval Christianity

Excerpt from E. Troeltsch, *The Social Teaching of the Christian Churches*, vol. 1, Allen and Unwin, 1931, pp. 246–56. (First published 1911.)

The Early Church never conceived the idea of a Christian unity of civilization. The life of the world in which it was placed was too independent, too settled and, above all, too complicated, too much under the dominance of the law and the State, and its economic conditions were too complicated, for such an ideal to have been either conceived or realized. At every point the path was blocked by the spirit of the ancient Polis and of the bureaucratic Hellenistic State. The fact that the Middle Ages created a unity of civilization, at least as an ideal, was due not merely to the development of the Church and of asceticism, but also to the life of the world itself, which in its new form fitted into the whole more easily than it had done hitherto. For even now the Church did not think in terms of social reform and social politics, or of shaping the connexion between the economic–legal substructure and the ethico-spiritual superstructure in harmony with her ideas, which it would have been her task to create, in spite of the opposing forces within the actual situation. In this respect the Church herself, and the Church in particular, was full of the most unpractical idealism. She seemed to think that if the spiritual government of the world were functioning properly, and if faith and love were functioning properly, and if faith and love were strong and healthy, then all difficulties would solve themselves. It is true that the Carolingian State and the Territorial Church system of the early Middle Ages had fused both these elements with each other. But the only person who had a vision of social reform was Charlemagne, and he was only able to take this view because the actual situation forced his State and the Church into a position of co-operation; and, moreover, because the situation itself made that kind of fusion possible. Again, both Church and

State became inextricably involved in each other's fortunes simply through the force of the circumstances which made this union possible. Therefore, when the Papal theocracy took over the supreme power from Kings and Emperors, it was simply entering into their inheritance. This all happened without further reflection, and without any deeper interference with life. The fact that the Church and the secular realm there co-operated harmoniously does not mean that the Church had consciously embarked upon a policy of social reform; it was simply the actual result of certain given circumstances. The real and the ultimate reason, therefore, for the possibility of an interior union, must have lain in the legal, economic and social conditions of the Roman-Germanic peoples themselves, who either accepted the Ethos of the Church without question or were ready to do so. However foreign and hostile the militaristic feudal spirit, with its warlike conception of honour, its emphasis on brute force, and all the coarseness and insecurity for life with which it was combined, may seem to the Christian spirit, still, on the other hand, there must have been something in these conditions which made it possible to effect such a change more readily than in either the ancient or the modern world. If we try to distinguish the unique element of the Middle Ages, as contrasted with ancient and modern times, it will then become clear why it was easier to accomplish this change, and therefore to make it possible to establish a relative Christian unity of civilization.

In the decaying Roman Empire, in spite of all its political upheavals, the main hindrance was still the continuance of the ancient idea of the State, the domination of a law which formally controlled all human relationships, the administration of a rationalizing bureaucracy, and, finally, the influence of a money economy which, although its force was exhausted, still made itself felt in its secularizing effects. This was a hindrance which continued even after the ancient pagan religious system had been destroyed. The Middle Ages, on the other hand, had no conception of the State at all in either the ancient or the modern sense of the word. Medieval economic life was based on agriculture; there was, therefore, no official class, or, rather, its officials were paid in landed property; officials thus became landowners who clung to the ownership of their land as a matter of private right. The military organization in particular, since it was impossible to use the old military levies for wars in distant lands, and for longer periods, was bound up with this system of feoffment and the sharing of immunities (or special charters of privilege). It was, however, only the great feudal lords, or the military levies which they had created, who were affected by this system. This explains why the military class, and, later on, the knightly class, became quite distinct from the peasant and bourgeois sections of the population. Thus there arose two main classes within the State; the Church and the clergy formed the third class, in so far as the clergy, represented by their leaders, did not enter into the ranks of the feudal lords.

The numerous gifts to, and classifications of ordinary freemen, due to economic, social and other similar reasons, had a similar effect, so that the ancient popular community of nobles and free peasants was transformed into the artificially restricted and most complicated, almost chaotic, system of feudal tenure, which was controlled by the authority of King and Emperor, and also by that of the Church, as supreme ruler and supreme feudal lord. In this system the Church claimed the princes as their feudal tenants, and absorbed the whole system into her hierarchically graded organization. On the other hand, under these various suzerainties, there were sections of the population which were bound to the Crown lands and the demesnes. These groups, however, were very different from the slaves of the Ancient World; they were simply bound to the soil, and to the various degrees of service which that entailed. The tendency towards personal freedom, however, increasingly developed, and the relationship of absolute submission gradually changed into one of mutual service and obligation, of personal contract and of loyalty. Under these circumstances there was no conception of the State as such, no common and uniform dependence upon a central power, no all-dominating sovereignty; no equal exercise of a public civil law; no abstract basis of association in formal and legal rules. At any rate, in so far as anything of that sort did exist at all, it was related only to the Church, and not in any way to the State. The dominant sentiment in human relationships was not obedience to authority, but contract, reverence, loyalty, faith – all of which were elements of feeling; the spirit of feudalism penetrated even into the serf-relationship; not even the army was based upon abstract law and obedience, but upon the good will and loyalty of the troops.

The groups which thus came into being then became united among themselves to all other groups belonging to the same class of society; this led to the organization of corporations, which ranged from the groups composed of the knights and nobles, down to those composed of free peasants, serfs, workmen attached to the court and manual labourers; and later it extended to the city industries. All these corporations possessed a law of their own, apart from the law of the State; to a great extent, indeed, they exercised their own right of jurisdiction in harmony with this law. Further, in these corporations or guilds there was a spirit of solidarity and of personal understanding and helpfulness, which, in spite of its traditional severity, was equally opposed to all legal formalism and appealed chiefly to the element of feeling. Finally, law in the narrower sense, civil and penal law, corresponded to this general spirit. Dispersed among many legal authorities, found by the assessors according to use and equity, to a great extent using a symbolism entirely opposed to the whole idea of abstract law, above all with no knowledge of the spirit of the Roman idea of property, or of abstract trade and money laws, this law was itself the expression of a society which had not yet been legally organized on a basis of formal rights and general equality. The Church alone had a written law and a formal process; this, however, was due to the special Divine character of the Church, and was strongly influenced by her standards.

This whole state of affairs was connected with the return to an economic system based on agriculture, for which the way had already been prepared by the period of late antiquity, and which was ultimately completed by the continental civilization of the Middle Ages. It was a return to simpler conditions of life, in which both personal relationships and the remains of the ancient socialistic collective life were predominant. The spirit of the ancient city state had been broken. The only vestiges which remained were the Stoic and Platonist elements which were preserved by the sacerdotal class, and those were the very elements which had already caused its destruction.

The agrarian character of this civilization, however, involved small and scattered settlements, the exclusion of the right of free change of domicile, as each region had to have its own lord, and each lord his own land, and ultimately every workman and manual labourer was obliged to have his own piece of soil; those who lost this were *déclassés*. This meant, however, that great importance attached to personal relationships, which developed a sense of solidarity in the ordering of life, and a widespread community feeling, expressed in mutual help and interdependence, in which all the people living in one place became a kind of united body, based on a spirit of mutual protection and mutual service. The elements which were lacking were the mobilization of life and of intelligence, independence of the direct gift of Nature, and confidence in rationalism which regulates and creates social conditions. In this situation everything seemed to be the gift of nature, the obvious way of life, and thus the result of the Divine ordering, whether as a good gift or as a penalty and judgement. The pilgrim, the traveller, the vagabond depend upon charity and hospitality, which thus seemed to supplement completely the normal arrangements of life by means of special demonstrations of charity. For a long time, even after the towns had come into existence, and had drawn to themselves masses of people from agrarian serfdom, there still prevailed in them, so far as it was possible, patriarchal authority and subordination, comradeship and mutual contract, that is, a spirit of mutual loyalty and respect, which was very different from the spirit of law in both the Ancient and the Modern World.

In the Ancient World the city state practically destroyed agricultural life and absorbed everything into itself; but the medieval industrial town long remained semi-agrarian in character; at a later stage we shall see the special significance of the medieval town in the development of the ethico-religious ideal.

Above all, the intellectual and ethical fundamental elements of the social type produced by a money economy were lacking. As yet there was no money economy worth the name. In the North, at least, it was very restricted until well into the urban period, and during the period when Catholic social ideals were being developed it was merely subordinate to a natural economy. That intellectual and moral type was also lacking which usually begins to make its own characteristic mark upon the minds of men, even when the money economy has not reached the stage of unrestricted calculating capitalism, or the spirit of gain for the sake of gain. Where this spirit predominates it makes all values abstract, exchangeable and measurable; it mobilizes property and, in a way of which no one hitherto had dreamed, advancing beyond the merely natural dependence of life, it groups together the economic values and the possibilities which they contain. The economic system based on money depersonalizes values, makes property abstract and individualistic, creates a rational law of trade and possessions, raises men above natural conditions of life, unites its fortunes with forethought, intelligence and calculation, replaces the idea of Providence and the spirit of mutual help and solidarity of those who are bound together in loyalty to one another, by products which are at all times ready for use; it produces great differences in possessions and in needs, and leads from the simple standpoint of the consumer to an active production of artificial values and conditions. It is the cause of the development of formal abstract law, of an abstract, impersonal way of thinking, of rationalism and relativism. As a result it leads to a restless and changing social differentiation which is based not upon the unchanging land, but upon accidental accumulations of money which can change anything into anything else. The personal relationships depending on nature and on social groups are dissolved; the individual gains an abstract freedom and independence, and, on the other hand, deteriorates into unknown forms of dependence which seem to be the powers of superior common sense and the sum of attractive possibilities. The individual makes up for the loss of concrete individuality, that is, of an originality which is infinitely differentiated and secured by corporate relations, by abstract individualism; that is, by the assertion of individual powers, from which it builds up rationally unions, group fellowships, institutions and enterprises, and to which it makes conditions rationally serviceable. These results came about very slowly and gradually after the rise of the money economy which began after the Crusades and was connected with the town industries.

During the period when the ecclesiastical social doctrines were being developed this spirit and type of capitalism did not exist at all. The society of that day inhabited regions which had been recently cleared; the population was sparse, the death rate high; means of communication were primitive and life itself was insecure. The social system was intelligently organized on an individualistic basis in direct dependence upon Nature, in associations which were based partly upon brute force, quite rationalistically conceived, and also üpon the sentiments of inward reverence and loyalty. Science and literature were limited to the smallest groups. Popular thinking was dominated by phantasy and symbolism. The need for unity in life and thought was extremely slight, and was in large measure satisfied by the idea of the unity of the Church and of Christendom, and also by the Christian view of the world, with its teaching on the Creation and the End of the world, and its central point in the institution of grace, the Church. Both in the spiritual and in the temporal realm the social fabric was held together by habit and custom, by reverence and faith, agreement and loyalty, by many of the customs involved in the holding of property in common, and by a mutual helpfulness, which, owing to the defective means of communication, and in the absence of a money-economy traffic in goods, is the natural basis for the existence of the individual group.

Medieval Society and the Christian Ethic

Medieval social structure, with its personal relationships open to everyone, with its graded system of estates and corporations, with its emphasis on the existing conditions of authority and their utilization for mutual service, with its emancipation of the individual within his appointed sphere, with its lack of abstract formal justice, with its exclusive groups and its fine shades of feeling in the sense of solidarity, with its fairly equal range of material need (which means at bottom that a man's wealth is proportionate to the number of people for whom he is responsible, and that power and position or prestige are dependent upon the possession of land and tenants), with its confidence in the spirit of mutual agreement, loyalty and reverence, with its tendency to humanize even the serf-relationship: this prepared a comparatively favourable soil for the realization of the ethical ideals of Christendom as they had been formulated under the guidance of the Church.

Even when art and science began to develop in closest contact with the Church, for a long time they both remained closely connected with the Church; in fact, there were no independent secular values of civilization at all which might have felt and claimed a Divine right to exist apart from the Church and her ideals. The only sovereignty that existed was that of the Church; there was no sovereignty of the State, nor of economic production, nor of science or art. The 'other-worldly' ideal of the Gospel had to contend against worldliness, love of pleasure, coarseness and violence, but it had no rivals in the realm of the spirit; nor did it come into conflict with any order of secular civilization containing its own law and authority which had an existence apart from the Church. Since civilized life was still so little developed, and was also constantly being broken up by almost uncontrollable impulses of passion and of unrestrained violence, it was quite possible to unite with it the pessimism of the Middle Ages, with its emphasis on sin and the sense of transitory existence, which formed the illusion of the sole supremacy of the religious values of life, and which was strengthened by every means imagination could devise. Man's relation to the world was conceived in terms of 'duty'. The whole outlook and conditions of life which existed at that time were not unfavourable to the growth of the new ecclesiastical social ideals. The conception of duty, the inwardness of an ethic which had no place for abstract law, but was primarily concerned with the cultivation of a right spirit in personal relationships, and the ideal Christian anarchism of a spiritual ethic – indeed, the whole Christian emphasis on the moral value of an 'inner' disposition and a spirit of love which finds expression in mutual help and service, and in a fight against the worship of mammon: all these elements took root in comparatively favourable soil.

Above all, the conditions of property and possessions were also favourable to this ethical system. As the Church itself was a great communistic institution, full of the spirit of solidarity and care for all, so every smaller group bore the same stamp of mutual love and loyalty and service. The charity of the Church, particularly that of the Religious Orders, was mainly needed for the service of the *déclassés*, the sick and the abnormal. On the other hand, the presence of such needy folk was considered normal and desirable, since they provided an opportunity for the exercise of charity; far from being hindered and set aside by a rational social policy they formed a normal Christian 'class' of their own, which was regarded as necessary for the whole. In any case, in theory and in ideal it is permissible to regard the matter in this way. Thus we can understand how it became possible to regard the secular life, as well as the ascetic life, as coming under the control of Christian standards; although in the ascetic life the conditions were more secure and favourable, yet it was possible for the secular life to be controlled by the Christian ethic. The only difference involved was one of degree, and that did not hinder the unity of civilization.

From another point of view, however, this social structure was closely connected with the warlike spirit of feudalism and with the feudal principle of honour; thus at this point it came into conflict with the Christian doctrine of non-resistance, of Christian humility and, above all, with the Christian idea of love. Here, too, there existed in reality a deep inward hostility towards the universal religious ethic of humanity. In these circumstances it seemed as though the Christian ideal could only be realized within a limited group; it was then that the cloister appeared to present the only conditions within which the Christian ethic could be practised without compromise. The attacks on the secularization of the Church, the attempts to make the incumbents of collegiate churches submit to the rule of the canons, and the ever-renewed assaults of asceticism, were all directed simply against the absorption of the ecclesiastical dignitaries themselves into the feudal system. This undercurrent of coarseness and violence, however, coupled with the world's conception of honour, constituted a foil for the ecclesiastical and ethical system, which impelled it to a vigorous assertion of its existence, and prevented it from degenerating into mere hypocrisy or sentimentality. The Church also undertook to transmute the feudal spirit itself into something ethical, in the ecclesiastical sense of the word, by making the order of knighthood a semi-spiritual dignity, and by consecrating its militarism to ideal ends – the defence of widows, orphans and the oppressed; by transforming the idea of honour into an obligation towards God and man, and into a virile loyalty to Christ and the Saints; and by directing the cult of women into the service of the Mother of God. In so doing the Church incorporated the military system and the use of force, by diverting it into Christian channels, into the ecclesiastical system of morals. This is the peculiar significance of the Crusades, which were organized by the Church with the aim of diverting into Christian channels the military element, together with all the social difficulty and conflict of the feudal world; from this point of view the Crusades were just as useful for external purposes as was asceticism for the inner life of the Church. The ethic of love could not do without the ethic of force, but, so far as it could, it placed it at the disposal of the service of love and of faith.

Although, in spite of this, a strong secular lay civilization, governed by the ideals of chivalry, came into being, this lay civilization was then either replaced by the bourgeois town civilization, or very greatly restricted. Finally, with the aid of the Mendicant Orders who helped the lower classes, this bourgeois civilization (just as in the case of chivalry, only with far greater effect and influence on history) was also guided into religious channels, which meant that the development of knightly civilization did not lead to a break between it and the ecclesiastical civilization.

Ethical Significance of the Medieval Town

We have now reached the point at which we ought to turn to the consideration of the ethical and spiritual significance of the medieval town. The ownership of the land which had grown up out of the loss of ancient popular freedom, out of the military organization, and out of the political needs of the monarchy, had never fully met the requirements of the Christian way of life, in spite of the fact that much of its organization was conceived in the Christian spirit. The reason for this lay mainly in the great differences of social position, in the feudal system itself and in its use of violence. Only when the city, which arose out of the decay of the system of territorial dominion and its residue, gathered into one the varied population which was made up of every conceivable kind of element, was the sphere prepared, within which the great advantages of medieval society could be cleansed from the coarseness and violence of feudalism.

The one vital need of city life – essentially an industrial asso-ciation – is peace, with which is combined freedom, and the sharing of each individual citizen in the life of the city as a whole, with freedom to work without disturbance and a right to acquire property by personal effort and labour. All these characteristics suggest a certain parallelism between the city and the claims of the Christian ethic. The town represented a non-military, peaceful community of labour, needing the military element solely as a means of protection, and devoid as yet of capitalistic and city features. As such it was a picture of the Christian Society.

From the standpoint of political and economic history, the period of town civilization, which begins with the twelfth century, is regarded mainly as a preparation and foundation for the modern world. At the same time, this period which is characterized by its great cathedrals and their intensive Church life; its religiously consecrated guilds and corporations; its social and political efforts for the spiritual and material welfare of its citizens; its Christian parochial schools and its charitable institu-tions; its peace and its public spirit – has a direct significance for the history of ethics and of religious life, and it constitutes the high-water mark of the development of the medieval spirit.

At first the main economic features of agrarian and rural society were retained, together with all that was in harmony with the ethic of the Church, while those persistent stumbling-blocks, militaristic feudalism and widely separated social grades based on the distribution of property, were absent.

In contradistinction to the ancient Polis, in which aristocratic landowners lived together, which developed its own political and commercial policy, and educated its citizens on the basis of slave labour, as men of independent means (whether large or small) and State pensioners, the medieval inland industrial town was a firmly established fellowship of labour and of peace, in which a modest amount of property of equal value was held by the citizens. The medieval town, with its strong sense of solidarity, thus proved to be far better adapted to the spread of the Christian ethic than the ancient Polis.

It was the city also which first produced that intensity and elasticity of intellectual life without which a vigorous develop-ment of the Christian world of thought is impossible; this is the

125

reason why, from the very beginning, Christianity was a religion of the city. But the medieval industrial town was still very closely connected with the conditions of the simpler agrarian life, and as a town of free labour and fellowship it was so far removed from the spirit of the ancient city state that the ideal of a secular life controlled by the Christian ethic thus took root more easily in the town. The later development of city life, however, did sever this relationship with Christian thought, especially in the Italian cities.

To sum up: it was thus at first actually due to pure coincidence that the social, economic and political conditions of medieval life made a comparatively thorough and direct Christianization of civilization possible.

Naturally, however, this practical coincidence did not exclude thoughtful examination of the facts. In theory the various elements were reconciled, and ideal rules for the regulation of ideal conditions were deduced from them. Only thus was the foundation laid, and the ecclesiastical unity of civilization achieved. This world of ideas became the permanent foundation of Catholic social doctrine.

8 E. Gellner

A Pendulum Swing Theory of Islam

E. Gellner, 'A pendulum swing theory of Islam', *Annales de Sociologie Marocaines*, 1968, pp. 5–14.

The sociology of Islam has a number of claims on the sociologist's interest. For one thing, Islam is, more perhaps than other religions, a blueprint of a social order. Hence the successes and failures of its implementation provide an interesting test case for theories concerning the relationship of belief and social reality. For another thing, Islam differs in various important ways from Christiantity which has perhaps, not surprisingly, been uppermost in the minds of European sociologists of religion. These two considerations are not unconnected: it is the total manner in which Islam is a social movement which perhaps most crucially differentiates it from Christianity.

It might be objected that, for instance, Christianity and Judaism can also be blueprints of a social order. But Christianity has a far greater tendency towards giving unto Caesar that which is Caesar's, and theocratic tendencies are only among many within Christianity, whereas they seem to be far more typical of Islam. Judaism, on the other hand, lacks the universalist and proselytizing tendencies of either. One might say that Islam is more total, in a number of dimensions: it does not restrict its appeal territorially; it does not restrict its application to some institutions only; and it does yet have a kind of independent existence in scriptural and normative record, and cannot simply be equated with the practices of a society in which it occurs. The first of these characteristics differentiate it from Judaism and much of Christianity. The third differentiates it from tribal religions, which *might* otherwise, in some cases, be held to be total in the second sense.

Two questions above all have inspired sociological curiosity about Christianity. The first: did it undermine the Roman Empire and classical virtue? Gibbon, Hume and Frazer thought it did.

St Augustine tried to refute the charge, but in modern times the decline and fall of the Roman empire is no longer a source of current sorrow and Christian apologists are not preoccupied with the issue. The second most popular question is: was a certain segment of Christianity crucial for the genesis of capitalism and hence of the modern world?

If we transpose these two questions to the context of Islam, the perspective we get on religion becomes quite different. Islam was not born inside an empire which then collapsed. It was born *outside* two empires, one of which it then promptly over-ran and the other it very nearly over-ran (and did over-run in the long run). Hence the first question scarcely arises in connexion with Islam. Islam appears to be a cement of empires, and not an acid corroding them.

The association of Islam with conquest, and above all early and rapid conquest, has one important sociological consequence: the absence of accommodation with the temporal power. Being itself Caesar, it had no need to give unto Caesar. Accommodation with the temporal world only takes place in *modern* conditions.

The second question of course arises only in a negative way. It arises in an inverse form, concerning the lack of preconditions for the emergence of the 'modern' world.

The best starting point for approaching the most interesting facet of the sociology of Islam is I think David Hume. In *The Natural History of Religion*, Hume presents several theories of religion, not necessarily consistent with each other. He begins with a rather conventional theory of a unilineal kind, of a progression from polytheism to monotheism. The status of this theory in his mind is not entirely clear: it may just be an historical account of what it so happens took place, without, as it were, theoretical or sociological significance. As it is also progression from a less rational view to a more rational one, and as he does not credit rationality with much influence over men's views (going somewhat beyond not crediting it with much influence over their actions), it is not quite clear what its place in the scheme is.

He does however proceed to a far more interesting theory, concerning a permanent oscillation in religious phenomena:

the *oscillation* between polytheistic and monotheistic views. Societies have a tendency, according to him, to proceed from polytheism to monotheism and then back again to polytheism, and so on, world without end.

The reasons he offers for this oscillation are interesting even though they are not quite satisfactory. The reasons are psychological, and this psychologistic approach is his chief weakness. The reasons for the progression from polytheism to monotheism are what one might call the Stalinist tendencies of the human heart. Within a population of spirits, etc., there will be some one who or which approaches a position of pre-eminence, however limited. Competition for his or its favours will lead the worshippers to credit him with even greater power and excellence, inevitably to the detriment of the rival spirits, etc. Thus an unique and transcendent and ineffable deity comes about: as a kind of product of an auction in competitive flattery.

But then, the pendulum swings back. A contrary process also takes place. This might be named the Sydney Stanley phenomenon, after the name of the chief personage investigated by the famous Tribunal during the postwar period. At the time, an interesting sociological argument was put forward: given the enormously great *and* unintelligible powers of the modern state, it was inevitable that petitioners, requiring the assistance of this enormously powerful but unintelligible entity for their ends, should seek the assistance of intermediaries claiming better acquaintance with the Kafka-esque intricacies of the approaches to what were then not yet known as the corridors of power. Hume sees the same process in the religious sphere: given that the deity is all powerful and yet hidden and unintelligible, what should be more natural than that a simple uninstructed worshipper should seek the aid of some spiritual intermediaries? The deity having been propelled by flattery into inaccessible and unintelligible regions, new lines of communication must be constructed, and these lead us back to a well-populated pantheon. And then the initial process can, in due course, start again.

The theory is clearly inspired in the first instance by the struggle of Jehovah against the Baalim, and by the struggle of the Protestants against graven images, and the awareness of the fact that the perpetuity of these struggles must arise from the presence of some counter force. Hume does however also make perceptive remarks about this process in Islam. This polarity, and the oscillation between the poles, seems to me the most interesting fact about Muslim religious life. One can start with Hume's doctrine of the oscillation without accepting his excessively psychologistic account of its mechanics.

Let us leave Hume for a moment and attempt a sociological characterization of the poles between which the oscillation takes place. Its proper characterization should, I think, be as follows.

On the one hand, let us, say, take a set or syndrome of characteristics which I shall call *P*. These are:

Strict monotheism
Puritanism
Stress on scriptural revelation and hence on literacy
Egalitarianism between believers
Consequently, absence of special mediation, which of course on its this-worldly side would involve hierarchy
Minimization of ritual or mystical extravagance; correspondingly, moderation and sobriety
Stress on the observance of rules rather than on emotional states.

On the other side, we may have a set or syndrome of characteristics which I shall classify as *C*:

Tendency towards hierarchy both within this and the other world
Consequently, priesthood or ritual specialization and a multiplicity of spirits in the other
The incarnation of religion in perceptual symbols or images rather than in the abstract recorded word
Consequently, tendency towards profusion of ritual and mystical practices rather than sobriety and moderation.
Similarly, an ethic of loyalty towards personality rather than respect for rules.

There is a further opposition of characteristics which need not be included in the definition but which perhaps sociologically follow from them: characteristics *P* are more favoured by an urban than by a rural setting in view of their requirements of literacy and perhaps for other reasons, whilst the characteristics of group *C* are more favoured by a rural than by an urban society.

It is at this point that one should perhaps introduce what seems to me the really striking contrast between Islam and Christianity: in Christianity the religious tradition characterized by Syndrome C is central. It had the greatest continuity of the time and the greatest extension territorially and in numbers. It is the religious traditions of characteristics P which are fragmented territorially and in organization, and which have perhaps a lesser continuity in time, or at any rate those extant at present have a lesser depth in time than has the main tradition.

Within Islam, this is inverted. The urban, literate or literacy-oriented, at least theoretically egalitarian Islam of the *ulama* of the towns is in some sense identical from one end of orthodox Islam to the other (restricting ourselves for the time being to Sunni orthodoxy), and is also somehow continuous over time. It is the hierarchical, less puritanical, emotionally and sensually indulgent Islam of the saints, holy men, etc., which is discontinuous in its organization, which undergoes fairly frequent and fundamental transformations, and so forth. *It* is the fragmented heterodoxy along the fringes.

This inversion is surely significant and deserves some sociological investigation.

Let us now leave religion and consider the political structure of the Muslim state. Leaving aside the question of the occasional presence of 'feudal' institutions, in general characteristics the typical Muslim state is very much unlike that of feudal Europe. I leave aside of course that degenerate use of the word 'feudal' which consists of applying it to any pre-industrial society with any kind of elaborate authority structure: this terminology, though no doubt by now ineradicable from political discussion, has perhaps little merit in sociology. In recent years, it has of course been replaced or supplemented by a new stereotype, that of 'oriental society', with its image of a pre-industrial bureaucracy supervising the endless digging and maintenance of irrigation channels. This model, whatever its merits elsewhere, does not seem to me to apply to the Islamic state any more than does the 'feudal' one.

The paradigm of the traditional Muslim state seems to be something like this: a society in which urban life and tribal life coexist. Towns are garrisons, centres of trade and of Muslim learning: they are also the location of the central power. The central power however does not fully control the rest of the society, either in a territorial or in a qualitative sense: for all that, the rest of the society remains in some sense one political or at least moral unit. Just this is one of the significances of Islam. The territorial limitations on the effectiveness of central power are simple: there is a penumbra of tribal lands which effectively resist central authority, tolerating neither its administrative agents nor its tax collectors nor, if they can help it, periodic visits by a peripatetic court accompanied by the army. In a qualitative sense, the central power is limited even in territories in which it is not so defied: tribes exist even within the Land of Government, and the representative of the central power is the local leader confirmed by the centre rather than a genuine bureaucratic nominee.

All this is of course implicit in the very notion of the persistence of tribes, if one means by tribes organizations extending in size well above the village level.

The dynamics of this kind of political system have been well schematized in the famous theory of Ibn Khaldun, which might be called the theory of the tribal circulation of élites. This theory presupposes an economic – and, one might add, spiritual and conceptual – dependence of the rural and marginal populations on the civilization of the city. The society as a whole operates at a level, and within a conceptual religious scheme, which makes the towns indispensable. At the same time, the organization and ethos of the towns make them inimical to social cohesion and hence military prowess. One might say that there is a tragic antithesis between civilization and society: social cohesion and the life of cities are incompatible. Only tribes have cohesion. Only cities have civilization. Tribes provide the political and military basis of empire. At the same time, the central power is based on cities. The consequence is this circulation of élites: every so often (in three generations, according to Ibn Khaldun), a new dynasty is born of some marginal tribe, whose social cohesion and vigour were preserved by its environment, both physically and socially speaking. Destroying the previous dynasty, it in turn bases itself on a town, either taking over the previous centre or building its own, as the Almoravides built Marrakesh. It in turn succumbs to urban life and is in due course replaced. The general pattern remains unchanged: only its personnel rotate.

The general pattern which is static has a certain neatness about it. It can be schematized as three concentric circles: in the inner circle, the tribes of government, those tribes connected by kin links or otherwise with the ruling dynasty, exempt from taxation and employed as a kind of taxation-enforcing army against other tribes; the middle circle consisting of those tribes who have taxes extracted from them; and finally the outer circle of those who do not allow taxes to be extracted from them. Urban life generally exists only within the inner two circles, and the towns are protected not by their own effort but by the governmental, central tribes.

Allowing for modifications and complications, this does seem to be the underlying pattern of the Muslim state. The picture I have drawn is based primarily on Morocco, where this pattern was unusually sharp and clearly conceptualized. The schema requires, as indicated, that the towns should be weak: either, of course, identified with a central power or on the other hand, in as far as they constitute a separate entity, dependent for their protection on the central power. They also seem relatively weak economically: there is a striking confirmation of this in the 'Keynesian' passages in Ibn Khaldun, where he credits the *court* with the crucial role which Keynes credits to the middle class, namely that of causing the upward or downward swing in economic fluctuations by its spending or refraining from spending.

It is perhaps possible to bring the political schema based on Ibn Khaldun into relation with the schema of religious life based on David Hume. Bringing them into relationship with each other will at the same time correct and complement the psychologistic bias of Hume's account.

The tribesman does indeed need spiritual intermediaries between himself and the ultimate deity. This is not merely because generations of theological flatterers have painted the deity in impossibly inaccessible transcendent colours. Part of the truth is of course that being illiterate the reasonings of the theologians and the recorded voice of the deity itself are not directly accessible to him. For him, it is indeed necessary that the Word should become Flesh. For he has no means of apprehending the disembodied word: a strictly platonic religion is difficult for him. But there is more to his need for a cult of personality than the provision of audio-visual aids for the illiterate devotees of a scriptural religion. The tribesman needs the sacred for purposes of arbitrating in inter-tribal and intra-tribal disputes (this distinction hardly applies in the case of segmentary tribes, anyway); he needs it to provide guarantees and sanctuary and underwriting for legal processes such as trial by collective oath, he needs it to provide continuity especially where tribal institutions of leadership are discontinuous and elective, he needs it to guarantee both spatial and temporal boundaries (and in the case of pastoral transhumant tribes, boundaries are *both* spatial and temporal) and so on. For all these purposes, the sacred must speak with an incarnate voice. It cannot content itself with enunciating abstract principles recorded in books and mediated by scribes and judges: there is no class of scribes and judges to do the mediating, and no one can read the books. The sacred must speak with a human voice. A hierarchical, specialized class of religious personnel is virtually indispensable. The personages in whom the sacred is incarnated have neither the means nor the motives for puritanism. The relationship they have with their devotees gives rise to an ethic of loyalty to a person, not the observance of an abstract rule. It would be impossible in these conditions, in the context of a highly articulated tribal structure, to develop an ethic of formal rules. The application of obligations in fact follows a complex sliding scale in terms of proximity of kinship. It is not so much the case, as laymen often suppose, that the tribesman distinguishes between an in-group to whom he has obligations and out-groups to whom he has none. It is rather that the tribesmen in a segmentary society know a series of superimposed in- and out-groups, so that obligations are graduated and enforceable according to context. This sliding scale morality cannot find Kantian expression. The 'cult of personality', on the other hand, comes naturally to it, for the various reasons indicated.

Theoretically, there is of course the possibility that these various requirements of the personalized sacred should be satisfied by the tribal structure, without drawing on the universalistic scriptural religion to which the tribe also gives its allegiance. This, however, would expose the tribe to the charge of heterodoxy. This is a very dangerous matter, for it provides a marvellous validation for aggression and dispossession. In any case, it is the essence of a sacred as functioning within the tribe, that it should suppose to have an external, independent validity, in order to justify its arbitrations and so forth. Of course, eclectism or syncretism are possible, and there might be two kinds of 'external' sacred. But, in fact, this solution has not been adopted, and one can see how unattractive it is. In fact, whatever its 'true' essence, Islam within the North African tribes assumes a form compatible with the requirement of tribal life. One can see – admittedly, in a regrettably *ex post* manner – that the characteristics grouped together as *C* are inevitable for tribal Islam, at least in most circumstances.

The situation is quite different in the town. This is how Bendix sums up Max Weber's argument on this point:

This religiosity of bourgeois strata seems to originate in urban life. In the city a religious experience of the individual tends to lose the character of ecstatic trance or dream and to assume the paler forms of contemplative mysticism or a low-keyed, everyday piety. For the craftsmen steady work with customers can suggest the development of concepts like 'duty' and 'recompense' as basic orientations towards life (*An Intellectual Portrait*, Doubleday, 1960, p. 114).

Thus it is not merely competitive flattery which leads the urban dweller towards a transcendent deity without intermediaries. The life he has around him is more anonymous, there are no stable personalities towards whom piety would take the form of loyalty. On the other hand, the townsman has a better chance of being literate, and a very good chance of being in contact with someone who is literate. The literate *ulama* can act as mediators of the Holy Writ. The personal charisma of freelance individual forms of the sacred are in competition with the religious value of literacy, and thus the *ulama* have an additional motive – the elimination of undesirable competition – in addition to the proclivity to flattery with which they are credited by Hume, to make them insist on a pure, transcendent deity speaking through its Word and not through ecstatic individuals.

I do not wish to argue that the situation is entirely symmetrical. It is not. While tribal rural life provides the opportunites only for personally mediated religion, urban life, while being the only place providing the medium for impersonal scriptural pure religion, provides opportunities for the other kind as well. Sufi mystics as well as *ulama* are to be found in towns. So while both forms are present in the town, only one is normally present in the countryside. Moreover, one must stress that the 'personal' form is different in the towns from the form it takes in the countryside. In the towns, it is essentially an escape from life; in the countryside, it confirms the local forms of life. The rural tribesmen are not really so very interested in mystical ecstasies or ritual specialists, though they have no objection to sensuous excesses. When they come to the annual festival, they combine it with the market and a jolly good party. The townsman on the other hand, has the market and also the benefit of the city lights available anyway: when he turns to the personalistic, he is seeking something *different*. The devotees of the personal saint are recruited in quite a different way in the town than in the tribe. In the tribe, affiliation is by group and is a kind of ascription; in the town, it is individual and elective.

We can seen now how the inversion of the relationship between characteristics C and P in Islam, by contrast with Christianity, ties up with what has been asserted about the centre of gravity of political power in the two types of society. If the central power is essentially town-based in Islam and the countryside tends to be tribal and is ever potentially or actually dissident, it is not surprising that the urban form of religion should be the central tradition and that a hierarchical personal and 'superstitious' form should be fragmented and deviant. If, generally speaking, pre-modern Christendom did have central state power with a rural basis, and the *towns* were an unforeseen potentially dissident growth within this structure, it is less surprising that the centrality and marginality of C and P should be distributed in the way in which they are.

Can the religious polarity also be connected with the dynamics of the system, apart from the stable structure which it has (as opposed to the unstable rotating personnel)?

The religious world has a rotation of its own or a series of possible rotations, in addition to playing a crucial part in the political collective circulation of elites sketched out above. Take this last role first of all: the arrival of a new dynasty carried in on the shoulders of the outer wolves, thereby turning themselves into sheepdogs, requires that outer wolves, or some significant number of them, should unite. Normally, the central power is protected from the wolves by their fragmentation. They are fully preoccupied with small local feuds and oppositions, and do not unite against it. The unification is only achieved by religious means. Whenever a religious idea is superimposed on tribal cohesion, or rather causes a tribal cohesion to work without tribal internal fission, a political crystallization takes place which can lead to the replacement of the old dynasty by the new. This part of the analysis is already present in Ibn Khaldun. It is thus seen that the start of Islam is re-enacted by new movements within Islam: Islam acts not as the corrosion of empires, but as the cement of their foundation. Where agents of a religious movement undo a dynasty, they do it not for its own sake, but in the interests of the establishment of a new one.

This is one way in which the religious element contributes to a political rotation. Note that, in order to unify tribal societies, a religious leader must possess something a bit *more* than the usual holy men embedded in the tribal structure. He can, for once, be puritanical, extreme and universal. He must possess justification for supplanting these many holy lineages and for unifying a large group of tribes. This unitarianism and puritanism, tacitly recognized but normally disliked by the tribesmen, provides the required justification. The tribesmen put up with it when it also justifies and makes possible conquests.

This, then, is the way in which the religious element contributes to the political rotation. But there is also a set of cyclical movements within the religious sphere itself.

For one thing, not all missionaries who go out to the tribes in the interests of greater religious knowledge and religious purity end up as unifiers and leaders of the tribes on a new movement towards the centre. Some simply settle down, as modest missionaries. In the end of course they finish as just another set of holy men performing a tribal function and losing their missionary one. This is a movement from missionary to leopard-skin chief, as it were: though in this case of course, the leopard-skin chiefs retain an Islamic colouring. But the reverse process can also take place. The holy men in the mountains are always being produced in excess of local demands. Competition between them drives many of them perpetually to seek new areas of activity. A talented former thaumaturge can start operation beyond the range of the tribal society which produced him. But if he starts operating in the towns, as sometimes he will, he is no longer working on well-articulated tribal groups: he is operating on a relatively amorphous urban mass. The urban lodge over which he or his deputy presides is no longer a kin centre embedded among others: it is a genuine club, a group of adepts selected by conversion and enthusiasm, who meet in given premises for purposes of extra devotion and other ritual activities. Some such leaders, when differentiating their product, may be pushed in the direction of the puritan end of the spectrum.

The point here is this: it is possible to distinguish within North African and perhaps other Islam between the holy lineages of the tribes and the 'religious orders', mainly of the towns. But a nominally identical movement will have both forms according to the context in which it operates and indeed may change from one form to the other over time, and have one form in one place and quite another elsewhere. There is nothing stable about this. The same terminology for leader, deputy, lodge and so forth will cover both phenomena, and thus indicate quite distinct social realities. Nevertheless, the fact that these distinct social realities are treated as a unity, not only by outside observers but even within the society, is itself a significant social fact.

The sociology of religion which is inspired primarily by Christianity distinguishes between churches, denominations and sects where churches, embracing the whole community, have placed the greatest hostages to secular fortune and are least severe in demanding, whereas the sects, opting out, can afford to keep strictly to the Word. In Islam, we see this inverted. It is the fragmented tribal 'church' which, though deviant and dissident, makes the greatest concessions to the requirements of a worldly order and can only be interpreted through it. It is the central tradition which manages to make the least concessions, despite being identified with the larger community.

III. Religion in Modern Industrial Societies

In contrast to the medieval period in Christian societies, modern societies where Christianity is prevalent tend to be characterized by a combination of religious pluralism and loss of religious control. In a few societies, such as Italy and Spain, one church, i.e. Roman Catholicism, does retain a monopoly or near-monopoly of religious surveillance. But most others are pluralistic – that is, they possess a number of competing religious orientations within the Judeo-Christian tradition. The U.S.A., Canada, Britain, West Germany, Holland, Ireland and Switzerland are examples. However, some of these appear to manifest a greater intensity of religious interest and religious commitment than others. Britain is on most indicators of religious interest and commitment much less religious than the U.S.A. or Holland, almost certainly in part because historically there has been a dominant State-linked religious institution in England, namely the Anglican Church. In contrast, in both Holland and the U.S.A. there has been a much greater equality and intensity of competition (or, indeed, conflict) between religious collectivities – notably between Catholicism and Protestantism.[1] Both Luckmann (Reading 9) and Wilson (Reading 10) survey various aspects of this kind of problem. Luckmann provides a brief survey of the empirical evidence favouring his thesis as to the decline of traditional religion; while Wilson discusses some major differences between Britain and the U.S.A. in respect of religious belief, practice and organization.

1. For full discussion see R. Robertson, *The Sociological Interpretation of Religion*, ch. 4, Blackwell, and Schocken Books, 1970.

Wilson emphasizes the degree to which religious developments occur in response to social changes. In the modern world, he argues, religious preconceptions are becoming less and less the basis for social organization and action. This he sees as a hallmark of the process of secularization.

9 T. Luckmann

The Decline of Church-Oriented Religion

Excerpt from T. Luckmann, *The Invisible Religion*, Macmillan, 1967, pp. 28–37.

During the past decades, and especially in the last ten years, many studies of churches, sects and denominations accumulated. Most studies originated in the United States, Germany, France, Belgium, England and the Netherlands, with a few coming from other countries such as Italy and Austria. In the European countries research concentrated, with a few exceptions, on Catholicism and the established or quasi-established Protestant churches. In the United States the sects received the major share of attention, although Judaism, Catholicism and the major Protestant denominations were not completely neglected.[1]

Despite the large number of studies it is not without difficulty that one may proceed to generalizations about the location of church-oriented religion in modern industrial society. With some exaggeration one may venture the remark that the wealth of data – in the absence of a common theoretical framework – proves to be more of an embarrassment than an advantage. Since most studies have concentrated on sociographic details it is easier to discern the local, regional, national and doctrinal peculiarities of the churches than the common social characteristics of church-oriented religion. To add to the difficulties, some authors have ecclesiastic if not theological commitments. It is, therefore, sometimes necessary to disentangle the data from a certain bias in interpretation. The fact that we cannot present all findings in detail here compounds the difficulties. If we are to gain an overall picture of church-oriented religion in modern society as a

---

1. Notable are Fichter's studies of Catholic parishes. Fichter was influential in initiating the trend from purely sociographic studies to parish sociology and his studies served as a model for most recent Catholic as well as Protestant parish investigations. Cf. Fichter (1951 and 1954).

first step toward an understanding of religion in the contemporary world, we must face the risk of some oversimplification. In order to minimize this risk, we shall present only such generalizations as are based on convergent rather than on isolated findings. Even after taking this precaution it is to be admitted that the generalizations cannot be taken as proven beyond all doubt. They are, however, conclusions favored by the weight of available evidence.[2]

In Europe it is common knowledge that the country is more 'religious' than the city. This is generally borne out by the findings of research in the sociology of religion. From church attendance figures to religious burial reports, various statistics which can be taken as indicative of church-oriented religion show consistently higher averages for rural than for urban areas. On the basis of such statistics only a small proportion of the urban population can be described as church-oriented. It is of some interest to note, however, that there is a long-range trend toward a decrease of church-oriented religion in rural regions, too. Consequently, the difference in church-oriented religion, while not completely leveled, is smaller now than several decades ago. It hardly needs to be added that this is merely part of a more general process. The transformations in the distribution of church-oriented religion are linked to increasing economic interpenetration of city and country, the growing rationalization of farming, the diffusion of urban culture to the country through mass media and so forth. It should be noted, however, that these transformations do not proceed at an even rate. In addition to local and regional circumstances of economic and political character the specifically 'religious' historical tradition of a region or congregation may speed up or retard the process.

According to another item of common knowledge women are more 'religious' than men and the young and old more 'religious' than other age groups. Research findings indicate that such opinions need to be revised at least in part. Indeed, women

2. Considering the limitations of this study an attempt to document the following by a complete bibliography would be impossible. A large bibliography can be found in Goldschmidt and Matthes (1962). For reviews of the field, see Glock (1959), Honigsheim (1957), Hunt (1958), Le Bras (1960), Goldschmidt, Griener and Schelsky (1959) and Lambert (1960).

generally do better than men on various indices of church-oriented religion, and the middle generation is, in fact, character-ized by lower participation and attendance rates than the young and the old. It is significant, however, that working women as a category tend to resemble men more closely in church orientation than, for example, housewives do. This hardly supports the view that women, children and old people have something like a natural inclination for church-oriented religion. The findings represent an important aspect of the social distribution of church-oriented religion rather than being indicative of the psy-chology of sex and age. In general terms, we may say, that the degree of involvement in the work processes of modern industrial society correlates negatively with the degree of involvement in church-oriented religion. It is obvious, of course, that the degree of involvement in such processes is in turn linked with age- and sex-roles.

The involvement of the working population in church-oriented religion – while lower than that of the rest of the population – is, however, itself significantly differentiated. Among the various occupational groups can be found important differences in participation. The indices are generally higher for agricultural, white-collar and some professional groups. These differences coincide roughly with the distribution of church-oriented religion among social classes. Farmers, peasants and those elements of the middle classes which are basically survivals of the traditional bourgeoisie and petite bourgeoisie are marked by a degree of involvement in church-oriented religion which is disproportion-ately higher than that of the working class.

In addition to church attendance, opinions on doctrinal mat-ters and so forth, some recent studies in the sociology of religion also investigated participation in various nonritual activities of the churches, ranging from youth clubs to charitable enterprises. These studies indicate that in Europe only a small fraction of the members of congregations join activities that lie outside of the ritual functions of the churches. While those participating in these functions – whom we may collectively call the ritual core of the congregation – represent only a relatively small part of the nominal membership of the parish, they are yet more numer-ous than those otherwise active in the church. The size of that latter group, the hard core of active members, varies from region to region and from one denomination to the other. It can be said that the major factors determining these differences are the ecology of the community and the distribution of social classes and occupational groups within the parish. The role which these factors play in the selection of the 'hard core' from the congregational membership as a whole, however, is not as important as the role these same factors play in the initial recruitment of the congregation from the reservoir of merely nominal members.

While some aspects of the relation between society and church-oriented religion are common knowledge, there can be little doubt that for the industrial countries of Western Europe the findings of the recent sociology of religion describe this relation with more precision. They establish a clear connexion between the distribution of church-oriented religion and a number of demographic and other sociologically relevant variables. In the foregoing we described the most important of these. We must, however, draw attention to the fact that the figures vary from country to country and from denomination to denomination. By most criteria Catholicism exhibits higher rates of participation than Protestantism. Some part of this variation can be attributed to differences in the degree of industrialization characterizing Catholic and Protestant countries, respectively, to the presence or absence of a tradition of militant socialism, to different forms of church–state relations and other factors. At the same time, there are considerable national and regional differences which cannot be attributed directly to demographic, economic or political factors. The level of participation in church-oriented religion seems to be exceptionally low in the case of Anglicanism. Or, to refer to another example, there are differences in the level of participation among French Catholic dioceses which can be attributed in part to sociologically rather intangible historical traditions. Note should be taken also of another factor, neglected in our present summary, that seems to be involved in the distribution of church-oriented religion: the proportion of the members of a denomination in the total population. With certain exceptions, so-called diaspora congregations are characterized by relatively high attendance and participation figures.

These remarks should not obscure the over-riding influence of economic, political and class variables in determining the distribution of church-oriented religion in present-day Western Europe. Before we proceed to draw conclusions about religion in modern society, the European data must be compared with the findings of research on religion in the United States.

For several reasons such comparison is difficult. First, the great variety of institutional expressions of religion in America has not yet been thoroughly and systematically investigated, although at least the major and most typical expressions and some of the sects, fascinating to the sociologist for one reason or another, did receive attention. Second, among the studies that were carried out some were guided by a pronounced positivistic bias. The third and most important reason is the unique social and religious history of America. For this, more than for any other reason, caution is indicated in summary characterizations of church religion in America, especially if they are to be used for comparison with the European findings. A sizeable number of processes and circumstances find no close parallel in European social history; for example, the absence of a feudal past and of a peasantry, the peculiar complex of conditions known as the frontier experience, the successive ethnically and denominationally distinct waves and strata of immigration, the rapid and nearly convulsive processes of urbanization and industrialization, the Negro problem and the early establishment of a dominant middle-class outlook and way of life. The religious history of the country includes equally distinct circumstances: the Puritan period, the early separation of church and state, followed by a persistent and peculiarly intimate relation between politics and religion, the era of revival movements, the prodigious development of sects and the transformation of sects into denominations.

If one views the findings of research on church religion in America against this historical background, it is surprising that they exhibit so much similarity to the European data. It is true that, at first, this similarity is not obvious. Fewer people seem to be involved in church religion than in Europe – if one bases the comparison on the European conception of nominal membership. Conversely, and no matter what criteria one uses, the figures for participation and involvement are much higher for the United States. The difference is especially striking in the case of Protestantism, since Catholic participation rates are relatively high in Europe, too.

Yet, on closer inspection, it appears that the same general factors determine the over-all social location of church religion, although the levels of participation may differ. The participation rates are again higher for Catholicism than Protestantism, especially if, in the latter case, one considers the major denominations rather than some of the smaller sects. And, again, differences between rural and urban areas can be found. The contrast between city and country exhibits a more complex pattern than in Europe and is not as striking, mainly because of Catholic concentrations in many metropolitan areas. The differences between men and women also follow the same lines, with the exception of the Jews. These differences, too, are less sharply drawn than in Europe. The differences in the involvement of the generations in church religion follow the European example only in part. Here, a number of factors, especially the pull of Sunday-school children on the parents – most pronounced in suburbia – complicates the basic pattern.

From the findings on church involvement of different occupational groups no consistent picture emerges. In any case, the data are too scarce to permit any generalizations. One may, perhaps, suspect that in this instance some deviations from the European pattern may be present. The differences between classes with respect to religion are less pronounced than in Europe. This may be attributable in part to the fact that class differences are less pronounced – and certainly less conspicuous – in general, despite an underlying structural similarity in the social stratification of the Western European countries and the United States. Although the major churches and denominations are, at the very least, middle-class oriented, the relatively sharp cleavage between a church-oriented middle class and an unchurched working class does not exist. This is, of course, not surprising, since the working class today merges almost imperceptibly into the outlook, way of life and religious pattern of the middle classes to a much greater extent than in Europe, although there are some indications of a process of *embourgeoisement* in the European working class. Such differences as still exist in the recruitment of church members and in participation are overlaid by the peculiarly American differentiation of prestige among the denominations. These differences find expression in the composition of membership of the denominations. Significantly enough, however, the status differences in the membership of the denominations are popularly much exaggerated. In this connexion the Negro–White cleavage in Protestant churches and congregations deserves to be mentioned. These observations are not valid for one social stratum: the rural and urban proletariat, the term not being understood in its Marxist sense. It consists in large part of Negroes, Puerto Ricans, Mexicans and others. This stratum is socially almost completely invisible and nearly unchurched. Even Catholicism, whose influence on the working class generally appears to be stronger than that of Protestantism, appears to have lost or is loosing its hold on this stratum. But this stratum is not part of the middle-class oriented working population and those parts that are not unchurched tend to be attracted to sects that are marginal to Protestantism both theologically and in its orientation to society.

Ethnic churches played a significant role in American religious history. Today, ethnic churches for persons of European background have either disappeared or are of subordinate importance. Only churches linked to racial minorities persist on the religious scene. Their function depends, of course, on the position of the minorities in American society.

One of the most important developments in American church religion is the process of doctrinal leveling. It can be safely said that within Protestantism doctrinal differences are virtually irrelevant for the members of the major denominations. Even for the ministry traditional theological differences seem to have an ever-decreasing importance. More significant is the steady leveling of the differences between Catholicism, Protestantism and Judaism. This process should not be taken as a result of a serious theological *rapprochement*. Furthermore, several areas of fairly sharp friction remain between Catholicism and the other religious bodies, especially in matters of public policy. There can be little doubt, however, that Catholicism, Protestantism and Judaism are jointly characterized by similar structural transformations – a bureaucratization along rational businesslike lines – and accommodation to the 'secular' way of life. In consequence of the historical link between this way of life and the Protestant ethos, the accommodation of Protestantism, as represented by its major denomination, has perhaps gone farther than that of the other religious bodies. It seems, however, that the difference is superficial (cf. Herberg, 1955). It is to be noted that, despite the trend toward a leveling of ideological differences and the increasing irrelevance of doctrine for the membership, the *social* differences in the traditions of Protestantism, Catholicism and Judaism continue to play a role. According to some findings they may be destined for perpetuation by endogamy. The way of life and the social basis for some central dimensions of subjective identification remain linked to subcultures designated by religious labels (cf. Lenski, 1961).

These observations may be summarized as follows. There are some aspects of church religion in America which are either unique or at least conspicuously different from the European situation. With one exception – the relatively high involvement of Americans in church religion – the differences seem less significant than the similarities. The correlations of various indices of involvement in church religion with demographic and ecological variables as well as with social role and status configurations follow a similar pattern in the European and American findings. This pattern represents the social location of church religion in the industrial countries of the West. If we may take these countries as paradigmatic, the pattern invites the conclusion that church-oriented religion has become a marginal phenomenon in modern society.

This conclusion meets one serious difficulty in the previously mentioned deviation from the pattern. The most 'modern' of the countries under discussion, the United States, shows the highest degree of involvement in church religion. To compound the difficulties, the high American figures of overt participation represent, in all likelihood, a fairly recent upward movement rather than a decrease from a yet higher previous level. In the face of these circumstances it is obvious that no simple unilinear and one-dimensional theory of 'secularization' in modern society can be maintained.

The difficulty is only apparent. In order to resolve it, it is only necessary to take into account the differences in the character of church religion in Europe and America. In Europe church religion did not undergo radical inner transformations and became restricted to a minor part of the population. As it continued to represent and mediate the traditional universe of religious ideas, its social base shrunk characteristically to that part of the population which is peripheral to the structure of modern society: the peasantry, the remnants of the traditional bourgeoisie and petite bourgeoisie within the middle classes, which are not – or no longer or not yet – involved in the typical work processes of industrial and urban society.[3]

In the United States, on the other hand, church religion has a broad middle-class distribution. The middle classes are, *in toto*, anything but peripheral to the modern industrial world. The distribution of church religion in America, nevertheless, does not represent a reversal of the trend toward 'secularization' – that is, a resurgence of traditional church religion. It is rather the result of a radical inner change in American church religion. This change consists in the adoption of the *secular* version of the Protestant ethos by the churches which, of course, did not result from concerted policy but is rather a product of a unique constellation of factors in American social and religious history.[4]

Whereas religious ideas originally played an important part in the shaping of the American Dream, today the secular ideas of the American Dream pervade church religion. The cultural, social and psychological functions which the churches perform for American society as a whole as well as for its social groups, classes, and individuals would be considered 'secular' rather than 'religious' in the view the churches traditionally held of themselves.[5] Comparing the European and American findings on the social location of church religion and allowing for the differences in the character of church religion in European and American society we are led to the conclusion that traditional church religion was pushed to the periphery of 'modern' life in Europe

3. For an interpretation, see Tenbruck (1959); cf. also Koester (1959), esp. p. 108.

4. A study which traces the symptoms of these changes has been done by Schneider and Dornbusch (1958).

5. For a description and interpretation of these functions, see Berger (1961).

while it became more 'modern' in America by undergoing a process of internal secularization. This conclusion requires further interpretation.

The configuration of meaning which constitutes the symbolic reality of traditional church religion appears to be unrelated to the culture of modern industrial society. It is certain, at least, that internalization of the symbolic reality of traditional religion is neither enforced nor, in the typical case, favored by the social structure of contemporary society. This fact alone suffices to explain why traditional church religion moved to the margin of contemporary life. The findings contradict the notion that the challenge of overt antichurch ideologies plays an important role. If the churches maintain their institutional claim to represent and mediate the traditional religious universe of meaning, they survive primarily by association with social groups and social strata which continue to be oriented toward the values of a past social order. If, on the other hand, the churches accommodate themselves to the dominant culture of modern industrial society they necessarily take on the function of legitimating the latter. In the performance of this function, however, the universe of meaning traditionally represented by the churches becomes increasingly irrelevant. In short, the so-called process of secularization has decisively altered either the social location of church religion or its inner universe of meaning. As we have formulated it, it may appear that these two alternatives are mutually exclusive. This is the case only for their hypothetical, extreme forms. In fact, less radical transformations of both the social location and the meaning universe of church religion may occur jointly.

References

BERGER, P. (1961), *The Noise of Solemn Assemblies*, Doubleday.

FICHTER, J. H. (1951), *Southern Parish*, vol. 1, University of Chicago Press.

FICHTER, J. H. (1954), *Social Relations in the Urban Parish*, University of Chicago Press.

GLOCK, C. Y. (1959), 'The sociology of religion', in R. K. Merton, L. Broom and L. S. Cottrell, eds., *Sociology Today*, Basic Books, pp. 153–77.

GOLDSCHMIDT, D., GREINER, F. and SCHELSKY, H. (1959), *Soziologie der Kirchengemeinde*, Enke, Stuttgart.

GOLDSCHMIDT, D., and MATTHES, J. (1962), Probleme der Religionssoziologie, *Kölner Zeitschrift für Soziologie und Sozialpsychologie*, special issue no. 6.

HERBERG, W. (1955), *Protestant, Catholic, Jew*, Doubleday.

HONIGSHEIM, P. (1957), 'Sociology of religion – complementary analyses of religious institutions', in H. Becker and A. Boskoff, eds., *Modern Sociological Theory in continuity and change*, Dryden, pp. 450–81.

HUNT, C. L. (1958), 'The sociology of religion', in J. S. Roucek, ed., *Contemporary Sociology*, Philosophical Library, New York.

KOESTER, R. (1959), *Die Kirchentreuen*, Enke, Stuttgart.

LAMBERT, R. D. (1960), 'Current trends in religion', *Ann. Amer. Soc. polit. soc. Scien.*, vol. 332, pp. 146–55.

LE BRAS, G. (1960), 'Problèmes de la Sociologie des Religions', in G. Gurvitch, ed., *Traité de la Sociologie*, vol. 2, Presses Universitaires de France, pp. 79–102.

LENSKI, G. (1961). *The Religious Factor*, Doubleday.

SCHNEIDER, L., and DORNBUSCH, S. M. (1958), *Popular Religion – Inspirational Books in America*, University of Chicago Press.

TENBRUCK, F. (1959), 'Die Kirchengemeinde in der enkirchlichten Gesellschaft', in D. Goldschmidt, F. Greiner and H. Schelsky, eds., *Soziologie der Kirchengemeinde*, Enke, Stuttgart.

10 B. R. Wilson

Religion in Secular Society

Excerpts from B. R. Wilson, 'Conclusion', *Religion in Secular Society*, Watts, 1966, pp. 221–33.

The concept of the Church, as it has been understood in the social sense, is one which acquired its full meaning and realization in European feudal society. It claimed within a given territory, the monopoly of spiritual power, just as the state claimed the monopoly of political and military power. In European history one Church presided over several nascent states and this but reflected its claim to transcendence and universality. For, although in the age of more emphatic nationalism the Church tended to become closely identified with the state, and this was especially true in Protestant Christendom – indeed to the point of accepting the dominant authority of the state – the earlier conception was of a Church unconfined by national or ethnic boundaries. But the Church relied, for the effective recognition of its claim to a monopoly of spiritual power, on the coercive power of the political authority.

As the institutions of society grew apart, and as religious institutions and functionaries lost, first their control of, and later much of their access to, various social activities – diplomacy, education, the regulation of trade, etc., so the civil authority gained in power, and, having less need for the good offices of the Church, was less disposed to protect its ancient privileges. The emergence of new classes with new skills and resources, who were unaccommodated in the Church, but whose social importance sometimes won for them the protection of princes, created a pluralism which became the first properly instituted invasion (there had been many unlegitimated invasions before) of the Church's claim to spiritual monopoly as far as the temporal sovereign's writ could run.

The ecclesiological theory of the Church remained. But

once tolerance was extended to organized dissenters the Church, sociologically viewed, was reduced to the status of a denomination, albeit for a very long time a dominant and privileged denomination. In America, despite the 'establishment' of particular confessions in various states, denominationalism was, from the very creation of the federation, the norm. Religious pluralism has its official foundation stone in the American constitution, although its modern beginnings go back to sixteenth- and early seventeenth-century Europe. The growth of religious diversity in the United States made evident the untenability of the social concept of 'the Church' in that society, although those religious organizations which inherited the ecclesiology and the associated liturgical practices, continued to behave as if they were in fact Churches. In political and social affairs, of course, they could not do so.

In Europe, where Established Churches did persist in most countries, loss of effective authority affected the Churches even in societies where there was near unanimity of religious belief. In Germany, Scandinavia, Holland, Switzerland and Britain, Protestantism created the conditions for an earlier manifestation of religious tolerance than occurred in Catholic countries, but as religion lost political influence, dissent, even in Catholic countries, became increasingly tolerated. More important, anti-clericalism became a significant manifestation of political radicalism.

What was begun by the tolerance necessary in increasingly diversified societies, was continued by the process of secularization itself. When large numbers effectively ceased to be religious, all religious movements were reduced to the status of denominations and sects. The process was, inevitably, the more painful in those societies in which the fiction of the concept of the Church had persisted. In America secularization drained the religious content, without too radically affecting the form, of religious institutions. So persistent indeed were the forms, that in that pluralistic society, sects could expect, especially in the nineteenth century when expansion and optimism were so manifest, to graduate into denominations and even to acquire for themselves the liturgical, architectural and (sometimes) the ecclesiastical styles which had previously been exclusively associated with those

153

more ancient religious institutions which had in the past been – and which still laid claim to being – Churches. Thus some commentators have, mistaking the form for the social reality, been prepared, rather inappropriately, to discuss the process not as one of denominationalism, but as one 'from sect to Church'. Church was, however, merely the high status towards which some sects were aspiring, without, however, any realistic prospect of attaining it.

In the secular society there are, strictly speaking, no Churches. There are denominations, some of which have special historic privileges, and some of which suffer some historic liabilities (for example, the preclusion of Roman Catholics from certain offices of state in England). But whereas denominational claims are, given the high level of manifest public support, sustainable in America, even these become difficult to sustain in Europe where the secularization process has not merely (or not so markedly) drained away the content of religious beliefs but has also caused public support to ebb. In some European countries those religious institutions which once boasted the name and the reality of Churches are, with secularization, faced with being reduced to the status of sects; that is to say, of being reduced to relatively small, heterodox groups who believe and practise things which are alien to the majority. They differ from sects, however, in lacking the intensity of commitment.

It is in response to this circumstance of secularization that the Churches of the past have sought to shore up their claims to status. Their dominant stratagem has been ecumenicalism. Since what secularization has eroded has been the intensity of specific belief, the sense of superiority and apartness, this solution has been all the easier to accept. Clearly, in this process, those Churches which have remained largest and which have managed to maintain their more traditional practices have some advantage. The ritual dance of ecumenism emphasizes steps known as 'drawing together' and 'growing together'. A close observer of the dance might notice that the gyrations and revolutions of some of the dancers are far more numerous in a short space of time than those of others. The attempt to discover a more firmly legitimated basis of faith and order – beginning with the Tractarian movement of the nineteenth century in

B. R. Wilson

England – has led to an attempt to restore the security of the past, however much of it may be done in the name of action appropriate to the present. The sentiments of returning to the first century of Christianity come readily to the lips of modern churchmen, even when they are emphasizing the need for change to keep up with the twentieth century, and restoring liturgical practices from the twelfth or thirteenth centuries (see Paul, 1964, and Wilson, 1965).

Yet if it is the Roman Church which, liturgically, ecclesiastically, and theologically stands to gain, it can do so in these departments only by surrendering control in others. What affects liturgy and ecclesiology and theology as an academic discipline, affects only the Church. It has little consequence for society at large. Where ethics are concerned, however, matters are rather different. The secular society, with its acceptance of more technical and scientific procedures, will not brook interference of the traditional kind, in, for example, matters relating to marriage and birth. It may eventually also reassert the control it was steadily acquiring until the past decade perhaps, over education, as the financial demands of modern education steadily outstrip the resources of private agencies – even of religious organizations. Other religious movements have in the main abandoned the attempt to influence society in these matters except by pious injunction. Eventually the Roman Church must do the same.

Ecumenicalism, then, is a response which might save the Churches from becoming sects, since 'from Church to sect' would appear to be the order of the day for religious organizations in secular society. Sects have always been anathema to churchmen, indeed to most Christians, even including those who, in the eyes of other Christians and of the secular world, are themselves sectarians. And this, even though there can be no doubt that the intensity of religious commitment, the most individually influential and pervasive religious view of the world undoubtedly exists in sectarian movements. Enthusiasm has never had much appeal to churchmen, and lay intensity has often been a matter for concern and reproach among those who have become professionals of religious organizations. The ecumenical alternative to sectarianism – although Christianity

155

was certainly sectarian in the now so-popular first century – is associated with the liturgical revival and the reassertion of the episcopacy even in denominations which began by disavowing both.

Both have a special appeal to the professionals of the Churches. They improve the claim to social status on the part of the ministry; they emphasize the antiquity of the religious role and hence reassure its performers of the legitimacy, permanence and usefulness of their chosen calling. Liturgicalism reasserts the monopoly of the professional, by providing him with the equivalent of skills and techniques which he alone is licensed to practise. Episcopacy ensures the promotion prospects of the cleric, and perpetuates the claim to high dignity, association with ruling *élites* and the maintenance of the religious institution in some nominal position of high social importance.

Given an organization with all the capacity for persistence displayed by the Churches – their claims on latent sentiment, their operation at crucial times of personal and familial crisis, their association with the kinship structure, and especially with the childhood of many people – one sees the clerical profession as a self-perpetuating incumbency. The forces of ecumenism are clerical forces, and the forces of the new ritualist movement are clerical forces. We witness the struggles of a professional for survival in the Protestant countries of Europe. The choice is principally between the loss of organizations, positions and social influence, as in the case of sects, or the maintenance of organizations, the multiplication of positions, the reassertion of professional expertise, and the close identification with the cultural goals and styles of secular society, as in the case of religious institutions in America. There is a third position and it appeals to a minority of the clergy in Europe. As the ministry becomes an entrenched but increasingly functionless intelligentsia, so this minority interprets its role increasingly as involvement with social and political affairs. From the secure base of religious livings, they sally forth on what are largely political crusades. This is the tradition of dissent, of course (even though it is often Anglican and Lutheran clergy who are involved), but it is not religious dissent. It is the use of a religious base for political action. In general, the choice of the clergy has been ecumenicalism, liturgicalism and the attempt to identify with the goals of secular society and to show where religious organization (even if not religious ideas and values) fits in.

The social basis which facilitates the development of ecumenicalism is the diminishing diversity of society. The disappearance of ethnic, regional and pronounced stratificational differences reduces the significance of the religious divisions which reflected them. That significance has, of course, been affected, too, by the process of secularization itself. Were secularization not involved it might be possible to predict a return to the Durkheimian case of a unitary religion expressing the social solidarity, cohesion and shared values of an undiversified society. Those functions of religion were manifested in a simple society, but we can seriously doubt whether, even with a less diversified society of the future, and with ecumenism, we shall in any sense return to the position in which religion would operate as the integrative agency of modern society.

The whole significance of the secularization process is that society does not, in the modern world, derive its values from certain religious preconceptions which are then the basis for social organization and social action. It is rather that ecumenical religion will, as Herberg suggests it does in America, merely reflect the values which stem from social organization itself. Even with its votaries in contemporary society, religion does not begin to compare in its influence with the total religious world view which prevailed in simple society, and the subsumption of all activities and all institutions in the religious orientation of the world. The diversification of society destroyed the dominance of religion, and redistributed its functions. The diminution of diversity (and it is a diminution in only certain areas, in fact) does not restore religion to its former pre-eminence, nor return to it the functions which it once performed.

Social cohesion, and some measure of social consensus – at least concerning innumerable patterns of action in everyday life – must prevail in all continuing societies which are not experiencing anarchy. But even if this cohesion were attributed to the primacy of shared patterns of values, norms, conventions and orientations to the world laid deep in the socialization process, still one need not suppose these values to be specifically religious or to be today actively supported by religious commitment and religious organization. It is clear, of course, that they owe, in origin and development, much to religious conceptions of society of the past.

We may rather turn to the complex dovetailing of our institutional arrangements; to the mixture of inducement and coercion which prevails within the work order of our society; to the largely autonomous body of duly instituted law; to the elaborate interaction of supply, demand, knowledge of the market, and knowledge of consumers, which structure much of the provision of a modern economy, to see what it is that maintains the cohesion of contemporary society. That certain values, norms, and conventions enter into this highly intricate picture is self-evident. That they have a primacy or a determinacy seems very much more disputable. That they are ultimately religious ideas, and rest on religious practice and institutions for their validity and legitimacy, seems highly questionable.

Social cohesion is but one of the functions which have been generally ascribed to religion. In this essay no attempt has been made to examine the fulfilment of these functions in modern society, but what has perhaps become broadly apparent is that the secular society does not appear to depend in any direct way on the maintenance of religious thinking, practices or institutions. In a society with diminished diversity in public affairs, and the relegation of various moral matters to the private domain, religion, too, may have become a largely private concern. Indeed religionists have increasingly tended to describe religion as an individual matter, and a personal matter. Such has been the drift especially of the more evangelical branches of Christianity. Does religion, then, become merely a matter for private predilection? Or a matter of individual demand for emotional support in circumstances of extremity? Do we then see a return, for the mass of men, to the occasional conformity of the past? Those occasions being primarily the occasions of trauma in the life cycle of the individual or of the nuclear family.

There is, however, one function which appears to have been vitally performed particularly by the Protestant manifestations of Christianity, and which assumed great importance in the development of modern society. The voluntary act of religious association implicit in Protestantism – in its various denominations and in many of its sects – entailed a distinctive commitment of goodwill to a group which was neither specifically kinsfolk nor neighbours. Without the primary affectivity of kinship relations, this goodwill had none the less to be manifested. Clearly, the implications for such a response are deeply laid in earlier Christianity: they are found in the parable of the Samaritan, and in the oft repeated dictum, 'We love him because he first loved us' which has applications for relations within the fraternity as well as for the relations of man to his God.

In Protestantism, however, was reacquired the voluntary character of earliest Christianity, and this has been of importance for the development of modern society. But Protestantism added something more to the detached goodwill which was implied in the formation of voluntary religious societies, and this it did by transcendental reinterpretation of the social roles of the new trading strata which were becoming important in late fifteenth- and early sixteenth-century Europe. The work ethic which was emphasized in Calvinism, in Puritanism generally and subsequently in Methodism and the various Holiness sects, was an ethic which rested on an essentially extraneous motivation to be committed to work. The disinterested devotion to the calling, relied on the detachment of work and material reward, and the assertion that work was a spiritual activity and a moral obligation. The strong informal assumption was that, whatever material ends were gained, the real end of fulfilling one's calling in this world was a heavenly reward. It was the uncertainty of that reward in Calvinism, and the strong informal assumption that, although God's will could not be known, achievement in this world was an intimation of the real blessings which God would bestow in the next, which induced the disposition to work (see Weber, 1930; Yinger, 1946; Parsons, 1949).

Thus, with work regarded as a religious and moral duty, material reward is, at least ideologically, displaced. A disinterested commitment is established. But, as Max Weber stressed, once these work dispositions had been established, and society had been resocialized for a new work order, the religious agent of this change was no longer necessary for its continuance.[1] Role performance, in the post-Protestant society, comes to rely on a secularized value structure in which work is no longer a sacred calling. Today a man works without the higher sense of purpose which the Protestant ethic communicated. Protestantism replaced the immediate material inducement to work by a more remote spiritual one, and this was perhaps a necessary ideological justification for that age; but in so doing it created a more involved nexus between what a man did and his reward for it. His remote prospective spiritual interest became effectively a type of disinterested commitment in the everyday activity of his life. The disappearance of a religious interpretation of economic activity may mean that role performance is now evinced without specific commitment and without devotion. The nakedness of the interest relation is borne home. Work, which ceased to be part of a life itself with the passing of agrarian society (that is for farmers), became a *calling* and was recognized as a distinctive activity of life, sanctified in religious terms, and was gradually transformed into being a *job*, supported strictly by the institutional order and an unmediated interest relationship.

It might be maintained that this development, which is clearly part of the secularization process, is itself part of the process of man's increasing rationality, his recognition of 'real' facts. One might, however, also ask whether work is made more bearable for the worker and its performance more valuable for society if disinterested devotion is lacking. Unreligious societies have attempted to find other ways of motivating men, of winning their disinterested goodwill: it is not clear that any appeals have been more effective than was that of the Protestant ethic.[2]

Disinterested devotion, or disinterested goodwill, has, however, significance for other things besides work relations. Although Victorian industrialism would not have been possible without a widely diffused work ethic, there may be a time when, in an age of automation, society's work order will function without these ingrained habits of work of the past. Even then, however, dis-

1. See Weber (1930), p. 70. At the end of Weber (1961, p. 270), he remarks, 'The religious root of modern economic humanity is dead, today the concept of the calling is a *caput mortuum* in the world.'

2. In this connexion, see Bendix (1956); and for an examination of some of these issues in a very different cultural context, see Bellah (1957).

interested devotion might still be necessary to society's functioning, at least as the radical alternative to institutional coercion.
Anyone who has compared the pattern of civic and political life
in underdeveloped countries with those of advanced society,
must be impressed by the differing degrees of disinterested commitment and detached goodwill which prevails in advanced
society, and the extent to which advanced societies rely on these
dispositions for their normal functioning. The maintenance of
public order and social control depend, in large measure, on the
diffusion of disinterested goodwill, and on a certain level of public
and individual honesty (as distinct from the purely communal
honesty which prevails in simple, often even in peasant, societies).
The extension of kin group and neighbourhood affectivity into
generalized and impersonal goodwill, has been an achievement
which has kept the corruption, crime, nepotism of modern society
within bounds. It has facilitated a pattern of very general socialization – all class, regional and ecological differences notwithstanding – in which a strongly internalized sense of impersonal
individual honesty has been very widely created. And in all of
this the teachings of Christianity, and originally the implications
of the teachings of Protestantism in particular and the voluntarism
of denominational allegiance, have played perhaps the most
important parts. Less advanced people rely very much more
on the social control of the group, on public surveillance of
individual behaviour; when those societies are urbanized and
industrialized, bribery and corruption become widespread
patterns of public behaviour. [. . .]

Secular society has little direct regard for religion. It would
be too early to say that it functioned without it, or that it could
ever do so. The secular society of the present, in which religious
thinking, practices and institutions have but a small part, is
none the less the inheritor of values, dispositions and orientations from the religious past. The completely secularized society
has not yet existed. Whether indeed our own type of society will
effectively maintain public order, without institutional coercion,
once the still persisting influence of past religion wanes even
further, remains to be seen. It may be, that in response to the
growing institutionalism, impersonality and bureaucracy of
modern society, religion will find new functions to perform – but

that, perhaps, would be not the religion which accepts the values of the new institutionalism, the religion of ecumenism, but the religion of the sects.

References
BELLAH, R. N. (1957), *Tokugawa Religion*, Free Press.
BENDIX, R. (1956), *Work and Authority in Industry*, Wiley.
PARSONS, T. (1949), *The Structure of Social Action*, Free Press, 2nd edn.
PAUL, L. (1964), *Deployment and Payment of the Clergy*, Church Information Office.
WEBER, M. (1930), *The Protestant Ethic and the Spirit of Capitalism*, Allen and Unwin.
WEBER, M. (1961), *General Economic History*, Collier.
WILSON, B. (1965), 'The Paul Report examined', *Theology*, vol. 68, no. 536, pp. 89–103.
YINGER, J. M. (1946), *Religion in the Struggle for Power*, Duke University Press.

IV. Mixed Patterns of Religion in the Modern World

In the introduction to the previous section on religion in modern industrial societies it was stated that religious pluralism was a rather widespread characteristic. Some sociologists also use the term to refer to the kind of pattern which is dealt with here in the essays of Geertz (Reading 11) and Willems (Reading 12). We prefer the term *mixed*, however, because Javanese society, with which Geertz deals, and Brazilian and Chilean societies, which Willems analyses, exhibit a mixing of religious tendencies which are relatively alien to each other. In Java we find Hinduism, Islam and indigenous, primitive religious forms mixed together; while in Brazil we find mixtures of Catholicism, old and new Pentecostal forms of Protestantism, Spiritualism, and the folk religions of Africans and Indians. The interesting interplay between syncretic, mixing forces, on the one hand, and conflicting, disintegrative forces, on the other hand, poses a number of sociological problems. Both essays show clearly how religious adherence is bound up with the system of social stratification in all three societies, Java, Brazil and Chile.[1]

1. Demerath's essay (Reading 19) in Part Four deals with patterns of religious observance in a very different kind of society, the U.S.A. The contrast between the U.S.A. and these other societies lies mainly, as far as the sociology of religion is concerned, in the fact that the content of religious belief and practice is clearly bound up with a rigidly traditional form of stratification in Java, Brazil and Chile. Syncretist *movements* are dealt with in Reading 21.

11 C. Geertz

Religion in Java: Conflict and Integration

Excerpts from C. Geertz, *The Religion of Java*, Free Press of Glencoe, 1960, pp. 4–6, 356–60, 363–75, 379–81.

There are two major government offices in Modjokuto, for it is the capital both of a district (*kewedanan*)[1] and a subdistrict (*ketjamatan*). The subdistrict, the lowest level to which the wholly appointive national bureaucracy reaches, administers eighteen villages all lying within ten miles of town. The district administers five continuous subdistricts, including that of Modjokuto itself, and is in turn subordinate to the regional (*kebupaten*) government, the capital of which is the nearby city of Bragang. In addition, the regional headquarters of the central government police is in Modjokuto rather than in Bragang, as are also the government pawnshop and the government hospital for the area. Offices concerned with the repair of roadways, the building and maintenance of irrigation systems, the improvement of agriculture and the administration of the market further swell the total of white-collar workers employed or underemployed by the government, as do the post office and the office of the local representative of the Ministry of Religion.

These five major occupational types – farmer, petty trader, independent artisan, manual laborer and white-collar clerk, teacher or administrator – represent the Javanese population of Modjokuto, grouped according to their economic activity. The crystallized typology of work patterns reflects the underlying organization of the economic system of the town of which it is an

1. The spelling of Indonesian words conforms to the current official orthography. Javanese words are spelled in accordance with the system currently employed by Balai Pustaka (a publishing agency of the Ministry of Education) in its publications in that language. This is identical with the orthography of Th. Pigeaud's *Javaans-Nederlands Handwoordenboek* (Groningen, n.d.), except that *oe* is replaced by *u*. Arabic words are also spelled in accordance with the Javanese system.

outcome. Similarly, the same population grouped according to their world outlook – according to their religious beliefs, ethical preferences, and political ideologies – yields three main cultural types which reflect the moral organization of Javanese culture as it is manifested in Modjokuto, the general ideas of order in terms of which the Javanese farmer, laborer, artisan, trader or clerk shapes his behavior in all areas of life. These are the *abangan*, *santri* and *prijaji*.

There are, it seems to me, three main social-structural nuclei in Java today: the village, the market and the government bureaucracy – each of them taken in a somewhat more extended sense than is common.

The Javanese village is as old as the Javanese, for it is likely that the first Malayo-Polynesian peoples to come to the island already possessed knowledge of agriculture. The evolution of the Javanese village to its present form has at each stage been regulated and expressed by a more or less unified religious system, itself, of course, evolving too. In the days before the Hindus, who began to come to the island around 400 A.D. or before, it seems likely that the sort of 'animism' common still to many of the pagan tribes of Malaysia comprised the whole of the religious tradition; but this tradition has proved, over the course of the centuries, remarkably able to absorb into one syncretized whole elements from both Hinduism and Islam, which followed it in the fifteenth century. Thus today the village religious system commonly consists of a balanced integration of animistic, Hinduistic and Islamic elements, a basic Javanese syncretism which is the island's true folk tradition, the basic substratum of its civilization; but the situation is more complex than this, for not only, as we shall see, do many peasants not follow this syncretism, but many townsmen – mostly lower-class displaced peasants or sons of displaced peasants – do. The *abangan* religious tradition, made up primarily of the ritual feast called the *slametan*, of an extensive and intricate complex of spirit beliefs and of a whole set of theories and practices of curing, sorcery and magic, is the first subvariant within the general Javanese religious system and it is associated in a broad and general way with the Javanese village.

The second major social substructure, the market, must be taken in a broad sense to include the whole network of domestic trade relationships on the island. For the most part, the interlocal aspects of this trade are in Chinese hands, the more local aspects in Javanese hands, although there is a good deal of overlap. The association of the Javanese trading element with a more puristic version of Islam than is common in Java stretches back to the introduction of the Mid-Eastern religion into the island, for it came as part of a great trade expansion, stimulated ultimately by the rise of the Age of Exploration in Europe, along the Java Sea. The coming of the Dutch crushed the lively Javanese trade which had sprung up in the north coast ports – Surabaja, Gresik, Tuban and others – as part of this expansion, but the trading culture did not wholly die; it persisted, although much changed and weakened, down to the present. The rise of reformist movements in Indonesian Islam in the early part of this century as part of the general nationalist movement which in 1945 finally brought Indonesia her freedom from Dutch rule revivified and further sharpened the sense for a purer Islam, less contaminated with either animism or mysticism, among the small-trader element in Javanese society.

The purer Islam is the subtradition I have called *santri*. Although in a broad and general way the *santri* subvariant is associated with the Javanese trading element, it is not confined to it, nor are all traders, by far, adherents of it. There is a very strong *santri* element in the villages, often finding its leadership in the richer peasants who have been able to make the pilgrimage to Mecca and set up religious schools upon their return. The market is, on the other hand, especially since the war and the disappearance of the Dutch demand for servants and manual workers, clogged with swarms of small *abangan* traders attempting to make a marginal living, although the greatest number of the larger and more vigorous traders are still *santris*. The *santri* religious tradition, consisting not only of a careful and regular execution of the basic rituals of Islam – the prayers, the Fast, the Pilgrimage – but also of a whole complex of social, charitable and political Islamic organizations, is the second subvariant of the general Javanese religious system which I shall present below.

The third is the *prijaji*. *Prijaji* originally referred only to the hereditary aristocracy which the Dutch pried loose from the kings of the vanquished native states and turned into an appointive, salaried civil service. This white-collar élite, its ultimate roots in the Hindu–Javanese courts of pre-colonial times, conserved and cultivated a highly refined court etiquette, a very complex art of dance, drama, music and poetry, and a Hindu–Buddhist mysticism. They stressed neither the animistic element in the over-all Javanese syncretism as did the *abangans*, nor the Islamic as did the *santris*, but the Hinduistic. In this century, the ascendant social and political position of this group so far as the native Javanese society is concerned (the Dutch of course occupied the genuinely dominant position until the revolution) has been weakened, access to the bureaucracy has become easier for the low-born but well educated, and an increasing number of nongovernmental 'white-collar' jobs has appeared. Further, it was upon this 'bureaucratic' group that the Dutch had their most direct acculturating influence, leading ultimately to the production of the highly secularized, Westernized and, commonly, somewhat anti-traditional political élite of the Indonesian Republic. As a result, the traditional court culture has weakened. Nevertheless, the *prijaji* variant not only remains quite strong among certain of the conservative elements in the society but also plays a basic role in shaping the world view, the ethics and the social behavior of even the most Westernized element in the still dominant white-collar group. The refined politesse, the high art and the intuitive mysticism all remain highly characteristic of Java's social élite; and, although somewhat attenuated and adjusted to changed conditions, the *prijaji* style of life remains the model not only for the élite but in many ways for the entire society.

Abangan, representing a stress on the animistic aspects of the over-all Javanese syncretism and broadly related to the peasant element in the population; *santri*, representing a stress on the Islamic aspects of the syncretism and generally related to the trading element (and to certain elements in the peasantry as well); and *prijaji*, stressing the Hinduist aspects and related to the bureaucratic element – these, then, are the three main subtraditions. They are not constructed types, but terms and divisions the Javanese themselves apply. They indicate the way the Javanese in Modjokuto themselves perceive the situation. [. . .]

There are several factors tending to exacerbate conflict among the three groups and several tending to moderate it. Among those exacerbating it might be included:

(a) Intrinsic ideological conflicts resting on deep-felt dislike for the values of other groups.

(b) The changing system of social stratification and increased status mobility which tends to enforce contact between individuals and groups formerly more or less socially segregated.

(c) The sharply increased struggle for political power to fill the vacuum left by the departure of the Colonial Government, which tends to embue religious differences with political significance.

(d) The need for scapegoats upon whom to focus tensions generated by a rapidly changing social system.

Those moderating the conflict include:

(a) The sense of a common culture, including the increasing importance of nationalism, which emphasizes what all Javanese (or Indonesians) have in common rather than their differences.

(b) The fact that religious patterns do not become embodied in social forms directly, purely and simply, but in many devious ways, so that religious commitments and other commitments – to class, neighborhood, etc. – tend to balance off, and various 'mixed type' individuals and groups arise which can play an important meditating role.

(c) A general tolerance based on a 'contextual relativism' which sees certain values as appropriate to context and so minimizes 'missionization'.

(d) The steady growth of social mechanisms for a pluralistic, non-syncretic form of social integration within which people of radically differing social outlook and basic values can, nevertheless, get along well enough with one another to keep society functioning.

Religion and Social Conflict

Antagonism among the several religious groups is easily enough documented. The strain is clearly greatest between *santris* and the other two groups, but significant tension between *prijaji* and *abangan* also exists. This general antagonism has almost certainly

169

increased markedly in this century, has sharply intensified since the Revolution, and is probably still increasing. But it is by no means an entirely new phenomenon. Since the days of the struggle between the Central Javanese kingdom of Mataram and the north coast harbor kingdoms (Demak, Gresik, Surabaja), at least, i.e. since the 16th and 17th centuries,[2] *prijaji* and *santri* have not seen eye to eye; and the resentment of the peasantry against the more or less exploitative ruling aristocracy and the shrewd urban-centered *santri* trading class is obviously of long standing. Nevertheless, at the moment, the conflict between the various groups is probably more intense than in the past and almost universally felt to be so by the Javanese themselves.

Ideological conflicts

The tension between *abangan* and *prijaji* is more subtly expressed than between these two groups and the *santris*, where the strain finds a more explicit outlet:

Talking of *santris*, Juminah (an *abangan* woman) told me of a taunting jingle the children shout at *santri* women. They just recite the first line, which has meaningless rhyming sounds, and keep the second, which carries the content, in their mind – thus not really saying out loud what they are thinking, although, as everyone knows the jingle, the intent is clear:

Mendung-mendung tjap gomèk
Kudung-kudung digawé lèmèk

Clouds, clouds, a Chinese holiday
A Moslem lady's head-shawl used as something to lie on.

The meaning is that, although they wear shawls (only *santri* women, and almost all of them, wear these shawls; they are in no way veils, however, but are merely draped over the top of the head) and make a great profession of piety, they are promiscuous.

Here the resentment is directed as it commonly is, against *santri* holier-than-thou moralism which *abangans*, particularly, tend to resent. But another aspect of the conflict, in so far as it is focused on ideological patterns, *santri* universalism and salvationism, also draws the pragmatic, relativistic *abangan*'s fire:

2. For a review of this period, see B. Schrieke, *Indonesian Sociological Studies*, The Hague and Bandung, 1955, part I, esp. pp. 80–82.

I talked the other evening to Mbok Min and her husband, who is a day-laborer in the rice fields when he finds work. They said that the *santris* say that if one doesn't chant the Koran one will end up in hell, but they, the Mins, don't believe it. As the Mins put it, heaven and hell are in the here and now. 'If you don't have enough to eat, if you steal and do bad things, if you are emotionally upset, then you have hell now.' . . . The village children nearby were yelling *traweh* (to announce the extra evening prayers during the Fast) and I asked the Mins innocently, what was that and they said, 'O, it is just for *santris* to pray every night in the prayer-house . . . The *santris* have 'Arab religion' but we don't hold with that. What is important is not chanting and all that business but doing right, not stealing and so on. The *santris* around here are always telling us we will end up in hell if we don't do just as they do.'

In *prijaji* attacks, the criticism of *santri* hypocrisy and intoler-ance is often combined with theoretical differences on patterns of belief:

He (an independent mystic *guru*) said that his 'science' was not religion like Christianity or Islam but real 'science' and so not easily to be dispensed to all comers like religion . . . He commented on the *santris*, whom he dislikes rather intensely, saying that people spend money to go on the pilgrimage which is just throwing money away. He said: 'They go to pray at the holy place and then come back here and are very honored. But the fact is that they haven't done anything to be honored for, because the real holy place is within the *batin*, the inner life. I make my pilgrimage to that. There is no need going off to Mecca when you can make a pilgrimage to God in your own inner life. Take the Mosque in Modjokuto. It can be ruined, can't it? Or fall down? Well, my mosque (pointing to his chest) cannot be ruined. It is in my heart and it is not like a building. Nothing can happen to it. And it is in there that I pray and that I come in touch with God.' He said that during the Japanese period, when the big riots occurred in Modjokuto, in which the Javanese populace stripped the Chinese stores of all their goods, all his pious *santri* neighbors joined in the looting, but he didn't. He told them not to, but they went ahead anyway and considered him a fool for abstaining. But now he still has a good job, whereas many of them have lost all they stole and are poor again. 'That's the way *santris* are,' he concluded. 'Hypocrites – all of them.'

From the *santri* side the attack is no less astringent. They accuse the *abangans* of being idol-worshippers and the *prijajis* of failing to keep themselves separate from God (a mortal sin of pride) and they have a marked tendency to consider everyone outside the fold a communist:

While talking with Abdul (a *kijaji*) he said that there were a lot of 'wild' religions around now, naming some of the sects in town. He said that they were all communist dominated and were a mixture of communism and 'Javanese science'. He said that he thought that the communist plan was to set up lots of little religions so as to generally confuse the religious situation, and then later they would say: 'See, religion just disorganizes things; away with all religions!' . . . He said that he had told one man that the 'native' beliefs of his sect really came from India, not from Java, and the man said he was talking like a colonialist. He told me that some time ago five communist youths came down from Surabaja and one of them said that when he became dictator all the *kijajis* would be done away with. Abdul said that there was a sect in Modjokuto called Islam Sedjati (Ilmu Sedjati) – 'true Islam' – but it really was 'false Islam'.

On the ideological level, the differences between *abangan* and *prijaji* are rather muted, both because of the general relativism of the two groups and because the *abangans* are not much interested in dogma in any case. Many *prijaji*, especially the better-educated ones, regard many *abangan* beliefs and practices as 'mere superstition'; and they generally regard the *abangans* as over-credulous. But the *prijajis* seldom express open disapproval of *abangan* beliefs and practices to the peasants directly. For the most part they deal with villagers as they always have – by minimizing direct contact with them as much as possible.

One exception to the non-interference policy is the *prijaji* attitude toward *abangan* beliefs centering around childbirth and to a lesser extent, around the role of women. Emancipated women of the *prijaji* group, organized into women's clubs, propagandize against birth practices and theories they consider unhygienic and in favor of modern Western methods as practised by the trained midwives attached to the hospitals. Similarly, they express disapproval of certain elements in the marriage ritual which symbolize the subservience of the women – such as the washing of the groom's feet by the bride, certain 'degrading' art forms – such as the *tajuban*, and, of course, polygamy – although this brings them into sharp conflict with the *santris* rather than with the *abangans*. Their efforts are, in any case, half-hearted, and, although ostensibly directed toward the peasants and town proletariat for whose welfare they feel responsible, are actually mostly aimed at advancing the status of women within the *prijaji* group itself.

In the other direction, the *abangans* are likely to regard most *prijaji* mystic theories as beyond their comprehension. They view *prijaji* religion with much of the grudging respect with which they view *prijajis* and the *prijaji* style-of-life generally – as undoubtedly admirable, but not necessarily attractive.

Class conflicts

The *prijaji–abangan* tension shows most clearly in relation to problems of status. *Prijaji* often accuse 'village people' of not knowing their proper place and so disturbing the organic balance of society, of having big ideas, and of unsuccessfully aping the *prijaji* style-of-life.

I asked the *prijaji* wife of the Modjokuto government animal-husbandry agent who lived in the houses around her, and she said, 'Peasants'. I said: 'When you visit around, where do you go?' She pointed in the direction of the center of town and said: 'Peasants aren't very good for mixing with . . . They say anything they want to – just follow their impulses of the moment. They talk about people; they don't keep secrets. *Prijajis* won't tell about anyone won't disclose secrets . . . Village people nowadays dress like *prijajis*. Sometimes you can't tell the difference. They even do their hair in the *prijaji* way . . . This first happened just about the time the Japanese came (1942–5). The Japanese used a lot of village girls for nurses, and this introduced them to wearing dresses, nice sarongs, etc. They buy one nice set of clothes and don't care if they have to wear rags when they're around the house and don't care if people see them always in the same set of clothes. *Prijajis* prefer to buy many sets of clothes, which may not be of top quality, so then they can change often; they feel ashamed if they are always seen in the same clothes . . . or village people will buy a bicycle. Nowadays many have them that didn't before, and they ride their bicycle in any old clothes.' Talking about the comparative situation of *prijajis* now and in the Colonial period, I asked which was a better time for them; and she said that from the point of view of those who are not 'convinced' (i.e. convinced nationalists) it was better before and many people complain nowadays. But those who are 'convinced' say that these times are like war times, and one cannot expect much. She said that in the Dutch time the *prijajis* who were at the level of

173

Police Chief and above wore trousers and spoke Dutch to their superiors. Her husband, as animal-husbandry agent, was in this group. Those who were below the Police Chief wore sarongs and spoke Javanese, and called the District Chief, etc. '*ndoro*' (roughly: 'master').

That the blurring of social demarcations began only in the Japanese period is, of course, not true; but that the blurring has been progressive and is continuing is obvious no matter at which aspect of the Modjokuto social system one looks. Although the claims of the more Jacobinic among the nationalists that sharp stratification contrasts have disappeared in Java, that the *prijaji* value system is dead or dying, and that power in Indonesia has been put into the hands of the masses – in other words, that the Revolution completely cut off Indonesia from her past – are very much over-stated, it cannot be denied that the Revolution seems if not to have begun at least to have stimulated wide-spread changes in the hierarchical patterns of prestige in terms of which Javanese society has been for so long integrated. The tracing of such changes, of their bases and their implications, cannot be carried out here; what is important to note is that such changes bring the *prijaji* and *abangan* (as well as the *santri*, who, so far as status is concerned, tends to side with the *abangans* against the *prijaji* claim to traditional privilege) world-views into more direct opposition than they have been in the past.

The traditional system of social stratification allowed mobility for individuals, as does every such system, but the system itself was stable and more or less unchanging; it was, in Schumpeter's image, like a hotel, always full but of different people. Today the system itself is changing, not just the people within it; and this changes the whole basis and perception of social mobility. It is no longer a situation in which a few favored individuals (or families) rise by a combination of luck and cunning out of the peasantry into the gentry but one in which mobility is a normal, expectable occurrence. Now, although the barrier between the governed and the governing (which was the major basis of the old system) remains real enough, it is considered crossable not merely by the extraordinarily fortunate or talented but also by anyone of normal ability and persistence. As a result, the bettering of his station is a legitimate and reasonable aim for a man to have, a meaningful goal toward which his life can be directed.

Further, since whole classes are moving now, even if the individual, so to speak, stands still, his class relationships do not remain constant. It is as though the floors in Schumpeter's hotel have begun to move and rearrange themselves. In such a situation, a sharp conflict between class-linked value systems is inevitable as the old pattern attempts to maintain itself in the face of the changing bases of social evaluation. [. . .]

Political conflicts

In addition to intrinsic ideological conflicts and increased status mobility, the intensified struggle for political power is a third divisive element which exacerbates religious conflict. In a colonial regime, particularly one so conservative in policy toward changes in native social structure as the Dutch, the subject people tend to be progressively cut off from the crucial political and economic roles in the system. Indirect rule, whether motivated by ethical or administrative considerations, is postulated on the supposition that traditional native institutions serve native interest better than any other institutions, particularly Western ones, are likely to do. This, in a sense, may well be true, and proponents of such a doctrine can point to the anomic results of more direct impact of Western forms on non-Western peoples in other parts of the world, say the Indian in the United States. Nevertheless, despite the theory, what actually occurs is not the mere stabilization of native society in its pristine forms, but rather, as the social system 'naturally' grows more complex, the European ruling group takes over each new role of functional importance as it appears, either filling it themselves or permitting certain others, typically non-European immigrants, half-castes, and a few specially chosen native aristocrats, to fill it, thus 'sheltering' the native society from the effects of change. In time, not only do the *loci* of all types of power shift more and more away from native hands as the 'Western' sector of the 'dual' (or 'plural') society grows in complexity and importance, but also the ruling group has to spend more and more time merely in keeping the native society intact. Traditional forms of life no longer exist naturally, as adaptive responses to their environment, but must be consistently and consciously shored up by special efforts on the part of the ruling group in the name

175

of 'native welfare'. Keeping the natives native becomes a full-time job.

When, at length, a political revolution occurs, as in Indonesia, the power vacuum suddenly revealed as almost all posts of crucial political importance are suddenly left vacant is tremendous and draws almost the whole of social life into it. (For various reasons, this occurs to a much lesser degree in the economic sectors; a fact which only magnifies the importance of the political in the eyes of the native population.) With the well- or cynically intended deceptions of Colonial rule removed, the real distribution of power becomes apparent to all; and, with the new understanding of what the score really is – an understanding confined in the pre-revolutionary period to a few nationalist intellectuals – the scramble for power becomes intense. Such heightened political struggle naturally results in a sharpened internal conflict between various religious groups. Religious positions become political ones – almost without alteration.

Mhd Rais spoke next (Rais is one of the dozen or so most important Masjumi national leaders; he was speaking at a mass meeting at the Regency capital to which all the local Masjumi leaders went). He said that he had read some nasty comments about him in the P.N.I. (the *prijaji*-dominated Nationalist party) press in Surabaja, but that he wasn't angry; he only laughed, because one couldn't expect politeness from the P.N.I. He started off on the PERMAI problem (a PERMAI leader had been reported in the press as saying that Islam was a foreign religion and Muhammad a false prophet, an event which was something of a *cause célèbre* for awhile), and rose to high pitch with a rhetorical challenge to the cabinet: 'Muslims are patient, but they won't be patient forever. You had better realize that they will take only so much and then they will fight. You must consider that your actions may bring about the flow of blood, that if you allow these insults to Islam to continue we may end up in a civil war.' . . . Then he attacked the proposals for separation of Church and state, ridiculed the religio-ideological theories of P.N.I. as empty of meaning, and said that the non-Islamic groups were urging marriage without going to the Naib, which would lead to a nation of bastards and Indonesia would become known as the bastard country . . . The other speaker started off by attacking the Communists in general terms, reading off the organizations he held were Communist dominated, and rising to heights of sheer spleen. He spoke entirely at a shout, pounded the rostrum, interrupted his speech to get the audience to shout *Allah Hu*

Akbar (God is most great) back at him, attacked the 'half-ripe intellectuals' who were for separation of Church and State, and in fact
attacked intellectualism in general, saying that the only thing one had
to do was fear God and follow the Moslem law. He attacked all non-
Islamic parties as infidel and said that Muslims who joined them were
breaking the rules of religion. He said that the idea of a secular state
was infidel; that Indonesia should not try to learn from Russia and
America, but just base its country on Islamic teachings . . .

A few comments must be made concerning this quotation. In
the first place, comparable remarks could be quoted for each
political group which would show little difference of intensity or
rationality. Secondly, speeches of this sort are not to be taken
over-literally as heralding immediate recourse to arms and
violence, for they are well within the limits of permissible political
hyperbole in present-day Indonesia. Thirdly, in each party there
are, in contrast to foot-stompers such as the one quoted, calmer,
more rational and more thoughtful leaders to whom such men
are as inherently unattractive as our Western political dema-
gogues are to our more responsible leaders. Nevertheless, despite
the qualifications, such demagogy is hardly without effect, and
the quotation does indicate both the rather intense level to which
political conflict has come in present-day Indonesia and the
manner in which it tends, in part, to focus around ostensibly
religious issues. [. . .]

Religion and Social Integration

If the divisive forces were the whole story, Javanese society would
have fallen into a war of all against all a good while ago. It is
necessary now to turn to the integrative elements in Javanese
society which tend to maintain it against the divisive elements.
Among the most important of these is the sense of a common
culture. This takes two main forms: a denigration of the present
in terms of the past, especially criticism of contemporary practices
by traditional standards of judgement, a practice mainly, but not
entirely, resorted to by older people; and the growing strength
of nationalism which attempts to appeal to sentiments of
national self-respect, solidarity and hope for a more 'modern'

style-of-life in order to curb social disorganization, which is characteristic mainly, but again not entirely, of younger people.

A night-long political discussion in a heavily *santri* village some fifteen or twenty miles from Modjokuto displayed both of these themes.

About ten or so, the *kijaji* showed up and started giving speeches of one sort or another, and a quite interesting discussion began . . . They started by lamenting the decline of traditional religious life, saying that only a few of the larger *pondoks* were still running in the old style and putting this decline down to laziness. The *kijaji* asked me about the general election in the United States and he said that there would be a hot time in the election here later (the election was then scheduled for early 1955). He talked about the Masjumi–N.U. split and said that it was too bad and then said something to the effect that he thought a 100 per cent Islamic state here was not possible because there were too many other groups; and so the Muslims should learn to get along with them. This statement met general agreement, one man saying that not all the Islamic law could be carried out in daily life; what was important was that Islam influence the State. There was some discussion then of Freedom (i.e. the post-Republican period), and the *modin* said that Djojobojo (a semi-legendary Javanese King) had predicted that when there was a Just King there would be good time for Islam and it would prosper. Then, surprisingly, he said that under the Dutch this was so – that they had just kings and Islam prospered. Someone said, 'Well, we have a President now, and we can't have a king again'; but the *modin* insisted that the old days were better than now because now party politics were tearing the country up. The *kijaji* agreed that the real differences between people in Indonesia were not those, say, between Christians and Muslims, but between political parties, and that one can't go back to the old days. He said that there were two ways that this prediction of Djojobojo could be read. One way was the way the *modin* had read it; literally, as meaning that there would have to be a real king in the future who was 'just' as a leader of the people, and then Islam would prosper. But another way to interpret it was that if all the people, the people as a whole, tried to be 'just', Islam would prosper – in a democracy the people is king, he said . . . The *kijaji* said that this was the Islamic view; he didn't know about the Christian view. One man then asked me, as the local expert on Christianity, I guess, if I could give them any information on this matter. I said that I thought that Christians would agree with the *kijaji*'s comment that if the mass of the people were just, religion would be well-off, hoping that this was a high enough abstraction for the purposes. But the *kijaji* suddenly changed his tune and said, 'Yes, but, often men have to die to achieve justice; blood has to be shed'; and then they launched into the Communists, saying that they were anti-religion, etc. . . .

Traditionalism and the inherited common culture

Traditionalists tend to lament the younger generation and refer to the greater stability and single-mindedness of people in the past. They invoke against the open expressions of discord the values for harmony and cooperation, for polite suppression of feeling and for proper behavior in terms of status values which still have some force for even the most 'modern' of young men. A treatment of Javanese religion in terms of its major variants, such as I have offered, tends to obscure the common value consensus upon which these variants are based and out of which they grow.

All Javanese – *santri*, *prijaji* and *abangan* – hold certain general truths to be self-evident, just as behind the division into Catholic, Protestant and Jew, Americans cling to certain over-arching values which in many ways make, for example, an American Catholic more similar in his world-view to an American Protestant than, say, to a Spanish Catholic. The high concern for status formality; the emphasis on rigid politeness and on dissimulation of emotion and avoidance of intense external stimuli; inwardness; a view of religion as phenomenological 'science' and of fasting as 'applied science'; the idea that resolution and fixity of will are one of the most important elements in living an effective life; the convinction that people (particularly if they are neighbors) ought to *rukun*, that is, cooperate and help one another (almost no one completely avoids giving *slametans*), and that religious beliefs of others ought to be viewed relativistically, as suitable for them if not for everyone – all these are beliefs and values which appear throughout Javanese society, even among the *santris*, whose departure from them is most marked.

In support of the last proposition I offer my notes on a speech by the head of Muhammadijah – in theory, one of the 'purer' Moslems in Modjokuto – to Aisijijah, the women's auxiliary of Muhammadijah, on the subject of the approaching general elections, a speech in which the influence of the general *prijaji-*

abangan 'Javanism' outlook is more apparent than the Middle-Eastern reformist Islam element.

He said that he was supposed to speak about the approaching General Election, but first he wanted to explain the intention of it. So he started out on a lecture on the nature of man. He said first that it was important to note that there was both the body and the soul. A body can't live without a soul; if it is lacking there is only a corpse. 'How do you know there is a soul? You feel it. For instance, if you are pinched, it hurts, and if you try to describe the hurt you can't – it just hurts. This is the supernatural thing within you, an *alus* object.' From here he went on to draw a stick figure on the blackboard, and to label the head with 'mind' and the body with 'heart'. 'The "heart",' he said, 'is what makes you feel unhappy, makes you want to do things, while the "mind" searches out ways for you to do it. It is the "heart" which feels the pinch of poverty and says, "I'll be a market-seller and get money"; but it is the mind which shows the way. Otherwise you would just keep wanting to be a market-seller and never do it.' Then he went into a sort of typing of the desires, using an Arabic classification. 'First, the desire to make yourself beautiful, to decorate yourself, to please yourself. Second, the desire to be a leader, to say to others: "Follow me, I will show you the way." Third, a liking for your own kind, your own nationality. Fourth, courage in the face of risk of loss. Fifth, fear.' He didn't say much about the first two but gave several illustrations for the third, love of one's own kind. He said, 'We all like our own children best, or our own cousins. Then we all like best our own organizations. We get invited to GERWIS (a leftist women's organization), but we are reluctant to go; we get invited to an Aisjijah meeting, and we want to go because we know we will see our friends there. When we meet an Aisjijah member on the street we feel different about them because we know they too are Aisjijah ... We like to be with Javanese because they are *alus*. All have brownish-yellow skin, not too black, not too white, just right. If you are in a group of Chinese, everyone doesn't talk much, but in a group of Javanese, everyone is talking happily. If you talk with a Chinese, it is as if you don't "meet the man"; you don't come in contact with the man. This is because he is from a different nationality. The fourth feeling, courage, means you have to be daring, be willing to take risks. If you go into business, you have to expect to lose as well as to make a profit. The fifth one is really not good, except as fear of God which lies behind everything, for it is dangerous to people and makes for loss. If I am selling in the market and I am afraid that everyone else is undercutting my prices, I lower mine and I lose. Actually none of these desires are good in themselves or bad in themselves. People may have a stronger concentration of one desire than of the other two. Everyone is different. The desire to please the self may be weak in one person and almost absent in another. Some people emphasize the desire to lead, and this is necessary in order to have leaders. You can have too much of one of these too (and he gave the Germans and the Italians and Hitler and Mussolini as examples of too much love of their own kind). Understanding or knowledge enters the eyes; then it goes to the head, the "mind", and from these to the "heart". This shows that understanding is not just reason but emotion.' He went on to talk about ideology and said that Islam meant '*slamet*' (well-being). Thus Islam means to wish in the heart intensely so as to reach *slamet* . . . He said: 'If we want a *slamet* life, we must go by the Islamic Ideology, which is based on the Koran and the Hadith. To do this we must study and struggle . . . We must struggle in three arenas: in the home, in society, and in politics. Politics concerns how we will be able to grasp the State. This must be done not by revolt but by election. Then if the State is in the hands of the Moslems, the fight for the *slamet* life can be carried on through the State Police, the Civil Service, the National Radio, the National newspapers (there are no State-owned newspapers, however), etc.; and obviously this will be much faster than merely struggling in the home. The changes one person can make in twenty years of effort in the home can be made in one year through politics.'

There are many characteristically *santri* aspects in this – the emphasis on 'business', the Fear of God and the Islamic State based on Koran and Hadith, the recourse to Arabic analysis rather than Hindu-Javanese ones, the split between 'body' and 'soul' rather than 'inside' and 'outside'. But what is striking is how much of *santri* ideology gets stated here in generally Javanese terms: the emphasis on a phenomenology of feeling, on *slamet* – well-being – as an end, the relativism based on different feelings for different peoples, the emphasis on concepts like '*alus*' and 'heart' (*ati*), and the like. Islam almost becomes another 'Javanese Science'. Only 'almost' of course; but the common vocabulary and the reliance on widely shared concepts, beliefs and values means that even if *santris* differ with their neighbors they are at least able to talk intelligibly with them and to agree on some of the ground-rules of dispute and on some of the basic truths – such as that everyone in life seeks *slamet* – upon which differences of opinion may then be elaborated. The integrative importance of such an underlying agreement is crucial. *Santris* may not like *abangans*, and *abangans* may have their doubts about *prijajis;* but they all prefer each other to Chinese or Europeans.

Nationalism and the projection of a new common culture

The more nationalistically inclined among the Javanese (who, of course, may be the same concrete individuals as the traditionalists in another context or mood) also rely somewhat upon the common traditional values, for the doctrines of nationalism are, in many ways, attempts to restate those values in a somewhat more generalized form; but over and above this, the nationalistic Javanese appeal to the kinds of aspirations stimulated by contact with the world outside of Java. At nearly every one of the almost daily meetings of one or another of the town's 'organizations', a term (*organisasi*, from the Dutch) used to refer to the various modern-type political parties, women's clubs, youth groups, lending cooperatives, social and charitable organizations, labor unions and so on which have proliferated spectacularly since the Revolution; at each major holiday, in addresses by local political officials; in the government newsreels and over the government radio; in the big-city newspapers, magazines and the like, which are more and more read in Modjokuto – whenever and wherever the opportunity offers – the din of the nationalist ideology is unremitting.

Rather than give an example from my notes, I translate below a newspaper report of a prospective celebration of the twenty-fifth anniversary of the women's movement which conveys a more vivid and precise sense of both the tone and content of this ideology as it is repeated day after day in Modjokuto than any summary could.

'One-Quarter Century Celebration'
Surabaja, 16 May. The Committee for the Celebration of One-Quarter of a Century of the Unity of the Women's Movement in Indonesia was set up on 24 November 1952 by the Women's Congress of Indonesia, in order to lay plans for the celebration of this anniversary on 22 December 1953.

As already announced by this committee, the 22nd of December marks the passage of 25 years since the Women of Indonesia united their will in support of the realization of the National Struggle. On 22 December 1928 for the first time the various women's organizations of Indonesia met in one Indonesian-wide Congress at Djokjakarta. This Congress reflected the deep-felt struggle for freedom that had spread throughout the entire Indonesian society. In that year the youth of Indonesia had already set forth the famous revolutionary slogan:

One People: Indonesian
One Country: Indonesia
One Language: Indonesian

The Women of Indonesia were also fired by this slogan, and for the first time there occurred a unification of the Women's Movement.

Thus this day, the 22nd of December, has been proclaimed The Day of the Women's Awakening. Before this historic day the various women's organizations were interested only in general advancement, but beginning 22 December 1928 the Women of Indonesia, fully conscious of their responsibilities, merged their movement with the national struggle.

Today, 25 years later, our country has attained its freedom. The Women's struggle does not end with that. And although, perhaps, in content and form it is somewhat different, its aim is unchanged; it is the Glory of our Country and People. The form and the content of the movement will continue to progress as Indonesian society progresses....
(*Suara Rakjat* [Surabaja], 18 May 1953.)

This sort of intensely felt but curiously abstract kind of ideological expression, with its emphasis on the unity of all groups, on struggle, and on social morality, is in part a symbolic masking of real value conflicts within the society, a kind of cultural protesting too much, by means of which conflicts which threaten to upset the social equilibrium can to a degree be kept out of conscious awareness or at least from open expression. But, in part, it is also an attempt to work out a set of values which, while related to traditional values and developed out of them, are less concrete and specific and so more able to deal with the wide range of situations in which a modern society inevitably finds itself. Thus a traditional value such as *rukun* is freed from its explicit and concrete context in the *slametan*, in carefully specified village 'public' labor on the roads and irrigation ditches, in traditionally frozen labor-exchange patterns in agricultural work,

183

and becomes generalized to celebrate cooperation in any context. In this form it serves two functions: it hides (to a degree) the real differences of opinion which exist, and it serves as a basis for the development of genuinely effective patterns of cooperation more widely applicable.

Supported by a new, if still weak, sense of national identity, a new, but still uneasy, sense of self-confidence, nationalism is thus becoming an important integrating factor in the society, most especially for the élite, for the educated youth and the urban masses. It is, in fact for some of the more engaged, a secular religion in the sense in which Marxism for the Soviet Union and 'Free-Enterprise' success ideology for the United States serves as such a religion for certain elements in those populations. '"Revolution" is still a holy word in Indonesia,' a professor at an Indonesian university told me. 'It is still a holy word in America?'

Mixed types and marginal groups: Social structural factors

In addition to the sense of a common culture, whether expressed in the vocabulary of traditional religion or of modern nationalism a second factor in preventing value differences between *prijaji*, *santri* and *abangan* from having the full effects which seem implicit in them is the fact, universal in the articulation of culture and social system everywhere, that value patterns are not institutionalized directly, purely and without distortion but, rather, are integrated into a differentiated social system in such a manner that the resultant social structure does not mirror the cultural organization in any simple way.

The first reason why this is true is that organizing forces arising from religion, stratification, geography, economics and so on do not all run in the same direction. A high-status *santri* has often more in common with a *prijaji* than with a low-status *santri*. An *abangan* who, confounding the probabilities, makes good in business, is likely to find himself seeing things the *santri* way to a degree, even if he can't be bothered with praying. And for a *santri*, as for all Javanese, a neighbor is a neighbor after all, even if he does burn incense to idols.

This cross-cutting, balance-of-forces nature of social life is what allows several antagonistic social and cultural elements to be contained within the same relatively balanced system. It is, in fact, the absence of such cross-cutting which bodes ill for the future of a social system. One of the most important reasons for the extreme instability of the relations between Javanese and Chinese, for example, is just such an ominous coalescence of racial, economic and religious factors all going in the same direction. The chances for open violence in such a situation are greater than in a case where the divisive aspects of racial and religious difference and inequality of wealth do not support but check one another.

The general failure for cultural and social forces to coincide exactly in any concrete society produces a type of individual one can only call 'mixed', and whose 'mixed' character lends to him a greater ability to mediate between contrasting groups. For example one of the first-rank leaders of N.U., the conservative Moslem party, in Modjokuto is in almost every other respect but the political a *prijaji*. Before the war he was a book-keeper, belonged to such moderate *prijaji* nationalist organizations as Parindra and Budi Utomo, and did not pray, go to mosque or know very much about Islam. In general he followed the *prijaji* variant of Javanese religion – its mysticism, aestheticism and rank-consciousness – as, despite externals, he still does. After the Revolution it was considered certain that he would appear as a leader in P.N.I. the nationalist party successor to the type of organization to which he belonged in the pre-war period, but he startled the entire community by joining N.U. and, for the first time in his life, by beginning to pray five times a day and to attend mosque.

What was involved here was not a religious conversion; this man is still as strong a *prijaji* as he ever was. He still looks down on most *santris* as fanatic and uneducated, regards his own position as frankly anomalous, and realizes that he doesn't 'fit' (*tjotjog*) where he is. The rest of his family does not even make the pretence of being *santri*. His wife does not pray; she keeps aloof from N.U. women's activities and continues to restrict her friendships to *prijaji* circles. We are *korbans* – 'victims', 'sacrifices' – both the man and his wife say, claiming that they gave up their more 'comfortable' position in the *prijaji* group to provide much-needed intellectual leadership to the ignorant and over-religious orthodox Moslem group, sacrificing personal happiness to contribute to the progress of the new Indonesia. Those who take a less kind view of this man's behavior say that he joined N.U. because, being one of the few educated members, he would be a major leader (he is the party's representative on the Regency governing board), whereas in P.N.I., with its greater supply of intellectuals, he would be only second rank. The details of the matter are, however, unimportant. What is important is that this man serves as a link between two culturally defined groups otherwise rather antagonistic by the simple expedient of being a member of both of them at the same time.

There are other people of the same sort: the now-retired Sumatran doctor, a *prijaji* by status but, like Sumatrans generally, a pious Moslem and so sympathetic to the *santris*; the *prijaji* store-owner who, although he dislikes Islam, mixes more with *santris* than with non-*santris* (his store is in the Moslem Kauman); the *abangan* village clerk in an otherwise entirely *santri* village administration; the *santri* high-official – the Bragang Bupati is an example – who naturally tends to move in *prijaji* circles.

But in addition to mixed-type individuals there are also mixed-type groups, cultural 'minorities', members of which are able to perform similar mediating roles. An example here is the small Protestant community in Modjokuto. Speaking broadly, there are two main types of Protestants (Catholics in Modjokuto are nearly all Chinese) within the town of Modjokuto: first, those who adhere to the Dutch Reformed Church, who are mainly *prijaji* in social status and style of life, many of them being or having been in the past white-collar employees of Dutch sugar concerns, the local H.V.A. hospital, etc.; and second, those who adhere to the more revivalistic Protestant sects (Seventh Day Adventist, Pentacostal, etc.), who, if they are Javanese – perhaps the majority of the members of such sects are either Chinese or non-Javanese Indonesians from Ambon, Flores, Sumatra, etc. – are fairly poor *abangans*. The second group is of only marginal social importance in Modjokuto, but the first serves as an important buffer between the major religious groups. Other cultural minority groups, such as certain Chinese and the above-mentioned non-Javanese Indonesians, serve similar functions, being as they are more-or-less neutral with respect to the major Javanese religious variants.

Groups which are products of recent social change and Western contact, and so to an extent secularized, also tend to fall 'in between' the major religious variants. The most important of these is undoubtedly the *pemuda* group, *pemuda* being an Indonesian word meaning 'youth'. The relatively sudden expansion of Western-type education in Indonesia in recent years has produced a 'youth-culture' whose members are marked by a deep-going restlessness, a sharp ambivalence *vis-à-vis* traditional Javanese values and an intense nationalism. They are often relatively free of commitment to any of the major religious systems described, a situation which leaves them both more independent of traditional constraints and more anxious and uncertain about how they ought to live – although rather unwilling to admit it. In Modjokuto, the secularization of this group has proceeded less far than in larger cities such as Djakarta and Surabaja, and most young men can still be classified as at least vaguely *santri*, *abangan* or *prijaji*. But it can hardly be denied that *pemudas*, even in Modjokuto, often find much more in common with each other, irrespective of religion, than they do with adults of their own (rather attentuated) religious persuasion. This emergent Indonesian 'youth-culture', made up of an intense, idealistic and perplexed group of young men and women who have suddenly been projected into a world they never made, is an important cross-cutting force in present-day Modjokuto, tending to off-set the conflict between religious views with the war between the generations.

Another social structural circumstance militating against the simple segmentation of society along religious lines is the fact that the *prijaji* are the traditional leaders of the society, the time-honored holders of power. The result is that the élites of all groups have a tendency to include at least some *prijajis*, either because *prijajis* attracted by power-wielding possibilities have moved into them or because their own leaders have become '*prijaji*-ized' as their personal power has grown. Peasant leaders, for example, are rarely peasants; most often they are lower *prijajis*; for, though the *abangans* have the numbers to form an impressive fellowship, they but rarely produce from among themselves men with the social skills to lead them, even in terms of their own values. The Communist party, as all others, is largely led by town-based clerks, not agrarian radicals. In the early days of the nationalist movements, almost all the leaders, even of the *santri* groups (Tjokroaminoto, the founder of Sarekat Islam being an example), were drawn from the civil-servant class because the latter had a virtual monopoly on education and because they bore the traditional trappings of authority.

The converse proposition holds as well. As individual *abangans* or *santris* gain in power because of their leadership of effective political groups, they tend naturally to adopt *prijaji* ways, which poses something of a problem, because in so doing they lose at least part of the specific ideological attraction which gained them power in the first place. The problem is particularly acute among the *santris*, whose values are so anti-bureaucratic, 'independent', and 'equalitarian' in nature; for they realize that as their leaders become civil servants due to *santri* political power, they become also less *santri* in outlook. This is not entirely integrative, however, because the more 'traditional' *prijajis* tend to resent such *parvenu* power holders and, as I have already remarked, some of the more conservative *literati* elements among them tend to hold aloof altogether from activity in the 'new society' for this reason. In part, what is occurring is a shift in traditional leadership patterns, in which lower *prijajis* particularly, those with more of a stomach for contact with people of all types and emerging leaders from non-*prijaji* groups are forming a new élite with a culture based to a degree on the old *prijaji* patterns and in part on the newer *intelligensia* culture connected with national-ism, more or less cutting out the purer *literati*.

Tolerance and pluralistic social integration

The last two points making for a moderation of religious conflict – tolerance based on 'contextual relativism' and the growth of social mechanisms for a pluralistic non-syncretic form of social integration – may be dealt with together for they are, in part, merely two sides of the same coin. Relativistic tolerance has been mentioned several times in this report as being characteristic of non-*santri* religious views, but even *santris* adhere to it despite the intense concern with missionization which tends to be characteristic of Islam. Traders and richer peasants are seen, by all groups, as more or less 'naturally' *santris*, civil servants as 'normally' *prijaji*, and poorer peasants and town proletariat as 'typically' *abangan*; and there is really little serious thought in any of the groups that there is much possibility of 'converting' the others. The *santris* may talk much about 'missionary work' (*tablég*) and rail about the heathenism of the non-*santri* group, but in fact almost all their missionary work is directed inward, towards the *santri* group itself, being designed to improve the doctrinal purity of those who are already committed rather than to gain new adherents. Most *santris* would be appalled at the idea of personally trying to talk a convinced *prijaji* or *abangan* into becoming a *santri*. Thus the three groups tend to become socially segregated to a degree and come to accept the *de facto*, if not *de jure*, existence of one another. In part, the displacement of religious conflict to the political level is based on just this deep-going reluctance of Javanese to urge their own beliefs on others who differ with them.

Thus, despite protestations to the contrary, it seems as if at least some members of each group are coming to the conclusion that a new synthesis based on the complete triumph of their own values throughout the entire society is not likely to occur, and that an open society is to replace a closed one. Such views, even in a half-concealed form, are not dominant as yet; and an American committed to a loose balance-of-interests system not only in government but in social organization generally is especially likely to over-emphasize them. Certainly the yearning for a new synthesis which will have some of the psychological and social comforts of the old syncretic unification of belief is easily to be found; it is perhaps the most widespread social sentiment and that upon which the Dar Ul Islam Moslem rebels, the Communists and the more xenophobic nationalists all play. Nevertheless, the realization that such a re-establishment of an organic society is not possible, or if possible not desirable, is becoming increasingly apparent to many people of all shades of opinion, albeit in an almost unconscious form. But if a society is to be formed in which groups of rather different outlooks on life and committed to varying basic values are mutually to co-exist, social mechanisms in terms of which the necessary continual adjustment and readjustment among such groups are to take place must be constructed.

The Holidays – Ceremonies of Social Integration and Conflict

The analysis of such mechanisms on the Modjokuto scene, aside from those already suggested, would take us too far afield into an analysis of the political system, the proliferating system of private associations, clubs, unions, parties and the like, and, in general, into the hundreds of specific social behaviors by means of which the Modjokuto people actually get things done. But symbolic of both the strains towards integration and the sharpened conflicts of the emerging society are the ceremonies, practices and beliefs focused around the increasingly important national holidays and those traditional holidays which are still of importance. The holidays mirror the religious, political, status and other conflicts upon which I have touched, reflecting the sharpened antagonisms which arise in any society which is changing its form; but they indicate also, dimly and uncertainly, something of the new forms which may emerge, presenting an indistinct and misfocused image of the value choices with which *abangan*, *santri*, *prijaji*, all three, are for the moment faced. As such, a brief treatment of them forms a useful conclusion to this description of Modjokuto religious belief and behavior.

Since the Revolution, the number of holidays has greatly multiplied, at least in theory if not in actual practice. Nationalist holidays, traditional holidays, religious holidays all crowd one another until it sometimes seems that, indeed, in Indonesia every day is a holiday. For example, there are Hari Lagu Kebangsaan (Holiday for the National Anthem), Hari Ibu Kartini (Princess Kartini's Day, Princess Kartini being a turn-of-the-century forerunner of the nationalist women's movement), Hari Peladjar Internasional (International Students' Day), Hari Pelawan (Heroes' Day, commemorating the victims of the Revolution), Hari Angkatan Perang (Armed Forces Day), Satu Mei (First of May; sometimes called Hari Buruh Internasional, International Worker's Day), Hari Gerakan Wanita (Women's Movement Day) and Hari Kemerdekaan (Freedom Day, Indonesia's 'Fourth of July', which, as it falls on 17 August is consequently commonly referred to as *tudjuh-belas-Augustus*) – all of them being more or less nationalist holidays, as is indicated both by the events they celebrate and by the fact that they have Indonesian names. Then there are special religious holidays which only part of the population celebrates: Idul Adha (Sacrifice Day, commemorating Abraham's sacrifice), Mi'radj (the day on which Mohammed ascended to heaven to address God), Maulud (the Prophet's birth- and death-day), etc., for the Moslems; Hari Natal (Christmas) and Hari Pentacostal (the Pentacost) for the Christians; and the first of Sura, the actual Javanese New Year, for a few scattered adherents to mystical sects. But the big holiday is still the traditional end-of-fast celebration Rijaja, the one holiday with an important significance to all Javanese. [. . .]

Rijaja: the end of fast holiday

In *Rijaja* almost every theme we have discussed in this report finds its place. The holiday, coming as a gala climax of the Fast month, manages to hold within itself the whole range of religious belief and practice characteristic of present-day Modjokuto. *Abangan*, *santri* and *prijaji*; ardent nationalist and subdued traditionalist; peasant, trader and clerk; townsman and villager – all can find somewhere in this syncretic of public festivals the sort of symbol congenial to them. This syncretism, this easy tolerance of religious and ideological diversity is, as I have repeatedly stressed, a fundamental characteristic of Javanese culture, the recent intensification of intergroup conflict to the contrary notwithstanding. But, recent or not, that conflict, too, finds its expression in *Rijaja*. In a sense, *Rijaja* is a kind of master symbol for Javanese culture, as perhaps Christmas is for ours; and, if one really understood everything one observed on *Rijaja* – a simple impossibility – one could say one understood the Javanese.

The central ritual act of *Rijaja* is a personal, individual begging of forgiveness patterned in terms of status differences. The child asks forgiveness of his parents, the young of the old, the worker of his boss, the tenant farmer of his landlord, the politician of his party chief, the former *pondok* student of his *kijaji*, the cured patient of his *dukun*, the mystical student of his *guru*. Each of these (relatively) lower status people goes to the home of the

191

higher status one, where he is received, usually with tea and snacks, where he formally begs the pardon of the host.[3] The meaning of this act is that the petitioner wishes the host to forgive from the depths of his heart any injuries, intended or unintended, which the latter has done to him in the past year, so as to lighten the weight of his sins. Having theoretically expiated his sins in the Fast, he now asks those against whom they were committed to forgive him for them. *Santris* sometimes say that this pattern is mildly heterodox, for only God can forgive sins; but it is probably the most universally practiced ritual in Modjokuto today. Even many Christians do it even though, strictly speaking, the holiday is Moslem.

Because of the inherent relativity of status, the celebration usually must spread over several days; and in any case higher status people tend to remain at home so as to receive petitioners until toward the end of the period, when they journey out to the few people who outrank them. Very high individuals, such as the doctors or the District Officer, may make very few if any visits; the village chief in the semi-urban village in which I lived spent three wearying days receiving guests in his home without going out at all.

Despite the nominally religious aspect of the forgiveness ritual, the visiting around is for most people a gala, quite unserious business. Everyone almost inevitably buys new clothes for *Rijaja* as we do for Easter, and prepares the best food he can for his guests. The visiting pattern is, thus, as much an opportunity to display one's clothes and one's fancy food as it is a sacred ritual, and the day is both holy day and holiday. The people move in colorful throngs through the streets and roadways, passing from house to house, stopping at each for only fifteen or twenty minutes, so covering a dozen or so in the day, sometimes even two dozen.

In the more urbanized circles one often finds a replacement of the individual visiting pattern by a kind of secular party – one high *prijaji* actually held one at which beer was served – called a

---

3. The most common phrase – in high Javanese – is *nuwun pangestunipun sedaja kalepotan kula, lair batin:* I request your pardon for my faults, inside and outside (i.e. your genuine, undissembled, pardon). This is often shortened to *lair batin.*

halal bihalal (Arabic for a mutual begging of pardon), which both simplifies the ritual almost to the point of disappearance and strongly emphasizes its festive aspects. Perhaps the final stage in this secularization process is the increasingly popular custom, more so in larger towns than in Modjokuto, where it is confined to the highest status levels, of not actually making the pardon-begging visit but merely sending a small card, rather like a Christmas card, with the pardon request printed on it in Indonesian.

There are, of course, other more explicitly religious rituals. As I have already mentioned, mass prayers are held at dawn in the town square and in the mosque; *santri* organizations give out the *zakat-fitrah* religious tax to the poor; there is a special *slametan* on *Rijaja* (as well as one five days after). Also, simply because it is such a universal holiday, one in which absolutely everybody participates (it is the one day in the year when the market closes down), *Rijaja* reflects the religious strains, conflicts and re-adjustments I have been discussing. Perhaps the most striking example of this is the fact that one cannot properly speak, in Modjokuto at least, of one single *Rijaja* day, for the various groups do not agree on the proper date. In 1954 some people celebrated the *Rijaja* on Wednesday, some on Thursday, and some on Friday, each holding that the other people were incorrect.

The immediate cause of this conflict is the different modes of calculating the day. We have already seen that there is a conflict over the proper mode of calculating the date between modernist and conservative *santris*: the modernists calculate ahead of time by means of astronomical data; the conservatives wait, with true caution, to see the moon appear. But they both agree that the proper day *is* the day the moon appears, and in 1954 this was Wednesday, 2 June. *Abangans* and *prijaji*, however, use the so-called *abogé* system of calculation, which is, in essence, but another *pétungan* numerological system like those described in the *abangan* chapter above.[4] The lunar year drifts, of course, in

4. In the *abogé* system, the 'a' stands for Alip, one of the eight years in the *windu* cycle (i.e. eight years, each with a different name, make up one *windu*), 'bo' stands for Rebo, one of the days of the week (Wednesday), and 'ge' stands for Wagé, one of the five market weekdays. This means

relation to this rigid mathematical calendar; so in 1954 this day came out to Friday, 4 June (actually, *Djumaat Wagé*). Now *Djumaat Wagé*, it just so happens, is an unlucky day generally, so that many *abangans* made their beg-pardon calls on Thursday, while many *prijaji*, regarding the unlucky notion as mere ignorant superstition, did their visiting on Friday, the proper day. The result was that the *santris* held *Rijaji* on Wednesday, the *abangans* (and a few *prijaji*) on Thursday, the *prijaji* (and a few *abangans*) on Friday, a phenomenon which gave rise to a tremendous amount of discussion and a sharp highlighting of some of the religious strains in contemporary Modjokuto life.

Despite all the disharmonies it reveals, *Rijaja*, simply because it is the most catholic, the most festive and the most genuinely collective of their ceremonies, reveals even more clearly, though less explicitly, the underlying unity of the Javanese people, and, beyond them, of the Indonesian people as a whole. With the exception of Hindu Bali and a few Christian and pagan areas, it is everywhere a major holiday. In a broad, diffuse and very general way it stresses the commonalities among all Indonesians, stresses tolerance concerning their differences, stresses their oneness as a nation. It is, in fact, the most truly nationalist of their rituals, and, as such, it indicates the reality and the attainability of what is now the explicit ideal of all Indonesians – cultural unity and continuing social progress.

---

that the year Alip always starts on Rebo Wagé, and knowing this, one can figure the day on which *Rijaja* falls in any year merely by extended, though simple, calculation. A shorter method is to take the day on which the year began and apply the *waldjiro* formula to calculate *Rijaja*, 'Wal' is Sawal, the month; 'diji' is *sidji*, 'one', 'ro' is *loro*, 'two'. This means that *Rijaja* (which falls on the first of Sawal) is calculated by counting one from the week day and two from the market day on which the year began. For example, if the name of the year is Éhé, it must have begun (i.e. the first of Sura) on Ngahad Pon. The first of Sawal, or *Rijaja*, then falls on Ngahad Wagé eight cycles (of thirty-five days each; seven times five) and 22 days later, because Wagé follows Pon in the five day cycle and you count: 'Ngahad-one'; 'Pon-one, Wagé-two'.

12 E. Willems

Religious Pluralism and Class Structure: Brazil and Chile

E. Willems, 'Religious pluralism and class structure: Brazil and Chile', *International Yearbook for the Sociology of Religion*, Westdeutscher Verlag, 1965, pp. 190–209. Translated by Ingeborg Herman.

To call the religious structure of Latin American countries 'pluralistic' may arouse strong objections. If the usage of this term can be justified at all, it indicates radical change; for the religious structure of Latin America, which here is understood as a cultural entity in the anthropological sense, was not historically pluralistic but monolithic. At least, religious unity was the cultural ideal present in the minds of the Iberian conquerors, in which they and their Creole heirs believed with a remarkable perseverance, and which initiated one of the most comprehensive and most difficult conversion movements in Western history. As a matter of fact, Iberian Catholicism, drawing its popularity and vitality mainly from its clinging to medieval forms of religiousness, became one of the most effective general denominators in a world of cultural differences, and nowhere in Latin America – with the exception of a few isolated tribal societies – was the integration of frequently numerous elements of autochthonous religions able to shift the balance of the supernatural picture of the world in favour of non-Catholic aspects. Even the African deities, who have continued to live on in several parts of Latin America up to this day, gained the identity of Catholic saints, and this double role extended their range of activity and secured cultural continuity with the Catholic world.

During colonial times the Spanish and Portuguese authorities tried everything to protect the monolithic religious system of Latin America against the effects of the Reformation. The thoroughness with which Brazil, for instance, was shielded against Protestant influences, is comparable only with the methods of modern health authorities aiming at the prevention of epidemic diseases being introduced to a country.

One of the effects of this age-old policy may be seen in the identification of Latin American culture with Iberian Catholicism, the existence of which is not really due to the puristic maintenance of its ritualism but to the strongly sentimental idea that Catholicism is an historic heritage which is passed on within families, from generation to generation, and whose familiar symbolism contributes to the social identification and emotional security of the individual. This explains the fact, appearing odd to the outside observer, that all those people who do not distinctly belong to another religious congregation call themselves 'Catholics' in censuses, although in countries like Brazil and Chile the number of practising Catholics (in the sense of the Church) scarcely exceeds 15 per cent of the total population. The statement of being without religion or not belonging to a religious congregation – if anybody would think of this at all – would most likely be interpreted as 'not typical of Brazilians' and 'not typical of Chileans'.

The interpretation of religion and church institutions as symbols of nationality took place in the nineteenth century. In both countries the Catholic church became the State church and, thus, the institutional path leading to the identification of nation and Catholicism was open. However, secularizing forces, undermining the previous unanimity of social consensus, were at work. The public promotion of Protestant immigration, mainly from Germany, indicated a reversal of the former attitude towards dissenters, even though this immigration strategy in both countries met with strong resistance (see de Carvalho, 1875, *passim*; Rosales, 1864, pp. 350, 365). Nationalistically justified anti-Protestantism flared up time and again and has by no means disappeared even today. In 1921 Jose Felicio dos Santos writes:

Protestantism is detested by the best groups of our people, even in non-Catholic circles. It is not only an enemy of our traditions, our national traditions, but it is also antagonistic to the traditions of our race. In the history of Brazil, Protestantism appears only in connexion with shame, spoilation, devastation and ruin . . .

And the following imputation of political intentions was repeated, more or less radically, by many Brazilians who were little or not at all interested in organized religion, including the Catholic church:

The North Americans continue with their secret expansion politics here in our country, and concurrently they go on exploiting us in their own country . . . It is not necessary to be Catholic to help the Church in its nationalistic mission . . . To defend the Church means to defend Brazil.

As late as 1938 we find a similar point of view in the book of a Brazilian Jesuit:

Aside from their early and shameful manifestations, the Protestant churches did not appear on the national scene until the spirit of Brazilianism had already taken on definite shape among our people, and with their propaganda they caused doubt and worry in many observers of our situation. The Catholic church, by contrast, appeared right in the very beginning of Brazilian history, and, influenced by the activities of secular and monastic clergymen, Brazil's history develops, as a number of historians not suspected of any friendly feelings for the Church, stated with sincerity. Thus, if we had no higher motives – which would be absurd – a sound and well-understood patriotism would suffice to make the Brazilians respect and promote the activities of the Catholic church.

These and many similar proclamations of an anti-Protestant attitude range from the insinuation that the missionaries were tools of American imperialism to the more sophisticated interpretation of Protestantism as an historic latecomer, for which there could be no role within the framework of an already established Brazilian culture. For many people a Brazilian Protestant is not really a Brazilian and conversion to a Protestant church equals a betrayal of the cultural heritage of the country. Around the turn of the century an American missionary stated that a factor working strongly against the

indigenous colporteur and his efforts is the contempt with which converts are looked at by the masses. Many people are of the opinion that it is right for a foreigner, who was born and raised in the Protestant faith, to maintain his religion and even to work for its extension. But it is unbearable if a native Brazilian, who was raised as a Roman Catholic, rejects his faith to become a Protestant; such persons are shunned, and some people think they are not worthy of any respect. For a foreigner it is difficult to understand the position of a native convert who resigns the religion of his country and his ancestors. Rome's claim to be the only true church with an infallible head, the regular and continuous transfer of spiritual authority to bishops and priests, and a complicated form of ceremonial service through the centuries, gained a strong influence on the attitude of the masses. Many religious rites and ceremonies became social customs and, thus, are inseparable from the reality of social life. To give this up means to expose oneself, to a great extent, to social disregard (Tucker, 1902, pp. 203 ff.).

Secularization of the Term 'Cultural Unity'

Not wishing to reproduce what has already been said about the first half-century of Protestant proselytism (Willems, 1963, pp. 311 ff.), we need to point out only that the spreading of the new religion in both Brazil and Chile developed very slowly and that functionally it was and still is connected with cultural changes characterizing the transition from an agrarian-paternalistic society of the past to the industrial society of the present. In Brazil the separation of Church and State came into being with the first republican constitution in 1891, in Chile not until 1925. Thus, freedom of religion actually already existing, was guaranteed by constitution. The maintenance of a uniform religious structure had fundamentally ceased to be a point of convergence of political consensus.

The ideological and political currents which gave rise to and were involved in this change cannot be further investigated here. Essential in this connexion is the fact that religion was less and less regarded as a symbol of political unity, although not in all social classes and regional cultures at the same time, of course. In the more traditionally ruled regions, such as North-eastern Brazil or the Chilean province of Coquimbo, this process developed very slowly, and in both countries a more obstinate adherence to religious traditions could be noticed among the middle and upper classes. These differences still exist today, but they are more pronounced in Chilean society than in Brazil.

Even though (due to this change) the basis for a religious pluralism was established, vehement resistance was offered to an institutional pluralism related to other cultural spheres. Since political emancipation the preservation of territorial unity, particularly in Brazil, was a problem worrying the statesmen of the imperium just as much as those of the republic. The reaction to actual and possible separatist revolutions or merely revolutions in which regional contrasts played a part, consisted mainly in the creation of a strongly centralized political structure.[1] The existence of ethnic minorities which, like the German-Brazilians, insisted on the preservation of their cultural heritage, since the time of the First World War led to the formulation of a monolithic-oriented ideology of general consolidation and assimilation. Differences in language, 'race', values and social institutions were interpreted as obstacles standing in the way of national unity. The pluralistic ideology of some ethnic minorities taking the view that the preservation of their own cultural heritage be more important to the country's development than assimilation to the Brazilian culture, was perceived as a menace to the national unity and as an actual political danger. Religion played a part in these issues only in so far as it – like the Protestant church associations of the German-Brazilians – advocated the preservation of the minority's traditions. As German schools, German clubs and co-operative societies were seen as adversaries to the monolithic national state, so was the Protestant church. Not that the oppression of the Protestant religion was demanded, but its 'nationalization', and above all, the introduction of the Portuguese language to sermons and rites.

The tendency towards moderation and a relative matter-of-factness seemingly puts Chile in strong contrast to Brazil (and many other Latin American countries). However, this difference exists mainly on the emotional and verbal levels. Aside from temporary phases of nationalistic exaltation in Brazil political action, particularly in the field of education, follows the guidelines of the assimilation ideology only hesitantly and with considerable aloofness. In Chile, by contrast, one can scarcely speak of such an ideology, but the educational system of that country is much more adequate for putting into practice the norms of a monolithic-culture politics, and political centralization has reached a point which makes institutional differentiation on the

1. Even in the Federal State of Brazil, there exist strong centralization tendencies, which are expressed, especially during political crises, through the position of the absolute supremacy of the Federal Government.

basis of provincial and local autonomy utterly impossible. As a matter of fact, Chile is much closer to the goal of monolithic cultural unity than Brazil. Even the fiercest nationalists cannot consider the minority problem of the country to be alarming – and regional differences appear less sharp than those of Brazil.

Regional Cultures, Social Structure and Religious Differentiations.

This raises the question of how the diversity of regional cultures is compatible with the idea of a monolithic national culture. If one separates the indisputable existence of regional cultures, markedly differing from each other, from the social ideals of nationalistic ideologies, there will be no doubt that the culture of Brazil (like that of Peru, Mexico, Bolivia and most other Latin American countries) is pluralistic.

As for the term 'regional culture' in Latin America (as in many other countries), it should be pointed out that the people living in its area have no ideas at all, or only very vague ones, about national inter-relationships. They do not belong – or if so, they do only to a limited extent – to the 'participating society', as we, together with Joseph Kahl, want to call those people

who go to school, read the newspapers, receive cash as remuneration for their work which they can change at any time and unrestrictedly, who buy goods in an open market in exchange for money, vote when the elections take place, thus deciding about competing candidates, and who express their personal opinions about many things that are none of their business. Especially important for the style of life of the participating society is the large proportion of people having an opinion about public affairs – as well as the expectation of these people that their ideas be considered (Kahl, 1962, p. 388).

Furthermore, if one distinguishes between the ideal of the monolithic cultural unity and the actually realized national unity, one will ask, above all, who the pillars of this unity are. It is a well-known hallmark of the social structure of Latin America, e.g. Brazil, that the conceptions of values, the behaviour pattern and the material culture of the upper classes do not have any essential regional differences. A member of the traditional upper class or of the urban bourgeoisie, who lives in Fortalexa or

Recife, is culturally much closer to other members of the same classes in Curitiba or Porto Alegre than to the peasants, cowboys or fishermen of his own region. The cultural splitting of social classes (which, of course, exists everywhere) in Brazil and Chile, as in the remaining parts of the continent, proceeds in such a way that the lower rural classes are to be seen as the carriers of the regional cultures and the upper classes as the carriers of the national culture. Up to the most recent time the attitude of the upper classes was exclusivistic in so far as almost all 'cultural affairs' (in the non-anthropological sense) were the monopoly of the upper classes. Since these classes concurrently had a political power monopoly, the existence of regional cultures did not represent a disquieting problem. It could be largely ignored. The ignorance and superstition of the lower classes were acknowledged with benevolence. One did not believe that these plantation workers, cowboys and small farmers would be able to represent their own interests in a responsible manner. Rather they were to be protected, with a fatherly but strong hand, against the consequences of their own ignorance and irresponsibility.

There were, however, moments in the more recent history of Brazil when such regional societies suddenly developed organizational capabilities which were interpreted as a political threat; and they were forcibly suppressed.

Two of these movements quite obviously had a messianic character and came into being under the influence of religious leaders. The 'Fanatics' Rebellion' of Canudos (da Cunha, 1944) in the north-east of Brazil, and the 'Holy War' in the interior of the southern state of Catarina (de Queiróz, 1957) could be suppressed only by means of the federal army after lengthy fights. These and numerous similar movements, being part of local history and having usually been ignored by the historians, point clearly to the fact that the religion of the lower classes is far from being orthodox, but rather is in continuous flux. Furthermore, they include – according to the model of typically messianic movements – revolutionary elements which are related to decisive changes in the conventional social structure (de Queiróz, 1960, p. 73).

The relevance of relationships between regional cultures, religious movements and social classes which become manifest in these unsuccessful attempts, becomes clear when one demonstrates the development of Protestantism and other religious currents. It could be expected that in view of the lesser differentiation of the regional cultures in Chile the present religious movements differ less from one another than those of Brazil. This is undoubtedly the case. In Chile all these movements are connected with the different types of Protestantism, but in Brazil there are two further movements, besides, a strong and highly differentiated Protestantism, which stretch over the whole country and have hundreds of thousands of followers: Spiritualism and Umbanda.

In both countries obviously a connexion between lower classes and religious movements exists, but in Chile their connexions with regional cultures are only very vague, whereas in Brazil they are distinctly recognizable. In traditional Chile one finds, as everywhere in Latin America, a substratum of unorthodox religious practices in a popular setting, like, for example, the proclamation of new saints, pilgrimages, the believing in miracles, faith-healing, etc. Certain aspects of Pentecostalism in Chile, including the overwhelming majority of the Protestants, show continuity with the people's Catholicism, although no member of the sect would ever admit this.

In terms of numbers, the development of these sects in Chile as well as in Brazil obviously points to a parallelism with certain economic and political processes which have contributed to a gradual emancipation of the lower classes from the paternalistic ties of the conventional social order.

Table 1

Development of Protestantism in Chile

Year	Total number of Protestants
1916	6,293
1925	11,591
1938	99,460
1949	264,667
1952	370,016
1957	370,428
1961	834,839

Source: Damboriena (1963), p. 16.

The inaccuracy of these figures is shown by the fact that, according to another source, the number of members belonging to the Iglesia Evangélica Pentecostal in 1957 already amounted to 500,000 (Damboriena, 1963, p. 63). From a number of indicators, which cannot be discussed in detail here, it is to be seen that at least the figures for 1952 and 1957 are much too small. The figure stated for 1961 most likely comes closer to reality, and it can be assumed almost with certainty that about 90 per cent of the 834,839 Chilean Protestants (roughly 11 per cent of the country's total population) belonged to different Pentecostal sects. According to numerous tests their members come mainly from the lower classes. It must, however, be added that here not only the laborers are involved but also the lower strata of the middle class, whose uncertain economic situation differs sharply from the relative stability of the European lower-middle class.

Table 2

Development of Protestantism in Brazil

Year	Total number of Protestants	Percentage of the total population
1890	143,743	1
1940	1,074,857	2·6
1950	1,741,430	3·35
1958	2,697,273	4·3 ?
1961	4,071,643	5·7 ?

This table was composed from various sources. The first three figures were taken from the general censuses. The data for 1958 are from a survey of the Protestant Federation of Brazil; and the figure indicated for 1961 was taken from Damboriena (1963).

The two most important sects in Brazil are the *Assembleia de Deus* and the *Congregação Cristã*. The first had one million followers in 1958, the latter half a million (Anon, 1959, pp. 6 ff.) In other words: in 1958, 55·6 per cent of all Brazilian Protestants belonged to these two sects. The total number of Pentecostalists is probably much higher, since there are at least a dozen other sects demonstrating a predominantly Pentecostal character.

In estimating the growth of this movement it has to be considered that in both countries the first Pentecostal parishes came into being in 1910. Their development was so slow that in 1932 only about 9·5 per cent of the Brazilian Protestants – excluding the non-proselytic German-Brazilian congregations – belonged to Pentecostal parishes (Braga and Grubb, 1932, p. 71). Although no figures are available for Brazil, it may be claimed that the pace of development was hardly faster there. Not until after the Second World War was the spread of this movement accelerated, which then, within the last ten years, grew like an avalanche. During these two decades the social structure of the two countries underwent more comprehensive and more decisive changes than ever before. Rapid industrialization, internal migration and population concentration in cities, the obsolete institutional structure of which was not ready to meet such changes, may be taken as the expression of this structural change.

The foundation of the society for Spiritualistic Studies of Confucius' Group in 1873 may be considered to be the beginning of an organized Spiritualism in Brazil. Although reliable data on the development of spiritualism are not available, it may be assumed with certainty that there was no mass movement before 1920. As the statistical data include only those Spiritualists belonging to the larger cult centres – and many followers, maybe the majority, assemble in smaller centres which cannot be statistically ascertained – the official figures are certainly much too small. According to the Brazilian census, the total number of Spiritualists increased from 463,400 in 1940 to 824,553 in 1950 (de Camargo, 1961, p. 176). Statistical authorities so far have not recognized the Umbanda as a religious congregation, and since this movement is institutionalized only to a minor extent, it is extremely difficult to give estimates. Most likely, however, the number of followers is much higher than one million.

Pentecostalism, Spiritualism and Umbanda gravitate around a common form of supernaturalism: the belief that supernatural beings descend to the living and temporarily take possession of their bodies. Following the biblical model, the Pentecostal sects believe that the fits of obsession of their followers, which express themselves in ecstatic conditions, visions, glossolalia and fainting fits, are caused by the Holy Ghost who descends to the members of the congregation and fills them with his 'gifts'. Occasionally it is the devil who takes advantage of the general confusion and suddenly enters the body of a believer. An extraordinary healing power is attributed to the state of obsession, which may affect the obsessed one himself as well as other persons having contact with him. Every Pentecostal parish quotes a rich treasure of stories about miraculous healings.

Brazilian Spiritualism in principle follows the teachings of Allan Kardec. During the sessions, which have developed into regular services, the media – following the ritual request of the cult leader – receive different kinds of ghosts. The 'ghosts of light' give advice on an enormous number of the believers' personal problems. Other 'sophisticated' ghosts contact the believers via the body of the medium and, by transferring a 'comforting atmosphere', exert healing or soothing influences. Sometimes, however, even 'evil spirits' plague those present with their wicked and obscene talk.

Umbanda is the result of a manifold syncretism combining African, American Indian, Catholic and Spiritualistic elements in a loosely arranged doctrine which allows flexibly for local variations. The basis is undoubtedly a religious tradition stemming from African origins and still persists in certain urban lower classes. This tradition is called *macumba*, *candomblé* or *Xangô*, depending on the region. Every African *Orixá* or god rules over a large number of spirits, and the medium – as in Spiritualism – becomes the carrier of the special capabilities of the spirit possessing his (the medium's) body. As in the *macumba*, many *Orixās* are identified with Catholic saints, which, of course, is in contrast to the teachings of Spiritualism. The main function of the media representing the spirits is – as in Spiritualism and Pentecostalism – of a therapeutic nature. But the social meaning of these creeds as well as of the social structure of the three sects exceeds, by far, their immediate purpose: all of them seem to embody the social and cultural characteristics which were refused to the lower classes.

Social Structure of the Sects

In strongest contrast to the Catholic church and to the rigid class structure of the two countries, the sects are organized in such a way that social distances are reduced to a minimum. If (at all) a ministry exists within the Pentecostal sects, it is neither organized in a hierarchy nor is it separated from the believers by a specific authority, by God's grace or by professional expertise. According to a literal interpretation of the principle of the 'ministry of all believers', religious office is open to all those who can look back to successful missionary activities. No importance is attached to theological education. In many a sect, especially in Chile, theological training is considered to be expressly pernicious; and one of the two main Pentecostal congregations, the Christian Congregation of Brazil, does not have any ministers. The elders in office are not remunerated and receive their authority directly from the Holy Ghost whose agreement is asked for every decision. The internal equality of the members corresponds to the autonomy and equality of the congregations themselves, which are not subordinated to a supreme church authority. Of course, sometimes the principle of equality is violated by ambitious leaders. In these attempts to rule over a sect authoritatively one may see the traditional Latin American behaviour pattern of the *caudillismo* or *caciquismo*. As a matter of fact, this behaviour is interpreted as *caciquismo* by the opposing members, and this tendency leads – also in accordance with the traditional pattern of revolt against established authority – to inner conflicts and schisms. The splitting and formation of new sects is always interpreted as liberation from an authoritarian and oppressive leadership and as a return to equality and unhampered spontaneity of their religious experience. The *Iglesia Pentecostal of Chile* and some other sects institutionalized the so-called propheticism in a way which complicated the stabilization of authority within the parishes and neutralized tendencies for undesired concentration of power in the person of the minister. Accordingly, any member is allowed to announce in front of the assembled parish a message inspired by the Holy Ghost. Such messages are often of a critical nature and may refer to the spiritual leadership of the parish. Since it is the Holy Ghost who speaks, nobody must escape from, or even forbid, the critical announcement.

While Pentecostalism could lean, without any hesitation, on the structural principle of Protestant congregationalism, Spiritualism and Umbanda were hardly in a position, organizationally, to face the sudden influx of thousands of new followers. The first trend was endlessly to multiply local cult centres, without an inner connexion. The Spiritualist movement was in a better position in so far as it had, in Allan Kardec's interpretation of the gospels and other writings, a normative basis, the validity of which was generally acknowledged. In addition, the 'father' of Brazilian Spiritualism, Francisco Candido Xavier, by means of authoritative messages, interpreted Kardec's teaching in such a way as to attract the Brazilian congregations. Xavier's writings reflect the nationalistic pride of their author who made a religion out of that which in Europe started as an intellectual hobby.

Efforts within Spiritualism resulted in the uniting of thousands of local cult centres into federations, of which in 1951 already twenty-one had been formed. Most of these organizations joined the Spiritual Federation of Brazil, but many rejected even this loose form of adaptation. The desire for local autonomy is stronger than unification efforts. After 1932 spiritualistic youth organizations also came into existence, and in 1949 the Youth Welfare Office of Brazil's Spiritualistic Federation was established, which is dedicated mainly to religious instruction. In São Paulo the two main federations have a centre for religious propaganda and social aid, which is frequented by about 10,000 persons per week. As far as the ability of Spiritualists for establishing and maintaining charitable educational and medical institutions is concerned, the following figures show that in this respect they compete successfully with other religious congregations.

Table 3

Institutions of Three Religious Federations in Brazil, 1958

Religion	Total number	Hospitals	Clinics	Asylums	Casualty wards	Schools	Others
Catholicism	1995	45	178	56	50	1008	658
Protestantism	1034	3	56	24	15	618	318
Spiritualism	1715	25	168	64	104	435	919

See de Camargo (1961), p. 137.

Contrary to Spiritualism, the doctrinaire basis of the Umbanda is so unstable and loose that the uniting of numerous local centres has proven extremely difficult. Neither the rituals nor the religious doctrine have unity, each *terreiro* (cult centre) has a system of its own, and each leader believes that he possesses the monopoly of absolute truth. Obviously the Umbanda represents local autonomy to an extent which surpasses that of Pentecostalism and Spiritualism by far. This tendency gains even more importance when the great number of *terreiros* is considered. According to Bastide (1960, p. 443), in the state of Guanabara alone (the former federal district) there were 30,000 of such centres several years ago.

The type of leadership, which developed within the Umbanda, in principle seems to be incompatible with the existence of superordinate organizations. The session leader, who speaks with the media, consults the spirits, expels them or gives them orders and assumes the role of a thaumaturgist; in the new sect (Umbanda) he takes the place that, in American Indian societies or in Africa, was held by the *pagē* (shaman). The disembodied ghosts have lost their position of supremacy; here it is the sorcerer who rules over the spirits (Bastide, 1960, p. 438).

In many respects the Umbanda leader resembles the American Indian shaman who competes with other shamans concerning the worldly presence of ghosts and those who believe in his position of power. He is not inclined to give even a fraction of his power to a federation, and if he does so, this happens only under the pressure of exterior conditions or in view of the impossibility of his rendering the social welfare services expected from him by his believers. As a matter of experience, there are local police commanders who wait for an opportunity to sue the less influential Umbanda leaders on the grounds of 'unlawful practice of medicine' or 'disturbing of the public order'. In such cases it is important, of course, to be able to claim legal protection, which only a federation can grant. Also, scarcely any of the many smaller Umbanda centres would be in a position to institutionalize the social welfare services which more extensive organizations can offer to their members. The largest and most productive organization is probably the Spiritualistic Federation of the Umbanda which, in São Paulo alone, has been joined by 260 *terreiros* (de Camargo, 1961, p. 53).

The Symbolic Subversion of the Traditional Social Order

From this sketchy description of the three religious movements it emerges clearly that they try to liberate themselves from the structural elements of the traditional social order, which are interpreted as sources of oppression and exploitation. By stressing organizational spontaneity and social self-help the paternalistic tutelage of the upper classes is rejected. The emphasized social equality within the sects negates the traditional class system.[2]

Attempts to assume power authoritatively are responded to with schisms which restore and, typically, overemphasize equality. The tendency to power centralization of the Brazilian and Chilean societies corresponds to the trend of unrestricted decentralization and local autonomy of the congregations. In other words, in a sovereignty-oriented society the sects stress their co-operative structure.

The theology of the three sects rejects the monopoly of the Roman Catholic church and its priestly hierarchy which is looked on as the bulwark of the traditional social order. The supernatural powers are directly accessible to every believer.

The possibility of direct and personal contacts with the supernatural world distinguishes the sects. The followers of Pentecostalism, particularly, hug themselves in self-descriptions, frequently including the words 'chosen people' or 'people of God'. The 'gifts of the Holy Ghost' – enlightenment, the gift of prophecy, glossolalia and visions, in which the contemplation of God plays an important part – separate the believer from others and give him a feeling of power which is in strict contrast to his social powerlessness. It is hardly surprising that the Pentecostal sects ignore, and often denounce as concomitants of a sinful worldliness, the conventional criteria of social differentiation, like wealth, family belonging, education and profession. As Walter Goldschmidt referring to similar sects in California, stated, the social reality is replaced by a putative social order in which the sect represents an élite called by God and confirmed by the 'gifts of the Holy Ghost'. In other words, the structure

2. 'The festive character of the Umbanda means fraternization. Among them are neither classes nor castes' (Zespo, 1960, p. 147).

and creed of the Pentecostal sects may be interpreted as a symbolic inversion of the conventional social order.

In a similar way the Spiritualists and Umbanda grant a feeling of power involving all those who get in direct or indirect touch with the world of ghosts. It is a compensatory mechanism that 'all of a sudden turns humble, small officials and maids into containers of enlightened spirits and carriers of sublime messages' (de Camargo, 1961, p. 125). Since every follower of Spiritualism has a moral duty to develop latent mediumistic capabilities, and since people who do not observe this commandment expose themselves to supernatural sanctions, this obviously means that the personal contact with the world of spirits is not considered a privilege of only a few persons but, on the contrary, is supposed to be accessible to the largest possible number of believers.

Also meaningful is the social rank of the spirits which are conjured up by the spiritualistic cult leaders. Usually they are individuals who had gained great success and social acknowledgement during their lifetime, thus belonging to a class which is not accessible to the majority of Spiritualists. This predilection for the socially prominent deceased is explained by the fact that these ghosts in their past incarnations had reached a great extent of perfection. The association of socially low-born believers with the spirits of famous dead who once belonged to the upper social classes may be interpreted as a reduction or negation of the class structure. In the comprehensive literature of Brazilian Spiritualism – there are publishing companies and book stores which specialize entirely in Spiritualistic literature – the argument of its spirits being superior appears again and again, especially when the Umbanda, whose association with 'inferior' ghosts is despised and exposed, are criticized.

As a matter of fact the position of the Umbanda is very difficult, and this difficulty includes contradictions which seem to be understandable only within the complex, ethnically differentiated, cultural context of Brazilian society. The transition from Macumba to Umbanda was characterized mainly by giving up African cult elements which were denounced by public opinion as signs of ignorance and backwardness of the largely coloured lower classes. Such cult elements were replaced by certain Spiritualistic principles granting the Umbanda an intellectual respectability and attraction which the Macumba lacked (Bastide, 1960, p. 432). Thus, one can speak of a social rise of the Umbanda, expressing itself not only by an avalanche-like increase in the number of its followers but, above all, by the growing self-respect of its coloured members as well as by an active participation of many persons belonging to the upper classes.

On the other hand, the Umbanda looks for association with quite another kind of ghost. Characteristic is the fact, for example, that during many sessions attended by predominantly coloured followers, it is the spirits of former slaves and their holders who descend to the media. Unhesitatingly the audience learns at these occasions that the spirits of the slaves have already reached the higher stages of perfection, whereas their masters are still tortured by the illusion of being incarnated. They carry heavy chains and in their attempts towards the first steps on the narrow path of spiritual elevation, need the greatest possible love and patience of the media and cult leaders (de Camargo, 1961, p. 125).

With great regularity the ghosts of *caboclos* (American Indians) and *Negros velhos* (old Negroes) appear, whom the Spiritualists reject as being 'low' or 'inferior'. The systematic revitalization of such ghosts within a movement worrying about its social status seems to make sense if one takes into consideration that the *caboclos* and *Negros velhos* take the place of the ancestors, so to speak, of the Umbandists, the majority of whom actually have American Indian and African forefathers. In giving these spirits a superposition in the religious symbolism, the Umbanda obviously express the desire to reverse the traditional social order and its conceptions of value. As this inversion appears to be impossible in reality, one places it in the world of ghosts, where the American Indians and Negroes hold the higher ranks of perfection and their masters – the traditional upper class – have to be satisfied with the lowest ranks.

At the same time this symbolic inversion is to be understood as an expression of Brazilian nationalism. The surprising success of the Umbanda is mainly due to the spontaneous efforts of the lower classes to revitalize the American Indian and African

211

cultural heritage of the Brazilian people and to liberate it from the historic ambivalence of the upper classes.

One must consider, however, that the spread of the three sects is only understandable if the very mystic atmosphere of religious traditions within the lower classes of Chile and Brazil is taken into consideration. The considerable internal migration continuously imports religious traditions into the cities. The popular mysticism that lives on there, in a way, forms the general atmosphere in which the alliance of men and spirits appears to be credible, thus colouring their efforts to build a 'better' society with strongly religious motives.

The social rise of the sect movements was preceded by that of historical Protestantism. Since most non-Protestants hardly distinguish between Pentecostal sects and other Protestant congregations, it can be rightfully claimed that Presbyterians, Methodists, Baptists and several smaller congregations had prepared, so to speak, the way for the social mobility of the sects. Social mobility is, of course, equal to a change in the relations connecting the persons or groups in this process with the surrounding society. It appears to be extremely difficult to make valid generalizations about the significance of these changes. The statements made by D. P. Kidder in 1845 on his experiences in Brazil are in sharp contrast to the reports of Brazilian Protestant historians. Kidder claimed that there was no Roman Catholic country in the world, 'where there was more tolerance of the Protestants' (Kidder and Fletcher, 1857, p. 143). On the other hand numerous cases of fanatic intolerance are reported, which often were accompanied by situations dangerous to the lives of the missionaries and their helpers (see Mesguita, 1940, pp. 56, 100, 133, 137, 217, 270, 287; Ferreira, 1959, p. 157; Buyers, 1945, p. 416). These contradictions can be explained in so far as the tolerance or intolerance of the population are a function of local or regional factors which in some districts still exist in a mitigated version.[3]

3. Similar regional and local differences are to be found in Colombia, which (of all Latin American countries) offers the strongest resistance to the missionary efforts of the Protestants. One of the leading Presbyterians, an American missionary, who is stationed as minister and schoolteacher in a medium-sized town of the Magdelena Valley, has informed us that in

The change – the strictest forms of which start from conflict, antagonism, discrimination, boycott, etc., and move, via the phases of mockery and indifference, in the direction of forms of co-operation and even selective preference – is due to the interaction of different factors.

1. In those parishes where the Protestants succeeded in gaining a footing, they formed at first small minorities which, like all minorities, were exposed to the vigilant criticism of a doubtful majority, only too willing to attribute weaknesses and mistakes of single Protestants to the total group. In this situation the Protestant parishes developed forms of social control which brought the behaviour of the individual believer – as a family member, employer, employee, client, business associate, etc. – under the effective and direct influence of Puritan morals. Gradually, the members of the Protestant parishes were considered conscientious businessmen, sober and industrious labourers, punctually paying debtors, and one started estimating highly the advantages of economic and professional relations with them.

2. In many parishes, mainly in Brazil, the constant proselytism of historic Protestantism scored great successes within the middle and upper classes of the population (Willems, 1963, pp. 330 ff.). These successes consolidated the social position of the Protestant groups and protected them against discriminating behaviour of hostile population circles. The two Presbyterian churches of Brazil were most successful in this respect.

3. Because of their educational efforts the Protestant churches slowly won the respect and acknowledgement of the non-Protestants. Originally the Protestant schools, especially the 'Gymnasien' (secondary schools), were meant to be instruments of religious proselytism. But soon it turned out that they were superior to the antiquated curricula and teaching methods of the Chilean and Brazilian schools, and non-Protestant families of the

the immediate vicinity visited by him and his helpers there are many parishes where they do not experience any resistance, whereas the intolerance in many neighbouring villages makes any mission activity impossible. It is also known that the highland districts within the wider boundary of Bogota feel very close to the Catholic church, while in the coastal districts a clear religious indifference predominates.

middle and upper classes started to send their children to the Presbyterian, Baptist and Methodist schools. The main concern of parents and students was by no means religious conversion but simply a 'modern' education. This influx of non-Protestants, who in most schools soon became the majority, was followed by an increasing secularization of the curricula. The proselytic tendencies slipped more and more into the background, but concurrently the Protestant schools gained numerous influential friends and defenders among the thousands of their previous pupils, who, without being Protestants, acknowledged the merits of the Protestant congregations and took up sides for their rights.

This rise in prestige of the Protestant churches had already reached the point of general tolerance and practical co-operation with non-Protestants, when the Pentecostal sects started to develop into a mass movement. As latecomers of Protestantism, they naturally did not have to fight the difficulties and obstacles characterizing the development of the historic churches. The missionary field was now wide open, and the sects invaded this field, which also comprised the historic churches, with unprecedented proselytic zeal. According to their teaching all the religions not aiming at an immediate mystic-emotional union with the 'spirit' are 'dead' or 'cold' religions which fell victim to the secularization and corruption of materialistic interests. The purity of their own doctrines requires a strict separation from the 'world' and its more or less 'corrupt' churches. In general, one can say that the relationships of the main Pentecostal sects with all the other churches and sects are dominated by this opinion. The ecumenical tendencies which led to understanding, partly even to co-operation and federations – in Chile as well as in Brazil – among the historic churches of Protestantism, are rejected by the Pentecostal congregations. In Chile this negative attitude is much stricter than in Brazil. The Chilean sects do not only fear the *mundanismo* of the historic churches; their conscious class character requires a rejection of intellectualizing influences, in which they apparently see a menace from the side of the better educated middle classes, to whom the Pentecostal supernaturalism is too 'naïve'. Aside from simply designed tracts and collections of hymns, Chilean Pentecostalism did not bring forth any religious literature, whereas the Brazilian sects – with the exception of the Christian Congregation – can praise themselves for having a relatively rich and specialized literature.

In Brazil the Pentecostal sects, the Spiritualists and the Umbanda are in proselytic competition with each other concerning potential followers from the same social classes. This rivalry and the unmistakable similarity of their supernaturalism resulted, as was to be expected, in tensions and mutual dissociation. While the Pentecostalists in Chile interpret the state of possession as a trance during which the person involved is not conscious of his deeds, the Brazilian sects refuse this concept. On the contrary, the Spiritualists are the ones – so they claim – who become irresolute tools of ghosts who, by their conviction, can only be of a devilish nature. They also believe that their own 'prophecies' are entirely different from the 'fortune-telling' of the Spiritualists. In particular, they do not share the assumption that the spirits obey human calls or order. The Spiritualists for their part despise the Umbanda in whom they do not see anything more than superstition and barbarian distortions of their own teaching. The Catholic church, of course, condemns the three movements sharply, but because of an enormous lack of priests, she is not in a position effectively to counteract them. In contrast to the Pentecostal sects being in open opposition to Catholicism, the members of Spiritualism and the Umbanda are composed of elements many of whom consider themselves Catholics. This continuity of religious belonging and participation is naturally not explicable on the level of official dogmatics. It does not even exist on this level, but in its substratum where – according to popular tradition – the contrasts lessen, where every supernaturalism is syncretistic and susceptible to additions and changes in interpretation.

One of the most important results of religious pluralism is the decomposition of the conventional vicarage system which in the past comprised the total parish. With the appearance of the Protestant churches and sects this unity dissolved into a multitude of religious corporations each of which, so to speak, forms a parish of its own. In many places in Brazil and Chile there is a Presbyterian, Methodist and Baptist parish beside the Catholic one.

The sects are usually represented in the form of the *Assembleia de Deus*, *Congregação Cristã* or in both of these forms. Besides, there may still be other congregations, like the Adventists, Jehovah's Witnesses and the Mormons. The spreading of the federation – organized Spiritualism and Umbanda – has been limited mainly to the larger city districts and their immediate surrounding. This confessional split does, of course, affect the public life of the parishes. The participation or non-participation in public affairs of many parish members is determined, to a considerable extent, by the ethics and norms of their faith. Most Protestants avoid national festivals which include drinking, dancing and chance (tombolas). As most churches and sects nowadays invite their members to take part in political elections and often even put up candidates of their own, the political parties frequently see themselves forced to take the criteria of this body of electors into consideration. It must be added, however, that the political participation of the non-Catholic churches, particularly the sects, is only just beginning. The distinct class character of the Pentecostal congregations is certainly likely to change the political structure of the parishes as their participation in elections increases. In Chile, we were able to find an obvious connexion between the *Iglesia Metodista Pentecostal* and the Radical Party. This alliance had meaningless practical consequences, as the overwhelming majority of the sect members were not even registered electors. These conditions are, however, in the process of changing fast, and it can be predicted with relative certainty that the religious pluralism in both countries will be felt as a political factor, probably in favour of parties which, without showing Communistic tendencies, will represent the interests of the lower social classes.

References
ANON (1959), *Brasil Evangélico*, Orgão Informativo do Confederação do Brasil.
BASTIDE, R. (1960), *Les Religions Africaines au Brésil*, Paris.
BRAGA, E., and GRUBB, K. G. (1932), *The Republic of Brazil: A Survey of the Religious Situation*, London, New York, Toronto.
BUYERS, P. E. (1945), *História do Metodismo*, São Paulo.
DE CAMARGO, C. P. F. (1961), *Kardecismo e Umbanda*, São Paulo.
DE CARVALHO, A. (1875), *O Brasil*, Porto.

DAMBORIENA, P. (1963), *El Protestantismo en América Latina*, vol. 2, Oficina Internacional de Investigaciones Sociales de FERES.

DA CUNHA, E. (1944), *Rebellion in the Backlands*, Chicago.

DE QUEIRÓZ, M. I. P. (1957), 'La guerre sainte au Brésil: le mouvement messianique au Contestado', *University of São Paulo, Faculty of Philosophy, Sciences and Literature Bulletin*, no. 187.

DE QUEIRÓZ, M. I. P. (1960), 'Aspectos Gerais do Messianismo', *Revista de Antropología*, vol. 3.

FERREIRA, J. A. (1959), *História da Igreja Presbiteriana do Brasil*, vol. 1, São Paulo.

KAHL, J. A. (1962), 'Soziale Begleite rscheinungen der Industrialisierung und Urbanisierung', in P. Heintz, ed., *Soziologie der Entrucklungslander*, Berlin and Cologne.

KIDDER, D. P., and FLETCHER, J. C. (1857), *Brazil and the Brazilians*, Philadelphia.

LIENHARDT, G. (1961), *Divinity and Experience*, Clarendon, Press,

MESGUITA, A. N. (1940), *História des Batistas do Brasil*, Rio de Janeiro.

ROSALES, V. P. (1864), *Recuerdos del Pasado*, Santiago.

TUCKER, H. C. (1902), *The Bible in Brazil*.

WILLEMS, E. (1963), Protestantismus und Kulturwandel in Brasilien und Chile, *Kölner Zeitschrift für Soziologie and Sozialpsychologie*, special edition.

ZESPO, E. (1960), *Codificação de Lei de Umbanda*, Rio de Janeiro.

Part Three Problems of Analysis and Interpretation

The four contributions to this part are all recent attempts to grapple with difficult analytic problems in the sociology of religion. Worsley (Reading 13) deals with the perennial problem of how the sociologist and anthropologist may most usefully define and delineate religious phenomena. Swanson (Reading 14) considers how we might best approach the sociological explanation of the subscription to beliefs in supernatural forces and entities. Stark and Glock (Reading 15) explore the issue of describing and measuring the religious commitment of individuals in modern societies. And Bellah (Reading 16) employs an ambitious analytic scheme to discuss the long-term evolution of religion from primitive to modern conditions. What these discussions have in common is a sensitivity to theoretical interpretation, explanation and methodological procedure. They may be seen in large part as a response to some of the general intellectual preoccupations of our time: what religion 'really is'; how we should recognize its rise and decline; and just what significance we should attribute to it. In some essays we see a continuation of the concerns exhibited by the classical sociologists: Bellah is influenced by Weberian perspectives; while Swanson's contribution is clearly in the Durkheimian tradition. Worsley, Stark and Glock are attempting to clear-up conceptual confusions. Worsley's concern is with the more general and fundamental issue of defining religion in such a way as to permit productive sociological inquiry into all types of society; while Stark and Glock address themselves more specifically to aspects of religiousness in Christian societies.

13 P. Worsley

Religion as a Category

Excerpts from P. Worsley, *The Trumpet Shall Sound*, McGibbon and Kee, 1968, pp. 21–35.

Weber's 'other-worldly' and 'this-worldly' orientations remain useful analytical categories as long as we realize that they are constructed with reference to the mental orientation of an actor, who still has to establish some operational balance between, on the one hand, his physical and social existence in this world and, on the other, his primary subjective orientation to the other, or next, world or to a wider, more inclusive cosmic universe.

The relationship of this world to the other or next world may be variously conceived by the believer:

(a) *part-to-whole:* this life is a mere speck of dust in a cosmos which may be conceived of as more or less shapeless, timeless, and directionless, or highly structured;

(b) *reflectional:* this life is the counterpart of an other-worldly existence, as in those primitive heavens where life is the same as on earth, only 'spiritualized';

(c) *emanational:* this life is a dependent variable of the Idea, as in Hegel;

(d) *contingent:* this life is a forerunner of another, 'higher', existence, a sequentially necessary passage through the 'vale of tears', during which the soul undergoes tests of moral–spiritual virtue, is ultimately judged, punished or rewarded, either at one blow (e.g. the Day of Judgement) or phased intervals (e.g. successive reincarnations), with the successful examinee either reaching the highest hierarchical grades or losing his personality and humanity – i.e. sin, defects, fleshly commitments – and becoming absorbed into timeless eternity.

The moral–ethical component is commonly found, since even the most transcendental religions usually recognize the world to the extent of recommending some, even if minimal, ways of behaving in this world, and towards one's fellow men, and not just towards God or in terms of orientation to the ultimate life. Religions thus concern themselves, in varying mixes, with ethical, cosmological, and eschatological problems, but by no means in the same way or with the same weight or place of emphasis; indeed, any of these concerns may be virtually omitted. As Macbeath (1952) has clearly shown, there are, for example, religions which are profoundly cosmological – in that they are very much concerned with the relationship of this world to the rest of the cosmos – but which are not all eschatological. Indeed, the Christian notion of eschatology, as being concerned with 'last things', itself needs to be broken into its constituent elements. It is, in any case, only one particular cultural conception of what the 'last things' are, and therefore a particular and parochial 'historical individual', rather than an analytical category.

The Christian 'last things' conventionally include death, judgement, heaven and hell. But the notion of judgement at or after death is by no means universally linked to conceptions of an after-life; the belief in heaven and hell is even more parochial. Indeed, great world religions have been quite uneschatological and amoral, in so far as they have no place for such conceptions as that of judgement in the after-life, and/or in so far as they do not necessarily tie their cosmological conceptions to any system of ethical prescriptions and moral injunctions about behaviour on this earth *at all*. The extreme case is the antinomian 'heresy', where the believer holds that this world is *only* a low-order, precursory phase of existence. To him, the demands of Caesar or of one's fellow men are as nothing, mere conceits and distractions – if not intrinsically sinful – which the truly spiritual man pays no heed to in his incessant orientation towards the true path, which he can only follow by emancipating himself from the demands of this earth. These true believers, then, *cannot* sin as far as the earthly order is concerned, because the earth's definition of sin is an arbitrary or irrelevant thing of Caesar's, or at best an invalid definition. The true believer can only sin within the framework of his own *religious* value system and relational system. The source of morality and, therefore, its requirements of man are other-worldly. Man's primary relationship is to God, not to man; the latter relationship is quite irrelevant, or, at best, secondary and derivative. (There is, of course, an eternal, immanent tension as far as the 'practical' implications of religious belief for action in the world are concerned, since a prime orientation to the other world always invites the criticism that institutionalized religion is deaf to the claims of justice. Conversely, what one might call relational or 'moral' religions – which insist that one must act out the implications of belief in one's relations with one's fellow men – tend to become embroiled in the partisan conflicts of this earth, and cannot, like transcendental religions, appeal to all and rise above the secular political battle.) The dissociation between this world and the other one may take the form of inversion, whereby the price of sanctity is not simply the flouting or by-passing of earthly rules in a 'neutral' fashion, as being 'of no consequence', but a crusading, militant, deliberate and systematic, sometimes nihilist, destruction and defiance of them.

The assumption that ethical values and moral behaviour on earth are always interwoven with religion, or that cosmology and eschatology are both necessary and related parts of religious world systems, is erroneous. It is empirically falsifiable from our knowledge of those religions that do not postulate an other-worldly source of moral rules and do not, for example, endeavour to enforce conformity to those rules by applying 'mystical' sanctions (in the anthropologist's sense of 'mystical' as 'pertaining to sacred things', to use a Durkheimianism). To assume otherwise is merely to substitute religion for sociology, to universalize, more or less unwittingly or arrogantly, the parochial values of the Judaeo-Christian-Islamic and certain other religious systems, with their particular combination of moral eschatology; an anthropomorphized Deity; the moralization of earthly life and the connecting of this to the after-life; the conception of supernatural intervention or involvedness in human affairs; a judgemental model of the relationship of this world to the next; and a single lifetime, temporal framework – a 'one-shot' conception of judgement.

Nadel's (1954) description of the religious outlook and institutions of the Nupe, to take one outstandingly well-studied instance alone, shows us a religion in which the link between the extra-human realm and this earth is lightly emphasized, both in terms of mystical sanctions for this-worldly behaviour and in terms of

223

the relative unimportance of religion as an exhaustive, overarching cosmological system. The 'otiose' High Gods of Africa may provide an *ultimate* 'mythological charter' for the cosmos and for man-on-earth within the cosmos, but just as 'long runs never come', so 'ultimate explanations' are rarely required or resorted to in day-to-day human affairs. More proximate entities, such as earth- or ancestor-spirits, or agents of magic and witchcraft, positive and negative, are the common manifestations of the other world.

Writers on religion all too often fail to make such distinctions in their eagerness to demonstrate the interrelatedness of beliefs, and the closeness of fit of these belief systems to the 'structure' (i.e. usually the formal morphological units) of the society. Only in rare cases, like Evans-Pritchard's (1937) study of the Azande, are particular beliefs fully set in their particular situational context. Hence, all too often we find an exaggerated unity of belief systems, as well as the imputation of exaggerated importance to such systems, or parts of them, sometimes implicit in the very process of presenting them *in abstracto* as 'the religion' or 'the cosmology' of a given people. (I pass over, as a separate issue, the functionalist mode of analysis in which it is assumed that the 'fit' between belief system and social structure is virtually one-to-one – or, at least, that the degree of congruence is non-problematic.)

Sequential presentation alone often implies a logic of priority *in the thought of the people* that may be quite illegitimate, certainly as far as everyday 'operational' behaviour (as distinct from situations where people are consciously enunciating a 'philosophy') is concerned.

It is necessary always to distinguish who 'they' are, who says what in what situation, and what the 'task orientation' of the various actors in the situation is, for 'religion' – in the form of esoteric ritual lore and theology – is differentially distributed throughout a society, or elements of it will be differentially distributed, or occur only in specific situations, contexts and 'niches', or be available differentially to different actors. I studied an Australian aboriginal tribe where the knowledge of the beliefs and rituals of 'their' culture on the part of most members was abysmal: as elementary and confused as that of the average

Church of England congregation member. Only the ritual specialists and leaders (and a few sceptics) possessed esoteric lore or thought about its meaning. V. W. Turner (1960) has shown how the key informant is often a man who, in our society, would be a professor of theology. Yet we would not, as sociologists, regard the verbalizations of a professor of theology as an adequate representation of even the 'religious' in our societies. A spurious unity is projected onto other people's belief systems by outside observers – sociologists and anthropologists – even though they are often familiar with that kind of sociological theory which relates exaggerated awareness of the compulsions of social norms to the observer's 'external' position.[1] They do not, however, always apply these insights to themselves as research workers observing other people's behaviour from outside. This over-systematization of belief is commonly accompanied by a spurious ontological 'priority' or hierarchy: the assumption that general cosmological, philosophical, etc., beliefs are somehow 'primary' or 'higher' (and must therefore be discussed first in any academic analysis). This is a natural disease of academics, a consequence, again, of their specialized role in the social division of labour as dealers in ideas. This proclivity is evident even in such an excellent set of studies as *African Worlds* (Forde, 1954). Douglas, for example begins (p. 9) by discussing 'Spiritual Beings: God', yet has virtually nothing to say of Him, but talks rather about humans, animals and spirits. Wagner opens (p. 28) with Cosmogonic and Cosmological Ideas: the idea of God, he says, is a 'very firmly established belief and of basic significance for the whole world view of the Abaluyia', though they were rather vague about the Creation process. The Kriges specifically emphasize the disinterest of the Lovedu: 'speculation about first beginnings of final causes . . . origins of the cosmic order and wonders of celestial phenomena do not exercise the Lovedu mind' (p. 59). Little remarks that 'the Mende have an essentially "practical" attitude to life', are

1. Cf. Merton's point that norms and values of non-membership groups are more visible than the actual behaviour within these groups, so that the non-member sees the official norms as more effectively binding than they are, and idealizes those who conform as 'the norm', etc. Hence the familiar phenomenon of the rigidity and zealousness of the recent convert. See Merton (1963), pp. 341–53.

uninterested in metaphysics, and are equally 'practical' *vis-à-vis* 'what we should term the supernatural world'. Yet he *begins* his analysis with a discussion of 'Beliefs in a Supreme Being and in Spirits' (pp. 112, 113). One could go on. True, there are indeed cultures, like that of the Dogon (pp. 83–110), that not only display elaborate riots of imagery and imagination in their religious beliefs (to which religion lends itself, potentially, since it is least controlled by mundane structural and cultural constraints), but the relationship of these complex elaborations of belief – usually recorded on collective ritual occasions from specialists – to the general stream of everyday life, and especially the life of those who are not ritual specialists, is not apparent from the literature (Berndt, 1951, 1952).

The most common distinction made by social anthropologists in their discussions of primitive thought is, firstly, that of 'primitive thought' itself as a separate kind of thought, a distinction attacked by Evans-Pritchard (1965, esp. ch. 4). The second major distinction is that between 'mystical' and 'empirical' action. 'Mystical' is a particularly unfortunate term, because of the special connotations, which it carries over from European and Asian religions, of individual, gnostic or ecstatic experience. But the distinction itself is even more unfortunate if it implies that there is a discrete type of actions that are distinguishable from 'mundane' action by the actors themselves. Primitive people accept that the world around them exists, and that it has its regularities, its appropriate rules and operations. But these norms are not solely technical ones, any more than we operate in a totally technical manner. We, too, are influenced by jealousy, lust, magical notions, status seeking, generosity, etc., even in our most scientific moments. For primitive cultures, the area of the extratechnical is wider and often more supernatural simply because the volume of scientific knowledge is smaller. But there is no basic difference in principle between the intrusion of quite non-technical considerations into technical situations demanding primarily technical responses in our lives, and the presence of magic in the activities of the primitive. Moreover, there are no non-social acts that are 'purely' technical: one cannot conceive of them. Drilling a hole in a piece of metal is done for some purpose, under someone's direction; to the worker, it means far more than the act of drilling alone: it may mean money, security, resentment of authority, pride in dexterity, etc., etc. Similarly, the world, for the primitive, is not a special, sealed-off, technical world, in which purely technical norms obtain. Nor does he even conceive of two distinct worlds at all: this world is not a separate realm, insulated from the other world in which 'mystical' actions are appropriate. (Indeed, in primitive heavens, people carry on doing quite mundane things: hunting, fighting, etc.) This earth, in fact, is not the same demysticized world that White men think of it as being – when they think about it 'scientifically', that is, for most of the time we also explain events by reference to 'luck', 'accident', etc., and even when we behave technically there are non-technical implications to, and dimensions of, our behaviour.

Similarly, to the man in a primitive culture, goals that we (in our 'scientific' capacities) label 'empirical' – planting potatoes, defecating or drinking beer – have to be achieved by performing both what we call 'ritual' actions as well as 'empirical' ones. But it is common for the same word – often, in Melanesian tongues, the term for 'work' – to be used to describe both kinds of action. In other words, the distinctions we draw, they do not.

Of course, though we may not necessarily invest quotidian actions with *supernatural* connotations as often, we, like 'primitive' peoples, never perform technical acts 'in themselves'. We do invest them with all sorts of other social meanings, which are not extraneous to the technical act but are always to be found and integral to it. The concept of pure technical action, therefore, can only be an ideal type, a dimension of concrete behaviour which includes many other dimensions. Even the scientist in his laboratory conducts his experiments in a social context: the laboratory itself is a complex social subsystem with its norms of behaviour, both those directly intrinsic to the performance of the work-task and other social norms. Thus, the scientist's white coat may have far more to do with status than hygiene. To this degree, our 'technical' acts are thoroughly invested with other complex, non-technical, social meanings.

The two kinds of activity – which we analyse out into two separate compartments – are thus abstractions from the social behaviour of men, which is of a piece until analytically broken down by the observer (or by the actor, who is then an observer of his own behaviour, a Me to his I). What we call 'ritual' action is therefore quite as 'empirical' as sleeping with one's wife, an act laden with social, including, in some cultures, ritual meanings.[2] There is no impermeable membrane between the 'mundane' and the 'magical', for the primitive is not a dualist, operating with a model of 'two worlds', nor a schizophrenic operating with different principles – empirical and mystical – in different situations.

Instead, he conceives of a single order of reality, in which man has only restricted powers, and access only to limited areas, but, through ritual, has some contact with and influence (often via mediating agents: the ancestors, etc.) over powers of a more far-reaching and compulsive kind. The activities of the ancestors are therefore quite 'empirical'. Indeed, by canons of evidence available to people with limited technical knowledge – and one must insist that they do seriously examine experience (and dreams, for instance, are real experiences) – there is ample confirmation of the existence of the ancestors and of their interest and intervention in human affairs. The spirits are at work in our real world, and, equally incontrovertibly, men go to the spirit world and return.

Therefore, although empirical acts are performed, what we call ritual acts are also integral, necessary and effective dimensions of social action. The actions we classify as 'ritual' may be more or less elaborated in certain situations, e.g. danger, uncertainty, unpredictability, etc., as Malinowski and others have shown. But this does not mean that the actors see these situations as calling for a special *type* of activity; they are simply situations calling for a *lot* of activity, and since one soon exhausts the limits of what technical means are available, further activity must inevitably be primarily non-technical, i.e. our 'ritual'. But, to them, they are all appropriate behaviours geared and oriented to achieving given ends, *tout court*, not empirical or ritual respectively as quite distinct types of action.

Thus, though the magic and ritual may connect with a 'background' theology, cosmology or philosophy, these remain very much unexamined and usually quite latent. What is uppermost,

2. For a similar analysis of the apparently purely physical act of (literal) sleep, see Aubert (1965).

most dominant and prominent in everyday interaction, is magico-religious practice.[3]

There is thus some truth in Marett's statement that religion in primitive society is as much 'danced out as thought out', even though the saying does undervalue the cognitive content of these religions.

Magic and ritual thus depend upon some wider theory of the world, of agency, of man, etc., but ethical, cosmological and eschatological beliefs are normally embedded in behaviour, not abstractly formulated. But if religion is not simply a set of beliefs,[4] neither is it simply a mode of group coherence, a system of ordering one's relations with groups and categories of one's fellow men and with 'Nature', as both the older structuralism-functionalism of, e.g. Radcliffe-Brown and the newer structuralism of Lévi-Strauss so often have it. It is, rather, a cluster of beliefs which are *used* in day-to-day social activities, with (variously) some of one's fellow men (not some abstract fellow man) in the contexts of changing situations focused on a diversity of social activities. Religion, then, is a stream of processes, not just an ideal operation in the soul, heart or intellect, or the ritual dance of puppets determined by the morphology of their social structure.

Because religion is intrinsically unbounded in its field of operation, because it is *ideal* as well as social, it is always potentially innovatory, and like all innovation, potentially hurtful to established interests. But religion, it ought to be said, is neither intrinsically conservative nor revolutionary. It can be infused with any kind of social content, notably political; there are both the religions of the oppressed discussed in this book, and the kinds

3. Anthropologists are quite right to reject the old-fashioned distinction between 'magic' and 'religion', where the former was conceived of as control via the supernatural, and the latter as the domain of extrahuman powers beyond human reach. These distinctions can easily be dismissed: magical actions necessarily imply some theory of the gods, spirits, 'life-force', etc. And religion is not just abstract theology; it is something acted out, i.e. it is usually most manifest as 'magic'! Even less is religion necessarily concerned with remote and inaccessible gods or spirits – the latter, indeed, are usually anthropomorphic: the living in another guise or phase of existence. See Firth (1945), ch. 6.

4. See Evans-Pritchard's (1934) classic castigation of the nineteenth-century 'Intellectualists'.

of religion that have been summed up in the label given to the Church of England as 'the Conservative Party at prayer'. The relationship of religious beliefs, let alone movements and organizations, to the established power system thus varies, and is not a matter for metaphysical pronouncement disguised as sociological generalization. It requires empirical investigation to see what the case is. We cannot know *a priori* (except to the extent that one can predict, e.g. that such-and-such a type of religion is appropriate to this or that social group).

Where religious movements are dissident or revolutionary, their innovatory potential can be held in check by the use of countervailing powers. Heretics can be burned at the stake. Powerful as this kind of deterrence can be, it is much more difficult, as has often been observed, to burn ideas, and burning people often only creates martyrs. Since men will continue to search for answers to eternal as well as novel problems, religion provides a channel of creative innovation. (I am not concerned here with the separate issue of whether such creativity and innovation is 'illusory' or otherwise, positive or negative, 'false' consciousness or 'real', etc.) Ultimately, too, the locus of religious experience is in the individual psyche, not in some Spencerian 'social sensorium', so that control over religious deviation from orthodoxy is singularly difficult to police, even with modern techniques of thought control and brainwashing.

Functionalist schemata cannot, naturally, find a meaningful place for these dynamic and subjective aspects of religion. Not even Nadel, in his brilliant and rather ignored *Nupe Religion*, has entirely escaped the determinism of functionalist analyses of religion. He does, on the other hand, clearly specify (a) the major 'competences' of religion; (b) the distinctiveness of the *religious* experience and of religious relationships within the context of all the other dimensions of religion as an *institution*; (c) the location of religious experience in the psyche of the actor; (d) the link, and distinction, between the meaning of the action to the individual actor and the consequences of this action for society, as well as the 'conditioning' of the religious experience and practice by society.

Nadel thus avoids many familiar and quite deadly traps. He speaks of four major 'competences' of religion:

(i) the capacity of religion to furnish certain supplements to [the] view of the world of experience which intelligence is driven to demand;

(ii) its capacity to announce and maintain moral values, or, more generally, an 'economic ethic', that is, its competence to guide 'the practical impulses for action';

(iii) its competence to hold together societies and sustain their structure; and

(iv) its competence to furnish individuals with specific experiences and stimulations (Nadel, 1954, pp. 259–60).

The use of the word 'competence', rather than 'function', appears to be deliberate, so as to avoid any implication that religion is some kind of inherent 'functional requisite', fulfilling specifiable 'functions'. Instead, it can (or commonly does, or potentially may – i.e. is 'competent' to) do various things which may, however, be done by other 'competential alternatives', to paraphrase Merton. By using the term 'competences', Nadel avoids the assumption too often hidden in the word 'function' that religion is somehow *peculiarly* or *necessarily* fitted to fulfil these 'requirements' of sociation. Furthermore, Nadel distinguishes between the first three competences, which 'refer to the nexus between religion and other, autonomous spheres of interest – the understanding of the universe; morality; maintenance of the given society.' (Analytically autonomous, presumably, not empirically. But, even so, a mistaken emphasis, since religion is not a separate 'province', separate from other provinces, as we have seen.) 'Maintenance of the given society' is a rather unfortunate functionalist backsliding, too, in so far as it clearly cannot embrace the radical and revolutionary religions of the disinherited (Lanternari, 1965). The label could perhaps be rephrased more adequately to refer to 'maintenance (and expansion) of the *collectivity of believers*'. A 'collectivity of believers' could be, at different extremes, members of an established church (in which case their solidarity *would* support, and be congruent with, the stability of the whole polity), or it could be a revolutionary micro-sect, in which case its 'subcultural' solidarity would be intrinsically dysfunctional for the wider polity, as Merton and most deviance theory have suggested.

But Nadel rightly observes that to analyse the links between religion and other autonomous spheres of interest – the understanding of the universe; morality; maintenance of the given society – does not help us distinguish just *what religion is*. Anthropologists and sociologists constantly show us its 'functions', 'competences', connexions, etc.; i.e. they concentrate, as they properly should as the central part of their task, on tracing out the effects of religion on the behaviour of collectivities (and vice versa) and the ways in which religious institutions condition the behaviour of individuals. They not only tend to eschew, notably, the philosophical problem of the meaning of religion, but even sometimes neglect the meaning of religion to the actor; the former problem they leave to the philosopher or the theologian, the latter to the psychologist. In the process, a serious overly sociological distortion emerges: by omitting to examine the meaning of religion to the actor, the group tends to be represented, in a reified way, as 'thinking', 'believing' or 'feeling'. A sociology that incorporates social action theory, however – as the older anthropological functionalism does not – cannot accept that the meaning of religious behaviour to the actor can be omitted, or taken as given, in any valid analysis of the cultural significance of religion. Collectivities do not think, or undergo religious experiences; men do. Even Durkheim's occasions of collective ritual are situations in which men respond to the situation. Their behaviour is, to be sure, profoundly and directly conditioned by the presence of many others, but not just by this: rather by the presence of many others who act and require one to act *in culturally prescribed ways*. Even so, the required or resultant religious behaviour is still mediated through and only meaningful within the individual psyche. There is no group psyche. Conversely, individual mystical experience is a highly social form of behaviour, conditioned usually by the internalization of sophisticated and culturally given theological notions embedded in a complex of values and beliefs about man, society, God, the cosmos, morality, etc.

Nadel, therefore, quite rightly points out that the first of three 'competences' are *not* somehow functionally necessarily and immanently tied to religion alone. Understanding of the universe, he points out, can be satisfactorily provided by science, for example; civic or political aims provide perfectly effective modes of handling the problem of social order; and 'ethical tenets would be just these and no more'. Empirically, and not *a priori*, man need not be religious to be moral, to order his thinking about the world, or to order his relations with his fellow men, Some metaphysicians and religious people, of course, hold otherwise, particularly with regard to the unanswerable, ultimate questions of creation, destiny and the significance of human life. The agnostic usually replies, in the face of these claims, that he does not know, but will not fill the gap by mythopoeic 'explanations', preferring instead the nobility – and agony – of permanently suspended judgement about such ultimacies,[5] much as Laplace, when asked by Napoleon what place there was for God in his intellectual map of the cosmos, replied 'Sire, I have no need of that hypothesis.'

The 'understanding of the universe' that is supplied by religion, then, is often of a very different order from that supplied by vulgar 'materialist' empiricism or by science; something else is involved. Again, the kind of morality that is part of a theological system of belief is of a different order from that of the agnostic: it derives its 'logic', its legitimation, its charter, its validation, from quite different sources. The social order buttressed by a dominant or established religion displays an overlapping of institutional orders, an extra dimension of congruence, that the secular polity lacks. Religious *Weltbilden*, religious ethics, religiously validated polities differ in kind, quite simply, from those in which this dimension is lacking. (It is important to repeat that it may be lacking – religion has 'competences', not 'functions'.)

The meaning of the action to the actor necessarily involves, then, some ideal-type specification of what religious, as distinct from non-religious, behaviour is. This is very simple and well known, though rarely stated in the sociological literature, which always tells us what religion does, or analyses its structural 'elements' (those which Nadel, following Durkheim, adequately identifies as 'doctrine', 'congregation' and 'observances'). Such writers may be correct, as sociologists, to avoid the metaphysical, philosophical questions of what religion is, in the sense of the truthfulness, or 'requiredness' or immanence of religion. What

5. Cf. Max Weber: 'it seems to me dubious whether the dignity of purely human and communal relations is enhanced by . . . religious interpretations'.

they cannot avoid as a fundamental sociological issue is giving consideration not only to the effects of religious commitment – the way in which religious commitment has consequences for one's relations to one's fellow men – but also to the way in which (a) the process of internalization in the psyche of the individual, (b) conceptions of what we call the supernatural and man's relationship to it, and (c) the content of belief are all culturally derived and socially prescribed.

Spiro (1964, p. 94) has recently defined religion as 'beliefs in superhuman beings and in their power to assist or harm man . . . . This belief . . . is the core variable which ought to be included in any definition of religion . . . [and] approaches universal distribution.'

It would be better to speak, however, of a superhuman 'realm' or of 'powers'. (Superhuman, that is, from our analytical point of view; not necessarily in the believers' own conceptual schema, for they may not distinguish their 'religious' beliefs from their other beliefs in the way that we do *for* them. They may have no conception at all of a 'natural' order as distinct from something called the '*super*natural': *we* have, and in using the distinction are supplying categories that depend upon our scientific distinctions, not necessarily the categories of the believers.) Moreover, Tylorian 'beings' may not be believed in, nor their intervention in human affairs. And in many religions 'power' of this kind can be mobilized: man is not confined, as far as his own action is concerned, to supplication. Otherwise, Spiro's emphasis upon the superhuman is useful, and forms a corrective to Nadel.

Nadel's fourth 'competence' – the *especially* religious – focuses upon the subjective emotional-psychic meaning of the religious experience to the actor, and is thus a quite different kind of analytical category from that we have used, which depends not on the actor's own categories, but on those of *our* scientific culture.

It is doubtful, however, that such experience is very common. The problem of eliciting the meaning of social action to the actor is a cardinal one in all sociology, of course, but it is particularly problematic where religious experience is concerned, since religious experiences may be held, both by the religious and the non-religious, to be 'inexpressible' (though even mystics seem to be able to communicate the substance, if not the 'reality', of their experiences, and, unless we believe that something mystical *is* involved, the psychic impact of the mystical experience does not seem so remote from other dimensions of experience as to suggest that it is any more impenetrable to imaginative empathy than someone else's sex experience).

Nadel (1954, p. 260) suggests that two elements seem to be discernible: 'something in the nature of an emotional state or a psycho-physical stimulation' and 'a more or less articulate assurance'.

Both the experience of the religious 'thrill' and of the 'assurance' are highly socialized and institutionalized events, even if they (obviously) occur to the individual and within his psyche. Even the 'individual' experience, that is, is a highly social phenomenon. [. . .]

The point, however, is not simply the social nature of individual mystical experience or of the experience of possession. It is that these are *special* forms of religious experience: that such ecstatic personal experience is rare, or foreign to many religions, or disdained or disapproved. It is, then, by no means a universal attribute of religion, and cannot be an irreducible part of the analytic definition of religion. But as the other three elements are only competential, and not necessarily found, what does religion consist of as distinct from other kinds of behaviour? In searching for the 'religious', Nadel arrives at individual sensation: James's famous 'thrill'. But most religious people probably never, or only rarely, experience it. Such experience may be encountered, but most religions do not, as cultural systems, encourage, require, expect or induce people to do so: for some 'church' religions, this kind of experience would be satanic, not holy – an individual-istic sin of hubris, something to be severely discouraged.

It seems much wiser, then, not to build into any definition this element of personal sensation, but rather to follow Spiro and simply observe that what distinguishes religious belief from other kinds of social belief is that, in some way or other (and that way may be oblique, remote or tenuous), it refers to, and looks for validation in, a dimension beyond the empirical-tech-nical realm of action. (This is, as we saw above, an analytical

235

distinction *not* necessarily present in the minds of the believers themselves.) But for most believers, most of the time, the other competences of religion may be quite predominant, and are not necessarily anything to do with the supernatural specifically. Hence, alternatives may be found for ethical codes of particular religions: morality can be detached from religion. But reference to what lies beyond man's knowledge, experience and control cannot.

References

AUBERT, W. (1965), 'Sleep: A sociological interpretation', in *The Hidden Society*, Bedminster Press, pp. 168–200.

BERNDT, R. M. (1951), *A Study of an Australian Aboriginal Religious Cult*, Cheshire, Melbourne.

BERNDT, R. M. (1952), *Djanngawul: An Aboriginal Religious Cult of North-Eastern Arnhem Land*, Routledge & Kegan Paul.

EVANS-PRITCHARD, E. E. (1934), 'The intellectualist (English) interpretation of magic', *Bulletin of the Faculty of Arts*, vol. 1, no. 2, Imprimerie de l'Institut Français d'Archéologie Orientale, Cairo.

EVANS-PRITCHARD, E. E. (1937), *Witchcraft, Oracles and Magic among the Azande*, Oxford University Press.

EVANS-PRITCHARD, E. E. (1965), *Theories of Primitive Religion*, Oxford University Press.

FIRTH, R. (1945), *Human Types*, Nelson.

FORDE, D. (ed.) (1954), *African Worlds: Studies in the Cosmological Ideas and Social Values of African Peoples*, Oxford University Press.

LANTERNARI, V. (1965), *The Religions of the Oppressed: A Study of Modern Messianic Cults*, MacGibbon & Kee.

MACBEATH, A. (1952), *Experiments in Living*, Macmillan.

MERTON, R. K. (1963), *Social Theory and Social Structure*, Free Press.

NADEL, S. F. (1954), *Nupe Religion*, Routledge & Kegan Paul.

SPIRO, M. E. (1964), 'Religion: problems of definition and explanation', in M. Banton, ed., *Anthropological Approaches to the Study of Religion*, Tavistock.

TURNER, V. W. (1960), 'Muchona the hornet, interpreter of religion', in J. B. Casagrande, ed., *In the Company of Man: Twenty Portraits by Anthropologists*, Harper & Row, pp. 333–55.

14 G. E. Swanson

Experience of the Supernatural

Excerpts from G. E. Swanson, *The Birth of the Gods*, University of Michigan Press, 1960, pp. 6–10, 15–29.

How shall we tell the supernatural from the natural? Some answer must be given to this question before one can venture a guess about the experiences from which an idea of supernature originates.

Supernatural forces take one of two forms. There is what we shall call 'mana' and there are spirits of various kinds.

Mana is a substance or essence which gives one the ability to perform tasks or achieve ends otherwise impossible. It increases natural abilities and confers supernatural skills. In itself, however, mana is an object, not a body of skills and abilities which are obtained through learning. Access to it is acquired, in the sense that a house or a wife or a spear are acquired, that is as a gift, as a purchase, or through the performance of appropriate acts.

When, for example, a Blackfoot Indian sought mana, he would go alone to some isolated spot. There, after fasting, prayer and exposure to the elements, a spirit might come and teach him a song or dance or might tell him that he would find some plant or animal which would, thereafter, be a source of good luck. Returning to his band, the Indian would employ these gifts to bring success in love or in hunting, to improve his performance as a warrior, to heal the sick or to aid in his other endeavors. It was common that he would incorporate objects of which the spirit told him into a medicine bundle, a convenient form in which to carry his talisman at all times. Such bundles could be purchased by those who lacked a spirit's visitation or who wanted to add to the charms which they owned. It is significant, however, that the spirits did not confer mana itself. Instead, they gave rituals or objects which enabled a man to make mana serve his needs.

237

Mana may be directed toward the achievement of the individual's purposes or those of a group. In either case, it is a substance which must be infused with human intentions or the intentions of spirits before its potentialities are realized. By itself, it does nothing. It is not able to organize events or to create them.

Spirits are supernatural beings. Unlike mana, they are personified. They have purposes and intentions of their own as well as the power to achieve their objectives.

Unfortunately for the construction of neat classifications, some personified supernatural forces fall between our categories of mana and spirit. Like mana they seem to have no objectives of their own, lying dormant until men activate them in the interest of human desires. At the same time, however, these forces are thought of as having the form of persons, animals, or other living creatures. We shall call them protospirits.

What makes mana, protospirits and spirits supernatural? How, for example, does mana differ from a medical injection or a machine which enables men to do what formerly was impossible? How does the nature of spirits differ from that of unusually strong or capable people who can master problems which are unsolved by others? The anthropologist Malinowski (1954) has taken great pains to show that primitives distinguish between the supernatural and other forces. Of what does that distinction consist?

Any answer to this question is speculative, but let us consider one which seems to fit the facts and which leads to interesting consequences. This answer says that behind natural events lies the supernatural – a realm of potentialities and purposes of which natural events are but concretions or expressions even as human behaviors or artifacts are expressions of the potentialities and purposes held by the men who produce them.[1] Let us suppose that mana represents the potentialities which underlie nature. Spirits represent organized clusters of the underlying purposes.

Now potentialities can serve a variety of purposes. In what is usually called magic, a person infuses mana with his own purposes. He activates the possibilities embodied in these

1. This conception is related to Plato's notions of immaterial essences which lie behind the appearances of reality.

transcendent conceptions, and thus influences the natural world by changing the supernatural. Spirits, representing purposes and possessing immediate access to the potentialities which underlie nature, can also manipulate natural events.

When he is confined to the world of nature, man is unable to produce what he wants merely by having the desire to do so, by informing the natural order with his purposes. Instead he must act upon it directly. He must create changes in the material universe which, of themselves, produce yet other changes until his objective is reached. At no point do his ideas or purposes, as such, intervene to change the environment. They must, in every case, be implemented by material action in the material world or that world remains as it was.

Supernatural forces are free of these limitations imposed on natural action in the material world. Many properties of the supernatural exemplify this freedom. A powerful spirit has but to desire rain and the waters fall. He can be at once in nature but not of it. Men will not perceive him directly through their senses. They will not find it inconsistent that he can be everywhere at once or that he can do many things at the same time. Not only do supernatural forces have powers not given to men, but, unless opposed by other and stronger spirits or by magic, the ends toward which those forces are directed are always accomplished. Finally, it is a common belief that the supernatural powers, unlike mankind, are immortal. They neither die nor become impotent with age.

These distinctions make it plain that we blur important differences in belief if we say that magic is only the science of primitives or that social movements like Fascism or Communism are of the same cloth as Christianity or Buddhism. There are similarities between magic and science. Both, for example, seek to understand and control nature. Likewise, both secular and religious movements may embody values which men seek with great devotion. But the underlying philosophy of science ignores the supernatural and secular creeds, as such, either ignore supernature or deny its existence. Magic and religion remain distinctive in having contacts with the supernatural as their goal. [. . .]

How can men's experience of their society produce the concept

239

of supernature? Because, says Durkheim, the relation of men to their society is like that of the worshipper to his god. Like the spirits, societies dominate their members by so controlling their thoughts and desires that individuals find intangible forces within themselves directing their conduct. Second, men feel strong, confident, and at peace with themselves when fulfilling their society's mandates. Third, as Lowie (1948, p. 155) puts it, 'all of a man's cultural possessions are the gift of society.' Society and culture go on though particular individuals perish. They provide an environment of directives and skills and values which persist in seeming perpetuity. And, Lowie continues to summarize:

In short, the individual consciousness finds an environment peopled with forces at once transcendentally potent and helpful, august yet benevolent; it objectifies its relevant impressions as we objectify our sensations, but with a significant difference: these sensations do not evoke the sentiment of awe, they correspond to the profane as contrasted with the sacred part of the universe . . .

Whatever the flaws in Durkheim's thought, and they exist,[2] it has the exceptional merit of directing our attention to a possibility quite in keeping with the character of supernature. It suggests that men develop a concept of personified supernatural beings directly from the model which their society provides. Unaware, as they generally are, of the extent to which overt behavior and inner impulse are formed by relations with other people, men find themselves in the hands of mysterious forces. Unlike other forces, these social customs seem to speak to individuals, chiding them for misbehavior, directing them to choose some goals rather than others, and rewarding their conformity. The thoroughly socialized individual has so acquired

2. Since I have neither reported nor employed Durkheim's applications of this scheme to the special case of Australian totemism, the familiar critiques of that application are not reviewed here. They are found in Lowie (1948), pp. 157–63. Other critical points mentioned by Lowie, namely that Durkheim's position identifies society with the crowd, or is incompatible with instances in which major natural phenomena are deified, or with the fact of individual religious experience, have also been left undiscussed. Such criticisms reflect misunderstanding of Durkheim's argument and its implications. A recent review of commentaries on Durkheim is given by Imogen Seger (1957).

these social standards that they are effective in directing his conduct even when he is quite alone.

And, we might add to Durkheim's discussion, unlike the law of the lever, or the principle of gravitation or other conditions of the physical world, these inner forces bear directly on a man's motives. They can be interested in what he intended as well as what he did.

Durkheim's position is plausible just because it begins to explain why men come to know intangible forces which can enter human lives, controlling will and action, and why these are forces with which people must come to terms. But much is left to be desired.

First, Durkheim's scheme does not suggest how spirits come to be unified and personified beings. Why should they not be experienced as powerful but disconnected impulses?

Second, what is the society that is venerated? Is it the composite of all the effects which contacts with one another have on people's conduct? Is it the pattern of such contacts? Is it but one special kind of social relationship to which people may belong? If there are gods of the winds or sea or the heavenly bodies, how can these somehow be the society in other guise when human actions do not exert obvious control over these natural forces? Is it all of the society that is venerated or just some of its aspects? Certainly the state or the economy or educational institutions are not considered supernatural in character by modern societies and we can find many primitive counterparts for this judgement.

Third, all spirits are not respected or venerated. Demons and devils may be feared, but they are not objects of moral respect. Other spirits are ignored or ridiculed or punished by those who believe in their existence. A satisfactory theory of supernatural beliefs must account for those relations between men and their gods. Durkheim's scheme does not provide the necessary explanation.

What I propose is to give tentative acceptance to the spirit, if not to the details, of Durkheim's position. I shall assume that some experiences with other people generate the concept of supernature and its two forms – mana and spirit. From that point, however, one must take a speculative path toward a more complete and plausible account than Durkheim provides. It begins

241

with a reconsideration of the nature of the supernatural, especially of spirits, and, after suggesting social experiences capable of producing a notion of personified supernatural beings, proceeds to extend the interpretation to include the presence of mana.

The Origin of Spirits

Spirits, we have seen, are organized clusters of purposes, each having a personal identity and access to mana. They are immortal. They may be invisible. They usually maintain their abilities through the years, not becoming feeble through age or illness. Only the powers of other supernatural beings limit the exercise of their skills. If we accept Durkheim's judgement that social experiences are the most likely source of supernatural concepts, to what social relationships do the experiences of spirits correspond?

Men may experience purpose in the acts of individuals or groups. That is, they find the behavior of individuals and groups directed toward goals, and learn that present conduct is shaped to promote the accomplishment of objectives. Purposes are the ideas people hold of what they will try to obtain in the future – a home, a lover, success in hunting, wealth, prestige, rectitude or whatever.

It happens, however, that people may have unintended effects on one another and that some influences they desire to wield are, nevertheless, denied them. Thus the exercise of purpose is not always clearly and cleanly seen as related to the consequences people have for each other's behavior. This fact has important implications for our work. If spirits are purposing beings, their influences flowing from their intentions, then we may expect that the social relations corresponding to supernatural beings must be those in which the connexion of intention and effect is evident.

But we can say more. The spirits are immortal. More accurately, their life span is greater than that of man. This qualification is entered because ancestors may take the form of spirits, at least in the thought of a generation or two of their descendants. It may be, however, that the dead sometimes cease to be considered as spirits once their names and deeds are lost to living memory.

When the purposes – the spirit – of an individual or group persist although the individual dies or the group's membership undergoes complete change, one must assume that those purposes continue to be embodied and active in survivors. Thus, when we seek the origin of spirits, we shall look for social relationships regarded as persisting across the generations. Individuals come and go. Groups may persist.

A further clue in our search is found in the fact that spirits have an identity. This does not mean that they are always named or that the peculiar traits of a particular spirit are invariably given a full and distinctive portrayal. It does mean that the notion of a spirit involves a particular and organized entity. The gods are individuals, not diffuse conditions. This fact suggests that we should look for *particular* groups as the source of the concept of spirit.

Finally, where there are several spirits, their purposes differ in some respects. They may protect different families or govern diverse aspects of nature or seek peculiar forms of attention from men and one another. These differences imply that we should search for groups with distinctive purposes.

To summarize, the characteristics of spirits suggest that we identify them with specific groups which persist over time and have distinctive purposes. What groups meet these specifications? Our next step is to propose an answer to this question.

There is a term in law and political science which seems to catch the qualities we seek. It is 'sovereignty'. A group has sovereignty to the extent that it has original and independent jurisdiction over some sphere of life – that its power to make decisions in this sphere is not delegated from outside but originates within it, and that its exercise of this power cannot legitimately be abrogated by another group. Although the term 'sovereignty' is commonly applied to nations or states, it can be applied to other groups as well.

In the United States, as in most societies, the family is a sovereign group. It has original and independent jurisdiction, within certain limits, over such matters as the education of the children, the practice of religion, the use of leisure and the choice of goods to be purchased. Similarly, among Americans, the national state has sovereignty over certain areas of importance, as have the several states, the counties, townships, local communities and other organizations.[3] In one society or another, clans, chiefdoms, extended families and many other types of organizations will be found to meet the criteria which identify a sovereign group.

To make the point still clearer, we may consider organizations which do not have sovereignty. These usually will include the armed forces, the schools and other agencies which are but specialized arms of sovereign groups, their purposes dictated by the organizations which have sovereignty and their powers delegated to them for the accomplishment of such purposes. We shall also include under this heading of non-sovereign, all groups devoted primarily to ritual or ceremonial functions, for the events they celebrate and symbolize are typically those of other agencies. Religious bodies would be in this category in most primitive societies, perhaps in all societies.

We shall assume that in so far as a group has sovereignty, it is likely[4] to provide the conditions from which a concept of spirit originates. The purposes of sovereign groups, like their special spheres of influence, tend to be distinctive and clear. By contrast, the purposes of non-sovereign groups are more likely to be seen as coming from a source other than themselves. The identity of the sovereign group is especially clear-cut just because its areas of control, and hence its purposes, are readily located. All we need add is the requirement that such a group shall persist over time.

3. The conception of sovereignty in a variety of groups was developed most fully by the pluralists. For a summary of their position and a good bibliography, see Coker (1934), pp. 170–74.

4. The phrase 'is likely' was chosen over some more positive phrase because one cannot rule out the possibility that conditions other than sovereignty may produce the same result. Since my thinking moved from the idea of 'spirits' to the social conditions which seem to embody the characteristics of spirits, I have not been forced to examine in detail the logical or psychological grounds by which an experience of sovereignty might lead to beliefs in *personified* supernatural realities. This reversed approach, while not necessary for these studies, presents interesting and difficult problems which a fuller account of religion must solve. As a temporary explanation, I would propose:

(a) Men associate purposing with the behavior of human individuals.

(b) When they find themselves in the grip of unseen and non-human purposing agents, men tend to think of those agents as superhuman persons.

This will almost certainly be the case for many groups in any stable and enduring society.

Nevertheless, a critic would be right in saying that these groups, as such, are not worshipped or venerated as supernatural. What features are associated with them that provoke the notion of supernature? The speculative solution of this problem is founded on some further observations about groups.

The Origin of Supernature

The argument to be outlined here states that people experience 'supernatural' properties in social life not merely because men are unwittingly controlled by social norms which they learn, but because social relationships inherently possess the characteristics we identify as supernatural. This argument is clearer if we let it flow from an illustration. Let us consider, therefore, the origin and organization of a particular social relationship, a marriage and let us suppose that we deal with the American case.

As in any voluntary relationship, the partners to a marriage join together because they facilitate one another's realization of objectives. I mean to imply that these considerations account for the union's existence whether the parties concerned know it or not. In the case of a marriage, one presumes that the partners enable each other to reach such goals as the rearing of children, achievement of status as full adults in the eyes of the community, the mutual exploration and development of their personalities, economic support, sexual satisfaction and, in some cases, a strengthening of the families from which they come.

In their first contacts, the individuals learn whether they can find such satisfactions in each other. They discover the kinds of relationships which best satisfy their needs. If a suitable form of interaction does develop, the man and woman who first committed themselves only to exploration now prepare to commit enough of such resources as affection, time and economic skills to maintain the relationship. In our example, we may think of dating before marriage as a period of exploration and of courtship as an extended period for completing the exploration and developing a stable relationship once preliminary investigation brings promising results. At some point in this process, the couple

245

must commit themselves to perform such acts as will make possible the continuing satisfaction of their desires or the marriage will not exist other than in name.

What is being described is the emergence of a pattern of inter-action between people, an exchange of desired behaviors, which can be used to reach certain goals and which is a prerequisite to such an accomplishment. This pattern incorporates an arrangement by which participants perform certain services for each other and, in return, receive services they desire. Presumably certain minimal arrangements of this kind are required for any relationship to persist. Once in existence, to return to the marital illustration, they allow the couple to work together in bearing and rearing children, entertaining guests, managing the economic affairs of a household and in endless other activities.

These underlying and requisite arrangements may be called the 'constitutional arrangements' or 'constitutional structure' of the relationship. The constitutional arrangements 'define' those affairs with which the organization may legitimately concern itself and the procedures by which its activities may legitimately be formulated and implemented. To put the matter a bit differently, constitutional arrangements 'state' a group's sphere of competence and the proper procedures for making and executing decisions. The words 'define' and 'state' are put in quotation marks to indicate that the achievement of a constitutional structure and the perception of its nature may or may not be self-conscious and symbolized in the experience of the participants. On occasion, as in the Constitution of the United States, some of the arrangements' more important features are given express statement. Similarly, the marriage vows make overt a part of those arrangements requisite to establishing a family. But it is typical that all features of the constitutional structure are not made explicit and, in such groupings as friendships, it may be that none of these features is symbolized.

How, then, do we know that constitutional arrangements exist? Locke, Hume, Rousseau and others invented historical episodes in which men first came together and, explicitly acknowledging their interdependence and the conditions under which they would live together, founded societies. Something like these fictive situations actually occurs at constitutional conventions or when articles of incorporation are drawn up and signed. But when is the constitutional structure of a marriage apparent? Of a friendship? Of a new sectarian movement?

The presence of certain minimal conditions under which an organization can continue in existence will come to light when there is a likelihood that such conditions will not be met. These are the constitutional problems of a marriage or a nation or of any other organization. The 'constitution' need not be written in order for the problems to exist and be recognized precisely as those which affect the group's continuation. Thus, a man and wife who cannot conceive of marriage to a person who is sexually unfaithful must revise the constitutional structure governing their relations or sever those relations if one of them is discovered having an extramarital affair.

It is the mark of a stable and legitimate[5] social relationship that the constitutional structure is consistent with the secondary, tertiary and other successive relations which are built on it. Only on rare occasions, furthermore, is it necessary in such a relationship to refer self-consciously to the constitutional structure itself to decide an issue. The operations which that structure permits are visible, not the constitutional structure itself. Constant examination by participants of their basic commitments to each other suggests that the foundations of the relationship are unstable. It is the nature of reform to debate the application of the constitutional structure, not its character. Revolution debates the validity of the constitutional structure itself.

Before relating all these observations to the concept of supernature, let us explore just a bit further the fact that not all aspects of a constitutional structure are made explicit and symbolic. This can be important in understanding the nature of mana and spirits.

We have seen that the constitutional structure, itself, emerges from the many interests and desires of the participants in a relationship. It expresses, implicitly or overtly, their minimal demands on one another if their interaction is to continue. But some interests and desires which lead to such demands go forever unrecognized. Others become more or less apparent as the

5. A legitimate social relationship is one in which the participants believe that the nature of their contacts with one another is right and just.

relationship continues. And close inspection would probably show that every taste and attitude and intention of the participants has some bearing, however distant, on the constitutional structure of every particular relationship in which it is involved. This vast, largely uncharted and unchartable body of dispositions and potentialities which each participant brings to a given relationship, and which changes with new experiences, provides the primordial conditions from which specific constitutional arrangements emerge.

The constitutional structure of a social relationship is like the notion of 'character'[6] in the individual. Despite the considerable differences in a person's behavior from one situation to another, we recognize certain attitudes and values as somehow enduring in his conduct and central to it. These predispositions have to do with the goals and means to which he is most thoroughly committed – those habits for whose maintenance he will pay the highest price. He need not be self-consciously aware of all or any such predispositions. Indeed, he typically is unaware of most of them. Yet they manifest themselves rather clearly when their existence is challenged and they provide a continuing, if subterranean, set of forces which orders many of his activities. As with a group's constitutional structures, these basic features of a person's identity are relatively organized areas of predispositions toward the environment, and are surrounded by tastes and desires which have been subjected to less searching evaluation from experiences in the environment. Such terms as Freud's 'primary process' have been used to refer to this analogue in the individual of what, in social life, we have called the primordial.[7]

6. The most detailed discussion of character in the individual is Reich (1945). See also Fenichel (1945).

7. Readers of the psychoanalytic literature may notice affinities between Freud's concept of the primary process and the primordial social relations described here. This pair of ideas may be considered as isomorphic despite the difference in their empirical referents. In both cases we deal with a set of active relationships which are hidden from the organs of consciousness. In social life, such organs may be equated with the constitutional structures. Neither the primary process nor the primordial relations ever become fully public. Further, their components are unaware of their own internal connexions and of the total pattern which they comprise. Separated from the constitutional structures (the social ego) and the ideal (the social superego), they exhibit many of the qualities which Freud attributes to primary

But how is all of this related to the supernatural? Let me suggest that the primordial links among men – vague, largely hidden, possessing unsuspected potentialities – correspond to the idea that the world is the expression or concretion of latent possibilities which, when infused with appropriate purposes, can be combined or rearranged or activated to serve human needs. This is the stuff that magic seeks to manipulate. By contrast, constitutional structures, and especially those of sovereign groups, are areas of partially organized and orderly influence in this primordial ocean. They represent the crystallization of purposes which spring from the nature of the primordial and whose consequences flow back into it. These constitutional structures are what men often conceptualize as personified and supernatural beings. Religion consists of behaviors directed toward influencing the purposes of such beings – of spirits.[8]

Both the primordial and the constitutional structures in which human life is immersed have properties which are also those that define the supernatural. As conditions which underlie the flow

---

process. They are not ordered or rationalized with respect to the operation of the constitutional structures. They are not regulated by having to be confronted with their consequences for public action. They are not ordered by being confronted with the fact that their consequences conflict with one another. They are not curbed by the perception that certain stages are required for their being put into effect – in this sense they are atemporal. They follow the paths which lead to the greatest likelihood of realization in public policy, ordered only by their own strength and by the likelihood of such realization. They seem almost indestructible – their roots being nourished constantly and reality never intervening to reveal their flaws. Those who participate in these relationships exhibit no doubts, negations or varying degrees of certainty concerning them. Perhaps, like the primary process, these primordial relations are easily condensed or displaced.

8. The distinction between magic and religion given here differs from some others in the literature. Thus Marion J. Levy (1952), pp. 243–4, 336, defines magic as the use of non-empirical means to achieve empirical ends; religion as the use of non-empirical means to gain non-empirical ends. This would place a prayer for health under the category of magic and a prayer to free souls from purgatory under the heading of religion. It would be impossible to classify situations in which empirical means, such as an offering of food, are used to gain non-empirical ends, such as a pleasant afterlife for deceased relatives. The definitions we shall use distinguish between magic and religion on the basis of the entities they govern, not the means by which those relationships are established or the ends which they are designed to accomplish.

of conscious experience and interaction, they are immanent in their guidance of the particular experiences of any given moment, yet transcendent in the continuity of their influence over many different experiences. Like relations in supernature, the relations within and between the primordial and constitutional structures are largely invisible and their effects are accomplished through the directives and limitations they set out for the conceptions of people who interact.

The influence of these structures upon participants in interaction is also like the supernatural in possessing powers not given to men. Their influence operates at all times. Without the application of any obvious or perceptible means, these structures determine people's relations and activities – both generating them and judging them. Further, these structures embody a wider 'knowledge' than any individual or group possesses in the sense that they contain more conditions and potentialities than those of which people are aware at any given time. The accomplishment of their purposes is inevitable as long as they are stable, for the only contingency required for that accomplishment is the presence of normal, well-socialized humans who are committed to the relationships which these structures undergird. They cannot, of course, be avoided or escaped by such humans. Here, then, we have entities which are not perceived in any direct sense, which may have some empirical site as their locale but not as their being, which have powers that transcend the means–ends processes of nature, which can affect nature without being of it, and which may or may not be experienced as having an enduring identity.

Any given social organization or group consists of a constitutional structure together with the inter-relations among participants which that structure permits and directs. Such inter-relations are an organization of activities for implementing and maintaining the constitutional structure. This has been illustrated in the example of a marriage.

Drawing together the pieces of this explanation of the supernatural we may conclude:

1. The experiences which seem closest to having the supernatural's characteristics are those connected with the primordial and constitutional structures of social relationships.

a. Like the supernatural, these structures embody purposes. They also embody those potentialities which can be put to work for beings who can infuse them with purpose.

b. Like the supernatural, these structures pervade the inner life and outer experience of men, directing and limiting human behavior as invisible, immortal, inescapable and vaguely understood forces whose effects on conduct seem to be produced by the direct induction of purpose.

2. The conception of spirits corresponds to experiences with the activities of sovereign organizations. More precisely, the spirits whom men approach do not represent particular sovereign organizations, as such, but their constitutional structures. Spirits stand for the complex and vaguely bounded constitutional structures which are given partial concretion in particular sovereign organizations and which exhibit consistencies and continuities of operation while always escaping complete and explicit embodiment in any human group. Spirits are likely to represent sovereign groups rather than other types of social organization because the purposes and spheres of influence of such groups, and hence of their constitutional structures, are more clearly available to the experience of participants.

3. The idea of mana is evoked by experiences with the primordial features of social life.

4. For our purposes, magic will consist of those behaviors designed to invest mana with a particular purpose; religion, of activities aimed at influencing, or responding to, the purposes of spirits.

Like other explanations this account of the supernatural will doubtlessly be shown to contain flaws. It is certain that it rests on many assumptions for which current evidence is inadequate. In any event, its value lies in its ability to organize facts which other schemes cannot interpret and, going further, to explain observations which cannot be integrated by alternative interpretations. Its value is further enhanced if it leads one to make verifiable predictions and if such verification is forthcoming.

References
COKER, F. W. (1934), 'Pluralism', *Encyclopaedia of the Social Sciences*, vol. 12, Macmillan.

FENICHEL, O. (1945), *The Psychoanalytic Theory of Neurosis*, Norton.

LEVY, M. J. (1952), *The Structure of Society*, Princeton University Press.

LOWIE, R. H. (1948), *Primitive Religion*, Liveright.

MALINOWSKI, B. (1954), 'Magic, science and religion', *Magic, Science, and Religion and other Essays*, Doubleday.

REICH, W. (1945), *Character-Analysis*, Orgone Institute, New York.

SEGER, I. (1957), *Durkheim and his Critics on the Sociology of Religion*, Bureau of Applied Social Research, Columbia University.

15 R. Stark and C. Y. Glock

Dimensions of Religious Commitment

Abridged from R. Stark and C. Y. Glock, *American Piety: The Nature of Religious Commitment*, University of California Press, 1968, pp. 11–19.

When we say someone is 'religious' we can mean many different things. Church membership, belief in religious doctrines, an ethical way of life, attendance at worship services, and many other acts, outlooks and conditions can all denote piety and commitment to religion.

Upon reflection, it becomes clear that the variety of meanings associated with the term religious, while they may well be aspects of a single phenomenon, are not simply synonyms.[1] For example, most people knowing that someone is an active church member would also expect him to be a firm believer in church doctrines and to be concerned about acting out his faith in his daily life. Going to church, believing and acting ethically are generally recognized as components of being religious. However, simply because a person is religious in one of these ways is no guarantee that he will be religious in others. There are active church-goers who do not believe, firm believers among the unchurched, and people who both believe and belong, but who could hardly be described as ethical. Deciding with any particular precision who warrants the designation 'religious' and who does not, turns out to be rather a complex problem.

The ambiguities in what religiousness can mean have led to serious failure in much research and writing on religious commitment. A good part of the recent dispute over whether American religion experienced a postwar revival or decline seems to have

1. The basic conceptual scheme presented in this chapter is elaborated in greater detail in Glock and Stark (1965), ch. 2.

[There are a number of competing schemes of dimensions of religiosity. The one presented here has its critics. For discussion see Robertson (1970), chs. 3 and 5. See also Reading 19 – *Ed.*]

been produced by different observers adopting different definitions. While some commentators pointed to increases in the proportion of Americans belonging to and participating in churches, others detected an erosion of biblical faith and asserted that religion was losing is authenticity. Since it seems likely that both of these changes were occurring simultaneously, whether one discerned a religious revival or decline depended at least partly on whether religiousness was defined in terms of practice or belief.[2]

Clearly, conceptions of religiousness are not the same to all men – either in modern complex societies or even in the most homogeneous primitive communities. This simple fact scarcely needs documentation. The evidence that people disagree about how the 'religious person' ought to think, feel and act is all around us.

Because of this great diversity, any investigation of the individual and his religion faces a formidable problem of definition – what shall we call religiousness and how shall we decide to classify persons in religious terms? There are several issues at stake in this matter. First of all there is the purely methodological problem of selecting criteria that may be applied unambiguously and systematically. However, since science mainly operates with nominal definitions, from a purely methodological point of view we could arbitrarily define religious commitment pretty much as we cared to. Our subsequent statements and findings, however, would only be applicable to religious commitment in the particular sense in which we defined it. But of course we aspire to do a good deal more than that; we want to make statements that will be agreed to have general applicability. Thus we come to a second consideration in defining our terms. This has to do with credibility or perhaps relevance. In order to make assertions about religious commitment that will be regarded as relevant it is necessary that readers agree that the way we define religiousness suitably represents the way they understand the term. If we want to have our statements taken as applicable to what is conventionally regarded as religious commitment then we must come to terms with conventional usage of the term religious commitment.

But, as we have just pointed out, the term religiousness is used

2. An analysis of the religious revival controversy is treated in detail in Glock and Stark (1965), chs. 4 and 5.

in a number of different ways and is subject to a great deal of ambiguity in conventional usage. Thus, to begin the task of defining and operationalizing religious commitment it is necessary to do a bit of linguistic analysis to determine the different things that *can* be meant by the term, or the different ways in which individuals *can* be religious. Subsequently, it becomes appropriate to try to discover whether religiousness manifested in one of these ways has anything to do with its being expressed in others.

By beginning with the broadest possible conception of what religious commitment can mean we are trying as much as possible to forestall rejections of our findings based on the belief that we are not really talking about religiousness. Social science research on religion is particularly subject to this kind of dismissal, especially from churchmen, and all dialogue is impossible so long as there is no initial agreement on a common language. Thus we shall try to begin with agreement at least on subject matter. Of course, we maintain no illusion that we can satisfy everyone. Clearly, for those who hold religiousness to be a purely metaphysical phenomenon, beyond the senses and not connected with what men think, or say, or do, our work will be totally irrelevant – mere materialistic concern with mundane appearances.

We are quite content to acknowledge that there may be a metaphysical element in religion which defies scientific scrutiny. But religion as we know it exists in the material world and cannot be comprehended wholly or even primarily in metaphysical terms·

If we examine the religions of the world, it is evident that the details of religious expression are extremely varied; different religions expect quite different things of their adherents. Catholics and many Protestants, for example, are expected to participate regularly in the Christian sacrament of Holy Communion. To Moslems, such a practice is alien. By the same token, the Moslem imperative to undertake a pilgrimage to Mecca during one's lifetime is alien to Christians. Similarly, Hindus are enjoined from eating beef, while Moslems and Jews reject pork, evangelical Protestants abstain from alcohol, and, until, recently, Catholics did not eat meat on Friday. These seem to be substantial variations, but we suggest that they are variations in detail. Beyond the differences in specific beliefs and practices, there seems to be considerable consensus among all religions on the general ways in which religiousness ought to be manifested. We propose that these general ways provide a set of core dimensions of religiousness.

Five such dimensions can be distinguished; within one or another of them all of the many and diverse religious prescriptions of the different religions of the world can be classified. We shall call these dimensions: *belief, practice, experience, knowledge* and *consequences*.

1. The belief dimension comprises expectations that the religious person will hold a certain theological outlook, that he will acknowledge the truth of the tenets of the religion. Every religion maintains some set of beliefs which adherents are expected to ratify. However, the content and scope of beliefs will vary not only between religions, but often within the same religious tradition.

2. Religious practice includes acts of worship and devotion, the things people *do* to carry out their religious commitment. Religious practices fall into two important classes:

Ritual refers to the set of rites, formal religious acts and sacred practices which all religions expect their adherents to perform. In Christianity some of these formal ritual expectations are attendance at worship services, taking communion, baptism, weddings and the like.

Devotion is somewhat akin to, but importantly different from ritual. While the ritual aspect of commitment is highly formalized and typically public, all known religions also value personal acts of worship and contemplation which are relatively spontaneous, informal, and typically private. Devotionalism among Christians is manifested through private prayer, Bible reading and perhaps even by impromptu hymn singing.

3. The experience dimension takes into account the fact that all religions have certain expectations, however imprecisely they may be stated, that the properly religious person will at some time or other achieve a direct, subjective knowledge of ultimate reality;

that he will achieve some sense of contact, however fleeting, with a supernatural agency. As we have written elsewhere, this dimension is concerned with religious experiences, those feelings, perceptions, and sensations which are experienced by an actor or defined by a religious group (or a society) as involving some communication, however slight, with a divine essence, that is, with God, with ultimate reality, with transcendental authority (Glock and Stark, 1965, chs. 3 and 8). To be sure, there are marked contrasts in the varieties of such experiences which are deemed proper by different religious traditions and institutions, and religions also vary in the degree to which they encourage *any* type of religious encounter. Nevertheless, every religion places at least minimal value on some variety of subjective religious experience as a sign of individual religiousness.

4. The knowledge dimension refers to the expectation that religious persons will possess some minimum of information about the basic tenets of their faith and its rites, scriptures and traditions. The knowledge and belief dimensions are clearly related since knowledge of a belief is a necessary precondition for its acceptance. However, belief need not follow from knowledge, nor does all religious knowledge bear on belief. Furthermore, a man may hold a belief without really understanding it, that is, belief can exist on the basis of very little knowledge.

5. The consequences dimension of religious commitment differs from the other four. It identifies the effects of religious belief, practice, experience, and knowledge in persons' day-to-day lives. The notion of 'works', in the theological sense, is connoted here. Although religions prescribe much of how their adherents ought to think and act in everyday life, it is not entirely clear the extent to which religious consequences are *a part* of religious commitment or simply *follow from it*.

For our present purposes, we will assume that the initial four dimensions provide a complete frame of reference for assessing religious commitment. But while it is possible to postulate these four aspects of religiousness on analytic grounds, relations among them cannot be explored without empirical data. It is scarcely plausible that they will be entirely unrelated. However, it is equally clear that being religious on one dimension does not necessarily imply being religious on another.

For all religions it can be said that theology, or religious belief, is at the heart of faith. It is only within some set of beliefs about the ultimate nature of reality, of the nature and intentions of the supernatural, that other aspects of religion become coherent. Ritual and devotional activities such as communion or prayer are incomprehensible unless they occur within a framework of belief which postulates that there is some being or force to worship. Similarly, it is plausible to call a rather ignorant believer religious, but not the knowledgeable skeptic. Or, the believer who has not undergone a religious experience could still be called religious, but a person who has religious experiences, but no religious beliefs, is likely to be called psychotic. Indeed, the believer who backslides when it comes to living up to his faith in everyday affairs, may still be defined as religious, but not so the ethical atheist. Thus, the belief dimension can be considered a particularly necessary, but often not sufficient, aspect of religious commitment.

In Christianity, it can be argued, religious practice is the second most valued aspect of religious commitment, not of such primary importance as is belief, but more cherished than the other three. However, in more mystical religions, and some extreme Protestant sects, more importance is placed on religious experience than upon practice.

It should also be noted that there is likely a certain incompatibility between the knowledge and experience dimensions. Religious bodies which place great importance on one seem inclined to give less importance to the other, although both dimensions are given some value in all religions. Modern Christianity seems to give less stress to religious experiences and more to religious knowledge.

While it seems true that these four aspects of religious commitment are not equally valued by religious institutions, all are valued to a considerable extent. Thus, any comprehensive effort to understand religious commitment, must consider each of them. In so doing it will be possible to construct extensive empirical descriptions of patterns of religious commitment, both among

American Christians in general, and as comparisons among the major denominations.

Before concluding this statement, something must be said about a well-known schema for classifying persons according to their religious commitment, and why we have chosen not to incorporate it into this study. This is Gordon W. Allport's important distinction between two types of religiousness, the 'intrinsic' and the 'extrinsic' (Allport, 1960). Allport's typology is presently enjoying a considerable vogue especially among psychologists. The basis of Allport's distinction is not merely the extent of a person's religious behavior (in the sense we have outlined in this statement), but the *motives* for his behavior, and to some extent the *consequences* of his religious behavior for other aspects of his life.

Allport (1960, p. 33) characterizes the extrinsic type of religiousness as:

utilitarian, self-serving, conferring safety, status, comfort and talismanic favors upon the believer. . . . People who are religious in this sense make use of God . . . [they are] dependent and basically infantile.

The intrinsic type, he describes as follows (p. 33):

This kind of religion can steer one's existence without enslaving him to his limited concepts and egocentric needs. One may call this type of religion 'interiorized' or 'intrinsic' or 'outward-centered'. In any case, it is the polar opposite of the utilitarian, self-centered, extrinsic view.

Allport's types crosscut the kinds of criteria of religious commitment we have developed earlier in this statement. Although in order to be religious in Allport's terms all persons must meet our criteria, he seeks to further exclude persons from being 'really' or 'authentically' faithful on the basis of their instrumental motives for piety or their lack of theological sophistication. While it is interesting that the mainstream of the Christian

3. The New Testament directly appeals to the deprived and promises them comfort. Similarly, conservative Christianity today shows no such 'choosiness', but explicitly seeks conversions on the basis of the personal good that follows from faith. Apparently this whole tradition, including hundreds of hymns such as 'What a friend we have in Jesus, all our sins and griefs to bear', falls on the 'inauthentic' side of the intrinsic, extrinsic distinction.

tradition has given major encouragement to the very sources of belief that Allport discredits,[3] these are, to be sure, most important distinctions. It seems both certain and important that folkish conceptions of faith will produce different interpretations of the world (e.g. of political values) than will sophisticated theologies. Similarly, it is very probably the case that people who adhere to faith out of need for psychic security will act upon their faith differently from persons whose commitment is based on high moral purpose.

But for all their importance it seems wise to exclude Allport's distinctions from our definition of religious commitment, for to include in the definition both the motives for commitment and the consequences which follow from it makes it impossible really to ask anything further about commitment. The purpose of all science, including social science, is explanation. But explanation is impossible unless there is something to explain. That is, it must be at least logically possible for assertions to be falsified; elements that are presumed to be related must logically be capable of independent variation. When a relationship between two concepts or elements in a theory is defined as true, independent variation is not even logically possible. For example, if by definition *only* intrinsic religious motives can produce authentic religious commitment, it is impossible to discover what kinds of motives most typically produce religious behavior, or even whether extrinsic motives can on occasion lead to authentic commitment. The reason for this is obvious, intrinsic religious motives and authentic religious commitment have been defined as equivalent. Similarly, if by definition *only* altruistic attitudes *can* follow from religious beliefs (otherwise the belief is inauthentic, extrinsic religion) then it is not possible to see whether the religious training, beliefs, and activities promoted by religious institutions typically do produce admirable results.[4]

4. It is recognized that Allport did not initially postulate these relationships as true by definition, but that he constructed his types through intensive psychological study of individual religiousness. However, the finished types present this 'true-by-definition' problem for anyone who seeks to employ them in their own research. While Allport's analysis may have provided justification for the types as generalizations – elements may be *related* in the manner which the types suggest – it is hard to estimate the extent to which he found deviant cases, that is, cases where the relations

did not hold. If the correlations were not virtually perfect, then while the data undoubtedly justified his types as generalizations, to adopt them *a priori* in our study would rule out the possibility of treating the elements of the types as variables. The possibility is open, at this point, for types along similar lines to emerge at the conclusion of our study to sum up our findings. But this is a way of describing findings, not of beginning analysis.

References

ALLPORT, G. W. (1960), *Religion in the Developing Personality*, New York University Press.

GLOCK, C. Y., and STARK, R. (1965), *Religion and Society in Tension*, Rand McNally.

[ROBERTSON, R. (1970), *The Sociological Interpretation of Religion*, Blackwell and Schocken Books.]

16 R. N. Bellah

Religious Evolution

R. N. Bellah, 'Religious evolution', *American Sociological Review*, vol. 29 (1964), pp. 358–74.

'Time in its aging course teaches all things.'
Aeschylus, *Prometheus Bound*

Though one can name precursors as far back as Herodotus, the systematically scientific study of religion begins only in the second half of the nineteenth century. According to Chantepie de la Saussaye (1904), the two preconditions for this emergence were that religion had become by the time of Hegel the object of comprehensive philosophical speculation and that history by the time of Buckle had been enlarged to include the history of civilization and culture in general. In its early phases, partly under the influence of Darwinism, the science of religion was dominated by an evolutionary tendency already implicit in Hegelian philosophy and early nineteenth-century historiography. The grandfathers of modern sociology, Comte and Spencer, contributed to the strongly evolutionary approach to the study of religion as, with many reservations, did Durkheim and Weber.

But by the third decade of the twentieth century the evolutionary wave was in full retreat both in the general field of science of religion and in the sociology of religion in particular. Of course, this was only one aspect of the general retreat of evolutionary thought in social science, but nowhere did the retreat go further nor the intensity of the opposition to evolution go deeper than in the field of religion. An attempt to explain the vicissitudes of evolutionary conceptions in the field of religion would be an interesting study in the sociology of knowledge but beyond the scope of this brief paper. Here I can only say that I hope that the present attempt to apply the evolutionary idea to religion evidences a serious appreciation of both nineteenth-century evolutionary theories and twentieth-century criticisms of them.

Evolution at any system level I define as a process of increasing differentiation and complexity of organization which endows the organism, social system or whatever the unit in question may be, with greater capacity to adapt to its environment so that it is in some sense more autonomous relative to its environment than were its less complex ancestors. I do not assume that evolution is inevitable, irreversible or must follow any single particular course. Nor do I assume that simpler forms cannot prosper and survive alongside more complex forms. What I mean by evolution, then, is nothing metaphysical but the simple empirical generalization that more complex forms develop from less complex forms and that the properties and possibilities of more complex forms differ from those of less complex forms.

A brief handy definition of religion is considerably more difficult than a definition of evolution. An attempt at an adequate definition would, as Clifford Geertz (1963) has recently demonstrated, take a paper in itself for adequate explanation. So, for limited purposes only, let me define religion as a set of symbolic forms and acts which relate man to the ultimate conditions of his existence. The purpose of this definition is to indicate exactly what I claim has evolved. It is not the ultimate conditions, nor, in traditional language, God that has evolved, nor is it man in the broadest sense of *homo religiosus*. I am inclined to agree with Eliade (1958, pp. 459–65) when he holds that primitive man is as fully religious as man at any stage of existence, though I am not ready to go along with him when he implies *more* fully.

Neither religious man nor the structure of man's ultimate religious situation evolves, then, but rather religion as symbol system. Erich Voegelin (1956, p. 5), who I suspect shares Eliade's basic philosophical position, speaks of a development from compact to differentiated symbolization. Everything already exists in some sense in the religious symbol system of the most primitive man; it would be hard to find anything later that is not 'foreshadowed' there, as for example, the monotheistic God is foreshadowed in the high gods of some primitive peoples. Yet just as obviously the two cannot be equated. Not only in their idea of God but in many other ways the monotheistic religions of Judaism, Christianity and Islam involve a much more differentiated symbolization of, and produce a much more complex relation to, the ultimate conditions of human existence than do primitive religions. At least the existence of that kind of difference is the thesis I wish to develop. I hope it is clear that there are a number of other possible meanings of the term 'religious evolution' with which I am not concerned. I hope it is also clear that a complex and differentiated religious symbolization is not therefore a better or a truer or a more beautiful one than a compact religious symbolization. I am not a relativist and I do think judgements of value can reasonably be made between religions, societies or personalities. But the axis of that judgement is not provided by social evolution and if progress is used in an essentially ethical sense, then I for one will not speak of religious progress.

Having defined the ground rules under which I am operating let me now step back from the subject of religious evolution and look first at a few of the massive facts of human religious history. The first of these facts is the emergence in the first millennium B.C. all across the Old World, at least in centers of high culture, of the phenomenon of religious rejection of the world characterized by an extremely negative evaluation of man and society and the exaltation of another realm of reality as alone true and infinitely valuable. This theme emerges in Greece through a long development into Plato's classic formulation in the Phaedo that the body is the tomb or prison of the soul and that only by disentanglement from the body and all things worldly can the soul unify itself with the unimaginably different world of the divine. A very different formulation is found in Israel, but there too the world is profoundly devalued in the face of the transcendent God with whom alone is there any refuge or comfort. In India we find perhaps the most radical of all versions of world rejection, culminating in the great image of the Buddha, and the world is a burning house and man's urgent need is a way to escape from it. In China, Taoist ascetics urged the transvaluation of all the accepted values and withdrawal from human society, which they condemned as unnatural and perverse.

Nor was this a brief or passing phenomenon. For over 2000 years great pulses of world rejection spread over the civilized world. The *Qur'an* (Koran) compares this present world to vegetation after rain, whose growth rejoices the unbeliever, but it quickly withers away and becomes as straw (57, 19–20). Men prefer life in the present world but the life to come is infinitely superior – it alone is everlasting (87, 16–17). Even in Japan, usually so innocently world accepting, Shotoku Taishi declared that the world is a lie and only the Buddha is true, and in the Kamakura period the conviction that the world is hell led to orgies of religious suicide by seekers after Amida's paradise (see Saburo, 1940). And it is hardly necessary to quote Revelations or Augustine for comparable Christian sentiments. I do not deny that there are profound differences among these various rejections of the world; Max Weber (1946) has written a great essay on the different directions of world rejection and their consequences for human action. But for the moment I want to concentrate on the fact that they were all in some sense rejections and that world rejection is characteristic of a long and important period of religious history. I want to insist on this fact because I want to contrast it with an equally striking fact – namely the virtual absence of world rejection in primitive religions, in religion prior to the first millennium B.C., and in the modern world.[1]

Primitive religions are on the whole oriented to a single cosmos – they know nothing of a wholly different world relative to which the actual world is utterly devoid of value. They are concerned with the maintenance of personal, social and cosmic harmony and with attaining specific goods – rain, harvest, children, health – as men have always been. But the overriding goal of salvation that dominates the world rejecting religions is almost absent in primitive religion, and life after death tends to be a shadowy semi-existence in some vaguely designated place in the single world.

World rejection is no more characteristic of the modern world than it is of primitive religion. Not only in the United States but through much of Asia there is at the moment something of a religious revival, but nowhere is this associated with a great new

1. One might argue that the much discussed modern phenomenon of alienation is the same as world rejection. The concept of alienation has too many uses to receive full discussion here, but it usually implies estrangement from or rejection of only selected aspects of the empirical world.

outburst of world rejection. In Asia apologists, even for religions with a long tradition of world rejection, are much more interested in showing the compatibility of their religions with the developing modern world than in totally rejecting it. And it is hardly necessary to point out that the American religious revival stems from motives quite opposite to world rejection.

One could attempt to account for this sequence of presence and absence of world rejection as a dominant religious theme without ever raising the issue of religious evolution, but I think I can account for these and many other facts of the historical development of religion in terms of a scheme of religious evolution. An extended rationale for the scheme and its broad empirical application must await publication in book form. Here all I can attempt is a very condensed overview.

The scheme is based on several presuppositions, the most basic of which I have already referred to: namely, that religious symbolization of what Geertz (1963) calls 'the general order of existence' tends to change over time, at least in some instances, in the direction of more differentiated, comprehensive, and in Weber's sense, more rationalized formulations. A second assumption is that conceptions of religious action, of the nature of the religious actor, of religious organization and of the place of religion in the society tend to change in ways systematically related to the changes in symbolization. A third assumption is that these several changes in the sphere of religion, which constitute what I mean by religious evolution, are related to a variety of other dimensions of change in other social spheres which define the general process of sociocultural evolution.

Now, for heuristic purposes at least, it is also useful to assume a series of stages which may be regarded as relatively stable crystallizations of roughly the same order of complexity along a number of different dimensions. I shall use five stages which, for want of better terminology, I shall call primitive, archaic, historic, early modern and modern.[2] These stages are ideal types derived

2. These stages are actually derived from an attempt to develop a general schema of sociocultural evolution during the seminar in which I participated, together with Talcott Parsons and S. N. Eisenstadt. This paper must, however, be strictly limited to religious evolution, which is in itself sufficiently complex without going into still broader issues.

from a theoretical formulation of the most generally observable historical regularities; they are meant to have a temporal reference but only in a very general sense.

Of course the scheme itself is not intended as an adequate description of historical reality. Particular lines of religious development cannot simply be forced into the terms of the scheme. In reality there may be compromise formations involving elements from two stages which I have for theoretical reasons discriminated; earlier stages may, as I have already suggested, strikingly foreshadow later developments; and more developed may regress to less developed stages. And of course no stage is ever completely abandoned; all earlier stages continue to co-exist with and often within later ones. So what I shall present is not intended as a procrustean bed into which the facts of history are to be forced but a theoretical construction against which historical facts may be illuminated. The logic is much the same as that involved in conceptualizing stages of the life cycle in personality development.

Primitive Religion

Before turning to the specific features of primitive religion let us go back to the definition of religion as a set of symbolic forms and acts relating man to the ultimate conditions of his existence. Lienhardt (1961, p. 170), in his book on Dinka religion spells out this process of symbolization in a most interesting way:

I have suggested that the Powers may be understood as images corresponding to complex and various combinations of Dinka experience which are contingent upon their particular social and physical environment. For the Dinka they are the grounds of those experiences; in our analysis we have shown them to be grounded in them, for to a European the experiences are more readily understood than the Powers, and the existence of the latter cannot be posited as a condition of the former. Without these Powers or images or an alternative to them there would be for the Dinka no differentiation between experience of the self and of the world which acts upon it. Suffering, for example, could be merely 'lived' or endured. With the imaging of the grounds of suffering in a particular Power, the Dinka can grasp its nature intellectually in a way which satisfies them, and thus to some extent transcend and

267

dominate it in this act of knowledge. With this knowledge, this separation of a subject and an object in experience, there arises for them also the possibility of creating a form of experience they desire, and of freeing themselves symbolically from what they must otherwise passively endure.

If we take this as a description of religious symbolization in general, and I think we can, then it is clear that in terms of the conception of evolution used here the existence of even the simplest religion is an evolutionary advance. Animals or pre-religious men could only 'passively endure' suffering or other limitations imposed by the conditions of their existence, but religious man can to some extent 'transcend and dominate' them through his capacity for symbolization and thus attain a degree of freedom relative to his environment that was not previously possible.[3]

Now though Lienhardt points out that the Dinka religious images make possible a 'differentiation between experience of the self and of the world which acts upon it' he also points out earlier (1961, p. 149) that the Dinka lack anything closely resembling our conception of the '"mind"', as mediating and, as it were, storing up the experiences of the self'. In fact, aspects of what we would attribute to the self are 'imaged' among the divine Powers. Again if Lienhardt is describing something rather general, and I think there is every reason to believe he is, then religious symbolization relating man to the ultimate conditions of his existence is also involved in relating him to himself and in symbolizing his own identity.[4]

Granted then that religious symbolization is concerned with imaging the ultimate conditions of existence, whether external or internal, we should examine at each stage the kind of symbol

3. One might argue that it was language and not religion that gave man the capacity to dominate his environment symbolically, but this seems to be a false distinction. It is very unlikely that language came into existence 'first' and that men then 'thought up' religion. Rather we would suppose that religion in the sense of this paper was from the beginning a major element in the *content* of linguistic symbolization. Clearly the relations between language and religion are very important and require much more systematic investigation.

4. This notion was first clearly expressed to me in conversation and in unpublished writings by Eli Sagan.

system involved, the kind of religious action it stimulates, the kind of social organization in which this religious action occurs and the implications for social action in general that the religious action contains.

Marcel Mauss, criticizing the heterogeneous sources from which Lévy-Bruhl had constructed the notion of primitive thought, suggested that the word primitive be restricted to Australia, which was the only major culture area largely unaffected by the neolithic.[5] That was in 1923. In 1935 Lévy-Bruhl, heeding Mauss's stricture, published a book called *La Mythologie Primitive* in which the data are drawn almost exclusively from Australia and immediately adjacent islands.[6] While Lévy-Bruhl finds material similar to his Australian data in all parts of the world, nowhere else does he find it in as pure a form. The differences between the Australian material and that of other areas are so great that Lévy-Bruhl is tempted to disagree with Durkheim that Australian religion is an elementary form of religion and term it rather 'pre-religion' (1935, p. 217), a temptation which for reasons already indicated I would firmly reject. At any rate, W. E. H. Stanner, by far the most brilliant interpreter of Australian religion in recent years, goes far to confirm the main lines of Lévy-Bruhl's position, without committing himself on the more broadly controversial aspects of the assertions of either Mauss or Lévy-Bruhl (indeed without so much as mentioning them). My description of a primitive stage of religion is a theoretical abstraction, but it is heavily indebted to the work of Lévy-Bruhl and Stanner for its main features.[7]

The *religious symbol system* at the primitive level is characterized

5. In his discussion of Lévy-Bruhl's thesis on primitive mentality, reported in *Bulletin de la Société française de Philosophie*, Séance du 15 Février 1923, 23e année (1923), p. 26.

6. Lévy-Bruhl's (1935 and 1938) were recently praised by Evans-Pritchard as unsurpassed in depth and insight among studies of the structure of primitive thought, in his introduction to the English translation of Robert Hertz (1960), p. 24. These are the only two volumes of Lévy-Bruhl on primitive thought that have not been translated into English.

7. Of Stanner's publications the most relevant are a series of articles published under the general title 'On Aboriginal religion' (1959–63), and 'The Dreaming' (1958). Outside the Australian culture area, the new world provides the most examples of the type of religion I call primitive. Navaho religion, for example, conforms closely to the type.

by Lévy-Bruhl as '*le monde mythique*', and Stanner directly translates the Australian's own word for it as 'the Dreaming'. The Dreaming is a time out of time, or in Stanner's words, 'everywhen', inhabited by ancestral figures, some human, some animal (Stanner, 1958, p. 514). Though they are often of heroic proportions and have capacities beyond those of ordinary men as well as being the progenitors and creators of many particular things in the world, they are not gods, for they do not control the world and are not worshipped.[8]

Two main features of this mythical world of primitive religion are important for the purposes of the present theoretical scheme. The first is the very high degree to which the mythical world is related to the detailed features of the actual world. Not only is every clan and local group defined in terms of the ancestral progenitors and the mythical events of settlement, but virtually every mountain, rock and tree is explained in terms of the actions of mythical beings. All human action is prefigured in the Dreaming, including crimes and folly, so that actual existence and the paradigmatic myths are related in the most intimate possible way. The second main feature, not unrelated to the extreme particularity of the mythical material, is the fluidity of its organization. Lienhardt, though describing a religion of a somewhat different type, catches the essentially free-associational nature of primitive myth when he says:

We meet here the typical lack of precise definition of the Dinka when they speak of divinities. As Garang, which is the name of the first man, is sometimes associated with the first man and sometimes said to be quite different, so Deng may in some sense be associated with anyone called Deng, and the Dinka connect or do not connect usages of the same name in different contexts according to their individual lights and to what they consider appropriate at any given moment (Lienhardt, 1961, p. 91).

The fluid structure of the myth is almost consciously indicated by the Australians in their use of the word Dreaming: this is

8. This is a controversial point. For extensive bibliography, see Eliade (1958), p. 112. Eliade tends to accept the notion of high gods in Australia but Stanner (1958, p. 518) says of the two figures most often cited as high gods: 'Not even by straining can one see in such culture heroes as Baiame and Darumulum the true hint of a Yahveh, jealous, omniscient and omnipotent.'

not purely metaphorical, for as Ronald Berndt (1951, pp. 71–84) has shown in a careful study, men do actually have a propensity to dream during the periods of cult performance. Through the dreams they reshape the cult symbolism for private psychic ends and what is even more interesting, dreams may actually lead to a reinterpretation in myth which in turn causes a ritual innovation. Both the particularity and the fluidity, then, help account for the hovering closeness of the world of myth to the actual world. A sense of gap, that things are not all they might be, is there but it is hardly experienced as tragic and is indeed on the verge of being comic (Stanner, 1959, p. 126; Lienhardt, 1961, p. 53).

Primitive *religious action* is characterized not, as we have said by worship, nor, as we shall see by sacrifice, but by identification, 'participation', acting-out. Just as the primitive symbol system is myth *par excellence*, so primitive religious action is ritual *par excellence*. In the ritual the participants become identified with the mythical beings they represent. The mythical beings are not addressed or propitiated or beseeched. The distance between man and mythical being, which was at best slight, disappears altogether in the moment of ritual when everywhen becomes now. There are no priests and no congregation, no mediating representative roles and no spectators. All present are involved in the ritual action itself and have become one with the myth.

The underlying structure of ritual, which in Australia always has themes related to initiation, is remarkably similar to that of sacrifice. The four basic movements of the ritual as analysed by Stanner are offering, destruction, transformation and return-communion.[9] Through acting out the mistakes and sufferings of the paradigmatic mythical hero, the new initiates come to terms symbolically with, again in Stanner's words, the 'immemorial misdirection' of human life. Their former innocence is destroyed and they are transformed into new identities now more able to 'assent to life, as it is, without morbidity'.[10] In a sense the whole

9. Stanner (1959), p. 118. The Navaho ritual system is based on the same principles and also stresses the initiation theme. See Spencer (1957). A very similar four act structure has been discerned in the Christian eucharist by Dix (1943).

10. Stanner (1960), p. 278. Of ritual Stanner says, 'Personality may almost be seen to change under one's eyes' (p. 126).

gamut of the spiritual life is already visible in the Australian ritual. Yet the symbolism is so compact that there is almost no element of choice, will or responsibility. The religious life is as given and as fixed as the routines of daily living.

At the primitive level *religious organization* as a separate social structure does not exist. Church and society are one. Religious roles tend to be fused with other roles, and differentiations along lines of age, sex and kin group are important. While women are not as excluded from the religious life as male ethnographers once believed, their ritual life is to some degree separate and focused on particularly feminine life crises (Berndt, 1950). In most primitive societies age is an important criterion for leadership in the ceremonial life. Ceremonies are often handed down in particular moieties and clans, as is only natural when the myths are so largely concerned with ancestors. Specialized shamans or medicine men are found in some tribes but are not a necessary feature of primitive religion.

As for the *social implications* of primitive religion, Durkheim's (1947) analysis seems still to be largely acceptable. The ritual life does reinforce the solidarity of the society and serves to induct the young into the norms of tribal behavior. We should not forget the innovative aspects of primitive religion, that particular myths and ceremonies are in a process of constant revision and alteration, and that in the face of severe historic crisis rather remarkable reformulations of primitive material can be made (Wallace, 1956). Yet on the whole the religious life is the strongest reinforcement of the basic tenet of Australian philosophy, namely that life, as Stanner puts it, is a 'one possibility thing'. The very fluidity and flexibility of primitive religion is a barrier to radical innovation. Primitive religion gives little leverage from which to change the world.

Archaic Religion

For purposes of the present conceptual scheme, as I have indicated, I am using primitive religion in an unusually restricted sense. Much that is usually classified as primitive religion would fall in my second category, archaic religion, which includes the religious systems of much of Africa and Polynesia and some of the

New World, as well as the earliest religious systems of the ancient Middle East, India and China. The characteristic feature of archaic religion is the emergence of true cult with the complex of gods, priests, worship, sacrifice and in some cases divine or priestly kingship. The myth and ritual complex characteristic of primitive religion continues within the structure of archaic religion but it is systematized and elaborated in new ways.

In the archaic *religious symbol system* mythical beings are much more definitely characterized. Instead of being great paradigmatic figures with whom men in ritual identify but with whom they do not really interact, the mythical beings are more objectified, conceived as actively and sometimes willfully controlling the natural and human world, and as beings with whom men must deal in a definite and purposive way – in a word they have become gods. Relations among the gods are a matter of considerable speculation and systematization, so that definite principles of organization, especially hierarchies of control, are established. The basic world view is still, like the primitives', monistic. There is still only one world with gods dominating particular parts of it, especially important being the high gods of the heavenly regions whose vision, knowledge and power may be conceived as very extensive indeed (Pettazzoni, 1956). But though the world is one it is far more differentiated, especially in a hierarchical way, than was the monistic world view of the primitives: archaic religions tend to elaborate a vast cosmology in which all things divine and natural have a place. Much of the particularity and fluidity characteristic of primitive myth is still to be found in archaic religious thinking. But where priestly roles have become well established a relatively stable symbolic structure may be worked out and transmitted over an extended period of time. Especially where at least craft literacy[11] has been attained, the mythical tradition may become the object of critical reflection and innovative speculation which can lead to new developments beyond the nature of archaic religion.

11. By 'craft literacy' I mean the situation in which literacy is limited to specially trained scribes and is not a capacity generally shared by the upper-status group. For an interesting discussion of the development of literacy in ancient Greece see Havelock (1963).

Archaic *religious action* takes the form of cult in which the distinction between men as subjects and gods as objects is much more definite than in primitive religion. Because the division is sharper the need for a communication system through which gods and men can interact is much more acute. Worship and especially sacrifice are precisely such communication systems, as Henri Hubert and Marcel Mauss (1899) so brilliantly established in their great essay on sacrifice. There is no space here for a technical analysis of the sacrificial process (see Evans-Pritchard, 1956, chs. 8–11; Lienhardt, 1961, chs. 7 and 8); suffice it to say that a double identification of priest and victim with both gods and men effects a transformation of motives comparable to that referred to in the discussion of primitive religious action. The main difference is that instead of a relatively passive identification in an all-encompassing ritual action, the sacrificial process no matter how stereotyped permits the human communicants a greater element of intentionality and entails more uncertainty relative to the divine response. Through this more differentiated form of religious action a new degree of freedom as well, perhaps, as an increased burden of anxiety enters the relations between man and the ultimate conditions of his existence.

Archaic *religious organization* is still by and large merged with other social structures, but the proliferation of functionally and hierarchically differentiated groups leads to a multiplication of cults, since every group in archaic society tends to have its cultic aspect. The emergence of a two-class system, itself related to the increasing density of population made possible by agriculture, has its religious aspect. The upper-status group, which tends to monopolize political and military power, usually claims a superior religious status as well. Noble families are proud of their divine descent and often have special priestly functions. The divine king who is the chief link between his people and the gods is only the extreme case of the general tendency of archaic societies. Specialized priesthoods attached to cult centers may differentiate out but are usually kept subordinate to the political élite, which at this stage never completely divests itself of religious leadership. Occasionally priesthoods at cult centers located interstitially relative to political units – for example Delphi in ancient Greece – may come to exercise a certain independence.

The most significant limitation on archaic religious organization is the failure to develop differentiated religious collectivities including adherents as well as priests. The cult centers provide facilities for sacrifice and worship to an essentially transient clientele which is not itself organized as a collectivity, even though the priesthood itself may be rather tightly organized. The appearance of mystery cults and related religious confraternities in the ancient world is usually related to a reorganization of the religious symbol and action systems which indicates a transition to the next main type of religious structure.

The *social implications* of archaic religion are to some extent similar to those of primitive religion. The individual and his society are seen as merged in a natural divine cosmos. Traditional structures and social practices are considered to be grounded in the divinely instituted cosmic order and there is little tension between religious demand and social conformity. Indeed, social conformity is at every point reinforced with religious sanction. Nevertheless the very notion of well-characterized gods acting over against men with a certain freedom introduces an element of openness that is less apparent at the primitive level. The struggle between rival groups may be interpreted as the struggle between rival deities or as a deity's change of favor from one group to another. Through the problems posed by religious rationalization of political change new modes of religious thinking may open up. This is clearly an important aspect of the early history of Israel, and it occurred in many other cases as well. The Greek preoccupation with the relation of the gods to the events of the Trojan War gave rise to a continuous deepening of religious thought from Homer to Euripides. In ancient China the attempt of the Chou to rationalize their conquest of the Shang led to an entirely new conception of the relation between human merit and divine favor. The breakdown of internal order led to messianic expectations of the coming of a savior king in such distant areas as Egypt on the one hand and Chou-period China on the other. These are but a few of the ways in which the problems of maintaining archaic religious symbolization in increasingly complex societies drove toward solutions that began to place the archaic pattern itself in jeopardy.

Historic Religion

The next stage in this theoretical scheme is called historic simply because the religions included are all relatively recent; they emerged in societies that were more or less literate and so have fallen chiefly under the discipline of history rather than that of archaeology or ethnography. The criterion that distinguishes the historic religions from the archaic is that the historic religions are all in some sense transcendental. The cosmological monism of the earlier stage is now more or less completely broken through and an entirely different realm of universal reality, having for religious man the highest value, is proclaimed. The discovery of an entirely different realm of religious reality seems to imply a derogation of the value of the given empirical cosmos: at any rate the world rejection discussed above is, in this stage for the first time, a general characteristic of the religious system.

The *symbol systems* of the historic religions differ greatly among themselves but share the element of transcendentalism which sets them off from the archaic religions; in this sense they are all dualistic. The strong emphasis on hierarchical ordering characteristic of archaic religions continues to be stressed in most of the historic religions. Not only is the supernatural realm 'above' this world in terms of both value and control but both the supernatural and earthly worlds are themselves organized in terms of a religiously legitimated hierarchy. For the masses, at least, the new dualism is above all expressed in the difference between this world and the life after death. Religious concern, focused on this life in primitive and archaic religions, now tends to focus on life in the other realm, which may be either infinitely superior or, under certain circumstances, with the emergence of various conceptions of hell, infinitely worse. Under these circumstances the religious goal of salvation (or enlightenment, release and so forth) is for the first time the central religious preoccupation.

In one sense historic religions represent a great 'demythologization' relative to archaic religions. The notion of the one God who has neither court nor relatives, who has no myth himself and who is the sole creator and ruler of the universe, the notion of self-subsistent being, or of release from the cycle of birth and rebirth, are all enormous simplifications of the ramified cosmologies of archaic religions. Yet all the historic religions have, to use Voegelin's term, mortgages imposed on them by the historical circumstances of their origin. All of them contain, in suspension as it were, elements of archaic cosmology alongside their transcendental assertions. Nonetheless, relative to earlier forms the historic religions are all universalistic. From the point of view of these religions a man is no longer defined chiefly in terms of what tribe or clan he comes from or what particular god he serves but rather as a being capable of salvation. That is to say that it is for the first time possible to conceive of man as such.

Religious action in the historic religions is thus above all action necessary for salvation. Even where elements of ritual and sacrifice remain prominent they take on a new significance. In primitive ritual the individual is put in harmony with the natural divine cosmos. His mistakes are overcome through symbolization as part of the total pattern. Through sacrifice archaic man can make up for his failures to fulfill his obligations to men or gods. He can atone for particular acts of unfaithfulness. But historic religion convicts man of a basic flaw far more serious than those conceived of by earlier religions. According to Buddhism, man's very nature is greed and anger from which he must seek a total escape. For the Hebrew prophets, man's sin is not particular wicked deeds but his profound heedlessness of God, and only a turn to complete obedience will be acceptable to the Lord. For Muhammad the *kafir* is not, as we usually translate, the 'unbeliever' but rather the ungrateful man who is careless of the divine compassion. For him, only Islam, willing submission to the will of God, can bring salvation.

The identity diffusion characteristic of both primitive and archaic religions is radically challenged by the historic religious symbolization, which leads for the first time to a clearly structured conception of the self. Devaluation of the empirical world and the empirical self highlights the conception of a responsible self, a core self or a true self, deeper than the flux of everyday experience, facing a reality over against itself, a reality which has a consistency belied by the fluctuations of mere sensory impressions.[12] Primitive man can only accept the world in its manifold givenness. Archaic man can through sacrifice fulfill his religious obligations and attain peace with the gods. But the historic religions promise man for the first time that he can understand the fundamental structure of reality and through salvation participate actively in it. The opportunity is far greater than before but so is the risk of failure.

Perhaps partly because of the profound risks involved the ideal of the religious life in the historic religions tends to be one of separation from the world. Even when, as in the case of Judaism and Islam, the religion enjoins types of worldly participation that are considered unacceptable or at least doubtful in some other historic religions, the devout are still set apart from ordinary worldlings by the massive collections of rules and obligations to which they must adhere. The early Christian solution, which, unlike the Buddhist, did allow the full possibility of salvation to the layman, nevertheless in its notion of a special state of religious perfection idealized religious withdrawal from the world. In fact the standard for lay piety tended to be closeness of approximation to the life of the religious.

Historic religion is associated with the emergence of differentiated religious collectivities as the chief characteristic of its *religious organization*. The profound dualism with respect to the conception of reality is also expressed in the social realm. The single religio-political hierarchy of archaic society tends to split into two at least partially independent hierarchies, one political and one religious. Together with the notion of a transcendent realm beyond the natural cosmos comes a new religious élite that claims direct relation to the transmundane world.

12. Buddhism, with its doctrine of the ultimate non-existence of the self, seemed to be an exception to this generalization, but for practical and ethical purposes, at least, a distinction between the true self and the empirical self is made by all schools of Buddhism. Some schools of Mahayana Buddhism give a metaphysical basis to a notion of 'basic self' or 'great self' as opposed to the merely selfish self caught up in transience and desire. Further it would seem that *nirvana*, defined negatively so as rigorously to exclude any possibility of transience or change, serves fundamentally as an identity symbol. Of course the social and psychological consequences of this kind of identity symbol are very different from those following from other types of identity symbolization.

Even though notions of divine kingship linger on for a very long time in various compromise forms, it is no longer possible for a divine king to monopolize religious leadership. With the emergence of a religious élite alongside the political one the problem of legitimizing political power enters a new phase. Legitimation now rests upon a delicate balance of forces between the political and religious leadership. But the differentiation between religious and political that exists most clearly at the level of leadership tends also to be pushed down into the masses so that the roles of believer and subject become distinct. Even where, as in the case of Islam, this distinction was not supported by religious norms it was soon recognized as an actuality.

The emergence of the historic religions is part of a general shift from the two-class system of the archaic period to the four-class system characteristic of all the great historic civilizations up to modern times: a political–military élite, a cultural–religious élite, a rural lower-status group (peasantry) and an urban lower-status group (merchants and artisans). Closely associated with the new religious developments was the growth of literacy among the élite groups and in the upper segments of the urban lower class. Other social changes, such as the growth in the market resulting from the first widespread use of coinage, the development of bureaucracy and law as well as new levels of urbanization, are less directly associated with religion but are part of the same great transformation that got underway in the first millennium B.C. The distinction between religious and political élites applies to some extent to the two great lower strata. From the point of view of the historic religions the peasantry long remained relatively intractable and were often considered religiously second-class citizens, their predilection for cosmological symbolization rendering them always to some degree religiously suspect. The notion of the peasant as truly religious is a fairly modern idea. On the contrary it was the townsman who was much more likely to be numbered among the devout, and Max Weber has pointed out the great fecundity of the urban middle strata in religious innovations throughout the several great historical traditions (Weber, 1963, pp. 95–8). Such groups developed new symbolizations that sometimes threatened the structure of the historic religions in their early form, and in the one case where a

279

new stage of religious symbolization was finally achieved they made important contributions.

The *social implications* of the historic religions are implicit in the remarks on religious organization. The differentiation of a religious élite brought a new level of tension and a new possibility of conflict and change onto the social scene. Whether the confrontation was between Israelite prophet and king, Islamic ulama and sultan, Christian pope and emperor or even between Confucian scholar-official and his ruler, it implied that political acts could be judged in terms of standards that the political authorities could not finally control. The degree to which these confrontations had serious social consequences of course depended on the degree to which the religious group was structurally independent and could exert real pressure. S. N. Eisenstadt (1962) has made a comprehensive survey of these differences; for our purposes it is enough to note that they were nowhere entirely absent. Religion, then, provided the ideology and social cohesion for many rebellions and reform movements in the historic civilizations, and consequently played a more dynamic and especially a more purposive role in social change than had previously been possible. On the other hand, we should not forget that in most of the historic civilizations for long periods of time religion performed the functions we have noted from the beginning: legitimation and reinforcement of the existing social order.

Early Modern Religion

In all previous stages the ideal type was based on a variety of actual cases. Now for the first time it derives from a single case or at best a congeries of related cases, namely, the Protestant Reformation. The defining characteristic of early modern religion is the collapse of the hierarchical structuring of both this and the other world. The dualism of the historic religions remains as a feature of early modern religion but takes on a new significance in the context of more direct confrontation between the two worlds. Under the new circumstances salvation is not to be found in any kind of withdrawal from the world but in the midst of worldly activities. Of course elements of this existed in the historic religions from the beginning, but on the whole the historic religions as institutionalized had offered a mediated salvation. Either conformity to religious law, or participation in a sacramental system or performance of mystical exercises was necessary for salvation. All of these to some extent involved a turning away from the world. Further, in the religious two-class systems characteristic of the institutionalized historic religions the upper-status groups, the Christian monks or Sufi shaykhs or Buddhist ascetics, could through their pure acts and personal charisma store up a fund of grace that could then be shared with the less worthy. In this way too salvation was mediated rather than immediate. What the Reformation did was in principle, with the usual reservations and mortgages to the past, break through the whole mediated system of salvation and declared salvation potentially available to any man no matter what his station or calling might be.

Since immediate salvation seems implicit in all the historic religions it is not surprising that similar reform movements exist in other traditions, notably Shinran Shonin's version of Pure Land Buddhism, but also certain tendencies in Islam, Buddhism, Taoism and Confucianism. But the Protestant Reformation is the only attempt that was successfully institutionalized. In the case of Taoism and Confucianism the mortgage of archaic symbolization was so heavy that what seemed a new breakthrough easily became regressive. In the other cases, notably in the case of the Jōdo Shinshū, the radical implications were not sustained and a religion of mediated salvation soon reasserted itself. Religious movements of early modern type may be emerging in a number of the great traditions today, perhaps even in the Vatican Council, and there are also secular movements with features strongly analogous to what I call early modern religion. But all of these tendencies are too uncertain to rely on in constructing an ideal type.

Early modern *religious symbolism* concentrates on the direct relation between the individual and transcendent reality. A great deal of the cosmological baggage of medieval Christianity is dropped as superstition. The fundamentally ritualist interpretation of the sacrament of the Eucharist as a re-enactment of the paradigmatic sacrifice is replaced with the anti-ritualist interpretation of the Eucharist as a commemoration of a once-and-for-all historical event. Even though in one sense the world is more devalued in early Protestantism than in medieval Christianity, since the reformers re-emphasized the radical separation between divine and human, still by proclaiming the world as the theater of God's glory and the place wherein to fulfill his command, the Reformation reinforced positive autonomous action in the world instead of a relatively passive acceptance of it.

Religious action was now conceived to be identical with the whole of life. Special ascetic and devotional practices were dropped as well as the monastic roles that specialized in them and instead the service of God became a total demand in every walk of life. The stress was on faith, an internal quality of the person, rather than on particular acts clearly marked 'religious'. In this respect the process of identity unification that I have designated as a central feature of the historic religions advanced still further. The complex requirements for the attainment of salvation in the historic religions, though ideally they encouraged identity unification, could themselves become a new form of identity diffusion, as Luther and Shinran were aware. Assertion of the capacity for faith as an already received gift made it possible to undercut that difficulty. It also made it necessary to accept the ambiguity of human ethical life and the fact that salvation comes in spite of sin, not in its absolute absence. With the acceptance of the world not as it is but as a valid arena in which to work out the divine command, and with the acceptance of the self as capable of faith in spite of sin, the Reformation made it possible to turn away from world rejection in a way not possible in the historic religions. All of this was possible, however, only within the structure of a rigid orthodoxy and a tight though voluntaristic religious group.

I have already noted that early modern religion abandoned hierarchy as an essential dimension of its religious symbol system.[13] It did the same in its *religious organization*. Not only

13. God, of course, remains hierarchically superior to man, but the complex stratified structure of which purgatory, saints, angels and so on, are elements is eliminated. Also, the strong reassertion of covenant thinking brought a kind of formal equality into the God–man relation without eliminating the element of hierarchy. Strictly speaking then, early modern (and modern) religion does not abandon the idea of hierarchy as such, but

did it reject papal authority, but it also rejected the old form of the religious distinction between two levels of relative religious perfection. This was replaced with a new kind of religious two-class system: the division between elect and reprobates. The new form differed from the old one in that the elect were really a vanguard group in the fulfillment of the divine plan rather than a qualitative religious élite. The political implications of Protestantism had much to do with the overthrow of the old conception of hierarchy in the secular field as well. Where Calvinistic Protestantism was powerful, hereditary aristocracy and kingship were either greatly weakened or abandoned. In fact the Reformation is part of the general process of social change in which the four-class system of peasant societies began to break up in Europe. Especially in the Anglo-Saxon world, Protestantism greatly contributed to its replacement by a more flexible multi-centered mode of social organization based more on contract and voluntary association. Both church and state lost some of the reified significance they had in medieval times and later on the continent. The roles of church member and citizen were but two among several. Both church and state had their delimited spheres of authority, but with the full institutionalization of the common law neither had a right to dominate each other or the whole of society. Nonetheless, the church acted for a long time as a sort of cultural and ethical holding company, and many developments in philosophy, literature and social welfare took their initiative from clerical or church groups.[14]

The *social implications* of the Protestant Reformation are among the more debated subjects of contemporary social science.

retains it in a much more flexible form, relative to particular contexts, and closely related to new emphases on equality. What is abandoned is rather a single overarching hierarchy, summed up in the symbol of the great chain of being.

14. Of course, important developments in modern culture stemming from the recovery of Classical art and philosophy in the Renaissance took place outside the main stream of religious development. However, the deep inter-relations between religious and secular components of the Renaissance should not be overlooked. Certainly the clergy in the Anglo-Saxon world were among the foremost guardians of the Classical tradition in literature and thought. The most tangible expression of this was the close relation of higher education to the church, a relation which was not seriously weakened until the late nineteenth century in America.

Lacking space to defend my assertions, let me simply say that I stand by Weber, Merton *et al.*, in attributing very great significance to the Reformation, especially in its Calvinistic wing, in a whole series of developments from economics to science, from education to law. Whereas in most of the historic civilizations religion stands as virtually the only stable challenger to the dominance of the political élite, in the emerging early modern society religious impulses give rise to a variety of institutional structures, from the beginning or very soon becoming fully secular, which stand beside and to some extent compete with and limit the state. The direct religious response to political and moral problems does not disappear but the impact of religious orientations on society is also mediated by a variety of worldly institutions in which religious values have been expressed. Weber's critics, frequently assuming a pre-modern model of the relation between religion and society, have often failed to understand the subtle interconnexions he was tracing. But the contrast with the historic stage, when pressures toward social change in the direction of value realization were sporadic and often Utopian, is decisive.

In the early modern stage for the first time pressures to social change in the direction of greater realization of religious values are actually institutionalized as part of the structure of the society itself. The self-revising social order expressed in a voluntaristic and democratic society can be seen as just such an outcome. The earliest phase of this development, especially the several examples of Calvinist commonwealths, was voluntaristic only within the elect vanguard group and otherwise was often illiberal and even dictatorial. The transition toward a more completely democratic society was complex and subject to many blockages. Close analogies to the early modern situation occur in many of the contemporary developing countries, which are trying for the first time to construct social systems with a built-in tendency to change in the direction of greater value realization. The leadership of these countries varies widely between several kinds of vanguard revolutionary movements with distinctly illiberal proclivities to élites committed to the implementation of a later, more democratic, model of Western political society.

Modern Religion

I am not sure whether in the long run what I call early modern religion will appear as a stage with the same degree of distinctness as the others I have distinguished or whether it will appear only as a transitional phase, but I am reasonably sure that, even though we must speak from the midst of it, the modern situation represents a stage of religious development in many ways profoundly different from that of historic religion. The central feature of the change is the collapse of the dualism that was so crucial to all the historic religions.

It is difficult to speak of a *modern religious symbol system*. It is indeed an open question whether there can be a religious symbol system analogous to any of the preceding ones in the modern situation, which is characterized by a deepening analysis of the very nature of symbolization itself. At the highest intellectual level I would trace the fundamental break with traditional historic symbolization to the work of Kant. By revealing the problematic nature of the traditional metaphysical basis of all the religions and by indicating that it is not so much a question of two worlds as it is of as many worlds as there are modes of apprehending them, he placed the whole religious problem in a new light. However simple the immediate result of his grounding religion in the structure of ethical life rather than in a metaphysics claiming cognitive adequacy, it nonetheless pointed decisively in the direction that modern religion would go. The entire modern analysis of religion, including much of the most important recent theology, though rejecting Kant's narrowly rational ethics, has been forced to ground religion in the structure of the human situation itself. In this respect the present paper is a symptom of the modern religious situation as well as an analysis of it. In the world view that has emerged from the tremendous intellectual advances of the last two centuries there is simply no room for a hierarchic dualistic religious symbol system of the classical historic type. This is not to be interpreted as a return to primitive monism: it is not that a single world has replaced a double one but that an infinitely multiplex one has replaced the simple duplex structure. It is not that life has become again a 'one possibility thing' but that it has become an infinite possibility thing. The analysis of modern man as secular, materialistic, dehumanized and in the deepest sense areligious seems to me fundamentally misguided, for such a judgement is based on standards that cannot adequately gauge the modern temper.

Though it is central to the problems of modern religion, space forbids a review of the development of the modern analysis of religion on its scholarly and scientific side. I shall confine myself to some brief comments on directions of development within Protestant theology. In many respects Schliermacher is the key figure in early nineteenth-century theology who saw the deeper implications of the Kantian breakthrough. The development of 'liberal theology' in the later nineteenth century, partly on the basis of Schliermacher's beginnings, tended to fall back into Kant's overly rational limitations. Against this, Barth's reassertion of the power of the traditional symbolism was bound to produce a vigorous response, but unfortunately, due to Barth's own profound ambiguity on the ultimate status of dogma, the consequences were in part simply a regressive reassertion of the adequacy of the early modern theological formulation. By the middle of the twentieth century, however, the deeper implications of Schliermacher's attempt were being developed in various ways by such diverse figures as Tillich (e.g. 1952), Bultmann (e.g. Jaspers and Bultmann, 1958) and Bonhoeffer (1954). Tillich's assertion of 'ecstatic naturalism', Bultmann's program of 'demythologization' and Bonhoeffer's search for a 'religionless Christianity', though they cannot be simply equated with each other are efforts to come to terms with the modern situation. Even on the Catholic side the situation is beginning to be recognized.

Interestingly enough, indications of the same general search for an entirely new mode of religious symbolization, though mostly confined to the Protestant West, also appear in that most developed of the non-Western countries, Japan. Uchimura Kanzō's non-church Christianity was a relatively early indication of a search for new directions and is being developed even further today. Even more interesting perhaps is the emergence of a similar development out of the Jōdo Shinshū tradition, at least in the person of Ienaga Saburo (see Bellah, 1964). This example indeed suggests that highly 'modern' implications exist in more than one strand of Mahayana Buddhism and perhaps several of the other great traditions as well. Although in my opinion these implications were never developed sufficiently to dominate a historical epoch as they did in the West in the last two centuries, they may well prove decisive in the future of these religions.

So far what I have been saying applies mainly to intellectuals, but at least some evidence indicates that changes are also occurring at the level of mass religiosity.[15] Behind the 96 per cent of Americans who claim to believe in God (Herberg, 1955, p. 72) there are many instances of a massive reinterpretation that leaves Tillich, Bultmann and Bonhoeffer far behind. In fact, for many churchgoers the obligation of doctrinal orthodoxy sits lightly indeed, and the idea that all creedal statements must receive a personal reinterpretation is widely accepted. The dualistic world view certainly persists in the minds of many of the devout, but just as surely many others have developed elaborate and often pseudoscientific rationalizations to bring their faith in its experienced validity into some kind of cognitive harmony with the twentieth-century world. The wave of popular response that some of the newer theology seems to be eliciting is another indication that not only the intellectuals find themselves in a new religious situation.[16]

To concentrate on the church in a discussion of the modern religious situation is already misleading, for it is precisely the characteristic of the new situation that the great problem of religion as I have defined it, the symbolization of man's relation to the ultimate conditions of his existence, is no longer the monopoly of any groups explicitly labelled religious. However much the development of Western Christianity may have led up to and

15. There are a few scattered studies such as Gordon Allport, James Gillespie and Jacqueline Young (1948), but the subject does not lend itself well to investigation via questionnaires and brief interviews. Richard V. McCann (1955), utilized a much subtler approach involving depth interviewing and discovered a great deal of innovative reinterpretation in people from all walks of life. Unfortunately lack of control of sampling makes it impossible to generalize his results.

16. Bishop Robinson's (1963) volume which states in straightforward language the positions of some of the recent Protestant theologians mentioned above, has sold (by November 1963) over 300,000 copies in England and over 71,000 in the United States with another 50,000 on order, and this in the first few months after publication. (Reported in *Christianity and Crisis*, vol. 23, 1963, p. 201.)

in a sense created the modern religious situation, it just as obviously is no longer in control of it. Not only has any obligation of doctrinal orthodoxy been abandoned by the leading edge of modern culture, but every fixed position has become open to question in the process of making sense out of man and his situation. This involves a profounder commitment to the process I have been calling religious symbolization than ever before. The historic religions discovered the self; the early modern religion found a doctrinal basis on which to accept the self in all its empirical ambiguity; modern religion is beginning to understand the laws of the self's own existence and so to help man take responsibility for his own fate.

This statement is not intended to imply a simple liberal optimism, for the modern analysis of man has also disclosed the depths of the limitations imposed by man's situation. Nevertheless, the fundamental symbolization of modern man and his situation is that of a dynamic multi-dimensional self capable, within limits, of continual self-transformation and capable, again within limits, of remaking the world including the very symbolic forms with which he deals with it, even the forms that state the unalterable conditions of his own existence. Such a statement should not be taken to mean that I expect, even less that I advocate, some ghastly religion of social science. Rather I expect traditional religious symbolism to be maintained and developed in new directions, but with growing awareness that it is symbolism and that man in the last analysis is responsible for the choice of his symbolism. Naturally, continuation of the symbolization characteristic of earlier stages without any reinterpretation is to be expected among many in the modern world, just as it has occurred in every previous period.

Religious action in the modern period is, I think, clearly a continuation of tendencies already evident in the early modern stage. Now less than ever can man's search for meaning be confined to the church. But with the collapse of a clearly defined doctrinal orthodoxy and a religiously supported objective system of moral standards, religious action in the world becomes more demanding than ever. The search for adequate standards of action, which is at the same time a search for personal maturity and social relevance, is in itself the heart of the modern quest for salvation, if I may divest that word of its dualistic associations. How the specifically religious bodies are to adjust their time-honored practices of worship and devotion to modern conditions is of growing concern in religious circles. Such diverse movements as the liturgical revival, pastoral psychology and renewed emphasis on social action are all efforts to meet the present need. Few of these trends have gotten much beyond the experimental but we can expect the experiments to continue.

In the modern situation as I have defined it, one might almost be tempted to see in Thomas Paine's 'My mind is my church', or Thomas Jefferson's 'I am a sect myself' the typical expression of *religious organization* in the near future. Nonetheless it seems unlikely that collective symbolization of the great inescapabilities of life will soon disappear. Of course the 'free intellectual' will continue to exist as he has for millennia but such a solution can hardly be very general. Private voluntary religious association in the West achieved full legitimation for the first time in the early modern situation, but in the early stages especially, discipline and control within these groups was very intense. The tendency in more recent periods has been to continue the basic pattern but with a much more open and flexible pattern of membership. In accord with general trends I have already discussed, standards of doctrinal orthodoxy and attempts to enforce moral purity have largely been dropped. The assumption in most of the major Protestant denominations is that the church member can be considered responsible for himself. This trend seems likely to continue, with an increasingly fluid type of organization in which many special purpose subgroups form and disband. Rather than interpreting these trends as significant of indifference and secularization, I see in them the increasing acceptance of the notion that each individual must work out his own ultimate solutions and that the most the church can do is provide him a favorable environment for doing so, without imposing on him a prefabricated set of answers.[17] And it will be increasingly realized that answers to religious questions can validly be sought in various spheres of 'secular' art and thought.

Here I can only suggest what I take to be the main *social*

17. The great Protestant stress on thinking for oneself in matters of religion is documented in Lenski (1961), pp. 270–73.

implication of the modern religious situation. Early modern society, to a considerable degree under religious pressure, developed, as we have seen, the notion of a self-revising social system in the form of a democratic society. But at least in the early phase of that development social flexibility was balanced against doctrinal (Protestant orthodoxy) and characterological (Puritan personality) rigidities. In a sense those rigidities were necessary to allow the flexibility to emerge in the social system, but it is the chief characteristic of the more recent modern phase that culture and personality themselves have come to be viewed as endlessly revisable. This has been characterized as a collapse of meaning and a failure of moral standards. No doubt the possibilities for pathological distortion in the modern situation are enormous. It remains to be seen whether the freedom modern society implies at the cultural and personality as well as the social level can be stably institutionalized in large-scale societies. Yet the very situation that has been characterized as one of the collapse of meaning and the failure of moral standards can also, and I would argue more fruitfully, be viewed as one offering unprecedented opportunities for creative innovation in every sphere of human action.

Conclusion

The schematic presentation of the stages of religious evolution just concluded is based on the proposition that at each stage the freedom of personality and society has increased relative to the environing conditions. Freedom has increased because at each successive stage the relation of man to the conditions of his existence has been conceived as more complex, more open and more subject to change and development. The distinction between conditions that are really ultimate and those that are alterable becomes increasingly clear though never complete. Of course this scheme of religious evolution has implied at almost every point a general theory of social evolution, which has had to remain largely implicit.

Let me suggest in closing, as a modest effort at empirical testing, how the evolutionary scheme may help to explain the facts of alternating world acceptance and rejection which were noted near the beginning of the paper. I have argued that the world acceptance of the primitive and archaic levels is largely to be explained as the only possible response to a reality that invades the self to such an extent that the symbolizations of self and world are only very partially separate. The great wave of world rejection of the historic religions I have interpreted as a major advance in what Lienhardt calls 'the differentiation between experience of the self and the world which acts upon it'. Only by withdrawing cathexis from the myriad objects of empirical reality could consciousness of a centered self in relation to an encompassing reality emerge. Early modern religion made it possible to maintain the centered self without denying the multifold empirical reality and so made world rejection in the classical sense unnecessary. In the modern phase knowledge of the laws of the formation of the self, as well as much more about the structure of the world, has opened up almost unlimited new directions of exploration and development. World rejection marks the beginning of a clear objectification of the social order and sharp criticism of it. In the earlier world-accepting phases religious conceptions and social order were so fused that it was almost impossible to criticize the latter from the point of view of the former. In the later phases the possibility of remaking the world to conform to value demands has served in a very different way to mute the extremes of world rejection. The world acceptance of the last two stages is shown in this analysis to have a profoundly different significance from that of the first two.

Construction of a wide-ranging evolutionary scheme like the one presented in this paper is an extremely risky enterprise. Nevertheless such efforts are justifiable if, by throwing light on perplexing developmental problems they contribute to modern man's efforts at self interpretation.

References

ALLPORT, G., GILLESPIE, J. and YOUNG, J. (1948), 'The religion of the post-war college student', *J. Psychol.*, vol. 25, pp. 3–33.

BELLAH, R. N. (1964), 'Ienaga Saburo and the search for meaning in modern Japan', in M. Jansen, ed., *Japanese Attitudes toward Modernization*, Princeton University Press.

BERNDT, C. (1950), *Women's Changing Ceremonies in Northern Australia*, Herman, Paris.

BERNDT, R. (1951), *Kunapipi*, Cheshire, Melbourne.

BONHOEFFER, D. (1954), *Letters and Papers from Prison*, S.C.M. Press.

DE LA SAUSSAYE, C. (1904), *Manuel d'Histoire des Religions*, transl. H. Hubert and I. Lévy, Colin, Paris.

DIX, G. (1943), *The Shape of the Liturgy*, Dacre.

DURKHEIM, E. (1947), *The Elementary Forms of the Religious Life*, Free Press.

EISENSTADT, S. N. (1962), 'Religious organizations and political process in centralized Empires', *J. Asian Stud.*, vol. 21, pp. 271–94.

ELIADE, M. (1958), *Patterns in Comparative Religion*, Sheed Ward.

EVANS-PRITCHARD, E. E. (1956), *Nuer Religion*, Oxford University Press.

GEERTZ, C. (1963), Religion as a cultural system, unpublished.

HAVELOCK, E. (1963), *Preface to Plato*, Harvard University Press.

HERBERG, W. (1955), *Protestant, Catholic, Jew*, Doubleday.

HERTZ, R. (1960), *Death and the Right Hand*, Free Press.

HUBERT, H., and MAUSS, M. (1899), 'Essai sur la nature et la fonction du sacrifice', *L'Année Sociol.*, vol. 2.

JASPERS, K., and BULTMANN, R. (1958), *Myth and Christianity*, Noonday.

LENSKI, G. (1961), *The Religious Factor*, Doubleday.

LÉVY-BRUHL, L. (1935), *La Mythologie Primitive*, Alcan.

LÉVY-BRUHL, L. (1938), *L'Expérience Mystique et les Symboles chez les Primitifs*, Alcan.

LIENHARDT, G. (1961), *Divinity and Experience*, Oxford University Press.

MCCANN, R. V. (1955), The nature and varieties of religious change, *Doctoral Dissertation, Harvard University*.

PETTAZZONI, R. (1956), *The All-Knowing God*, Methuen.

ROBINSON, J. (1963), *Honest to God*, S.C.M. Press.

SABURO, I. (1940), *The Development of the Logic of Negation in the History of Japanese Thought*, Tokyo. (In Japanese.)

SPENCER, K. C. (1957), *Mythology and Values: An Analysis of Navaho Chartway Myths*, American Folklore Society.

STANNER, W. E. H. (1958), 'The Dreaming', in W. Lessa and E. Z. Vogt, eds., *Reader in Comparative Religion*, Row, Peterson.

STANNER, W. E. H. (1959–63), series 'On Aboriginal religion', in *Oceania*, vols. 30–33.

TILLICH, P. (1952), *The Courage to Be*, Yale University Press.

VOEGELIN, E. (1956), *Order and History, Vol. I: Israel and Revelation*, Louisiana State University Press.

WALLACE, A. (1956), 'Revitalization movements', *Amer. Anthrop.*, vol. 58, pp. 764–70.

WEBER, M. (1946), 'Religious rejections of the world and their directions', in H. H. Gerth and C. Wright Mills, eds., *From Max Weber*, Oxford University Press.

WEBER, M. (1963), *The Sociology of Religion*, Beacon.

Part Four **Religion and Social and Cultural Differentiation**

The contributions to this Part deal mainly with special aspects of the sociology of religion. They are either concerned with religion in relation to some specific aspect of the wider society, such as political allegiance, or with some special aspect of religious institutions. Some of the essays focus on complex, industrial societies in which religious belief and practice is markedly differentiated from other sectors of social life, while others deal precisely with situations in which the degree of differentiation of religion from other spheres is low and where specialization within the religious sphere is relatively small. The one possible exception to this general description is Reading 17 by Eisenstadt on the significance of Protestantism in the transformation of Western societies in the period following the sixteenth-century Reformation. This sets the scene, both historically and sociologically, for a number of the subsequent items. Each section is briefly introduced.

I. Religion and Societal Change

Of all the themes dealt with over the years by sociologists of religion, Weber's thesis about the link between Protestantism and the work ethic of capitalist societies is undoubtedly the most well-known. It has been debated by sociologists, historians, religious intellectuals and economists for about sixty years – and the controversy shows little sign of abating. In one sense the debate is largely an historical one. Is there sufficient evidence to confirm that the religious teachings of emergent Protestantism, especially in its Calvinistic forms, had the social consequence of establishing a new orientation to economic activity – an orientation which stressed the sacrosanct virtues of thrift, discipline and careful calculation? For the sociologist the issue is a more general one – revolving around the problem of the degree to which religious ideas may operate as independent sources of motivation and social and cultural innovation. For many years the controversy initiated by Weber focused on these historical and sociological problems mainly in terms of Weber's specific emphasis upon the relationship between religious commitment and the economic orientations and actions of individuals. In recent years, however, attention has shifted to a more comprehensive level of analysis. Sociologists have increasingly discussed such themes as the significance of religious change in effecting reformations in the value systems of societies, the consequences of religious groups being placed in subordinate, minority positions in societies and so on. In Reading 17 Eisenstadt touches upon such themes within the context of exploring the contribution made by Protestantism to changes in the political structure of specific societies. His piece is especially valuable as a synthesis of recent debates and findings.

17 S. N. Eisenstadt

The Protestant Ethic Thesis

Excerpts from S. N. Eisenstadt, 'The Protestant ethic thesis in analytical and comparative context', *Diogenes*, no. 59 (1967), pp. 25–46. (Reprinted in S. N. Eisenstadt, ed., *The Protestant Ethic and Modernization*, Basic Books.)

I

Weber's famous 'Protestant Ethic' thesis – the thesis published originally by him as 'Die Protestantische Ethik und der Geist des Kapitalismus' in *Archiv für Sozialwissenschaft in Sozialpolitik*, in 1904–5 (vols. 10 and 11) and reprinted in his *Gesammelte Aufsätz für Religionssoziologie*, in 1920 (see also Weber, 1930) – which has allegedly attributed the rise of modern, as distinct from pre-modern, types of capitalism[1] to the influence of Protestantism and especially of Calvinism, has provided – probably more than any other single *specific thesis* in the social sciences – a continuous focus of scientific controversy.

This controversy has burst aflame anew in each decade, each generation of scholars seeing in it a continuous challenge. Although in each generation there were those, like Robertson (1933) in the twenties, Fanfani (1934) in the thirties, and Samuelson (1961) in the fifties, who denied it any validity, yet somehow even such denials had to be stressed anew, each generation having to grapple with the fact that so many still attributed to this thesis some central importance in the social sciences in general and in the understanding of modernity in particular.

In the last fifteen years or so, with the upsurge of the great interest in development and modernization beyond Europe, interest in this thesis has arisen once more. Many seek in the existence or non-existence of some equivalent to the Protestant ethic the key to the understanding of the successful or unsuccessful modernization of non-European countries.

In order to be able to understand what it is in this thesis that

1. On Weber's distinction between pre-modern and modern capitalism, see Weber (1961), p. 4.

may be of such critical importance it will be worth while to survey very briefly some of the major stages of the controversy around it, even if it would of course be impossible to present here a complete history of this controversy.

We may very broadly distinguish between two types of controversial arguments with regard to the Weberian thesis, corresponding to some extent, but not entirely, to chronological stages in its development.

The first stage of this controversy, best summarized in Fischoff's (1944) article and in Baerling's (1946) book (see also Tawney, 1956; Elton, 1963, pp. 312 ff.), has mostly, although not entirely, dealt with the analysis of the alleged direct causal connexion between the Protestant–Calvinist ethic on the one hand, and the development of capitalism on the other. At this stage the Weberian thesis was attacked at almost all the quotients of the assumed equation. Some have stressed that most of the initial Calvinist communities – be it Calvin's Geneva itself, the earlier Calvinist communities in the Netherlands, in Scotland or in the Palatinate – did not favor the development of new, more autonomous economic orientations or organizations, that in their manifest attitudes to economic activities they did not go much beyond the more severe medieval Catholic orientations, and that in some respects they were even more conservative and restrictive towards such activities, mainly because of their predilection for the extreme, totalistic religious regulation of all aspects of life which made them take all these matters more seriously than late-medieval Catholicism.

On the other end of the equation it was often stressed that the first great upsurges of capitalism developed in pre-Reformation Catholic Europe – be it in Italy, Belgium or Germany – and that they were much more 'developed' than those in the first Protestant or Calvinist countries. On the contrary, economic retrogression or retardation very often set in in many of these communities, as for instance in Calvin's Geneva, to no small degree due to the restrictive orientations of the Protestant communities mentioned above.

Others have cast doubt on the specific 'mechanism' through which, according to Weber, Calvinist belief became transformed into or linked to motivation for this-worldly economic activities, namely the psychological derivatives of the idea of predestination, the great anxiety which this idea created among believers, urging them to undertake in a compulsive way this-worldly activities to prove their being of the elect.

While some tended to cast doubt on the very relevance of any aspect of Calvinist religious orientation for the development of modern frameworks and activities, others like Hudson (1949, 1961) and lately the Georges (1958, 1961) have tended to point to other orientations in the Calvinist *Weltanschauung*, such as the emphasis on individual responsibility, on the general orientation to 'this world' (as against the 'other-worldly' orientation of many other religions), as well as the general shattering of the traditional *Weltanschauung*, as possible ways or mechanisms through which the Protestant, Calvinist Puritan or Denominational outlook could facilitate the development of modernity.[2]

Others who admitted the 'predilection' of Protestantism for various aspects of the 'modern' world – be it economic, scientific or modern political activities – tended to attribute this predilection to structural situations and exigencies within which Protestantism was put as a result of the wars of religion or the Counter-Reformation, to its being in a minority position in these countries, or to the indirect impact of Protestantism on the over-all institutional structure of these countries in the direction of growing pluralism and tolerance. They often did stress that the tendency of many Protestant groups – Huguenots in France or in exile, Protestant sects in Holland and England – to participate more actively than their Catholic or even Lutheran neighbors in modern capitalistic activities developed, usually later, in the seventeenth to eighteenth centuries, and that it was very often due to reasons which had but little to do with the original Calvinist belief but was mostly related to such factors as persecution, forced emigration and exile and denial of possibilities of participation in central politics and cultural spheres.

Still others tended to emphasize that the tendencies of Protestants to participate in these activities were later developments, not necessarily typical of the mainstream of Calvinism or Protestantism, but more characteristic of its transition into a more

2. In this vein, see also the older works of Hauser (1963). Several of the relevant studies can be found in Green (1959).

pluralistic, tolerant, semi-secularized world and of the decline of its strong religious commitments than of its own initial inherent religious tendencies. For these writers it was often the *weakening* of the original totalistic religious impulses of the Puritans that provides the basic link between Protestants and modernity.

Tawney's (1926) classical study, which was intended as a sympathetic defense of Weber's thesis against many of the earlier critics like Robertson, was basically a detailed study of exactly such processes of the continuous change of the motivational orientations of Puritan groups in the direction of secularization, of growing emphasis on economic motives and activities within a society which became more and more 'tolerant' and secular.

In almost all criticism of this type or at this stage we can thus find an ambivalent attitude to Weber's thesis. On the one hand we find a critique of the direct causal relationship between the rise of Protestantism and the development of economic activities which has allegedly been explained by Weber in the concrete European or American setting. But on the other hand, most of these critics, with the exception of the extreme negativists, do admit that despite all this there was indeed 'something' in the Weberian thesis. In one way or another they acknowledge the existence of some 'insight' or kernel of truth in Weber's thesis without, however, defining exactly what this kernel may indeed be, outside some of the very broad, general terms mentioned above.

II

In order to be able to understand more fully this 'kernel' it is necessary to go to the second type of argument, or to the second phase of controversy. This type of argument can already be found in the earlier works of Troeltsch (1912, 1931) and Holl (1927, 1959). Although these two scholars were in a way in seemingly opposing camps – Troeltsch supporting Weber's thesis and Holl at least partially denying it – yet they did to a large extent have something in common. Neither Troeltsch nor Holl was mainly concerned with the analysis of the mechanisms of the alleged direct causal relation between Protestantism and capitalism activity. Troeltsch fully acknowledged that the initial impetus of Calvinism was what would be nowadays called a totalistic one, i.e. an attempt to establish a new civilization totally regulated by religious precepts.

But for him the major problem was not whether these initial orientations did promote or even facilitate the various types of such modern activities but rather what their influence was once they did not succeed in establishing the first totalistic impulses.

Holl's major concern or polemic against both Weber and Troeltsch was mostly in defense of Lutheranism, which has often been depicted as the more conservative force in the Reformation, with but few transformative powers, as against the more dynamic and revolutionary Calvinism. Against this view Holl claimed that, from a broad comparative point of view (a view which in his work includes the analysis of the Eastern Church), Lutheranism did indeed contain a dynamic, transformative tendency of its own which, while differing from that of Calvinism, being more centered on the individual and less on the *religious community*, could yet, given appropriate conditions, contribute greatly to the formation of forms of modern life and culture.[3]

But this type of approach to Weber's thesis has been largely neglected since then and only recently has it been taken up again, often without any reference to these earlier studies, in different ways by various scholars. Of these a brief discussion of the work of Trevor-Roper, Luethy and Walzer[4] can best serve for the purposes of our analysis.

Luethy, and to some extent Trevor-Roper, denies the correctness of Weber's thesis in the economic field proper. They claim that economic development in Europe was independent of the specific direct impact of Protestantism. They show, for instance, as others did before them, that the first initial impact of Protestantism on economic life was, as Calvin's Geneva shows, a restrictive one. But they admit, indeed they stress, that especially England,

3. On these differentiations between Lutheranism and Calvinism, as seen also from the point of view of Weber's strong emphasis on Calvinism, see Nelson (1965). See also Müller-Armack (1959). More recently a similar thesis with regard to Lutheranism has been taken up by Ritter (1938, 1950 esp. ch. 3).

4. See Trevor-Roper (1965a), Luethy (1964) and Walzer (1964, 1965). See also Luethy (1965), pp. 58–99, where parts of his work on the Protestant Bank, most relevant from the point of view of a *general* discussion of the Protestant Ethic thesis, have been reprinted.

the Netherlands, and to some extent the Scandinavian countries were more successful, after the Counter-Reformation, in developing viable, continuous, flexible modern institutions, whether in the economic, political or scientific fields, than most of the Catholic countries like Spain, Italy or even France which were the first to develop many modern institutional frameworks.

At one level of argument it seems as if to them, as to some of their precursors, this was mostly due to the structural implications or exigencies of the victory of Protestantism and not necessarily to anything inherent in the religious orientation of Protestantism in general or of Calvinism and Puritanism in particular.

But at another level of argument the picture is already somewhat different. This, for instance, Luethy transposes Weber's theory almost entirely to the political field. For him the major impact of Protestantism on European history has been in the political field. This impact was effected, according to him, through the direct reference to the Bible as a source for new bases of legitimation of authority as well as through the new structural impetus to the development of pluralistic settings which developed through the outcome of the Counter-Reformation or the Wars of Religion.

In principle the type of criticism that Luethy directs against Weber could easily be directed against his own thesis. It could easily be shown that the original political impulse of either Lutheranism or Calvinism was not in a 'liberal' or democratic direction but rather in a more 'totalistic' one. But whatever the correctness of such criticism of details, it would be largely misdirected, because Luethy's analysis does not deal with the direct economic or political impact or 'results' of the activities of certain religious groups or beliefs but rather, as has already been the case by Troeltsch and Holl, with its transformative effects.

From this point of view Luethy's more specific work (1959–61; esp. vol. 2, p. 786) on the Protestant Bank is very significant. Here he shows how the ultimate difference between 'Catholic' finance and 'Protestant Banks' was based on the degree to which the latter were not tied to the given political order but were conceived as an autonomous sphere of organized activity, supported by the legitimation of economic calculus. This legitimation could be derived from the Calvinist ethic, but it developed in Geneva mostly after the downfall of the initial totalistic-religious régime in Geneva, while in France the reliance of the monarchs on the (mostly foreign) Protestant banks also developed only after the expulsion of the Huguenots on the one hand and the bankruptcies of the Royal ('traditional Catholic') finances, on the other hand.

Parallel indications have been developed even more fully by Walzer's independent analysis of the two groups instrumental in the shaping of Puritanism in England, the intelligentsia (ministers, students and lay intellectuals) and the gentry. He shows that originally the impulses of Calvinism were directed not in the economic field, but in the political one and that in this field they were also initially mostly totalistic.[5] But then he continues to show, in very detailed analysis, how, after the initial failure of these totalistic orientations, when the Puritans became a persecuted minority, and especially an *exiled* minority of 'intellectuals', there took place a transformation of their orientations in the direction of the reconstruction of new rules, organizations, new patterns of human connexions and new society and polity.

III

Thus Luethy's work on the Bank and Walzer's analysis of the Puritan intelligentsia indeed contain very important indications for the full re-examination of the Weberian thesis in its broadest analytical and comparative applications.

The crux of this re-examination lies in shifting the course of the argument from an examination of the allegedly direct, causal relation between Protestantism and capitalism (or other aspects of the modern world) to that of the transformative capacities of Protestantism.

It is of course true that originally the Reformation was not a 'modernizing' movement. It did not have very strong modernizing impulses; it did indeed aim at the establishment of a new,

5. See Walzer (1965). A similar emphasis on the political activities of some, especially French and Scottish Protestants, can be found in Burrell (1960) and Trevor-Roper (1963).

The transformative potentials, in the political field, of the Puritan idea of the covenant have been explored previously by many people. See among others, Hudson (1949, 1961) and Breuer (1950).

purer 'medieval' socio-political religious order. Originally Protestantism was indeed a religious movement aiming at the religious restructuring of the world. It was just because of these strong 'this-worldly' religious impulses that from the very beginning they were caught up with, and in, the major socio-political, economic and cultural trends of change which European (and especially Western and Central European) society was undergoing from the end of the seventeenth century on: the development of capitalism, the development of Renaissance states, absolutism and the consequent 'general' crisis of the seventeenth century, the crisis between 'state' and 'society', the development of a secular outlook and science (Trevor-Roper, 1965b).

The Reformation did not directly cause any of these developments, although in many indirect ways it did of course contribute to the weakening of the traditional framework of European society. Many of these crises or developments stemmed from the same broad roots as the Reformation – from the crisis of Catholic civilization in general and the Catholic Church in particular. But their specific cause, as well as the groups which fostered them, whether the humanistic like Erasmus, the new international merchants like the Fuggers, did on the whole differ from the reformers, although sometimes overlapping and often very much serving as important mutual reference groups. But however strong the concrete interrelationships between these various groups and the various 'crises' which they fostered, neither was a *direct* cause of the other.

The significance of the Reformation and of Protestantism is to be found not in the fact that it directly caused or gave rise to new types of economic, political or scientific activities, but in its contribution to the restructuring of European society, a restructuring which developed as a result of all these crises but which came, in the post-Counter-Reformation period, to a fuller fruition in the Protestant than in the Catholic countries, because of some of the transformative potential of Protestantism as it developed in these settings. This crucial impact of Protestantism in the direction of modernity came after the failure of its initial totalistic socio-religious orientations.

Thus the special importance, from a broad comparative point of view, of Protestantism could be seen in that, for a variety of reasons to be shortly examined, it did contain within itself the seeds of such transformation, and that in its specific setting these seeds could bear fruit and greatly influence the course of European civilization on the way to modernity. [. . .]

IV

This shift of the locus of the discussion and controversy about the Weberian thesis from the analysis of the direct-causal links between Protestantism and capitalism (or other types of modern institutions) to the analysis of the broader transformative powers or tendencies of Puritanism or Calvinism puts this discussion, to begin with, in a broader perspective of the totality of Weber's work. As Mommsen has recently put it very succinctly:

To Max Weber the exemplar among such religious movements that 'change the world' was Puritan. Although he investigated other variants of Christianity and other great world religions from the standpoint of the social consequences of their teaching, none in his opinion had influenced the course of human development in quite such a revolutionary manner as had Puritanical religiosity (Mommsen, 1965, p. 31).

But beyond this it puts this discussion in a broader *general* comparative and analytical perspective.

Already in Weber's general work on sociology of religion the major emphasis was not on the direct religious injunctions about different economic behavior but on the more general 'Wirtschaftsethik' of each religion, i.e. on those broader types of orientations inherent in the ethos of each religion which influence and direct economic motivation and activities.

But the shift to the analysis of the transformative capacities of different religions contains an additional element, namely the possibility that, under certain conditions, different religions may foster new types of activities, activities which go beyond the original direct 'Wirtschaftsethik', i.e. there may take place a transformation of the original religious impulses which may in turn lead to the transformation of social reality.[6]

This shift does necessitate a reformulation of the problems for

6. One of the interesting analyses which deals explicitly with such transformative capacities of religious movements after their initial failure is that of G. Sholem (1946, 1958).

comparative analysis in general, for the consequent re-examination of the Weberian thesis, even within the context of Weber's over-all work, in particular. In addition to asking about the 'Wirt-schaftsethik' orientation of different religions, or of the religious orientations of different social groups,[7] it is necessary to ask about the *transformative* capacity of different religions (or, for that matter, of secular ideologies), i.e. their capacity for internal transformation which may then facilitate the development of new social institutions and individual motivations in directions differ-ent from their original impulses and aims.

Here several problems stand out. The first problem is what it is within any given religion (or ideology) that creates or may account for the existence of such transformative capacities. The second question is in what directions such transformative capaci-ties may develop. Last comes the question, what are the conditions in the society within such religious or ideological groups develop which facilitate or impede the institutionalization of such trans-formative capacities or orientations?

With regard to all these questions only very tentative and pre-liminary answers can be given both with regard to Protestantism and even more with regard to other religions. But even such pre-liminary answers perhaps may indicate some of the possibilities of such an analytical and comparative approach.

V

With regard to the first question, what it is in the nature of Protestantism that creates such transformative potential or capa-city, to a large extent the answer has been given by many scholars, although it probably needs further elaboration and systematization.

All of them seem to agree that this potential or capacity does not seem to be connected to any single tenet of the Protestant faith, but rather in several aspects of its basic religious and value orientations.

The most important of these are its strong combination of 'this-worldliness' and transcendentalism, a combination which orients individual behavior to activities within this world but at

7. This is a central aspect of Weber's work which is analysed by Andreski (1964). See also Yang (1964) and van der Sprenkel (1964).

the same time does not ritually sanctify any of them, either through a mystic union or any ritual act, as the final point of religious consummation or worthiness. Second is the strong emphasis on individual activism and responsibility. Third is the unmediated, direct relation of the individual to the sacred and to the sacred tradition, an attitude which, while strongly emphasizing the importance and direct relevance of the sacred and of tradition, yet minimizes the extent to which this relation and individual commitment can be mediated by any institution, organization or textual exegesis.[8] Hence it opens up the possibility of the continuous re-definition and re-formulation of the nature and scope of this tradition, a possibility which is further enhanced by the strong transcendental attitude which minimizes the sacredness of any 'here and now'.

These religious orientations of Protestantism and Protestants (and especially Calvinists) were not, however, confined only to the realm of the sacred. They were closely related to and evident in two major orientations in most Protestant groups' conception of the social reality and of their own place in it, i.e. in what may be called their status images and orientations (Pauck, 1961; Niebuhr, 1959).

Most of the Protestant groups developed a combination of two types of such orientations. First was their 'openness' towards the wider social structure, rooted in their 'this-worldly' orientation which was not limited only to the economic sphere but which also, as we shall see later, could encompass other social fields. Second, they were characterized by a certain autonomy and self-sufficiency from the point of view of their status orientation. They evinced but little dependence from the point of view of the crystallization of their own status symbols and identity on the existing political and religious centers.

VI

With regard to the second question, namely that of the directions in which such transformative capacities can be effective, the

8. This point has been analysed with great skill, with regard to the Armenians in the Netherlands and their potentially more revolutionary and open orientations, by L. Kolakowski (1965).

picture is already much more complicated, certainly much more so than as presented by Weber himself.

The first such level of institutional aspect, probably least dealt with by Weber, which Protestantism tended to transform was that of the central political symbols, identities and institutions. By the very nature of the totalistic reformatory impulses of the Protestants these institutions constituted natural foci of their orientations and activities. The very basic theological tenets, whether of Luther, Zwingli or Calvin, or whatever the marked differences between them in their attitudes to political institutions, contained some very strong ingredients for the reformulation of the relation between state and 'society', between ruler and ruled, and redefinition of the scope and nature of the political community.

The initial failure of their totalistic attempts did not abate or nullify these impulses. On the contrary, the structural roots of the various crises of European society in the sixteenth and seventeenth centuries, and especially the crisis of 'state *v.* society,' as well as the political exigencies of Protestant communities in various European states, facilitated and even reinforced this continuous orientation towards the political sphere and towards activities within it.

And indeed the Protestant Reformation did have a great initial impact on the central political sphere. Certainly this impact was not necessarily intended by the rulers who adopted Protestantism. Yet it did have important structural effects which greatly facilitated the further development of a more flexible and dynamic social system.

Of crucial importance here was the search of the rulers for new legitimation as well as their attempts to forge new symbols of collective identity.

On both these levels, that of legitimation of new patterns of authority and of forging new symbols of national identity, there developed, through the initial religious impact of the major Protestant groups and especially through their transformation, the possibilities of the reformation of the relations between rulers and ruled, of patterns of political participation and of the scope and nature of the political community.[9]

9. One of the earlier expositions of this view can be found in Lindsay (1945).

These orientations also contained possibilities for the restructuralization of the central legal-institutional institutions and of their basic premises, centered around the idea of covenant and contract and around the reformulation of many concepts of natural law which led to a much more differentiated view of the legal state and autonomy of voluntary and business corporations, freeing them from the more restricted view inherent in traditional natural law (Little, 1963). And indeed, in the first Protestant societies – England, Scandinavia, The Netherlands – and later in the United States, through the incorporation of Protestant orientations and symbols, perhaps even before the full development of motivations to new types of economic or scientific activities, there developed a transformation of the central symbolic and political sphere and of the basic interrelations between the political and social spheres. This not only reinforced the existing relative autonomy of these spheres but created new, more flexible types of political symbols, new bases of political obligations and more flexible political institutions.

Here the comparison with Catholic countries, especially during and after the Counter-Reformation, is extremely instructive. The ingredients of almost all the elements – new bases of legitimation and new national symbols, autonomy of religious institutions (as evident, for instance, in the Gallican Church) – existed in most of these countries on the eve of the Reformation and even to some extent throughout the Counter-Reformation. And yet in these countries, such as Spain and France or even earlier in the Italian states of the Renaissance where the very first types of modern statecraft developed, these potentially diversifying orientations were stifled in their development not only by various external exigencies (like the vicissitudes of warfare among the small Italian principalities and the deflection of trade routes from them) but also by the maintenance of the older, Catholic symbols of legitimation, of the traditional relations between Church and State, and by viewing both of them as the natural or preordained mediators between man and community on the one hand and the sacred and natural orders on the other.[10]

10. See for instance Castro (1954); and also, for a Catholic analysis, very interesting from this point of view, Daniel-Rops (1961a and b).

VII

But the transformative effects of Protestantism were not limited only to the central institutions and symbols of society but also to other aspects of the institutional structure of modern societies, and especially to the development of new types of roles, role structure and role sets and to motivations to undertake and perform such roles. The essential core of Weber's Protestant Ethic thesis, as distinct from Weber's wider discussion of the transformative effects of Protestantism, focuses on one aspect of this problem – the development of the role of the economic entrepreneur and of the specific setting within which this role could become institutionalized.

Here again it is obvious that many of the basic ingredients of this role and of its new specific goals have of course existed before, and have even continued to develop, to some extent, in Catholic countries. But it is true that in the period after the Counter-Reformation these developments, even when quantitatively initially *not different* from the later developments in the Protestant countries, could not free themselves, as Luethy's work on the Bank shows, from their dependence on the political center, in terms both of their goal-orientation and legitimation. In the Catholic countries these frameworks could not attain such autonomy and could not foster the consequent continuous impetus for further, more differentiated development. It was mostly in Protestant countries, or among Protestant (Calvinist) communities that these roles acquired a new type of autonomous legitimation and were able to develop a relatively independent organizational framework.

It was also mostly among the Protestant communities that another crucial aspect of the crystallization of new roles took place, namely the relatively intense development of motivation for the undertaking of such roles and goals and for identifying with them.

Thus we see that the transformative potential of Protestantism could effect the development of new roles in three different directions: first, in the definition of specific new roles with new types of goals, defined in autonomous terms and not tied to existing frameworks; second, in the development of broader institutional, organizational and legal normative settings which could both legitimize such new roles and provide them with the necessary resources and frameworks to facilitate their continuous working; and last, in the development of new types of motivation,[11] of motivations for the understanding of such roles and for identifying with them.

Although these three aspects of the development of new roles and role complexes are very closely interwoven and interrelated (and were perhaps not fully distinguished by Weber), yet they have to be kept distinct, because to some degree at least they can develop to different degrees.

But whatever the exact aspects of such new roles, which tended to develop under the impact of the transformative tendencies of Protestantism, as has already been briefly mentioned above, they did not develop only in the economic sphere but in a much greater variety of institutional spheres. They could indeed develop in the political sphere proper, giving rise to new types of active political participation and organizations in the form of parties, community organizations and public service (Scotland, The Netherlands, France) (Burrell, 1960). They could also develop in the cultural and especially scientific and educational sphere.[12] In the economic sphere proper they could develop in other ways distinct from capitalist-mercantile or industrial entrepreneurship proper, as for instance, in the transformation of the economic activities of the gentry (Stone, 1965, p. 10).

Here again in all these spheres the beginning and possibilities of such new roles existed before Protestantism, but it was more in the Protestant countries as against the Catholic ones that they developed in terms of organizational autonomy of goals, organizational structure and legitimation.

VIII

We may now pass very briefly to the third question, namely that of the conditions under which such transformative capacities of

11. On the importance of the relations between the motivational and the organizational aspects of the development of roles, see Bellah (1963).

12. The influence of Protestantism on science has constituted another continuous focus of research and controversy derived from the Protestant Ethic thesis. See for instance, Merton (1938), Feuer (1963), van Gelder (1961), Rabb (1962) and Kearney (1964).

Protestantism (or of other religions) could indeed become 'absorbed' or institutionalized.

In very broad terms it seems that the possibility of such institutionalization is greater the stronger the seeds of the autonomy of the social, cultural and political orders are within any society. The existence of the autonomy of the cultural order facilitates the development of new symbolic realms which can support and legitimize central institution building while the autonomy of the sphere of social organization facilitates the development of new organizational nuclei which help in the crystallization of some viable new institutions without disrupting the whole fabric of the pre-existing order, thus enabling the new order to build to some extent on some at least of the earlier forces.

It is indeed in the realm of European and especially Western European Christian culture that we find the strongest tradition of autonomy of the major institutions of the cultural, political and social orders, and it is here indeed that the first and most continuous impetus to modernization did develop. But the course of modernization was not of course either even or continuous or the same in all, even Western and Central European, countries.

The specific transformative potentials of Protestantism can be seen in the fact that it took up these seeds of autonomy and pluralism and helped in recrystallizing them on a higher level of differentiation than in the Catholic countries, like Spain and France, where the potentially pluralistic impact of various modern trends, including Protestantism, was inhibited by the formation of the Catholic state during the Counter-Reformation.

But even within the Protestant countries there existed great variations. The transformative orientation of Protestantism did not necessarily develop fully and in the same direction among all Protestant groups in all countries, though to some minimal extent they probably occurred in most of them. The concrete development and institutionalization of such orientations depended to no small degree on the interaction between the orientations and placement of the major Protestant groups on the one hand and the pre-existing social structure, and especially on the extent of 'openness' of the existing political and cultural centers, of the broader groups and strata and on their initial reaction to religious innovations. The exact scope of such institutionalization differed greatly according both to the nature of the groups (i.e. aristocracy, urban patriciate, various 'middle' groups, urban proletariat or peasantry) which were the bearers of Protestantism on the one hand and their placement within the broader social structure in general and with regard to the political and cultural center in particular, on the other.

The transformative capacities of the Protestant groups were smallest in those cases where they attained full powers – when their more totalistic restrictive orientations could become dominant – or in situations where they were downtrodden minorities.[13]

Contrariwise, both the scope of new institutional activities which different transformed Protestant groups developed, and the extent to which they were successful in transforming central spheres of the society were most far-reaching in those situations in which the various Protestant groups were in a position of what may be very broadly called 'secondary' élites, close to but not identified with, the central élites, and in so far as Protestant groups and orientation became integrated into wider national communities which developed on the basis of the prior autonomy of the Estates becoming the only bearers of such new political or national identity.[14]

The various interactions between different transformative potentialities and existing structural flexibility could give rise to paradoxically similar, or divergent, results. The influence of Lutheranism, allegedly more conservative than Calvinism, took a variety of forms for example. In the German principalities Lutheranism was indeed very restrictive, because the existing political framework was not an appropriate setting for the development of a new national identity and community or for the development of more autonomous and flexible status orientations in the broader strata (see Drummond, 1951; MacNeill, 1954; Ritter, 1938, 1950, ch. 3, esp. pp. 133–70; Adam, 1938). Here, the 'traditional' or autocratic rulers of the small principalities adopted the new religious orientations, and in this context the more conservative

13. On their situations as minorities, see among others Scoville (1950) and Wayne-Nafziger (1965).

14. Of special interest in this respect are the developments in the Netherlands, the relation between Protestants and the development of the Dutch nation. See Geyl (1960, 1961), Schöffer (1964a and b) and Roords (1964).

among these orientations became predominant, often restricting further institutional development.

But in the Scandinavian countries these religious orientations were integrated into new, wider national communities and developed on the bases of the prior autonomy of the Estates. While they certainly did not impede the development of an absolutist state in Sweden, they did help to make possible the subsequent development of these states in a more pluralistic direction (Holmquist, 1922; Schrey, 1951; Schweiger, 1962; Ritter, 1950).

Similarly paradoxical results, also demonstrating the importance of restrictive prior situations or frameworks, are evident in the institutionalization of Calvinism. Of special importance here is the Prussian case, where the institutionalization of these orientations by the absolutist, autocratic Hohenzollerns did not facilitate the development of a flexible and pluralistic political framework, though it did support development of more activist collective political goals (Kayser, 1961).

References

ADAM, A. (1938), 'Die nationale Kirche bei Luther', *Archiv für Geschichte der Reformation*, vol. 35, pp. 30–62.

ANDRESKI, S. (1964), 'Method and substantive theory in Max Weber', *Brit. J. Soc.*, vol. 15, pp. 1–8.

BAERLING, R. F. (1946), *Protestantisme en Kapitalisme, Max Weber in die Critick*, Wolfers, Groningen-Batavia.

BELLAH, R. N. (1963), 'Reflections on the Protestant ethic analogy in Asia', *J. soc. Iss.*, vol. 19, pp. 52–60.

BREUER, J. G. (1950), 'Puritan mysticism and the development of liberalism', *Church History*, vol. 17.

BURRELL, S. A. (1960), 'Calvinism, capitalism, and the middle classes: some afterthought on an old pattern', *J. mod. Hist.*, vol. 32, pp. 129–41.

CASTRO, A. (1954), *The Structure of Spanish History*, Princeton University Press.

DANIEL-ROPS, N. (1961a), *The Protestant Reformation*, Dent.

DANIEL-ROPS, N. (1961b), *The Catholic Reformation*, Dent.

DRUMMOND, A. L. (1951), *Protestantism since Luther*, Epworth.

ELTON, G. R. (1963), *Reformation Europe, 1517–1559*, Collins.

FANFANI, A. (1934), *Cattolicesimo e Protestantesimo nella Formazione del Capitalismo*, Milano. English translation, *Catholicism, Protestantism and Capitalism*, Sheed Ward 1935.

FEUER, L. S. (1963), *The Scientific Intellectual*, Basic Books.

FISCHOFF, E. (1944), 'The Protestant ethic and the spirit of capitalism', *Social Research*, vol. 11, pp. 54–77.

GEORGE, C. H. (1958), 'Protestantism and capitalism in pre-revolutionary England', *Church History*, vol. 27, pp. 351–71.

GEORGE, C. H., and GEORGE, K. (1961), *The Protestant Mind of the English Reformation, 1570–1640*, Princeton University Press.

GEYL, P. (1960), *Noord en Zuid*, Utrecht-Antwerpen.

GEYL, P. (1961), *The Netherlands in the 17th Century*, Benn.

GREEN, R. W. (1959), *Protestantism and Capitalism*, Heath.

HAUSER, H. (1963), 'La modernité du XVIe siècle', *Cahiers des Annales*, vol. 21.

HOLL, K. (1927), *Gesammelte Aufsätze zur Kirchengeschichte*, vols. 1 and 2.

HOLL, K. (1959), *The Cultural Significance of the Reformation*, Meridian.

HOLMQUIST, H. (1922), 'Kirche und staat im evangelischen Schweden', *Festgabe für Karl Müller*, Mohr, Tubingen, pp. 209–2077.

HUDSON, W. (1949), 'Puritanism and the spirit of capitalism', *Church History*, vol. 18, pp. 3–16.

HUDSON, W. (1961), 'The Weber thesis re-examined', *Church History*, vol. 30, pp. 88–9.

KAYSER, C. R. (1961), Calvinism and German political life, *unpublished Ph.D. thesis, Radcliffe*.

KEARNEY, H. F. (1964), 'Puritanism, capitalism and the scientific revolution', *Past and Present*, vol. 28, pp. 81–101.

KOLAKOWSKI, L. (1965), 'La genèse et la structure dans l'étude des idéologies religieuses', in M. de Gandillac, L. Goldmann and J. Piaget, eds., *Entretiens sur les Notions de Genèse et la Structure*, Mouton, pp. 307–23.

LINDSAY, A. D. (1945), *The Modern Democratic State*, Oxford University Press.

LITTLE, D. (1963), The logic of order – an examination of the sources of Puritan–Anglican controversy and their relation to prevailing legal conceptions in the 16th and 17th centuries, *unpublished Doctor of Theology Thesis, Harvard University*.

LUETHY, H. (1959–61), *La Banque Protestante en France*, 2 vols., SEVPEN, Paris.

LUETHY, H. (1964), 'Once again: Calvinism and capitalism', *Encounter*, vol. 22, pp. 26–38. [Reprinted in Luethy (1965).]

LUETHY, H. (1965), *Le Passé, Menace Présente*, SEVPEN, Paris.

MACNEILL, J. T. (1954), *The History and Character of Calvinism*, Oxford University Press.

MERTON, R. K. (1938), 'Science, technology and society in seventeenth-century England', *Osiris*, vol. 4.

MOMMSEN, W. (1965), 'Max Weber's political sociology', *Int. soc. Scien J.*, vol. 17.

MÜLLER-ARMACK, A. (1959), *Religion und Wirtschaft*, Kohlhammer.

NELSON, B. (1965), 'Max Weber's sociology of religion', *Amer. soc. Rev.*, vol. 30, pp. 595–601.

NIEBUHR, H. R. (1959), *The Social Sources of Denominationalism*, Meridian.

PAUCK, W. (1961), *The Heritage of the Reformation*, Free Press of Glencoe.

RABB, K. (1962), 'Puritanism and the rise of experimental science in England', *J. world Hist.*, vol. 17.

RITTER, G. (1938), 'Das 16. Jahrhundert als weltgeschichtliche Epoche', *Archiv für Geschichte der Reformation*, vol. 35.

RITTER, G. (1950), *Die Neugestaltung Europas in 16. Jahrhundert*, Druckhaus Tempelhof, Berlin.

ROBERTSON, H. R. (1933), *Aspects of the Rise of Economic Individualism*.

ROORDS, D. J. (1964), 'The ruling classes in Holland in the seventeenth century', *Britain and the Netherlands*, vol. 2, pp. 109–33.

SAMUELSON, K. (1961), *Religion and Economic Action*, Heinemann.

SCHÖFFER, I. (1964a), 'De Nederlandse revolutie', *Zeven Revolution*, de Bussy, Amsterdam, pp. 9–29.

SCHÖFFER, I. (1964b), 'Protestantism in Flux during the revolt of the Netherlands', in J. S. Bromley and E. H. Kossman, eds., *Britain and the Netherlands*, vol. 2, pp. 67–84.

SCHREY, H. H. (1951), 'Geistliches und weltliches Regiment in der Schwedischen Reformation', *Archiv für Geschichte der Reformation*, vol. 42, pp. 146–59.

SCHWEIGER, G. (1962), *Die Reformation in den Nordischen Landern*, Kozel Verlag, Munich.

SCOVILLE, W. C. (1950), 'The Huguenots and the diffusion of technology', *J. polit. Econ.*, vol. 9, pp. 294–311.

SHOLEM, G. (1946), 'On the Sabbatean movement of the 17th century', *Major Trends in Jewish Mysticism*. [Reprinted 1956.]

SHOLEM, G. (1958), *Shabbetai Tzui*, 2 vols. (Hebrew).

STONE, L. (1965), 'Review of C. Hill's *Intellectual Origins of the English Revolution*', *New York Review of Books*, August.

TAWNEY, R. H. (1926), *Religion and the Rise of Capitalism*, Harcourt, Brace.

TAWNEY, R. H. (1956), 'Religion and economic life', *Times Lit. Supp.*

TREVOR-ROPER, H. R. (1963), 'Scotland and the Puritan Revolution', in H. Y. Bell and L. Ollard, eds., *Historical Essays 1600–1750; presented to David Ogg*, pp. 78–130.

TREVOR-ROPER, H. R. (1965a), 'Religion, the Reformation and social change', *Hist. Stud.*, vol. 4, pp. 18–45.

TREVOR-ROPER, H. R. (1965b), 'The general crisis of the seventeenth century', and 'General crisis: a symposium', in T. Ashton, ed., *Crisis in Europe*, Routledge. pp. 59–97 and 97–117.

TROELTSCH, E. (1931), *The Social Teachings of the Christian Churches*, 2 vols., Allen & Unwin. (New edition 1956.)

TROELTSCH, E. (1912), *Protestantism and Progress*, Williams and Norgate. (New edition 1958.)

VAN DER SPRENKEL, B. (1964), 'Max Weber on China', *History and Theory*, vol. 3, pp. 348–70.

VAN GELDER, H. (1961), *The Two Reformations in the Sixteenth Century*, Nijhoff, The Hague.

WALZER, M. (1964), 'Puritanism as a revolutionary ideology', *History and Theory*, vol. 3, pp. 59–90.

WALZER, M. (1965), *The Revolution of the Saints*, Harvard University Press.

WAYNE-NAFZIGER, E. (1965), 'The Mennonite ethic in the Weberian framework', *Explorations in Entrepreneurial History*, second series, vol. 2.

WEBER, M. (1930), *Protestant Ethic and the Spirit of Capitalism*, trans. T. Parsons, Allen & Unwin.

WEBER, M. (1961), *General Economic History*, Collier.

YANG, C. K. (1964), 'Introduction' to Max Weber, *The Religion of China*, Free Press.

II. Religion and Politics

The previous Reading by Eisenstadt has illuminated some of the major historical relationships between religion and politics. In the contribution which follows (Reading 18) Alford deals with connexions between religious commitment and political disposition in four modern societies: Canada, Australia, Britain and the U.S.A., with particular reference to the distinctive political behaviour of Catholics. Basically, Alford is interested in the conditions which tend to produce or inhibit the religious grounding of political behaviour.[1]

1. In Reading 21 Fernandez deals with the relationship between religion and politics within specific religious movements.

18 R. R. Alford

Religion and Politics

Excerpt from R. R. Alford, *Party and Society*, Rand McNally, 1963, pp. 49–58.

The connexion between religion and politics arises as a problem only in nations which are not religiously homogeneous. Classical political thinkers such as Aristotle took it for granted that religious homogeneity was a condition of political stability, and they were right. Where opposing beliefs about ultimate values enter the political arena, they exacerbate struggles by preventing compromise.[1] In modern non-homogeneous societies, three changes (occurring in different degrees in different societies) may have moderated conflicts over ultimate values: secularization, the weakening of religious belief in general; compartmentalization, the separation of religion from other areas of life; and homogenization, the convergence of many religions upon a vaguely defined consensus on teaching and practice.[2] Actually all of these processes, or contradictory forms of them, may be going on simultaneously.

The largely Protestant societies such as the Anglo-American countries have possibly moved farther along these three paths of change than other countries. Protestantism, with its emphasis upon the separation of Church and State, undoubtedly has

1. For a modern form of the argument that religious homogeneity is necessary for political stability, see Leicester Webb (1960a and b). Western societies, as he sees it, are unified by certain political values closely associated with Christianity: the idea of justice and the concept that the polity is something toward which men who are conscious of moral freedom and responsibility will naturally be drawn.

2. See Gerhard Lenski (1960), p. 9, for this usage of the term 'compartmentalization'. However, Lenski later uses the word for the opposite phenomenon: the tendency for the whole of life to be organized around religious membership. He cites the Netherlands and Lebanon as the best examples of the latter (pp. 326 ff.).

encouraged a secular norm in the behavior of parties and voters. Even where religious issues and motives exist, they have had to remain covert, because they are illegitimate in the political realm.

In this respect, the Anglo-American countries differ greatly from the continental European countries. Religious parties do not exist in the Anglo-American countries, in sharp contrast to such continental nations as Italy, France, Belgium, Norway and the Netherlands. No parties based almost exclusively upon an appeal to religious values and identifications have gained any appreciable strength in the Anglo-American countries. Although some parties have gained most of their support from particular religious groups (the nationalist parties *Bloc Populaire* and *Union Nationale* in Quebec, and the splinter Labor party in Australia gain the great bulk of their support from Catholics), the parties have never based their appeals or programs upon this characteristic of their supporters. This difference between the Anglo-American countries and some of the continental European ones is almost a defining characteristic of the former: they are 'secular, homogeneous' political systems.

One reason for this difference may be suggested. In the continental countries where religious parties are strong, religious freedom was won at the same time and was linked with the achievement of political freedom. The consequence was that to this day, religion, class and politics have been closely linked. In Britain, on the other hand, these issues emerged separately and were solved separately; as a result, not only were Church and State legally separated, but also the development of legitimate issues and parties connecting the two was prevented.

Certain features of the Reformation in England in the 1500s, unlike those of the Reformations on the continent, may have contributed to the relatively high degree of separation of church and state and the legitimacy of religious pluralism in British political culture. Since varying political stratagems rather than a constant religious ideal initiated the English Reformation, a number of religious options came to exist. The political authority in England undertook to break Catholic power without any single religious ethic or ideology guiding its efforts; it followed a continually oscillating course of strategy *vis-à-vis* the Church in the period 1530–60. The crown of England itself passed through many hands during this period, and every change of government brought a sharp change of position regarding the Church. After three decades of policy fluctuation, the political authority could no longer re-establish a single dominant religion. A minority of the population remained firmly Roman Catholic, but other minorities just as firmly adhered to one or another of the many church reforms and systems of dogma which had been pressed upon the English people in the preceding decades. The English state had by the 1560s missed its historic opportunity, as no other European state had, to take religious decisions out of the hands of the people. Religious pluralism and the separation of the state from a single coercive church were thereby established in England – and subsequently in its colonies – as in no other country.[3]

Thus, a firmer historical basis for the secularization of politics has existed in the Anglo-American countries than in certain continental nations. In the colonies, the institutional domination of Protestantism was even less of an issue, and the Catholic church has never been more than a minority religion except in certain regions such as Quebec.[4] It must be emphasized again, however, that political secularization need not imply the secularization of the whole society. These are two parallel processes which need not be associated.[5]

Another reason for the rise of religious parties in continental Europe and their lack, so far, in the English-speaking countries has been the simple fact that the latter are predominantly Protestant, the former, predominantly Catholic. Where Catholics have made up a majority of the population, and therefore have had an opportunity to carry out Catholic social policies by political means, Catholic parties have arisen and Protestant parties have

3. Taken from a summary of results in Schoeffler (1960), pp. 322–4. I am indebted to Reinhard Bendix for this source.

4. See S. M. Lipset (1960), pp. 83–5 for a discussion of the ways in which historical resolution of issues colors subsequent political struggles.

5. In the Netherlands, for example, the percentage describing themselves as 'free thinkers', with 'no fixed religion', or as 'churchless' has increased steadily in each subsequent Census since 1879 to a high of 17 per cent in 1947. Although undoubtedly this figure does not indicate the 'real' degree of secularization – since in a country where so few are areligious there must be some pressure to admit being religious – even this trend does not accord with the contrary trend toward religious parties. See Fogarty (1957), p. 357.

formed in reaction.[6] In the Anglo-American countries, the autonomous authority of the Catholic church to educate its own members has not been seriously challenged, and that church, as a consequence, has not made militant attempts to influence political life. A *modus vivendi* has been worked out which has not only strengthened the legitimacy of the national political system, but has made it unnecessary for religious parties to emerge. No religious group of any size in these systems has challenged one fundamental premise of a legitimate democratic state: either a secular political culture must exist in a society with more than one important religious group, or homogeneity of religious basis. It is a measure of the viability of Protestantism, combined with British political institutions and traditions, that each of the Anglo-American countries has to a great degree been able to assimilate the Catholics into a secular political culture.

This achievement stands out even more when the particular situation of Quebec in Canada is considered. Here most of the conditions favoring the development of a religious party are present: a minority religious group is the majority within one of the two largest political units within a federal state; ethnic differences are present; a different language is spoken; and a sense of opposition is felt toward a political party with a historical association with another religion and ethnic group (the Conservatives, based upon English Protestants). Yet no religious party has developed; rather, nationalistic parties flourish. In Latin Europe, in contrast, the connexion between a distinctive ethnic culture and Catholicism has produced strong Catholic parties (Burks, 1952).

In Canada alone of the four Anglo-American countries might we expect such a consequence. Catholics in the United States and Australia are more diverse ethnically and geographically than in Canada, and in Britain the secession of Ireland deprived that issue of its saliency (although even the Irish issue had more of a nationalistic than a religious flavor). This example indicates again that something distinctive about the political culture of the Anglo-American countries effects even the regions and religious groups presumably most isolated from its influence. Quebec has

6. See Lipset and Linz (1956) for some of the general formulations of this section.

taken the path of an extreme emphasis upon 'Canadianism', stressing cultural autonomy within the framework of the Canadian federal union rather than struggling for a separate religiously homogeneous state or forming a religious party.[7]

French-Canadian nationalist parties have not even stressed their religious differences with English-Canada, although they could have easily done so. This failure to emphasize a possible source of regional political solidarity is another mark of the difference between the political culture of the Anglo-American and continental systems. The 1942 nationalist party in Quebec – the *Bloc Populaire* – grew in spite of the refusal of Catholic Action and Cardinal Villeneuve in Quebec to support the party. It clearly had a possible religious appeal and base, however, for the lower clergy welcomed it, seeing the new party as a possible avenue for reversing the 'effects of the wartime industrialization upon French-Canadian family life and morals' (Wade, 1955, p. 956). A religious appeal could conceivably have offset the new party's internal divisions over economic policy. Some of the leaders were crusaders for nationalization of industry, some were big businessmen, and an overriding appeal for religious unity could have temporarily dissolved those differences; yet none was made.[8]

Thus, the primary fact about the political relevance of religion in the Anglo-American countries is that it is *not* the primary fact of political life. The problem then becomes the extent to which religious groups exhibit distinctive patterns of political behavior, and to link this to differences and similarities in social and political processes. While the designation 'secular and homogeneous' applies when comparing these societies with others, religion is

7. Clearly Quebec's policies are determined by many factors, including the fear of joining the 'melting pot' United States, but the point here is simply that its nationalistic tendencies have not been reinforced by a serious attempt to raise religious issues. Religion has been only one of the aspects of French-Catholic culture which have been seen by Quebec nationalists as necessary to maintain.

8. The assimilation of Quebec to a secular political culture must not be overstressed. The Catholic Church in Quebec has a number of rights not possessed by other churches. In addition, there are Catholic trade unions and other religious penetrations into institutions normally secularized in the Anglo-American countries. This in itself makes the extent of political secularism more notable.

relevant to political behavior in these countries, although in varying degrees.

The distinctive political behavior of Catholics will be of chief concern here. Catholics in each of these countries are more likely to vote for the major Left party than are Protestants. In the United States, they are disproportionately Democratic; in Great Britain and Australia, Labor; in Canada, Liberal.[9]

Possible causes of the distinctive political behavior of Catholics in these four countries lie partly in their special religious beliefs which find expression in political issues, but also partly in their position historically as an immigrant and low-status minority in each country. Even in Britain, the Catholics have largely been of Irish descent and have been treated and have regarded themselves as an ethnic minority. Catholics entered the other countries as immigrant minorities and went into low-status occupations. These several characteristics have combined to produce a tendency to vote for the Left party. The Right parties have tended to represent the upper classes, which have also been Protestant and from majority ethnic groups; the Left parties have tended to represent the lower classes, which have been more likely to be Catholic and have minority ethnic status.

Some of these reasons for political differentiation along religious lines are likely to disappear, but some are relatively permanent – again depending on general processes of secularization and homogenization in the society at large. Distinctive Catholic values and institutions are not likely to disappear: thus the issues of religious education and political representation are always present in these countries. These issues take different forms in each nation, and to the extent that they exacerbate Catholic consciousness of minority status, either culturally or religiously, their voting patterns may deviate from those of Protestants. The historical association of a party with a low-status immigrant group may disappear more readily as Catholics move up in social status and ethnic differences disappear. To put it another way, the purely religious dimension of distinctive

9. For the United States, see Berelson *et al.* (1954), pp. 71, 333; A. Campbell *et al.* (1960), pp. 301–6. For Great Britain see P. Campbell *et al.* (1952), p. 63; Eysenck (1954), p. 21. For Australia, see Overacker (1952), pp. 305–6; Spann (1961). For Canada, see Dawson (1954), p. 510; Filley (1956).

political behavior may emerge more clearly after the class and ethnic associations disappear.

The lack of legitimacy of either religious parties or explicitly religious political appeals or even explicitly religiously motivated voting in the Anglo-American countries does not necessarily mean that distinctive patterns of religious voting are likely to disappear even if the Catholics become completely assimilated ethnically and socio-economically. A compelling argument for the continuation of a Catholic deviation is the continuing failure of the Anglo-American societies to live up to Catholic social policies. The very notion of the separation of Church and State is against traditional Catholic stands.[10] Until the State becomes Catholic or Catholics abandon certain fundamental tenets – such as religious education, opposition to birth control and other positions – such issues will always be a potential source of religiously based political cleavage. This distinctiveness does not necessarily have to be exhibited by loyalty to their traditional party, of course.

Catholic voting behavior in these countries is under a complex set of contradictory cross-pressures. Assuming that there is an association between class and party, and one between religion and party, almost every possible combination of class position and party identification involves cross-pressures for Catholics. The matter is further complicated by the contradictory tendencies within Catholicism itself, for it is at one and the same time profoundly conservative religiously and, sometimes, powerfully progressive socially. The very success of the Church in holding its members close may intensify these cross-pressures, since religion cannot as easily become compartmentalized for Catholics as for Protestants.

Middle-class Catholics are under cross-pressures because their class position and the conservative component of Catholicism pre-disposes them to vote Right. But the historical association of their minority status and ethnic position with the Left party leads them to vote Left.[11] Working-class Catholics are also under

10. The attempts by American Catholic intellectuals such as John Courtney Murray to reconcile pluralism with Catholic social theology are testimony both to the secular norm of the Anglo-American societies and the necessity for Catholic theology to remain essentially unquestioned.

11. Apparently, not only middle-class status but also subjective middle-class identifications are necessary to reduce Catholic distinctive political behavior, at least in the United States.

cross-pressures because the class and ethnic components of their status and the progressive component of Catholicism predispose them toward a Left vote, but the conservative element of Catholicism draws them toward a Right vote. The political consequences of these complex cross-pressures have not been satisfactorily analysed comparatively and are beyond the scope of this volume. However, cross-pressures have been held to lead to withdrawal from political activities.[12]

Two recent studies have found, in contrast to the earlier one, that Catholics do not withdraw from voting in situations of predicted cross-pressures. A study of voting among Catholics in Kingston, Ontario, in 1953 and 1955 found that Catholics in a conservative political climate voted as heavily as anyone else. And a study of middle-class Catholics in Detroit in 1957 and 1958 found that they did not withdraw from political activity (Meisel, 1956; Lenski, 1960, p. 132).

The conclusions to be drawn from these specific findings may be: (1) that the cross-pressures upon Catholics have lost their importance; or (2) that Catholics are not under cross-pressures because one of the presumed bases of pressure is not one in reality or because through some other process the person or group is 'shielded' from such pressures; or (3) that the cross-pressure theory is invalid – membership in groups with differing political predispositions does not tend to reduce the level of political activity or does so only under certain special circumstances.

The conservative influences of Catholic religious beliefs and values are shown by a number of studies. Contrary to what one might expect, Catholics (in the United States and Canada, at least) who usually attend services and are involved in church-related activities are *not* more likely to vote for the traditional Left party of their group; they are, indeed, less likely to do so than those more removed from their church. Conversely, Catholics more involved in the social and associational life of the Catholic community (apart from its religious dimension), as one

12. The finding of the 1940 Erie County study in the United States was that persons in cross-pressured situations voted less often and delayed their voting decision more than persons not under cross-pressures. See Lazarsfeld (1948).

might expect, are more likely to vote for the traditional party than those less involved in such community life.[13]

These studies indicate the dual and sometimes contradictory political effect of Catholicism as an aspect of an ethnic subculture and Catholicism as a distinctive set of values embodied in religious institutions. Unfortunately, within the range of data available for this study, no specification of these consequences in the Anglo-American countries can be undertaken.

It need not be assumed that distinctive voting patterns are the only expression of religious values in politics or that a religious party is incapable of adjusting to changing situations. In the Netherlands, although the support given to various parties has changed little in the last 50 years, governmental coalitions have changed in their composition, and varying social philosophies have been implemented. Although almost all Catholics vote for the Catholic party, for example, conflicts of interest between Catholic workers and Catholic employers take place *within* the Catholic party. Shifts of power and influence are reflected in changes of leadership and, thereby, shifts of the alliances within the parliamentary coalitions (from alliances with the Protestants to cooperation with the socialists, or vice versa). Such methods may allow political differences to be resolved as effectively as do the methods more common in the Anglo-American countries.[14]

13. See Lenski (1960), p. 165, and Meisel (1956), pp. 492–4, for parallel findings for the United States and Canada on this point. Meisel found that sisters and lay nurses in Canada were more likely to be Conservative voters than were rank-and-file Catholics. Lenski found that Detroit Catholics who attended church frequently were more likely to be Republican than non-attending Catholics, but that Catholics who associated frequently with Catholics were more Democratic than Catholics who associated frequently with Protestants.

14. I am indebted to Carlos Kruytbosch for pointing this out to me. See Fogarty (1957), for a detailed analysis of the religious parties in continental Europe.

References

BERELSON, B., *et al.* (1954), *Voting*, Chicago University Press.

BURKS, R. V. (1952), 'Catholic parties in Latin Europe', *J. mod. Hist.*, vol. 34, pp. 269–86.

CAMPBELL, A., *et al.* (1960), *The American Voter*, Wiley.

CAMPBELL, P., *et al.* (1952), 'Voting behavior in Droylsden in October, 1951', *J. Man. Sch. econ. soc. Stud.*, vol. 20.

DAWSON, R. M. (1954), *The Government of Canada*, University of Toronto Press.

EYSENCK, H. J. (1954), *The Psychology of Politics*, Routledge & Kegan Paul.

FILLEY, W. (1956), 'Social structure and Canadian political parties: the Quebec case', *West. polit. Quart.*, vol. 9, pp. 900–914.

FOGARTY, M. (1957), *Christian Democracy in Western Europe, 1820–1953*, Routledge & Kegan Paul.

LAZARSFELD, P. F., *et al.* (1948), *The People's Choice*, Columbia University Press.

LENSKI, G. (1960), *The Religious Factor*, Doubleday.

LIPSET, S. M. (1960), *Political Man*, Doubleday.

LIPSET, S. M., and LINZ, J. (1956), The social faces of political diversity in Western democracy, *unpublished MS, Center for Advanced Studies in the Behavioral Sciences*, Stanford.

MEISEL, J. (1956), 'Religious affiliation and electoral behavior: a case study', *Canad. J. Econ. polit. Sci.*, vol. 22, pp. 481–96.

OVERACKER, L. (1952), *The Australian Party System*, Yale University Press.

SCHOEFFLER, H. (1960), *Wirkinger der Reformation*, Klostermann, Frankfurt.

SPANN, R. N. (1961), 'The Catholic vote in Australia', in H. Mayer, ed., *Catholics and the Free Society: An Australian Symposium*, Cheshire, Melbourne, pp. 115–41.

WADE, M. (1955), *The French-Canadians, 1760–1945*, Macmillan.

WEBB, L. (1960a), 'Churches and the Australian community', in E. D. French, ed., *Melbourne Studies in Education, 1958–1959*, Melbourne University Press. pp. 89–113.

WEBB, L. (1960b), Politics and polity, *Australian National University Lecture*.

III. Religion and Social Stratification

The relationships between degrees of religiousness and position in the class and status structure, and between the nature of religious belief and social class position, have been intensively discussed and probed for well over a hundred years. The apparent religious apathy of the European working classes as they developed in the first half of the nineteenth century was the object of much study during that period. Modern sociological discussion owes much to the seminal essays of Max Weber and in particular his analyses of the religious dispositions of underprivileged social strata. In Reading 19 Demerath examines in detail the often contradictory evidence of the relationship between intensity or structure of religious commitment and social class position in American society.

19 N. J. Demerath, III

Religion and Social Class in America

Excerpt from chapter 1 of N. J. Demerath, III, *Social Class in American Protestantism*, Rand McNally, 1965, pp. 1–25.

Two hallmarks of American religion are its susceptibility to non-religious factors and its resulting variety. In the absence of any state church, religion is particularly vulnerable to influences such as social class. This has been a central theme in observations of American society since the beginning of the 19th century. In 1832 Alexis de Tocqueville (see 1954) commented that the denominational competition in American religion lent it a unique vitality. Only a few years later Harriet Martineau (1962, esp. pp. 332–55) witnessed the same competition but saw it as contributing more hypocrisy than vitality, and she pointed an especially accusing finger at an unscrupulously tyrannical clergy. Contemporary observers have also agreed on the perception of diversity while disagreeing over its effects. On the one hand, Talcott Parsons (1960, ch. 10) has urged that denominationalism provides an adaptable religious system to meet the needs of a variegated society. On the other hand, H. Richard Niebuhr (1929) deplored denominationalism as a fragmentation of the true religious spirit.

While denominationalism is not our concern, it reflects the influence of social class, and this is very much to the point. It is no secret that class has had more than passing effect on American religion. Not only is this a theme among foreign journalists, social theorists and theologians, but it has also commanded the attention of empirical analysts. By now, it is almost *de rigueur*, and certainly a commonplace, to begin studies of American religious variation with a table showing the relation between social class and denominational affiliation. This study is no different, and Table 1 is drawn from data that originally appeared in the National Council of Churches' Information Service.

Table 1

Social Class Profiles of American Religious Groups

Denomination	Upper	Class Middle	Lower	N
	%	%	%	
Christian Scientist	24·8	36·5	38·7	(137)
Episcopal	24·1	33·7	42·2	(590)
Congregational	23·9	42·6	33·5	(376)
Presbyterian	21·9	40·0	38·1	(961)
Jewish	21·8	32·0	46·2	(537)
Reformed	19·1	31·3	49·6	(131)
Methodist	12·7	35·6	51·7	(2100)
Lutheran	10·9	36·1	53·0	(723)
Christian	10·0	35·4	54·6	(370)
Protestant (small bodies)	10·0	27·3	62·7	(888)
Roman Catholic	8·7	24·7	66·6	(2390)
Baptist	8·0	24·0	68·0	(1381)
Mormon	5·1	28·6	66·3	(175)
No preference	13·3	26·0	60·7	(466)
Protestant (undesignated)	12·4	24·1	63·5	(460)
Atheist, Agnostic	33·3	46·7	20·0	(15)
No Answer or Don't Know	11·0	29·5	59·5	(319)

From Schneider (1952), appendix, p. 228.

Based on a national sample, the table orders the major United States religious groups by decreasing status. At the high-status extreme, nearly one-fourth of the Christian Scientists, Episcopalians, and Congregationalists are from the upper class; fewer than one-half are from the lower class. At the other end, fewer than one-tenth of the Roman Catholics, Baptists and Mormons are from the upper class; roughly two-thirds are from the lower class.

Although the particulars of the relationship will vary over time and between different areas of the country,[1] Table 1 is

1. Temporal variation in status composition is a theme as old as the sociology of religion itself. Religious groups frequently begin as lower-class splinter movements, but undergo upward mobility in the quest for stability and community influence. As one example of geographical variation, note the contrast between the lower-class Methodism of Warner's Catholic-dominated Yankee City (Newburyport, Massachusetts) and the middle-

generally representative of myriad studies of local communities as well as of large national samples. There are, however, two important caveats which bear upon the present study. First, even though denominations can be ranked by status, there is no justification for converting relative rankings into absolute categorizations. Episcopalians may be *relatively* upper class, but more than 40 per cent are from the lower class. Baptists may be *relatively* lower class, but they claim their Rockefellers as well. Status heterogeneity within denominations is crucial in this study, for it is less concerned with gross differences among groups and more concerned with the subtler distinctions within them.

A second qualification concerns the difference between religious preference and religious involvement. These are not identical, and it is possible that their relations to social class may be dissimilar. Thus, lower-class Episcopalians may be more religiously involved than their more heralded upper-class co-members. At the same time, although the Baptists are generally lower class, the upper-class adherents may control the church organization.

But if research on actual religious involvement is more important for our purposes, it is also less common and less precise compared to studies of class and religious preference. Perhaps because of its relative sparseness, its neglect of denominational distinctions, its oversight of the differences between various kinds of involvement, and its general quality as a research 'aside', research on involvement has harbored an unexposed contradiction. The majority of studies find those of high status (middle and upper class) more religiously involved. Yet an important minority report that those of low status (working and lower class) are more involved.

The Case for High-Status Religiosity

American religion, especially Protestantism, has been widely held to be an activity of the middle and upper classes. The

class Methodism in the South. In fact, a number of southern Methodists are concerned about their 'exclusiveness' as a high-status church. While they may be guilty of a bit of status up-grading, a meeting of Methodists in Richmond, Virginia, recently recommended increased attention toward the lower classes. 'Methodists told church in danger of "class" label', *Richmond Times-Dispatch*, 14 July 1960.

argument rests principally on three indicators of involvement: church membership, attendance at church services, and participation in the church's formal activities. On each of these measures, persons of high status appear to be more deeply involved than those of low status.

Before moving to the actual studies, two comments are appropriate. First, although the empirical relations are relatively unambiguous, their meaning is open to question. Throughout I will try to show that the three measures do not exhaust, nor always illuminate, the concept of religious involvement. Rather than stop short at the data themselves, I will try to probe beneath them.

A second comment concerns my use of the term 'high status' to refer to the combined middle and upper classes. This is partly a reflection of my concern with the latent debate between those who see the greatest involvement among the middle and upper classes and those who see it among the working and lower classes. More important, however, is another conflict within the former camp alone. While all of the studies in this section agree that those of high status are more involved than those of low, they disagree on the relative involvement of the middle and upper classes themselves. Some have described a *linear* relation where involvement increases consistently with increasing status so that the lowest class is the least involved and the upper class is the most. Others, however, have reported a *curvilinear* pattern. Here there is a slight drop-off in involvement among the upper class, and the middle class is most involved, though both high-status groups are more committed than those of low status. This is a minor but persistent inconsistency that I will deal with in the conclusion of this section. Until then I will note its occurrence but stress the larger difference between the high- and low-status groups over all.

Religious identification

It was not until the 1930s that social scientists began to examine variations in religious involvement or religiosity[2] empirically.

2. The term 'religiosity' is a convenient shorthand for the phrase 'religious involvement'. The usage here, however, should not be confused with Harold Laski's where it is used to suggest hypocritical, self-centered religion at odds with the 'pure' religious motive.

Because information on church preference and membership was easily available from questionnaire surveys and from the churches themselves, this was one of the first measures explored. Because social class had already proved a potent explanatory factor, it was one of the first correlates examined.

Hadley Cantril (1943; see also Pope, 1953), a pioneer of the national poll, used data similar to those in Table 1. Pooling four surveys from the Office of Public Opinion Research and Gallup's American Institute of Public Opinion, he went beyond the question of informal religious preference and investigated the more formal issue of actual membership. Cantril was especially concerned with the class differences between Protestants and Catholics. He divided the aggregate sample into three categories: Protestant church members, Catholic church members and non-members. Needless to say, he found that Protestant members had generally higher status, though the difference was not large in the South where Protestant fundamentalism is strong among the lower classes.

But the more important finding for our purposes concerns the non-members. Membership *per se* was not Cantril's focus; hence he lumped Jews into the non-member category. Yet, despite the high status of Jews generally, the non-members were still lower in status than the Protestant and Catholic members combined. In other words there was a generally positive or direct relation between membership and social class. Although the extreme upper class had a slightly lower rate of membership than the middle class, the two high-status groups combined had a higher rate than the lower classes. The finding, while curvilinear, gave early support to the larger pattern of high-status religious involvement.

Subsequent support is available from the so-called community studies with which empirical sociology cut its teeth in the late thirties and forties. Lloyd Warner's (Lloyd Warner and Lunt, 1941) Yankee City series and Robert and Helen Lynd's (1929) celebrated study of Middletown confirmed the pattern described by Cantril. Although the upper classes were slightly less frequent church members than the middle classes, both had higher rates of membership than the lower classes.

Studies of other communities give still more support. Louis

Bultena's (1949) analysis of Madison, Wisconsin, James West's (1945) investigation of Plainville, Lee G. Burchinal's (1959) examination of a small midwestern farm community, Warner's (1949) analysis of the similarly midwestern Jonesville and Hollingshead's (1949, 1953) more sophisticated analysis of Elmtown (Warner's Jonesville) corroborate a higher rate of religious identification among the high-status townsfolk. Unlike the findings of Cantril, the Lynds and Warner in his work on Yankee City, however, the relations with class in these latter studies are linear. Here the upper classes have the highest rates of church membership, with the middle classes next and the lower classes last. This difference between linearity and curvilinearity will be taken up later. Meanwhile, the larger and more consistent difference between the combined high-status groups and the lower classes is of paramount concern.

Table 2 presents Hollingshead's results for Elmtown. Although Hollingshead is better known for his focus on Elmtown's youth,

Table 2

Religious Affiliation and Social Class in Elmtown

	Social Class			
	I and II	III	IV	V
% Members	97%	94%	87%	71%
N	(35)	(158)	(312)	(230)

he also published material on the general population of the community which sought to refine Warner's technique of assessing social class. For each person, Warner relied upon class ratings from a select body of informants who were mostly upper-middle-class housewives. Hollingshead also used ratings but, to avoid any bias, from informants scattered throughout the class hierarchy. The table, then, is the product of a more reliable analysis. Classes I and II are the upper- and upper-middle-classes, and these are combined because of the small number of cases. Class III, of course, is the solid middle class, class IV represents the skilled and working class and class V includes those of extremely low status, generally either unskilled laborers or unemployed. The relationship is clear and, in this case, linear. Fully 97 per cent of the topmost classes are church members; this declines consistently to only 71 per cent among the lower class.

Note that Hollingshead's percentages of identification are high for a nation in which the over-all level of formal church membership is under 65 per cent. Of course, this is largely because of Hollingshead's inclusion of informal religious preference as well as formal church membership. It is also because Hollingshead deals with a small town, and rates of religiosity and the size of the community are inversely related in our society. It is no accident that most American Protestantism has its strongest roots in a rural or frontier past.

From another view, however, these community studies raise more serious issues. It is true that each finds the lowest percentage of church members among the lower classes and the greatest proportion within the combined high-status group. But this alone does not insure an unambiguous interpretation. The studies also find social class to stand in a similar relation to every other type of voluntary association, whether social clubs, community service groups, political parties or the P.T.A. In every instance the lower classes are the most withdrawn. The conclusion is reinforced by Mather (1941), Komarovsky (1946) and Wright and Hyman (1958).

The question, then, is whether church affiliation has a religious significance beyond that of organizational affiliation in general. It is possible that church membership *per se* is a particularly poor measure of religiosity. Membership need not connote a commitment to religion. It may stake a status claim or serve as a vehicle for mobility as the cynics suggest and as Underwood (1957, esp. pp. 246–50) observes. It may be a prerequisite for something as basic as credit or a job, as witnessed by Pope and Weber.[3] Or it may simply represent a penchant for formal associations. In fact, it can be argued that the churches have sought to capitalize upon all of these motives. Lloyd Warner and Lunt (1941), Robert Lee (1962) and Charles Page (1952) have all noted that churches increasingly recruit members through a

3. Pope (1942), pp. 322–5, provides a specific instance in which the churches served as clearing-houses for mill employees. Weber (1958), makes a similar point after his travels through the United States in 1904, when he visited relatives who were backwoods farmers in North Carolina.

network of activities that are more secular than sacred. The proliferation of church recreation leagues is the referent in Page's phrase, the 'basketballization' of American religion. William H. Whyte (1956, p. 372) describes the appeal of age-group social clubs in the churches of the middle-class organization men in Park Forest, Illinois. There, during 1955, a modern jazz concert and a folk sing were the most successful gatherings of one congregation. Finally, many persons have suggested that the churches function as ladders of social standing; memberships change in response to actual, anticipated and illusory mobility.

But, of course, church membership is not antithetical to religious commitment. Moreover, the foregoing does not explain the low membership rates of the lower classes. One possible explanation here, however, is that the churches engage in selective recruitment. While their doors are open to all, as Table 1 attests, they may be especially keen on the higher-status member because of his ability to staff important positions of lay responsibility and because of his contribution to the congregation's image in the community. And yet the lower classes are not simply the abject victims of neglect or discrimination. Many prefer a more spontaneous religion and pay little attention to actual membership or even to a consistent organizational allegiance. Neither of these are important to the celebrated lower-class revivals and 'storefront' sects. Here there is great turnover and, even when membership is tallied, there is little inclination (and few channels through which) to report it to the larger Protestant councils who add the summary totals.

As further evidence for religiosity among non-church members and further testimony of the gap between formal membership and informal preference, consider the aforementioned research of Bultena (1949) in Madison, Wisconsin. While Bultena found a slight positive relation between membership and social class, he also inspected the non-members on their own terms. Roughly one-fifth of the Madison adult population in 1949 were not church members. But of these, fully 60 per cent expressed both a specific denominational preference and a high degree of private religious concern. Clearly membership is not coterminous with religious feeling or personal commitment, nor is it a prerequisite. It may represent only the most secular aspect of the high-status religious experience, and it may be irrelevant to much of lower-class religiosity. At best it is only one among many measures of involvement. At worst, it may harbor a systematic bias that affects the lower classes for whom religion may be important while membership is not.

Church attendance

Since the early 1940s, church membership has given way to church attendance as the most prominent measure of religiosity. The question, 'How often have you attended church in the past month?' is now fully entrenched in the standard repertoire of survey items. It has been related to everything from political preference and academic success to sexual compatibility. Throughout there is the assumption that attendance is an accurate gauge of religious involvement generally; indeed, for some researchers, the two are seen as identical. And yet here again the measure is far from unassailable. Although all of the studies cited show that those of high status are more frequent attenders than those of low status, the question of meaning remains. As we shall see, a low rate of attendance is not tantamount to irreligion. Attendance, like membership, assesses only one part of the religious experience.

One of the first studies to examine the relationship between church attendance and social class was the Lynds' (1929) analysis of Middletown (Muncie, Indiana). Using a dichotomous distinction between the business (white collar) and working (blue collar) classes, the Lynds found that 55 per cent of the business-class adults attended church at least three times a month, but only 25 per cent of the working class attended that frequently.

More recent community studies provide corroboration. Hollingshead's (1953) work in Elmtown uses more elaborate class distinctions as in Table 2 and finds a positive linear relationship between class and attendance that is similar to the relation between class and membership. Burchinal's (1959) findings for attendance are almost identical. Finally Gerhard Lenski's (1961, pp. 102–3) recent analysis of *The Religious Factor* in Detroit shows that the middle classes have a higher percentage of regular attendance than the working class, using a two-category class system similar to the Lynds'.

Further support comes from national polls. In 1951, the *Catholic Digest* (polls release) found that only 62 per cent of the lower class attended church but some 75 per cent of the upper class did so. A 1955 poll by the American Institute of Public Opinion reports a similar if somewhat weaker relationship. Analysis of more recent data from the A.I.P.O. again supports a positive, linear relationship between class and attendance. Here the relation was even stronger than that reported by the *Catholic Digest*.

Finally, two analyses of the actual members of single denominations have also examined the relation between class and attendance. Glock, Ringer and Babbie (1967, esp.ch. 5) inspect several measures of religiosity in their unpublished study of Episcopalians. So does Yoshio Fukuyama[4] in his study of urban Congregationalists. Both studies are consistent with previous research in their findings that the lower classes have the lowest rate of attendance, although Glock and Ringer find a curvilinear relation in which the middle classes have the highest rate and the upper-class members suffer a relative dip. Two things are important here. First, the issue of linearity versus curvilinearity apparently confounds the research on attendance as well as the research on membership. Second, the class differences in attendance are generally smaller among those who are church members than among the general population. This last observation is a useful point from which to begin a critical assessment of the research on attendance.

I have already mentioned Burchinal's results concerning class and attendance for the community at large. But the most arresting feature of Burchinal's study is his simultaneous examination of status, attendance and church membership. Dividing his small-town sample into two groups, church members and non-members, he finds that there is only a very slight relationship between social class and attendance within the categories of members and non-members considered separately. Thus, although

4. See Fukuyama (1961). Actually, Fukuyama's study closely parallels much of the present research. It appeared after the present essay was conceived, however, and provides a form of independent replication, though its brevity precludes the kind of extensive exploration intended in the following.

I have earlier indicated that membership is not the only criterion of religious involvement and may include some bias, it seems to be an important intervening[5] factor in the relation between class and attendance. The implication is that attendance may not simply reflect personal religious need, but rather the extent to which one is subject to the pressures of the church as an organization. Certainly non-members are less exposed to these pressures. This may account for as much of their low attendance as does their low status. Here, then, is one reason for restricting the generalizability of research on attendance. Much of this research ignores the factor of membership. Attendance may also reflect only a more formal and institutionalized aspect of religion and not the religious experience as a whole.

Church attendance is, of course, often pictured as pharisaical by those who are alienated from religion altogether. But without going to such extremes, there is evidence to suggest that not all attendance is religiously motivated and that the non-attenders are not exclusively Godless. Consider again the Lynds' research on the church-going practices of Middletown. With their customary thoroughness, they report not only the statistics but also some of the reasons for the statistics as supplied by the townspeople themselves. The business-class (high-status) attenders give several explanations of their behavior. Among them are the following:

You can usually hear a good sermon when you go to church, and I really have more respect for myself when I do attend church. (*or*) Why, it just never occurred to me to question church-going! (*or*) I would hate to live in a community where there was no church. I must confess I am not as interested in church or in church work as a good many. Lots of the time I am just plain bored by church, but feel I ought to go.

5. Technically, the term 'intervening' has temporal connotations. An intervening factor occurs before either the independent or the dependent variable and dictates the course of their relationship. In this case, it is difficult to make assertions regarding time order. Since membership is frequently inherited from one's parents, there are a number of persons for whom it is indeed an intervening influence in the strict sense. On the other hand, there will also be persons who begin by attending a given church and only later join it. Here the term is imprecise. Without getting into semantic difficulties, the over-all point is that membership has an effect on the relationship between attendance and social class. Time order is less important than the fact of multivariate interaction.

(*or*, *finally*) I haven't any very definite beliefs, but feel about going to church pretty much the way I do about bringing up children; I'm afraid not to go for fear my child will be missing something valuable if she is not established in habits of going to church and Sunday School (Lynd and Lynd, 1929, pp. 366–7).

Note the major themes of unquestioned loyalty, boredom, external obligation, and the need for self-respect. By contrast, the working-class non-attenders seem less inhibited about resisting social convention. They explain their lack of attendance like this:

I feel just awful and I'm ashamed, but we never go. The reason people don't go to church as much as they used to is lack of discipline in the home and lack of interest. Then there's other things: unless a person is prominent in the church or socially, people in the church have no interest in her. (*or*) Just never got interested in going to church, though I go to revivals and things like that. (*or*) There's too much dressing up for church these days; he used to go in his overalls just as good as anybody. But now it won't do for people to go without being all dressed up and we just haven't got the clothes for that. (*or*, *finally*) People are mostly hypocrites. If they really believed the things they say in church they would do something about all the things that are wrong. If all the people who have called themselves Christians for 2000 years had really believed in Jesus and his way of living, they'd 've made the world a mighty different place from what it is now (Lynd and Lynd, 1929, pp. 362–6).

It is true that the Lynds had the ears of skeptics and I have picked selectively from their quotations. Nevertheless, these remarks suggest the possible independence of church attendance on the one hand and religious concern on the other. Attendance may play vastly different roles in the religious experience of different classes – or, indeed, no role at all. For some of the high-status attenders, actual religious feeling is strikingly absent. At the same time, all of these lower-class non-attenders can hardly be classified as irreligious. There is one who enjoys revivals and another who is agitated over religious hypocrisy.

Actually most of the authors cited in this section make similar qualifications of the meaning of the relation between class and attendance. In addition to Burchinal and the Lynds, Hollingshead reports that social class bears no relation whatsoever to belief in God. Attendance and belief are both important facets of religiosity, however, and if social class is not consistently related to both, one must probe deeper for a more complicated relation between class and religiosity as a whole. As we shall see later, Glock and Ringer, and Fukuyama also report that class stands in different relation to other facets of involvement. Clearly attendance does not exhaust the domain. It is possible that it, like membership before and like parish activities to follow, reflects only the 'doing' dimension of religiosity and not the important aspect of religious 'feeling'. The relation with class seems dependent upon the distinction.

Parish activities

In moving from church attendance to activities within the organization, we are moving in a secular direction. I have already noted that the churches sponsor many groups which compete with the attractions of the non-church community. In addition to such common activities as the choir, the Sunday School staff and the ladies' aid, a parish will frequently sponsor a basketball team, a bowling league, a great-books discussion group and possibly a circle or two of group therapy. Moreover, every congregation relies upon its laymen to staff important positions of responsibility which keep the organizations going. These might include positions on the finance committee and the building committee, and the representatives of the denominational lay councils on a national level. Among these activities, one might distinguish between recreational activities and responsibilities. However, persons of high status appear to dominate both.

Some of the earliest speculation on the relation between class and religion centers in this area. Max Weber's[6] comparative analysis of Confucianism, Hinduism, Judaism and emerging Protestantism makes the point that religious movements carry the near indelible stamp of the status group that founded them. For example, some Protestant groups such as the Episcopalians, Presbyterians and Congregationalists have their roots in a bourgeois reaction to Catholicism and seem to have retained this high-status trademark. Extending Weber's argument, a corollary applies to more recent denominations that began as lower-class

6. For a useful summary of Weber's work in this area, as well as a detailed bibliography, see Bendix (1960), pp. 71–265.

sects in the wake of the Reformation. Thus, within any religious movement, the highest-ranking status group will assume lay leadership and dictate the religious mood. This would apply to the Baptists, the Methodists and the Lutherans, for example.

Weber's argument rests on the premise that parish activities are more than incidental to the religious spirit of the congregation. For one thing, they provide more intimate contact with the religious leadership and, thereby, an avenue of influence. For another, many of these activities are instrumental in getting things done. Laymen are often ascribed a knowledge of finance and secular concerns that extends beyond the pastor's. They often have the opportunity to turn the church as an organization to their own designs.

Qualitative evidence that this has occurred is available in several historical analyses of developing churches and denominations. S. D. Clark's (1948) study of Canadian Methodism reveals the growing pressures of the high-status laity and the growing disaffection of the lower classes. Paul Harrison's (1959) more recent analysis of the American Baptist Convention affords another instance of this. Although it began as a lower-class sect, the Baptist movement has taken on higher-status members who have exerted increasing influence towards modernization. According to Harrison, not only has much of Baptist fundamentalism been subdued, but its principle of local autonomy for each parish has been subverted. Bureaucratization has quietly gained sway at the national level.

But apart from qualitative evidence of influence in strategic spots, there is also quantitative evidence of greater high-status participation in activities generally. Glock, Ringer and Babbie (1967) find that the association between class and parish activity is no different than that between class and membership or church attendance. While women are typically more active than men, and the upper class is less involved than the middle class, it remains true that those of generally high status participate more than those of low status.

Although parish activity does not have the currency of attendance as a measure of religiosity, Glock and Ringer are not alone in their general findings. Fukuyama (1961) reports a generally similar relation between class and activity among Congregationalists. Hollingshead's (1953) aforementioned study of adult religion in Elmtown confirms the lower classes as the least active in church organizations. Harold Kaufman (1953) has found both participation and lay leadership positively related to class in a rural farm community in upper New York state. It might be noted, however, that these latter three studies differ from Glock and Ringer's work with urban Episcopalians in two respects. First, neither Fukuyama, Hollingshead nor Kaufman reports a curvilinear relation as do Glock and Ringer; in each case, the extreme upper class is the most active and the association is consistently linear. Second, because Glock and Ringer as well as Fukuyama, are dealing with church members alone, the relation between class and activity is weaker than those reported in Hollingshead's and Kaufman's studies of whole communities. Once more, membership seems to be an important factor in the relation between class and involvement.

But there is a more important qualification of the association. Like membership and attendance, the meaning of parish activities is unclear. I have already mentioned the secular quality of most activities. This alone creates suspicion of attempts to use them as measures of religious involvement as a whole. A more empirical caveat can be inferred from Glock and Ringer's study. Their concern is not solely with religious involvement in itself, but also with involvement in the church versus involvement in other aspects of the community. Now it is true that class is positively related to parish activity when other commitments are not considered. But if one compares high- and low-status adherents on the *proportion* of sacred to secular activities, the differences reverse. Thus, the low-status parishioner spends a larger amount of his organizational investment on the church than does the high-status member. Kenneth Lutterman (1962, esp. ch. 8, pp. 37–8) provides similar evidence for investment of a more literal sort in his study of financial giving to churches. Although the low-status church member may give less money to the church on absolute grounds, he gives a higher percentage of his income. In short, even a small donation or a single activity may be more salient for the lower-class member because it is less rivalled by commitments of other sorts. Again, then, there are reasons for doubting the case for high-status religiosity.

347

Linearity v. curvilinearity

Although all of the studies cited agree that the higher classes generally are the most active, several dispute the linearity of the association. Warner and Lunt, Cantril, Bultena, and Glock and Ringer have all found that involvement is highest among the middle classes. This is at odds with the studies of Fukuyama, Hollingshead, West, Kaufman, Burchinal, the *Catholic Digest*, and later reports of the American Institute of Public Opinion that find religiosity at its peak among the extreme upper classes.

Now survey research is subject to myriad idiosyncracies which make comparisons among studies risky. It is possible, for example, that the discrepancy between Cantril, Warner, and Glock and Ringer, on the one hand, and Fukuyama, the *Catholic Digest*, and the American Institute of Public Opinion, on the other, is adducible to different definitions of social class. The latter studies use a broader definition of upper class, and, thus, include many of the highly involved middle-class types as well.

But the disparity in the remaining studies may reflect something else. All of the studies reporting the upper class most involved deal with predominantly farming communities of less than 6000 persons. By contrast, all of the studies that find the middle classes most involved deal with samples drawn largely from urban areas with populations in excess of 50,000. There are, of course, considerable differences between America's Elmtowns and Middletowns. One particular difference seems crucial here. Most small towns do not observe a sharp demarcation between the middle and upper classes. Not only are rural upper classes 'less upper' than their urban counterparts, but they are also more visible and better integrated into the community as a whole. In fact, the small-town upper classes are the community leaders, and this is necessarily manifest in such key community institutions as the churches.

On the other hand, urban areas are better able to sustain a distinction. The upper class is more socially distant through pronounced educational and power advantages. It is also less visible since its members are usually ensconced in retreats such as the board of directors of a business firm, foreign travel, exclusive country clubs, and a self-sustaining social world that is frequently endogamous. The urban upper class may rule the productive community, but it tends to withdraw from the community's voluntary activities. As if filling a vacuum, the middle classes provide the leadership here and, again, this is manifested in the churches.

Sinclair Lewis supplies a biting distinction between the upper- and middle-class religious styles in his stereotyped city of Zenith. The speaker is advising the Reverend Mr Gantry on the local social clubs:

> Yeh, but the owner of the Advocate, and the banker that's letting Win Grant run on till he bankrupts, and the corporation counsel that keeps 'em all out of jail, you don't find *those* malefactors going to no lunch club and yipping about Service! You find 'em sitting at small tables at the old Union Club, and laughing themselves sick about Service. . . . I couldn't get you into the Union Club. They wouldn't have any preacher that talks about vice – the kind of preacher that belongs to the Union talks about the new model Cadillac and how hard it is to get genuwine Eyetalian vermouth. But the Tonawanda – they might let you in. For respectability. To prove that they couldn't have the gin they've got in their lockers in their lockers (Lewis, 1960, p. 373).

This distinction between the populations of the discrepant studies is only speculative, but it does provide one possible reconciliation.

Of course, the problem of the relative involvement of the upper and middle classes pales beside the larger issue of the religiosity of the lower classes versus the higher classes generally. Here, as we have seen, the statistics are clear enough, yet they are qualified by three major considerations. First, church membership, attendance and parish activity all relate to formal participation in the church as an organization and not necessarily to private religious feelings. Second, the relation of class to attendance (and possibly parish activity) is partially an artifact of differential exposure to organizational pressures rather than a simple reflection of personal religious needs. Finally, the same type of religiosity may mean one thing to high-status parishioners and quite another to those of low status. Thus, church membership may be irrelevant to the more spontaneous religion of the lower classes. Here revivals may supplant formal church attendance, and even a small amount of parish activity may be more meaningful since these people are less active in secular groups.

The Case for Low-Status Religiosity

All of the qualifications of high-status involvement would seem hollow indeed if there were no empirical support in the opposite direction. The present section suggests, however, that this has not been mere cavilling. Although studies reporting the lower classes most involved are in the minority, their sparseness is no measure of their significance. Accuracy rather than bulk is the final arbiter.

Actually, some of the studies already mentioned include side-remarks on low-status religiosity – remarks that are overwhelmed in the final tally. The Lynds, for example, divide their treatment of Middletown religion into four chapters: dominant religious beliefs, where and when religious beliefs are carried on, leaders and participants in religious rites and, last, religious observances. The fourth of these is by far the most elaborate. It was cited in the last section for its description of the business class as the most frequent church-attenders and most likely church members. But the first chapter offers a contrast in dealing with religious beliefs. The Lynds summarize as follows:

First, members of the working class show a disposition to believe their religion more ardently and to accumulate more emotionally charged values around their beliefs. Religion appears to operate more prominently as an active agency of support and encouragement among this section of the city. A second point is the shift in the status of certain religious beliefs during the past generation – notably the decline, *particularly among the business class*, in the emphasis upon Heaven, and still more upon Hell (Lynd and Lynd, 1929, p. 329; Demerath's italics).

The Lynds observe further that the secularization of Middletown religion has occurred at different rates for the two classes. When asked if 'it is wrong to go to the movies on Sunday', roughly a third of the working-class high schoolers replied 'yes', as compared with only a sixth of the business-class students.

A second research that finds both positive and negative relations between status and religiosity is Gerhard Lenski's (1961) recent analysis of a small sample of Detroiters. The study is concerned more with the effect of religiosity on status than vice versa, yet it reports not only that attendance is directly related to class but also that other forms of involvement are inversely related to class. Persons of middle-class occupations and college educations are slightly less likely to be doctrinally orthodox and devotionally active than those with working-class occupations and without college educations.

Another study that harbors a discrepancy between high- and low-status religiosity is Glock and Ringer's research with Episcopalians. In addition to church attendance and organizational activity, they used a third measure of involvement pertaining to the 'intellectual dimension'. This refers to the parishioner's knowledge of traditional doctrine and the extent to which he reads religious literature. Whereas church attendance and parish activity are at their lowest ebb among the lower classes, the situation is reversed for intellectual involvement. Among women, the lower class scores highest with 51 per cent intellectually involved, and this decreases to 41 per cent among the lower-middle, 34 per cent among the upper-middle, and 28 per cent among the upper class. Among men, the percentages run in the same order from a peak of 32 per cent for those of low status to a depression of 17 per cent for those of extremely high status.

Conflicting relations with status also occur in Fukuyama's analysis of Congregationalists. Fukuyama delineates four types of religiosity which he labels the cultic, cognitive, creedal and devotional. The cultic is an amalgam of church attendance and organizational activity and its positive relation with class has already been reported. The cognitive represents the parishioner's knowledge of religious doctrine and the affairs of his congregation. The creedal signifies personal allegiance to traditional doctrine, regardless of one's detailed knowledge. Finally, the devotional connotes personal prayer and reliance upon religion beyond the church itself.

Table 3 presents the relation between each of these facets and social class. As we learned previously, the *cultic* is positively related to class, and gives a range from 53 per cent involved among those of generally high status to only 35 per cent among those of low status. The relation is also positive for the *cognitive*

Table 3

Social Class and Four Types of Religiosity among
Congregationalists

Four Dimensions % Highly Involved	Socioeconomic Status		
	High	Moderate	Low
	%	%	%
Cultic	53	43	31
Cognitive	28	24	15
Creedal	27	28	31
Devotional	16	23	32

Abstracted from Fukuyama (1961), p. 159.

dimension, although it is important to note that, unlike Glock and Ringer's 'intellectual commitment' above, this dimension refers only to knowledge itself and not to involvement in it. Moreover, it refers to knowledge of the congregation as well as to knowledge of the doctrine. That one *knows* the financial state of his parish does not mean that he will develop a deep-rooted attachment to it. As with knowledge of most things, religious knowledge should increase with familiarity and with education. Since the high-status parishioners are apt to be active in parish administration and well educated, this helps to account for their high score. However, the other two dimensions of religiosity offer contrasting relations with class. Both *creedal* and *devotional* religiosity increase among progressively lower-status groups, although this is only pronounced for the latter. Both refer to a more inward religiosity that is concerned less with the formal church and more with personal feelings. Fukuyama (1961, p. 159) concludes that 'different social classes differ not so much in the degree to which they are religiously oriented but in the manner in which they give expression to their religious propensities'.

A last study that finds the lower classes more religiously involved is my own survey in Winchester, Massachusetts (Demerath, 1958). Actually, in this area the individual's own status has less bearing upon his religiosity than does his parents' status – succor to the argument that one's religion is a product of one's rearing and changes little in substance thereafter. Nevertheless, both forms of status are negatively related to fundamentalism in religious beliefs,[7] and, in both cases, the lower classes are less tolerant of religious relativism. Roughly one-third of the high-status group believe in either or both heaven and hell; this increases to more than two-thirds among the low-status respondents. When asked their hypothetical reaction to their child's desire to change his religious affiliation, a similar pattern obtains. The lower class is apt to be reproachful, while the middle and upper classes are more permissive.[8] Finally, those of low status have a higher frequency of personal prayer and even perceive prayer differently. They see it as a spiritual duologue and divine source of guidance. The higher-status respondents interpret it more as self-administered therapy in the secular psychiatric sense.[9]

And yet here, as with high-status religiosity, there are grounds for dispute. Although the Lynds, Lenski, Glock and Ringer, Fukuyama and my own previous research suggest that the lower classes are more religious when religiosity is measured by personal belief and private practice, two final studies provide some doubt. One of these is Gerhard Lenski's (1953) early analysis of social class and 'religious interest' in a representative sample of the Indianapolis area. Certainly interest alone is more personal and less institutionalized than formal membership, attendance and parish activities. But when Lenski related interest to four separate measures of status, he found more ambiguity than consistency. When class is measured by occupational prestige, the

7. The doctrine of predestination provides an interesting exception among Catholics. High-status Catholics are more frequent believers on this item alone when compared to low-status Catholics. But, of course, predestination is antithetical to traditional Catholic theology and the absence of belief among the lower classes reflects orthodoxy rather than apathy.

8. In this connexion, see Nunn (1964). Nunn finds that the coalition is most common among lower-class parents. This is one of several unique measures of religiosity that might be added to the support for the argument that lower-class religious involvement is greater than middle- or upper-class involvement. I am indebted to Warren O. Hagstrom for this reference.

9. Cf. Gurin, Veroff and Feld (1960), pp. 372–6. Here it is reported that those of low status are more apt to resort to prayer in periods of emotional stress. Hence we have still another measure of religious involvement that indicates that the lower-class are far from alienated from religion altogether.

family's total financial worth and the respondent's education, the lower classes are slightly more interested than the middle and upper classes. When class is measured by the household's yearly income, the high-status respondents show more interest. Although one can argue that the differences are generally in the predicted inverse direction and no smaller than the differences that Lenski later accepted in Detroit, here he rejects all of the findings as statistically insignificant.

The second study which provides grounds for suspicion is Rodney Stark's[10] analysis of national polls in Great Britain and the United States. Surprisingly, Stark finds that *both* participation and belief are positively related to social class in each country. Thus, the higher one's status, the more one is likely to attend church regularly and the more one is likely to claim belief in God. The latter finding is, of course, the puzzle since its positive relationship is a blatant contradiction of the negative association described by others.

How can we explain these discrepancies? One tack is to point out the considerable difference between such nebulous items as 'belief in God' and 'religious interest', on the one hand, and more precise questions such as religious reading and the interpretation and extent of personal prayer, on the other. The forme questions will elicit positive answers from all but the most confirmed atheists, and atheism has never been the vogue in American upper-class circles. The latter questions, however, provide more range. They allow the researcher to discriminate between the more traditional and the more secularized positions. It may be that the essential difference between classes lies at this more delicate level.

Another explanation for the disparity concerns the populations studied. Both Lenski and Stark examined samples that were designed to represent whole metropolitan areas and whole nations. By contrast, my own research in Winchester focused on a small town in New England where the Catholic church sets

10. Rodney W. Stark, 'Class, radicalism and church attendance in Great Britain', a paper delivered at the meetings of the American Sociological Association, Washington, D.C., September 1962. This paper includes only part of the results mentioned. [For subsequent publication details see p. 454 of this book – Ed.]

much of the religious tone for the lower classes. The Lynds looked at only a single small city where church membership was the norm in the 1920s. And Glock and Ringer and Fukuyama were concerned only with affiliated Episcopalians and Congregationalists. The difference here points to an important hypothesis concerning lower-class religion in general. If a lower-class individual is committed to religion at all, his internal involvement is likely to be higher than that of his higher-status church-fellows. On the other hand, there is a large segment of the lower class that has no religious commitment whatsoever. Perhaps because these people have found functional alternatives to religion in political extremism,[11] trade unions or the extended family, they are markedly different and must be held apart in any assessment of the church's importance to its members. Neither Stark nor Lenski compartmentalized the two lower-class groups, and this resulted in a low over-all rate of religiosity. My research in Winchester dealt with an anomalous town where the distinction may not have been so important. Glock and Ringer and Fukuyama focused only on those who had some religious commitment in the first place.

11. It is important to note that some of the most militant anti-clerical and, indeed, anti-religious movements are both lower-class and politically to the left. The American Rationalist Federation, for example, has deep roots in European socialism. Many of its branches comprise lower-class European ethnics who rally around rationalism for an identity that is distinct from the persecuting state churches of their native countries. In Europe itself, the ties between organized free thought and left-wing politics are even stronger. For example, the West German 'freie Gemeinde' are particularly powerful but also particularly communistic in political coloration. The author is currently beginning research on this end of the religious spectrum.

References
BENDIX, R. (1960), *Max Weber: An Intellectual Portrait*, Doubleday.
BULTENA, L. (1949), 'Church membership and church attendance in Madison, Wisconsin', *Amer. soc. Rev.*, vol. 14, pp. 384–91.
BURCHINAL, L. G. (1959), 'Some social status criteria and church membership and church attendance', *J. soc. Psych.* vol. 49, pp. 53–64.
CANTRIL, H. (1943), 'Educational and economic composition of religious groups', *Amer. J. Soc.*, vol. 48, pp. 574–9.
CLARK, S. D. (1948), *Church and Sect in Canada*, University of Toronto Press.

DEMERATH, N. J., III (1958), Religious participation, attitudes and beliefs in an adult sample, *unpublished A.B. honors thesis, Harvard College.*

DE TOCQUEVILLE, A. (1954), *Democracy in America*, Vintage, vol. 2.

FUKUYAMA, Y. (1961), 'The major dimensions of church membership', *Rev. relig. Know.*, vol. 2, pp. 154–61.

GLOCK, C. Y., RINGER, B. B., and BABBIE, E. R. (1967), *To Comfort and to Challenge*, University of California Press.

GURIN, G., VEROFF, J., and FELD, S. (1960), *Americans View their Mental Health*, Basic Books.

HARRISON, P. M. (1959), *Authority and Power in the Free Church Tradition: A Social Case Study of the American Baptist Convention*, Princeton University Press.

HOLLINGSHEAD, A. (1949), *Elmtown's Youth*, Yale University Press.

HOLLINGSHEAD, A. (1953), 'Selected characteristics of classes in a Middle Western community', in R. Bendix and S. M. Lipset, eds., *Class, Status and Power*, Free Press, pp. 213–24.

KAUFMAN, H. (1953), 'Prestige classes in a New York rural community' in R. Bendix and S. M. Lipset, eds., *Class, Status and Power*, Free Press, pp. 190–203.

KOMAROVSKY, M. (1946), 'The voluntary associations of urban dwellers', *Amer. soc. Rev.*, vol. 11, pp. 686–98.

LEE, R. (1962), 'The organizational dilemma in American Protestantism' in H. Cleveland and H. D. Lasswell, eds., *The Conference on Science, Philosophy and Religion: Ethics and Bigness*, Harper, pp. 187–211.

LENSKI, G. (1953), 'Social correlates of religious interest', *Amer. soc. Rev.*, vol. 18, pp. 533–44.

LENSKI, G. (1961), *The Religious Factor: A Sociologist's Inquiry*, Doubleday.

LEWIS, S. (1960), *Elmer Gantry*, Deu.

LLOYD WARNER, W., and LUNT, P. S. (1941), *The Social System of a Modern Community*, Yale University Press.

LLOYD WARNER, W., et al. (1949), *Democracy in Jonesville*, Harper.

LUTTERMAN, K. J. (1962), Giving to churches: a sociological study of the contributions to eight Catholic and Lutheran churches, *Unpublished Ph.D. dissertation, University of Wisconsin.*

LYND, R. and LYND, H. (1929), *Middletown*, Harcourt, Brace.

MARTINEAU, H. (1962), *Society in America*, Doubleday, Anchor.

MATHER, W. A. (1941), 'Income and social participation', *Amer. soc. Rev.*, vol. 6, pp. 380–83.

NIEBUHR, H. R. (1929), *The Social Sources of Denominationalism*, Holt.

NUNN, C. Z. (1964), 'Child control through a "coalition with God"', *Child Dev.*, vol. 35, pp. 417–32.

PAGE, C. (1952), 'Bureaucracy and the liberal church', *Rev. Relig.*, vol. 16, pp. 137–50.

PARSONS, T. (1960), *Structure and Process in Modern Societies*, Free Press.

POPE, L. (1942), *Millhands and Preachers*, Yale University Press.

POPE, L. (1953), 'Religion and the class structure', in R. Bendix and S. M. Lipset, eds., *Class, Status and Power*, Free Press, pp. 316–23.

SCHNEIDER, H. (1952), *Religion in 20th-Century America*, Harvard University Press.

UNDERWOOD, K. W. (1957), *Protestant and Catholic; Religion and Social Interaction in an Industrial Community*, Beacon.

WEBER, M. (1958), 'The Protestant sects and the spirit of capitalism', in H. Gerth and C. Wright Mills, eds., *From Max Weber, Essays in Sociology*, Oxford, Galaxy Books, pp. 302–22.

WEST, J. (1945), *Plainville, U.S.A.*, Columbia University Press.

WHYTE, W. H. (1956), *The Organization Man*, Simon & Schuster.

WRIGHT, C. R., and HYMAN, H. H. (1958), 'Voluntary association membership of American adults: evidence from National Sample Surveys', *Amer. soc. Rev.*, vol. 23, pp. 284–94.

IV. Religious Collectivities

In this section the contributions deal with religious movements and organizations. One of the favourite themes of sociologists of religion during the past 40 years or so has been that deriving from Max Weber's distinction between *church* and *sect*. Basically, the terms have been used to distinguish religious organizations which are supportive of the culture and social structure of the society in which they operate and those which in some form or other reject the nature of the wider society. Some useful and important work has been done in this tradition of analysis; but, on the other hand, much of the discussion has been sterile and unproductive, in the sense that the church–sect theme has become something of a sociological obsession. In any case the distinction between church and sect derived very much from a Christian perspective and sociologists have had the greatest difficulty in applying it productively to non-Christian societies. Most of the more fruitful discussions of the problem of developing an adequate sociological classification or typology of religious organizations movements have been the work of American sociologists and most of these discussions have been undertaken in reference to American society. We have chosen here to present contributions which range across a number of different types of society and not to become too involved in the over-developed church–sect theme – although Wilson's article (Reading 20) on sects touches succinctly on some aspects of the controversy. Wilson is mainly concerned to extend our understanding of religious sects – organizations or movements which regard themselves as religiously 'special' and unique and are typically set apart from the wider society. His article is a follow-up to a very well-known contribution (Wilson, 1959) to the analysis of sectarian movements in industrial societies. His intention here is to widen our perspective and knowledge by looking additionally at pre-industrial and primitive societies; although the movements he considers from these kinds of society are frequently local responses to the impact of industrial societies. Fernandez's piece (Reading 21) tackles the problem of delineating different types of religious movement in Africa, with special reference to the problem of the relationship between religious and political pre-occupations and goals – a problem which a number of anthropologists and sociologists have confronted when analysing movements which developed in response to European colonization and intrusion (see particularly Worsley, 1968).

References

WILSON, B. R. (1959), 'An analysis of sect development', *Amer. soc. Rev.*, vol. 24, pp. 3–15.

WORSLEY, P. (1968), *The Trumpet Shall Sound*, McGibbon & Kee, and Schocken Books, revised edn.

20 B. R. Wilson

A Typology of Sects

B. R. Wilson, 'A typology of sects in a dynamic and comparative perspective', *Archives de Sociologie de Religion*, vol. 16 (1963), pp. 49–63. Translated by Jenny M. Robertson.

In spite of the work of J. M. Yinger and Peter Berger (to say nothing of those who deal with religious movements in non-industrial societies) it is still too often claimed that the sect–church dichotomy (with the addition sometimes of the 'cult') is an adequate tool for analysis in the sociology of religion (Berger, 1954; Simpson, 1955, 1956; Sundkler, 1948; Yinger, 1946, 1957). Since Yinger established types of sects and types of churches, our work has in fact outgrown Troeltsch's dichotomy. We are now beginning to use categories which do not depend exclusively on the opposition between the conservative church and the perfectionist sect, types in which Troeltsch had seen 'a logical outcome of the Gospels . . .' (Troeltsch, 1931, p. 341). If the sociology of religion is to move forward, we must create categories which allow us to study comparatively the social functions and development of religious movements. As a consequence, such studies must shun categories dictated too specifically by the characteristics of a particular theological tradition. Obviously, the types we can use are still drawn mainly from the material at our disposal, especially from Christian movements. But it is imperative that we should try to enlarge their application, and, if needs be, modify their formulation in the light of this extension of their meaning, so that we shall have a series of analytical instruments which will no longer be centred on a particular civilization and religion (in this case, Christian).

One of the principal obstacles to this development lies in the fact that the sociology of religion is a field in which sociological thinking and religious thinking are not always distinguished clearly. The interest which theologians take in this special field and the education they have received are likely to perpetuate the use of specific categories which are indifferent to sociologically significant distinctions. This is not to say that the contributions of theologians to the field are without value. Sometimes they provide valuable insights; but they often also introduce elements of confusion. In one recent study, Martin E. Marty (1960) has characterized sects as oriented negatively to the wider society and 'cults' as positively oriented. This distinction is pre-eminently sociological. It is not a question of their conception of God, which is a distinction of a theological nature. Nevertheless, it seems to me we need a more refined typology of responses to the outside world. There are variations of positive or negative orientation which interest the sociologist.

Sects are ideological movements having as their explicit and declared aim the maintenance, and perhaps even the propagation of certain ideological positions. One must, therefore, admit that those whose interest lies above all in ideological questions (the source and credibility of ideas about God, and justification of practices in his name) have a legitimate interest in the study of sects. But sociological distinctions are not simply based on the distinctions of theological belief and practice, and certainly not on the *odium theologicum* which tries to characterize sects as extremist. In a valuable contribution to our conception of the denomination as a type, D. A. Martin places the denomination in opposition to the sect, without always giving enough attention to the diversity among sects. He describes them as if they were always revolutionary or introversionist, perhaps using as his authority for this the classifications proposed by Troeltsch. Martin writes: 'While the denomination is characterized by moderation, the sect is either communist or anarchist, revolutionary or quietest, nudist or uniformed, ascetic or licentious, completely sacramental or non-sacramental, worshipping in a wild communal rant, or, like the Seekers, utter silence' (Martin, 1962). Martin thus character-izes sectarian eschatology as adventist and sects as revolutionary, except in the case where too great a disillusionment has made them quietist. It is always easy to criticize a typology by under-lining the case which does not correspond to the proposed classifications; but Martin's is too gross. Sects are not easily marshalled into a few dichotomies. The Brethren, Quakers and Christadelphians are neither communist nor anarchist; the different Darbyist groups, Jehovah's Witnesses, Church of God in British Isles and Overseas, the holiness movements do not worship in a wild rant nor in total silence; the Assemblies of God are neither ascetic nor licentious. But who would deny that these are sects? In fact, this kind of analysis takes the part as the whole; it overlooks the way in which separate elements combine together, and almost completely ignores the various possibilities for the transformation of sects.

From the sociologist's point of view, there are three sorts of drawback to the theological or doctrinal classification of sects. First of all, such a classification limits the possibilities for the comparative study of sects within different religious traditions. In the second place, it prevents recognition of other significant aspects of the character of sects, for the doctrine may persist when the social organization and the orientation of the movement have changed. Thus, classification which grows from doctrinal description does not sufficiently take into account the organizational and dynamic aspects of sects. Thirdly, because it is theological, this kind of classification runs the risk of stigmatizing the sect and characterizing it in terms which are essentially normative.

The sociologist can use diverse principles of classification to study sects. The structural aspect has perhaps not been thoroughly explored, although it may perhaps not offer a wide enough view of the phenomenon. I wish here to develop a classification I used in a previous study of the transformation of sects (Wilson, 1959), in the hope that this typology can be shown to be of use in the analysis of sectarian movements in non-Christian and non-Western environments. I also wish to attempt a first, tentative step, and only by way of experiment, in applying this typology to religious movements at the fringes of Christianity. This classification takes as its central criterion the sect's *response to the world*. It is hoped that we shall find there an adequate principle of classification, capable of advancing the comparative study of sects and also of sect development.

One clearly sees that our criterion of response to the outside world constitutes a variable influenced by doctrinal thought, although it is not perhaps determined by that alone. It recognizes the ideological character of sects, without nevertheless neglecting

363

the way of life of the sect's members, which also necessarily affect the manner in which they accept, reject, neglect or attempt to transcend, to improve or to transvaluate the opportunities which worldly society may offer. Here we have a factor which can effect change without producing specific doctrinal changes, in response simply to the social changes affecting the members of the sect. Of course, a certain specific type of response is more likely to be seen in certain age groups, in certain social classes, among people with particular educational backgrounds or in certain ecological contexts. It might also be more attractive to one sex than another; it will suit better a rural situation, or an urban or a suburban one. And it may arise and develop at one stage rather than at another of the social and cultural history of the sect under review. In this article we shall not be able to examine all these variables individually. But we shall intimate certain relationships between different types of sects and different stages of cultural development.

I should now like to propose a seven-fold classification of sects. Four of these types have already been put forward; but here I distinguish characteristics in quite a different way from that which I adopted in my previous research. I define each type in terms of its response to the world, of the kind of reaction which dominates the customary practices and its members' beliefs. For each of these types is suggested the typical theological position in Christian sects, by giving a few specific examples of these movements. We define also the activities to which they typically devote themselves and refer to the biblical texts which they favour. The reader will understand that I do not claim that all these texts hold the same importance in Christian tradition, but that I seek simply to illustrate the way in which sects attempt to integrate with this tradition. I have not tried, except very tentatively and where the evidence is perfectly clear, to suggest from which social groups these sects recruit.

The *conversionist* sect is the typical sect of 'evangelical', fundamentalist Christianity. Its reaction towards the outside world is to suggest that the latter is corrupted because man is corrupted. If men can be changed then the world will be changed. This type of sect takes no interest in programmes of social reform or in the political solution of social problems and may even be actively hostile towards them.

Its judgement on man and events tends to be moralizing, because it is believed that man is entirely responsible for his actions. It rejects all causal explanations which take into account the influence of environment on behaviour, or any other determinist explanation. Typical activities of this type of sects are revivalism and public preaching at mass meetings rather than door to door. The leaders of the sect mobilize the group and use techniques of mass persuasion in order to convert individuals. The dominant note in the atmosphere of the group is of an emotional, but not ecstatic, nature. Among Christian sects, the texts regarded highly are those which encourage the preaching of the Gospel throughout the world. They attach great significance to the relationship between the individual and a personal saviour, a relationship expressed in direct emotional terms rather than in a symbolic or ritualistic manner. They hold the total understanding of the doctrine to be less important than the profound feeling of the essential personal relationship. In the same way as they interpret the Scripture literally, the sect's members tend to take this relationship literally. For them the Saviour is a person, a sort of benevolent and suffering Superman. The Salvation Army, in the first stages of its existence, the Assemblies of God and other pentecostal movements, as well as independent evangelical sects, are examples of this type of sect.

One recognizes the *revolutionary* type in the eschatological movements of the Christian tradition. Its attitude towards the outside world is summed up in a desire to be rid of the present social order when the time is ripe – if necessary, by force and violence. Its members are awaiting a new order under God's direction. They will then become the holders of power as the friends and representatives of God. This type of sect is hostile at one and the same time to social reform and instantaneous conversion. It is not opposed to causal explanations, in so far as one accepts its own assumptions of causal categories. It tends to explain the world in determinist terms, just as it tends to consider the fate of individuals as pre-determined. In the Christian tradition, we have therefore a position which is more Calvinist than Arminian. One meets here less tendency to moralize than among the *conversionists*, for reproaches are out of place when one likes to consider all events as the accomplishment of a divine plan. The members of these sects occupy themselves actively in prophetic exegesis, in comparisons of inspired texts and between the predictions of the sect and contemporary events. They often have long-drawn-out internal debates elaborating prospects of the future. Conversion is considered to be an occasional and gradual occurrence, and comes about only when the stranger to the sect has familiarized himself completely with the complexity of sect belief and is convinced of its truth. Permission to belong is not given freely, and the revolutionary sect, when it is fully institutionalized, seeks to maintain itself in a state of vigilance and doctrinal purity. Its meetings are matter-of-fact, unemotional occasions. These are occasions to praise God decently and without emotional excess, for speaking of one's calm certainty that the promises will be fulfilled. The biblical texts in favour in these circles are directly eschatological or else obscure visions from prophetic books which can be interpreted as relevant predictions for the present period. They see God as a divine autocrat, as a leader, a dictator whose impenetrable will imposes itself on the progress of the universe. One finds in these sects little feeling of a direct relationship with divinity. On the contrary, their members have the feeling that they are God's instruments, waiting for the decreed moment, agents of His work and will. Jehovah's Witnesses, Christadelphians and the Fifth Monarchy Men (England, seventeenth century) are typical representatives of these ideas.

The pietist sects represent the *introversionist* type whose response to the world is neither to convert the population nor to expect the world's overturn, but simply in retiring from it to enjoy the security gained by personal holiness. This type is completely indifferent to social reforms, to individual conversion and to social revolutions. None of these elements seems significant to these sects in their view of their position and task on this earth. The introversionist sect may accept, especially in its early stages, some particular inspirational experiences and retain them for objective phenomena significant for the entire group, or consider them as purely individual revelations which might help the growth of personal piety. These groups are concerned more with deepening than widening spiritual experience. One finds among them a certain disdain for those 'without holiness' and with little or no desire to introduce them to it. These movements' meetings are 'assemblies of the saved' (gathered remnant). The community will support the individual and hold him in its bosom, rather than push him to seek his mission in the outside world. These groups, if Christian, put great weight on biblical texts which exhort the faithful to be a law unto themselves and to live apart from the world. They conceive of a divinity of the type of the Holy Spirit rather than in a more personalized way. The real relationship in this case is less than between sinner and saviour, rather that between outpouring vial and receiving vessel. Typical examples of this category of sects can be seen in certain 'holiness movements', as well as in European pietist movements of the eighteenth century.

Manipulationist sects, which I previously called gnostic, are those which insist especially on a particular and distinctive knowledge. They define themselves *vis-à-vis* the outside world essentially by accepting its goals. They frequently proclaim a more spiritualized and ethereal version of the cultural ends of global society but do not reject them. These sects instead try to change the methods appropriate to attaining these ends. They sometimes claim that the only way of achieving this is to use the special knowledge taught by the movement. That is the only true and worthwhile way of acquiring health, wealth, happiness and social prestige. Although reinterpreting 'worldly' activities, these sects offer special techniques and verbal modes of assurance which justify the pursuit and attainment of cultural goals. These movements are thus of the type sometimes called 'cults', and which Marty[1] depicts as positively oriented towards the outside world. They offer, by means of publicity, facilities for learning their systems but do not provoke conversions since the important thing is for them to acquire spiritual attitudes rather than to offer specific activities or relationships. The group life of these movements is often reduced to an absolute minimum, their gnosis being impersonal. Anyone may accept it and use it for his personal ends

1. See Marty (1960). This author suggests that 'cults' collapse in the absence of a charismatic leader. But this type of leader is far from being a constant factor in the movements Marty embraces under this name. They often prosper in a completely impersonal context – such is the case in the various branches of New Thought and Rosicrucianism.

since its efficacy is not dependent on any relationship or on any mystical process. When the members of these movements come together, the chief function of their assembly seems to be not so much for worship or devotion as to claim prestige and social status for successes achieved using the special teachings of the sect. These movements are often syncretist, even within the Christian tradition. But they use evangelical texts such as those where Christ affirmed that he had many other things to say, but that men could not bear to hear them. Divinity is understood, implicitly or explicitly, as a source of laws or principles to apply in one's daily life. The idea of a personal saviour is reduced here to a minimum and one notices the absence of any emotional relationship with God, or a relationship of authority. Provided he can take the trouble, anyone can learn the doctrine, which can be applied universally. These sects take little interest in eschatology. They are interested in results in this world, and the hereafter seems to them simply an enhancement of present joys. Typical groups of this type in Christian countries are Christian Scientists, Unitarians, Psychiana, Scientology and Rosicrucians.

The types I now wish to add to this classification are those found within the Christian tradition, but which also can be found elsewhere.

Thaumaturgical sects are movements which insist that it is possible for men to experience the extraordinary effect of the supernatural on their lives. Within Christianity, their principal representatives are spiritualist groups whose main activity lies in seeking personal messages from the spirits, obtaining cures, effecting transformations and performing miracles. These sects define themselves in relation to the wider society by affirming that normal reality and causation can be suspended for the benefit of special and personal dispensations. They resist acceptance of the physical process of ageing and death and come together to affirm a special exception from everyday realities which assures each individual and his loved ones of perpetual well-being in the next world. For the present, they procure immediate advantages by accomplishing miracles. In several ways these groups differ little from manipulationist sects, except that their response to the world is less universalist and more personal. Moreover, they do not claim a special gnosis, but tend rather to call upon spirits and other powers to perform oracles and miracles. The ends they seek can be defined in terms of compensation for personal losses rather than the specific quest for cultural goals. Here religious activity is not far removed from magic. When these groups assemble, they form an audience in which the majority hope for personal benefits or watch others obtain them. If they are Christian, these groups put great weight on the various miraculous happenings in the Scriptures. The Gospel according to St Mark especially appeals to them. Their most characteristic activity is the 'seance' or public demonstration. The relationships they seek tend to be more with lost relatives than with God or a saviour and their conception of a saviour is seldom elaborated. We find among these groups the national Spiritualist Church and the Progressive Spiritualist Church.

The *reformist* sects seem to constitute a case apart. But the dynamic analytic approach to religious movements demands a category corresponding to those groups which, though sectarian in more than one respect, have affected transformations in their early response towards the outside world. Originally revolutionary, this attitude may have become introverted later. The history of the Quakers is a typical example of this. Revolutionary at the start and becoming introvertionist during the eighteenth century, they have gradually adopted a reformist position. This type of sect, possessing a very strong sense of identity, studies the world in order to involve itself in it by good deeds. It takes unto itself the role of social conscience. The sect also accepts a place in the world without being of the world or touched by its impurity. It associates with the world but keeps apart from it. The favourite texts of these sects, even if they do not hold fast to them, are those according to which faith without deeds is in vain and which support the view that the sect is itself the leavening of the lump. Their doctrinal position is mitigated, subsumed by their humanitarian orientation and their reformist tendencies towards the outside world. The Christadelphians may at some time in the future end up by being transformed into this kind of sect, even though their doctrinal position is much more extensive and could not be easily abandoned. The interest in this category lies in the importance it would seem to have for the study of the transformations of sects when the structure persists although the response to the outside world is modified.

The *Utopian* sect is perhaps the most complex type. Its response to the outside world consists partly in withdrawing from it, and partly in wishing to remake it to a better specification. It is more radical than the reformist sect, potentially less violent than the revolutionary sect and more constructive on a social level than the conversionist sect. It sets out through its activities to construct the world on a communitarian basis. It does not seek only to establish colonies but also proposes a programme for the reorganization of the world along community lines. Thus it aims at a sort of social reconstruction, but of a kind essentially different from that of such groups as the Quakers. It does in fact propose measures for social reorganization, and not only improvements and reforms within the existing framework of society. In the case of a Christian movement, the favourite biblical texts may be those of the Acts recounting the establishment of the primitive Christian community in Jerusalem. But sects of this sort are unlikely to have a clear conception of divinity. They may be conversionist in some measure but the converts they want are of a distinctive kind. As a consequence of the demands made of their members, they are likely to be rather suspicious of the candidates for conversion, rather like the monastic Orders. Among Christian groups (or more or less Christian) of this type, one might name the Tolstoyans, the Community of Oneida, the Brüderhof and perhaps also certain sections among the Christian Socialists.

In the case of Utopian sects, it seems necessary to distinguish between those which consider the founding of 'colonies' as their essential religious mission, as the specific means of attaining grace, and those for whom this represents but one reasonable means. Thus groups such as certain Mennonites, the Amana Society and the Shakers, communal in practice, have become so in response to particular circumstances, rather than as part of their original vision. Their practice of communal living does not constitute their response to the outside world, but their defence against it. This was in particular the appropriate way in which to adapt to the colonial (American) society into which they had immigrated, and which threatened to disperse them and assimilate them in piecemeal fashion into the irreligion of

the 'frontier' situation. The practice of communal life, sometimes assisted by linguistic distinctiveness, became for these
groups an important means of protecting their way of life from
that of the wider society; and in a society where land was cheap
and awaited only clearing, vicinal segregation by means of communal living became an almost natural means of defence. Of
course, it could have happened that communal living assumed
a very great significance for a movement and one should not
neglect its importance as a decisive factor in the creation of a
specific kind of change in introversionist movements. Gradually,
as the original inspiration becomes less active – as was the case
with the Shakers and the Amana society, introverted groups
which at their inceptions claimed special spiritual gifts – communal living may then become an end in itself.

It would seem that, when sects do persist, they always undergo
processes of mutation; some of the reasons for this have already
been studied. Because sects cannot cut themselves off completely from the world they are influenced by external factors.
But the internal causes are perhaps even more significant: the
response of the founders towards the outside world becomes
difficult to maintain for successive generations. The latter may
equally re-evaluate and reinstate the devices of isolation set up by
the founders, and what were in the beginning only institutional
defence mechanisms may gradually become intrinsically important and no longer just as a means. Communitarianism, first
adopted as protection, or the ideology and practices of the sect
can thus be transformed from defence to response. It may in
turn become the object of new mechanisms of defence and
rationalization, and doctrinal or spiritual legitimation may,
consequently, take the place of something which originally was
purely circumstantial. Thus one can observe the internal consequences and even the *systematic ideological consequences* of
what was at the beginning simply defensive action, and an
institutional adaptation is brought about. Communal living alone
is not enough to characterize as Utopian the sects which adhere
to it, any more than the squabbles between the Doukhobors
and government agents of British Colombia would justify
the inclusion of these sectarians among revolutionary groups.
To decide otherwise would introduce a foreign criterion of

organization into our classification,[2] and reduce its usefulness in the study of the processes of transformation within sects.

Any typology of sects must point up, and not hide, the fact that sects pass through processes of change. It is not only a question of the process of denominalization, which is the typical change within conversionist sects (see Wilson, 1959). All organizations are prone to suffer an attentuation in commitment to their original values and this is especially true among protest movements. The sect manifests this tendency most particularly in its response to the world. Indeed, the structures, duties and official doctrine are much more resistant to change. But the attitude towards the outside world, which constitutes the major issue of debate between the sect and the wider society, may itself shift imperceptibly. An extremely clear illustration of this type of change can be found in the case of the revolutionary sect which, while remaining essentially a sect, may gradually change its attitude towards the outside world. An intense revolutionary spirit is difficult to maintain, especially when it depends upon the expectation of a supernatural sign, the date of which is of necessity frequently postponed. The revolutionary sect appears to be susceptible to two kinds of development. In the first case, the sect may bind its fate so tightly to the idea of active revolution that it does actually stage a rebellion: in that case it seems impossible to preserve the original religious position in its primitive form, even approximately. Sudanese Mahdi-ism, the Marching Rule Movement of the Solomon Islands,[3] the Taiping rebellion (see Wallace, 1956) and perhaps the case of the Fifth Monarchy Men (England, seventeenth century) seem to furnish examples of this type of transformation. The change into a military force tends to lead to the suppression of the sect by state authorities or to turn it into a secret party, precarious in its existence, and henceforward more political than religious. The second possible mutation may be harder to trace. It is difficult

2. Clark (1937) presents a classification in which the communitarian sects are regarded as a distinct species.

3. One might hesitate to classify this movement as a sect. Worsley's (1957, pp. 170 ff.) account suggests that in spite of its millenarian aspects, this movement had distinct political aims since its birth. Allen (1951) seems to suggest that the movement had a much less well-developed political consciousness at its birth.

to maintain over a long period the hope of a divine appearance or a cataclysm, and it may perhaps be easier to keep it up by recruiting new adherents, enthusiastic for what to them is a new perspective, than to recruit a second generation or successive generations of members from among the children of members. But if the sect is well protected and has a good chance of maintaining its internal recruitment, then its response to the world will probably take on new aspects in spite of the persistence of doctrinal declarations, interpretations of the Scriptures or ritual. It seems that the revolutionary sect which persists, in these circumstances, becomes more passive, more withdrawn and that it then grows nearer in fact to the position of the introvertionist sects. The change wrought among the Quakers would seem to be of this order. It is the same as is being wrought at the present time, up to a certain point, among the Christadelphians. These changes do not always go unnoticed within the sects and are often resisted there. Indeed, these processes themselves produce schisms within revolutionary sects rather in the same way as we have seen the process of denominationalization engender schisms in conversionist sects. Thus, among Christadelphians today, and in spite of the reintegration of certain old schismatic groups, tensions can be observed between those holding an introvertionist conception of the movement and those, especially the young, who would prefer ideas of social reform. Some of the latter have moreover been expelled on these grounds. And alongside this can be seen the persistence of older revolutionary ideas. The Quakers have undergone other mutations – from revolutionary sect they become introversionist and social reformist. This came about not only because the Quakers individually were interested in good deeds but by the fact of the movement's concerted action in its entirety. A significant characteristic of the reformist position must be seen in the fact that it does not use this type of good works as a means of proselytizing. The reforming work becomes the *raison d'être* of the sect, the central point of its mission and of the image it has of itself – a changed response to the world.

Of course one can best study the typical changes of sects in terms of internal factors (disappointment of eschatological hopes, recruitment of a second generation). But the influence of the wider society must not be omitted in studying the birth and transformation of sects. It is obvious that sects of the manipulationist and introversionist type can only come about at certain stages of social and cultural development. A manipulationist sect can come into being only when metaphysical thought has extended into the religious and philosophical traditions of a society. Sects of this type tend to succeed among semi-intellectuals who have some knowledge of scientific or philosophical reasoning and imitate it up to a point. Manipulationist sects are universalist and this also is a cultural variable found only at relatively advanced stages of cultural development. These sects comprise more 'educated' people; they are unlikely to originate from the working classes. They tend to offer visions of prestige and power, as well as the short cuts for achieving them. They attract groups who have some ambition in this direction. The special means offered by the sects to attain these goals are defined in terms of verbal techniques and metaphysical theories. They use a language which attracts confidence and creates assurance, and their pre-occupation with the explanation of their theories tends to exclude all other activity. Well-being in this world, perceived in terms of health, wealth, comfort and social status, constitutes the practical sanction for these sects' teaching. The achievement-oriented society offers its rewards through extremely competitive processes. In response, these sects offer new methods which allow an escape from tensions and the achievement of cultural goals, especially for those who are sensitive to social status, and struggle to attain it. Sects of this type were particularly significant during the nineteenth and twentieth centuries in industrial societies (see Griswold, 1954; England, 1954; Wilson, 1961).

For quite different reasons, the introverted attitude also tends to be manifest only in certain kinds of social circumstances. The retreat from the wider society and the rejection of its dominant religious teachings and practices are only possible when the social institutions have reached a certain degree of autonomy from each other, and in circumstances where religious expression and practices have ceased to constitute a necessary public performance. The idea of private life must be established before an introversionist religion can originate, especially in its non-communitarian forms. In monasticism the retreat from the world was practised under the auspices of the dominant social ideology and led to a style of life separated from the world outside, but one could also say that it was undertaken in the name of that world. In the case of the introversionist sect, the retreat constitutes a more radical 'contracting out', even though it does not renounce all social contacts, but essentially only the customary and dominant religious and moral consensus. It can thus only originate in a society already partly secularized, or in a society where military conquest, for example, has put in doubt the traditional religion and made possible some differentiation. Participation in secular activities can continue, but if this leads to difficulties in the field of religious practice then communitarian tendencies and segregation might, in favourable circumstances, occur. But introversionist sects have not always been able or wished to become communitarian; their method of retreat seeks to establish a personal religious privacy, not vicinal segregation. They do not consider that this isolation is necessarily endangered by secular activities if these are deemed 'necessary'. Thus certain holiness movements and strict Darbyists admit that their members need to expose themselves to the affairs of the world, while keeping their private lives pure of the contamination of that world. While conversionist and revolutionist sects insist on a doctrine of witness and its public expression, the introversionist sects deny the value of such activity and reject its theoretical implications. Introversionism seems to have constituted an attitude which was tenable in seventeenth-century Europe, but it is clear that the social climate is today less favourable to this kind of religious attitude. Compulsory education, sanitary and social regulations, increased economic control of individual activity on the part of the State, the extension of taxes, obligatory military service or the use of certain procedures approved by nations to secure exemption from it – all these factors bring the sectarian into closer involvement with the wider society. The development of mass communications and the reliance which governments have upon them, the extension of the division of labour, the development of large scale man-power recruitment, the disappearance of the small business – all this makes effective isolation more and more difficult. The diffuse dependence of the individual on society makes his withdrawal harder all the time and the individual's widening social experience, his access to a great variety of cultural, social and leisure activities probably reduce the relative attractions of a life of retreat. Organic solidarity does not necessarily lead to increased allegiance to society and its goals, but it does make complete independence more difficult to attain or even to contemplate. These circumstances may, at least for some time, produce among the sects responses which facilitate the persistence of those already 'established', but at the same time make less likely the growth of new sects, at least of the introversionist type, and perhaps also of the revolutionist type.[4]

If we now leave the Christian world for what one might call the mission territories, we can quickly see that manipulationist sects and introversionist sects are not likely to develop there.[5] Indigenous sects, which abound in these societies, are either revolutionist or thaumaturgical. These two kinds of responses are primitive and simple. Thaumaturgical practice characterizes primitive religion and magic, and when societies reach the degree of complexity where religious deviation becomes possible, thaumaturgy becomes an almost inevitable part of it. Nevertheless, healing sects often owe much to the thaumaturgical tradition of Christianity itself. Sects of this kind are born in primitive societies in reply to social change and to deterioration in the traditional culture. One of the aspects of this phenomenon is the introduction of new ideologies which become in turn a source of religious ideas and practices accessible to purely native religious movements. The 'Zionist' sects of South Africa (see Sundkler, 1948; Dougall, 1956; Hunter, 1936) illustrate this syncretization of pagan and Christian thaumaturgical practices, as do the so-called Pocomania sects of Jamaica (Simpson, 1956). But it is quite unlikely that manipulationist or introversionist sects will come into being among the indigenous populations of these two territories, of which one is more or less detribalized and the other is an under-developed non-tribal society.

4. For an examination of the social circumstances favouring the survival of sects, see Wilson (1958).

5. The only example of a sect in an under-developed country (excluding nativistic attitudes) which I have found possible to classify as introversionist, in so far as I have the facts, is the 'Apostles of Aiyetoro' on the Nigerian Seaboard. The evidence reported by a periodical is too meagre to make a decisive case. See Anon (1951), pp. 387 ff.

We frequently find the revolutionist type of religious movements in these mission territories, and it has been called, or called itself 'Ethiopian' (Cook, 1933; Westermann, 1937; Roux, 1945; Sundkler, 1948; Shepperson, 1952; Schlösser, 1949; Thwaite, 1936). The Ras Tafari movements of Jamaica are movements similar in their salient features. They insist in the typical manner, but in varying degrees, on the adventist or chiliastic expectation, on the coming reversal of roles between the adherents and their enemies, and all share the same awaiting of the millennium (Simpson, 1955). In certain contexts these movements have been identified with a type of incipient nationalism, or, where the term 'nationalism' is anachronistic, they are at least taken for semi-political movements. One may well consider some of them in these terms but in other cases to call them such is to go beyond the evidence. Many of them are nearer to those revolutionist sects which are not completely institutionalized. They do not necessarily lead to revolutionary activity but look forward to a revolutionary transformation of their society, or at least of their own circumstances. In general, they believe that a supernatural intervention in their favour will bring about the revolution.

Researchers accept the consideration that revolutionist sectarianism is a response to a situation of cultural strain. There seems some reason to suppose that this is a spontaneous response of oppressed or colonized peoples who make their wish-world into their response to the real world. But we cannot always be sure that this type of movement constitutes a spontaneous response, and if we wish to draw a clear picture of the circumstances and cultural conditions to which revolutionary sects respond, we need to be able to dissociate the effects of cultural contact from those of cultural diffusion. Even very slight cultural contact seems capable of producing recognizable effects at the level of religious interpretation.[6] But the responses of revolutionary sects as such may be provoked and stimulated by missionary activity, even by that of a more or less orthodox kind.[7] We must

6. Berndt and Firth both consider that autochthonous movements arise independently of all foreign influence after very slight contact, or even in reaction to rumours from places where there has been slight cultural contact; see Berndt (1952, 1954) and Firth (1935).

7. Evidence from the beginnings of missionary activity in Polynesia is presented in Koskinen (1953). See also Lane (1927).

also consider another factor: the fact that the Christian Scriptures carry a very clear revolutionist element, which forms the doctrinal core of European and American revolutionist sects. These have often actively proselytized in under-developed countries and have disseminated their teaching far and wide. Paradoxically they are not alone in having communicated ideas of the return of Christ and the millennium, since these teachings are also after all part of the message of the many fundamentalist groups we can call conversionist. Nevertheless, in the context of mission territories, it could be that doctrines relatively less significant in the European or American situation may be just those most easily accepted by native peoples.

Thus several pentecostal sects, some of which call themselves holiness movements, and other fundamentalist groups, among them the Darbyists, have been working in Jamaica since 1919; the Seventh Day Baptists (in Nyasaland), the Brethren Church (in Nigeria), the so-called Open Bible Standard Church Group (French West Africa) and many other groups were at work in Africa around 1955. The Seventh Day Adventists were reported to have about two thousand missionaries in the missionary lands at this time, and the American Assemblies of God had about seven hundred and fifty. These two groups have made a considerable number of converts in different parts of Africa and in other territories (see Thiessey, 1955, pp. 411 ff.; Pierce Beaver, 1954; Price and Mayer, 1956; Price, 1957). Already in the period around 1930, the penetration of the Seventh Day Adventists into the mission fields of more orthodox groups provoked complaints (Burton, 1936; Keesing, 1941, pp. 225 ff.). The Mormons and Jehovah's Witnesses maintain a substantial but secret number of lay missionaries in these countries, and the latter try to transform all their converts into as many 'publishers' of their particular form of adventism.

The native sects manifesting the direct influence of the Christian missions are legion. In a certain number of cases their leaders are indigenous people irritated by the limited opportunities for prestige and power offered by the missions in which they were educated. Such was the case of Kimbangou (see Lerrigo, 1922; Schlösser, 1949; Comhaire, 1953, 1955; Balandier, 1955); and that of Simon-Pierre Mpadi Chilembwe, whose career owed much to the radical and volatile Joseph Booth, a fundamentalist missionary of changing views, who are prototypes of the mission-influenced leaders of a native revolutionist movement (Shepperson, 1954). The Kitawala, a Rhodesian version of the Jehovah's Witnesses movement, furnished further evidence of the direct influence of revolutionist Christianity on the dissident religious attitudes of indigenous peoples (Quick, 1940; Schlösser, 1949; Cunnison, 1951).[8] And examples in this direction are not lacking for Melanesia, Polynesia and China.[9]

It remains for us to establish in which of their aspects the native revolutionist movements constitute simply a response to cultural contacts without borrowing the eschatological and messianic ideas of Christianity. The nativist movement, the promise of the return of ancestors and their customs, seems to constitute a response of this type.[10] The cargo cults seem also to arise without ideological borrowing. These two movements are of the revolutionist type, but perhaps we have less proof in the case of the returning Messiah as an indigenous myth giving birth to religious activity, although this has been suggested regarding the case of the Manseren cult of Biak in New Guinea.[11] If some revolutionist sects originate outside all Christian influence we have evidence of the wider usefulness of our categories, which

8. Shepperson (1952) suggests that these movements have become somewhat different from the Jehovah's Witnesses of Europe and America.

9. The 'Manseren' revolt in Papua, led by Stephanus during the Second World War, manifested distinct signs of Christian influence, according to Pos (1950), pp. 561 ff. (On Manseren see fn. 11.) Williams (1934) suggests that misunderstood missionary teaching played some part in the movement.

As for Polynesia, see Winks (1953), Thompson (1908), Brewster (1922), pp. 141 ff. and 236 ff., and Cato (1947).

As for Asia, see Boardman (1951) and Krader (1956).

10. Nativistic movements of this sort have been called 'revitalization movements' by Wallace (1956). They did perhaps appear spontaneously as autochthonous movements in response to cultural contact. The American Ghost Dance should be classed among them and perhaps also the Taro in British New Guinea.

11. See de Bruyn (1951), Bodrogi (1951), and Chinnery and Haddon (1917). There seems to be agreement in thinking that the belief in the return of the Manseren Koveri as a saviour precedes Christian missionary activity. It is perhaps a response to a previous conquest. Later the 'cult' borrowed Christian elements. Fletcher (1891) considered that the Indians had their own messianic myths of a returning cultural hero.

are no longer culture-bound. In order to study this question, and some other connected problems, we must analyse the indigenous sects and make sure of distinguishing between their different elements. We could then link the latter to the conditions of cultural contact and to levels of social development. Köbben (1960) has begun an analysis of this type. It seems probable that in less advanced societies the possibilities of response to the outside world are limited, and that only two of them (revolutionist or thaumaturgical) constitute possibilities of original response in pre-literate societies. These two responses, it will be noted, permit considerable elements of fantasy. Both clearly existed in the history of Christianity; although the thaumaturgical response has given rise to fewer sectarian organizations as such, it has existed within the Christian tradition in cult movements of one kind or another, or as residual paganism. As a primitive position and as a transformation of the revolutionist position the introversionist sect seems only to manifest itself in certain conditions of social development. For manipulationist sects, conditions favouring their appearance seem to be those in which the religious, intellectual and educational monopoly of traditional religious functionaries has been broken, and in circumstances which make status insecurity common and social mobility possible, at least for a certain number.

The conditions for the appearance of the other three types of response to the world seem even more strictly limited. It seems that conversionist sects are linked with the development of individualism and this perhaps constitutes the condition *sine qua non* of their appearance. The reformist response appears to be essentially derivative. One can consider it partly as a process in the secularization of sects, at any rate as an accommodation to the concerns of the outside world. If Utopian conceptions can be formed to some degree in revolutionary sects, the idea of undertaking social action with a view to establishing a new society arises only at a stage of social development in which one can see traditional cultural values in the perspective of a certain realistic relativism. Thus it seems that the birth of this type of sect is also itself limited to certain general circumstances of social development. Few of our types, it seems, can be observed among the religious deviations one finds in pre-literate societies. This fact should not deter us in the attempt to discover the relevance of these types for the analysis of religious movements within the other major world religions, as well as in the Protestant development of Christianity from which our types are primarily derived.

References

ANON (1951), 'A visit to the Apostles and town of Aiyetoro', *Nigeria*, vol. 36.

ALLEN, C. H. (1951), 'Marching rule : a nativistic cult of the British Solomon Islands', *South Pacific*, vol. 5.

BALANDIER, G. (1955), *Sociologie actuelle de l'Afrique noire*, Presses Universitaires.

BERGER, P. L. (1954), 'Sociological study of sectarianism', *Soc. Res.*, vol. 21, pp. 467–85.

BERNDT, R. M. (1952), 'A cargo movement in the Eastern Central Highlands of New Guinea', *Oceania*, vol. 23, pp. 40–65 and 137–58.

BERNDT, R. M. (1954), 'Reaction to contact in the Eastern Highlands of New Guinea', *Oceania*, vol. 24, pp. 190–228.

BOARDMAN, E. P. (1951), 'Christian influence on the ideology of the Taiping rebellion', *Far Eastern Quart.*, vol. 10, pp. 115–24.

BODROGI, T. (1951), 'Colonization and religious movements in Melanesia', *Acta Ethnograph. Acad. Scient. Hungar.*, vol. 2, pp. 259–90.

BREWSTER, A. B. (1922), *The Hill Tribes of Fiji*, Lippincott.

BURTON, J. W. (1936), *Missionary Survey of the Pacific Islands*, World Dominion Press.

CATO, A. C. (1947), 'A new religious cult in Fiji', *Oceania*, vol. 18, pp. 146–56.

CHINNERY, E. W. P., and HADDON, A. C. (1917), 'Five new religious cults in British New Guinea', *Hibbert J.*, vol. 15, pp. 448–63.

CLARK, E. T. (1937), *The Small Sects in America*, Abingdon.

COMHAIRE, J. L. (1953), 'Religious trends in African and Afro-American urban societies', *Anthrop. Quart.*, vol. 26, pp. 95–108.

COMHAIRE, J. L. (1955), 'Sociétés secrètes et mouvements prophétiques au Congo belge', *Africa*, vol. 25, pp. 54–8.

COOK, L. A. (1933), 'Revolt in Africa', *J. Negro Hist.*, vol. 18, pp. 396–413.

CUNNISON, I. (1951), 'A Watchtower assembly in Central Africa', *Int. Rev. Miss.*, vol. 40, pp. 456–69.

DE BRUYN, J. V. (1951), 'The Manseren cult of Biak', *South Pacific*, vol. 5, pp. 1–11.

DOUGALL, J. W. C. (1956), 'African separatist churches', *Int. Rev. Miss.*, vol. 25, pp. 257–66.

ENGLAND, R. W. (1954), 'Some aspects of Christian Science', *Amer. J. Sociol.*, vol. 59.

FIRTH, R. (1935), 'The theory of "cargo" cults: A note on Tikopia', *Man*, vol. 55, pp. 130–32.

FLETCHER, A. C. (1891), 'The Indian Messiah', *J. Amer. Folk-Lore*, vol. 4, pp. 57–60.

GRISWOLD, A. W. (1954), 'New thought: a cult of success', *Amer. J. Sociol.*, vol. 59.

HUNTER, M. (1936), *Reaction to Conquest*, Oxford University Press.

KEESING, F. M. (1941), *The South Seas in the Modern World*, Allen and Unwin.

KÖBBEN, A. J. F. (1960), 'Prophetic movements as an expression of social protest', *Int. Arch. Ethnograph.*, vol. 49, pp. 117–64.

KOSKINEN, A. (1953), 'Missionary influence as a political factor in the Pacific Island's, *Suomalaisen Tiedeakatemian Tolmituksia, Annales Academiae Scientiarum Fennicae*, Sarja Ser. B, vol. 78 (Helsinki).

KRADER, L. (1956), 'A nativistic movement in Western Siberia', *Amer. Anthrop.*, vol. 58, pp. 282–92.

LANE, G. H. (1927), *Fox Pitt Rivers, The Clash of Cultures and the Contact of Races*, Routledge.

LERRIGO, P. H. J. (1922), 'The prophet movement in the Congo', *Int. Rev. Miss.*, vol. 11, pp. 270–77.

MARTIN, D. A. (1962), 'The denomination', *Brit. J. Sociol.*, vol. 13, pp. 1–14.

MARTY, M. E. (1960), 'Sects and cults', *Ann. Amer. Acad. polit. soc. Scien.*, vol. 332, pp. 125–34.

PIERCE BEAVER, R. (1954), 'Expansion of American Foreign Missionary activity since 1945', *Miss. Res. Lib. Occas. Bull.*, vol. 5, no. 7.

POS, H. (1950), 'The revolt of "Manseren"', *Amer. Anthrop.*, vol. 52.

PRICE, F. W. (1957), 'The younger churches: some facts and observations', *Miss. Res. Lib. Occas. Bull*, vol. 8, no. 7.

PRICE, F. W., and MAYER, K. E. (1956), 'A study of American Protestant Missions in 1956', *Miss. Res. Lib. Occas. Bull.*, vol. 7, no. 9.

QUICK, G. (1940), 'Some aspects of the African Watch Tower Movements in Northern Rhodesia', *Int. Rev. Miss.*, vol. 29, pp. 216–26.

ROUX, E. (1945), *Time Longer than Rope*, Gollancz.

SCHLÖSSER, K. (1949), *Propheten in Afrika*, Limbach, Brunswick.

SHEPPERSON, G. (1952), 'Ethiopanism and African nationalism', *Phylon*, vol. 14, pp. 9–18.

SHEPPERSON, G. (1954), 'The politics of African Separatist Movements in British Central Africa, 1892–1916', *Africa*, vol. 24, pp. 233–46.

SIMPSON, G. M. (1955), 'Political cultism in West Kingston, Jamaica', *Soc. econ. Stud.*, vol. 4, pp. 133–49.

SIMPSON, G. M. (1956), 'Jamaican revivalist cults', *Soc. econ. Stud.*, vol. 5, pp. 321–42.

SUNDKLER, B. G. T. (1948), *Bantu Prophets in South Africa*, Butterworth.

THIESSEY, J. C. (1955), *A Survey of World Missions*, Inter-Varsity Press.

THOMPSON, B. (1908), *The Fijians: A Study of the Decay of Custom*, Heinemann.

THWAITE, D. (1936), *The Seething African Pot*, Constable.

TROELTSCH, E. (1931), *The Social Teaching of the Christian Churches*, Macmillan.

WALLACE, A. F. C. (1956), 'Revitalization movements', *Amer. Anthropol.*, vol. 58, pp. 264–81.

WESTERMANN, D. (1937), *Africa and Christianity*, Oxford University Press.

WILLIAMS, F. E. (1934), 'The Vailala madness in retrospect', in E. E. Evans-Pritchard *et al.*, *Essays Presented to C. G. Seligman*, Kegan Paul, pp. 36–79.

WILSON, B. R. (1958), 'The appearance and survival of sects in an evolutionary social milieu', *Arch. soc. Relig.*, vol. 5, pp. 140–50.

WILSON, B. R. (1959), 'An analysis of sect development', *Amer. soc. Rev.*, vol. 24, pp. 3–15.

WILSON, B. R. (1961), *Sects and Society*, Heinemann, and California University Press.

WINKS, R. W. (1953), 'The doctrine Han-Hanism', *J. Polynes. Soc.*, vol. 62, pp. 199–236.

WORSLEY, P. (1957), *The Trumpet Shall Sound*, McGibbon & Kee.

YINGER, J. M. (1946), *Religion in the Struggle for Power*, Duke University Press.

YINGER, J. M. (1957), *Religion, Society and the Individual*, Macmillan.

21 J. W. Fernandez

African Religious Movements

Excerpt from J. W. Fernandez, 'African religious movements – types and dynamics', *Journal of Modern African Studies*, vol. 2 (1964), pp. 531–49.

Our object here is threefold. We shall first attempt to establish an elementary typology,[1] as simple as is clearly possible, of religious movements in Africa. We shall next examine one type more fully – the so-called 'syncretist' movements of equatorial Africa – in the interest of exposing their particular configuration and dynamic changes. We shall finally try to assess the present and future place of these religious movements in the sequential processes leading to nationalism, Africanism and Pan-Africanism – the processes, in other words, leading from the communal to the modern, the stateless to the state societies in Africa. In this way we can perhaps say something useful about the relation of religion to politics in so far as this relationship is evident in African religious movements.

I

Two points must be made to simplify the discussion of types. First, only those movements will be discussed which may be defined against a background of Christian evangelization. Religious movements formed under the impetus of Islamic evangelization, such as prophet movements in the Mahdist tradition, will be ignored, though they are of importance, particularly in Sudanic Africa.[2] It was Christian evangelists in their

1. The types we propose are simple not complex ideal types. They are not mutually exclusive. The features defining the type are fewer than those possessed by any member within the type. The discussion is from the observer's rather than the participant's point of view.

2. See Jamil (1963) and Fisher (1963). It is clear that Islam in the Maghreb and West Africa can almost be regarded as one long succession of religious movements.

travels throughout the bush who were, from the earliest moments of colonization, generally the most effective agents in making Africans fully aware, first, of the attitude of deprecation taken by the dominant colonial society towards their culture, and second, of the political domination that lay behind the missionaries, ready to support their right of evangelization on those occasions when Africans attempted to repel them.[3] This emphasises the relevance of the background of Christian evangelization to our discussion. The colonial administrations, concerned always to establish their district and regional administrative centres, were less given to travelling and thus made more superficial contact in the bush. The Christian missionaries, in most cases then, were the first real agents of domination and deprecation, in reaction to which most religious movements arose.[4] The thoroughgoing identification of the evangelical with the colonial and imperial enterprise in the minds of Africans has been often remarked. Historically, however, Christian evangelization was frequently the first term of this identification, colonial administration the second.

We cannot presume, however, in discussing the types of religious movements which arose under Christian domination to find their origins solely in this unique situation. It is clear, given the turmoil, extensive migrations and kaleidoscope of succeeding dominations and subordinations in African history and pre-history, that revitalization movements of a religious character were a fairly frequent traditional pattern. Herskovits (1962, p. 418) argues that 'many of the separatist movements are to be thought of as reinterpretations of the prophet movements

3. What is remarkable in the evangelization of Africa is the general tolerance with which it was at first received. This testifies to African religious eclecticism and to the identification of Christianity with the material benefits of European civilization. The failure of evangelical Christianity to produce these goods was one of the frustrations which gave rise to religious movements which have sought these by other means. Most clearly evident in the Cargo Cults of Melanesia, this is present as well in Africa. George Shepperson notes the similarity between the Cargo Cults and Nyasaland religious movements, and refers to Livingstone's view that 'Africans identified the coming of the missionary with the arrival of a cornucopia of material goods' (Shepperson, 1962, pp. 19 and 146).

4. We ignore here the impact of traders, which in most cases was transitory, and their contacts limited to the trading situation.

widely prevalent in Africa long before European control'. While noting this continuity we shall consider the movements only in response to the colonial, predominantly Christian presence.[5]

If we compile a list of types of African religious movements we recognize at once that we are confronted with too broad and redundant a typology. A partial compilation would include prophetism, faith healing, prophet healing, Bible church, Ethiopian, Zionist, messianic, millenarian, separatist, contra-acculturative independent, syncretist and nativist, to go no further. It is a considerable challenge to reduce this plethora to the four basic types we propose – reformative, separatist, nativist and messianic – because the various regions of Africa have become attached to the typologies that have grown out of original local research. Thus Sundkler's (1961, pp. 38–43) typology, Ethiopian-Zionist, has currency in Southern Africa. Yet, as Parrinder (1953, p. 108) points out, it is not really satisfactory elsewhere. For one thing, other areas do not have the same racial problems as South Africa. These have been a dynamic factor in separatism there and are expressed in the term Ethiopianism. For another thing, all areas have not had the same close contact with New World revivalism and millenarianism: this contact was primarily with the American Negro separatist churches such as the African Methodist Episcopal Church in the United States or the various Negro Baptist Churches. Pentecostal revivalists such as the Christian Catholic Apostolic Church of Zion Illinois, the Adventists and especially the Jehovah's Witnesses, whose watchtower doctrines have had such an impact on Central Africa, were also important. No one can deny, within the framework of South African history that Sundkler's two terms are appropriate in typing the religious movements that occurred there. We must seek for terms, however, that are less bound to a specific area and a specific history.

5. Kopytoff (1963) identifies the Holy Water movement in the south-western Congo as just one in a long series of re-examinations of religious and magical technology with the object of replacing the outmoded and fatigued with more vigorous forms. Because of a very few items like the Holy Water itself we tend, he points out, to see this as a specific response to the colonial situation. But the colonial situation was not the first disaster and frustration faced by the Suku.

The classic typology for movements of the kind we are considering here remains that of Ralph Linton (1943). By such movements he means 'any conscious organized attempt on the part of a society's members to revive or perpetuate selected aspects of its culture'. Linton discusses two sets of criteria – whether the movements are perpetuative or revivalist, and whether they are magical or rational. He combines these sets into the four theoretical types – revivalistic–magical, revivalistic–rational, perpetuative–magical and perpetuative–rational. A recent and particularly cogent criticism of Linton by Worsley (1957, pp. 267–76) points out, however, that practically all religious movements are ready to adopt new elements, invent new ritual or reinterpret the old and hence the categories perpetuative and revivalistic suggest a state of affairs so delimited as to be uninformative. Worsley also criticizes the term rational, pointing out that it risks evoking an old argument as to logical and pre-logical mentality. What looks magical to us may be perfectly rational in another less sophisticated frame of reference with other premises. Reason should not be after all a function of range of awareness.

Nevertheless movements do differ as to the degree to which they perpetuate the old or incorporate the new. The clue to a more appropriate set of characteristics to which to refer a typology is found in Linton's statement that 'what really happens in all nativistic movements is that certain current or remembered elements of culture are selected for emphasis and given symbolic value' (Linton, 1943, p. 231). If this is true, the question arises, Whence does the particular movement obtain its symbols? From its own cultural tradition, or from the culture of the society or societies with which it is in contact? We find ourselves thus on a continuum, or a continuous series of gradual stages between movements which exploit primarily their own tradition and movements which are largely committed by acculturation to the symbols of the contact culture. The continuum thus lies between the two poles of a traditional or an acculturated symbolism.

But the larger question remains as to how these symbols are used: whether instrumentally or expressively. This suggests a second dimension, which may be defined as follows. An instrumental type of religious movement chooses the elements for symbolic use in a realistic and goal-minded fashion and with a view to perpetuating them under existing conditions. We find fairly pragmatic attempts to compensate for the deprivations and other frustrations involved in the situation of subordination, without endangering the continuity and survival of the religious group, since it is seen as the only institution that can achieve its goals. In an expressive type of religion the emphasis is upon escape by symbolic displacement from the situation which is causing frustration. This is done by means of symbolic forms in ritual and ceremony, song, drama and dance. Intense involvement of the participants in these activities draws their attention away from the frustrations and deprivations of their everyday situation. In such movements the group as an entity is not all-important. It and its activity are but means to this symbolic displacement.

In an expressive movement there is no calculated attempt to deal with a difficult situation directly. Rather the frustrations involved often spontaneously produce supernatural and visionary experiences in persons of charismatic qualities.[6] These movements rely on intense evocation of the supernatural and are given over to enthusiastic religious behaviour. Their emotional tone is high and they count heavily on ritualization. Their leaders are preoccupied with internal concerns and not with representing the group to the larger situation of which it is a part. Moribund elements of culture may be revived, not in anticipation of practical advantages, but as part of a magical formula which will miraculously change a frustrating environment and return it to a pristine condition. In all cases these movements exhibit an unrealistic reliance on their ability to create and constitute their own universe through expressive symbolism.

In summary, then, movements whose emphasis is primarily instrumental keep enough cognisance of the total situation to which they are reacting to remain adapted to it and thus guarantee their survival. They are exocentric – well aware of their place in a larger field. Movements whose emphasis is expressive

6. The expressive-instrumental continuum is basic in the work of Talcott Parsons (1951, p. 348). He says of the expressive orientation: 'The essential point is the primacy of "acting out" the need disposition itself rather than subordinating gratification to a goal outside the immediate situation.'

institute kinds of behaviour which compensate the individuals for the deprivations they feel at the moment; but they remain pre-occupied with these compensations, their symbolic gratification, without reference to the outside world of time and place, of which they are a part. They are not so much concerned with their group survival as they are with directly reducing the frustrations and anxieties with which they are living.[7]

We have some examples of what we mean in the Gabon religious cults studied by the writer (Fernandez, 1964). These cults, ordinarily typed syncretist, are in two different places along the expressive–instrumental continuum. Those concerned with expressive satisfactions insist on ritual procedure regardless of administrative disapproval of certain practices such as use of the corpse or ritual flagellation. Other cults, more instrumental in orientation, attempt to modify their practices to some extent to accord with the directives of the government and local adminis-tration. It is the latter who have had, quite naturally, greater survival value but they have not provided the range of symbolic satisfactions available in the former. For example the expressive groups have always freely taken the alkaloid stimulant, *eboga* (tabernenthes eboga), an important guarantee of a satisfying ritual experience. The instrumental-type cults have been, because of their awareness of administrative disapproval, more sparing in the use of this drug, denying thereby some ritual satisfactions to their members for the sake of the survival of the group. The price of survival has been the pain of accommodation.

We may now locate the four types of religious movements proposed earlier in relation to our two bi-polar continua. Nativist movements are those oriented towards a *traditional* symbolism, which they manipulate *expressively*. Messianic movements generally employ an *acculturated* symbolism, which despite their acceptance of historic time they manipulate *expressively*, conjuring up millennial satisfactions. Separatist

---

7. It should be repeated that this is an analytic distinction; no religious movement is exclusively instrumental or expressive, nor could it be. We are concerned with the relative primacy of one mode or another of action. Knowledge of the relative primacy is of value in assessing the order of priorities in a movement's economy and is useful in predicting its capacity to survive.

movements employ an *acculturated* symbolism, which they tend to manipulate *instrumentally*. Reformative movements find their base in a *traditional* orientation, with which, because of their *instrumental* orientation, they deliberately and creatively combine an acculturated symbolism. This theoretical placing of the four types may be indicated in a diagram using two co-ordinate axes.[8]

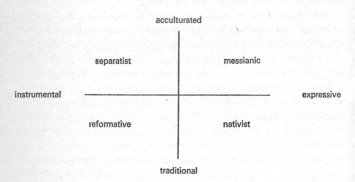

Figure 1

We now turn to individual cases. Every concrete movement may be located in a particular position on the co-ordinate system of the diagram, though there are difficulties caused by overlap and interpenetration.

Separatism. Most of the movements within this category have the organizational characteristics of a church. They place, in fact, heavy emphasis upon the social organization and co-ordination of the membership. They are concerned with the group's status in the larger society and think usually, though not

8. Herbert J. Spiro (1962) makes highly illuminating use of such a scheme in his article. Walter Zessner (1961) makes a similar presentation, called by him geometric vectorial symbolism. Such diagrams have, he maintains, inherent advantages over descriptive language. Both schemes are more comprehensive than the one presented here. They attempt to assess the cycle of activities within a system, they embody more dimensions, and they imply what is equilibrium and disequilibrium, symmetry and asymmetry, in a given system. I am elsewhere elaborating the scheme presented here.

necessarily, of improving that status.[9] Usually they separated from European-dominated parent organizations for non-religious reasons. In respect to Christian symbols, religious belief and ceremony, they continue to adhere very closely to the practices of the parent organization and they remain therefore fairly orthodox in liturgy and theology. The separation from the parent body was designed to make possible greater status in church organization, which was achieved. Members of the best examples of movements of this kind, the African Congregational Church and the Bantu Methodist Church in South Africa, are very conscious of their social status within the larger community, and are anxious that their religious behaviour should be instrumental in promoting or maintaining it. Many of the African churches which are classed as Ethiopian by Sundkler would fall fully into this category, as would all of the native churches recognized by the South African Government. If, for reasons of continuing frustration or weak leadership and organization, fission occurs in a separatist church, and Sundkler testifies to the extent of this, it is likely that the newly formed groups will forget their concern with orthodoxy and tend more and more to a syncretism and perhaps eventually to nativism. Also, continuing frustrations may lend importance to visionary experiences and give the movement substantial qualities of messianism. The dynamism of these movements has been amply portrayed by Sundkler, to whom the problem of orthodoxy is a main concern.

Other examples of this type of movement may be mentioned. One is the Church of the Lord Aladura, which had its beginnings among the Yoruba in Lagos in the twenties, and has since spread to the other three regions of Nigeria, and to Ghana, Sierra Leone and Liberia as well (Turner, 1962). Here again we are dealing with founders who were all *bona fide* members of the Church Missionary Society affiliates in West Africa, but who claimed to

9. Such separatist movements as the *Apostolowa Fe Dedefia Habobo* (the Apostolic Revelation Society) in Ghana, as described by Baëta (1962), pp. 77–93, have many of the instrumental characteristics of improvement associations. On the other hand South African separatist churches, though sensitive to their relationship to the larger society, strongly support apartheid and the social *status quo*. Sundkler (1961), pp. 310–11, however, makes clear that this support is strongest from those movements of a Zionist, that is, messianic, disposition.

have become dissatisfied with the immorality of European Christianity as evidenced by the foolishness of the First World War and compounded by succeeding metropolitan barbarities. Nevertheless the leaders of this movement have been resistant to the symbolism of traditional African religion, and greatly desire to be accepted by the Christian community. Evidence of their concern with Christian orthodoxy has been their habit of enrolling their leaders in a two-year course at the Missionary Bible Institute in Great Britain.[10] The African Methodist Episcopal Church of South Africa and Rhodesia, the Watchtower Society of Jehovah's Witnesses (as opposed to any of the Kitawala or Watchman offshoots) and John Chilembwe's Providence Industrial Mission, all fall within the separatist division, though at rather different positions (see Taylor and Lehmann, 1961, ch. 9 and pp. 227–38; Cunnison, 1951; Shepperson and Price, 1958).

A final example of the separatist type is the African Greek Orthodox Church in Uganda, founded by Reuben Spartas in the twenties in dissidence and protest against the paternalism of missionary Anglicanism. At first linked with the Marcus Garvey movement and the African Orthodox Church in the United States, the remarkable thing is that by a long series of skilful negotiations Spartas finally gained in 1946 corporate acceptance by the Greek Orthodox Church. Thus, as Welbourn (1961, ch. 5, esp. pp. 80–81) points out, both Romans and Anglicans in Uganda are faced not with a purely local schism, but with a recognized branch of a world church in their midst. What is demonstrated in this course of events for our purposes is the goal-minded, instrumental and acculturated orientation of the movement, which eventually resulted in a full return to orthodoxy.

Nativist movements contrast in every way with separatist movements. In so far as they begin in the context of Christian colonization, they express a fundamental disaffection with Christian symbolism and with the way Christianity confronts the supernatural. These movements turn to tradition for effective

10. Recent research by Mitchell (1963) shows a preoccupation with alleviating the physical and spiritual sufferings of members by expressive techniques. His insistence that the Aladura movement must be studied from 'the perspective of the Protestant religious system' confirms in our view, however, its separatist character.

ritual and more penetrating belief. They are, like messianic movements, often preoccupied with directly healing or easing the multitude of physical and spiritual ills that afflict Africans, and they do this by ecstatic techniques and highly emotionalized ritual. In a purely nativist movement the sources of these techniques and rituals should be exclusively traditional. But, as Worsley has indicated, this is rare in the situation of culture contact which gives rise to religious movements. We almost always have a syncretism. Thus the churches which Sundkler calls 'Zionist' in South Africa would seem to fall into this category, although a good many traditional curing practices have been prohibited.

Moreover, in the type-movement of South African 'Zionism', the *ama Nazaretha* or Nazarene Church of Isaiah Shembe, there is a patent search for a new messiah, partially made out in Shembe himself. Though the nativist orientation is strong here, so also is the messianic tendency. An indication of the strong traditional orientation is seen in Shembe's construction of an old-type Zulu village, Ekuphakameni, in order that his followers might worship and be cured in appropriate surroundings. The kinds of conditions created by European cities and farms could only further sicken his people (Sundkler, 1961, pp. 93–9). Another example of a nativist movement with overtones of messianism was Mau Mau in Kenya and, before it, Maji Maji in southern Tanganyika. The various modern anti-witchcraft movements which have been so abundant in Africa in recent years, and the Congo 'Holy Water' movements discussed by Kopytoff, also fall in this category (see Richards, 1935; Marwick, 1950; Field, 1960; Kopytoff, 1962).

Reformative movements are those which have preserved a strong sense of the viability of the traditional African religious attitude with its associated symbolism.[11] However, these move-

11. The term reformative is taken from Voget (1956, p. 250) who defines it as a 'conscious creative attempt on the part of a subordinate group to obtain a personal and social reintegration through a selective rejection modification and synthesis of both traditional and alien cultural components'. He suggests that these movements are the most stable and enduring – most successfully providing for dignified accommodation with universalistic pan-ethnic implications. In fact Pan-Africanism may well rest most solidly on an instrumental approach consciously combining old and new. This kind of posture is, of course, difficult to maintain.

ments have been inescapably aware of Christianity and the attractiveness of some of its symbolism, and have therefore made calculated attempts to integrate Christian elements into their beliefs and ritual. A prime example of this type of movement is Bwiti in Gabon (Balandier, 1955, 1957; Fernandez, 1964); a marginal example is *lalouisme* or the Abadice Cult in the southern Ivory Coast (Paulme, 1962). The air of calculated recreation in all these movements is reflected in the name Abadice – coined from ABC – as well as their susceptibility to the obvious advantages of Western civilization. In the case of Bwiti we find, over time, the gradual reinterpretation and creative elaboration of an ancestor cult, Bieri, in the presence of Christianity. The orientation remains traditional, with the purposeful accretion of Christian elements. We may mention, as a movement marginally reformative in the direction of separatism, the National Church of Nigeria and the Cameroons, which was organized by Azikiwe's N.C.N.C. as its religious wing – mainly, to be sure, for instrumental political purposes, but also with the purpose of preserving a denigrated African tradition.

A better example of reformatism from Nigeria would be the Reformed Ogboni Society among the Yoruba. This traditionally had important social and political functions as a secret society, which have been much reduced, while its religious dimensions have been carefully syncretized with Christian elements (Parrinder, 1953, pp. 175–81). The Reformed Ogboni Society indicates in its very name the important feature of these movements, their sense of continuity with African tradition and, at the same time, their readiness to reform themselves by appeal to acculturation.

Messianic movements are commonly seen as those that arise out of intense xenophobia – in most cases the hated object is European and colonial domination. The prophet or black messiah, responding to visionary experiences, which confirm his election and provide him with charismatic personality, works upon this emotion in expressive ways. A *Weltanschauung* is created, irrespective of the actuality in which the movement exists, and the prophet guarantees for his followers either a return to the golden age of African culture or the coming of a future millennium. The unrealistic promises and expressive practices of these movements reduce the frustrations of social domination and cultural deprecation by elaborating a compensatory universe. It is of interest, and may be due to African pragmatism, that a pure example of this type of movement is rare, though many African religious movements have moved through a messianic stage. It is of further interest that messianic movements characteristically reject a good portion of their own traditional religious practice. This is true of *kimbanguisme*, which in its early form was a messianic movement largely influenced by missionary protestantism (Andersson, 1958, p. 49). Other movements which through their expressive character and acculturation fall into this quarter of the diagram would be the Society of the One Almighty God in Uganda, with its adamant reaction to medicine of all kinds (Welbourn, 1961, pp. 31–53), and the Elliot Kamwana and Bamulonda movements in Rhodesia and Nyasaland (Taylor and Lehmann, 1961, pp. 238–47; Shepperson, 1962, pp. 149–52). As marginally messianic we would include Alice Lenshina's Lumpa Church (Taylor and Lehmann, 1961, pp. 248–68; Rotberg, 1961) and the Musama Disco Christo Church of Ghana (Baëta, 1962, pp. 28–67). It is clear that the expressive orientation and messianic qualities of the Lenshina movement encouraged the fanaticism to which it succumbed in its recent confrontation with the Government. Because of the heightened emotion characteristic of these movements, the unrealistic expectations they create in their followers, and their neglect of the larger situation of which they are a part and to which they have reacted but remain unattuned, they are usually short-lived. Their organizational thrust is customarily expended in ritual and cosmological elaborations, and not in more viable social and political forms.

II

It will be useful now to examine more closely a type which appears with frequency in the literature – the so-called syncretist cults of western equatorial Africa. Since syncretism – that is, the coalescence of differing religious forms – appears in all the movements so far indicated, it is not an apt term for a typological scheme.

Our discussion up to this point intimates that movements

frequently do not stay placed in one quarter of the diagram, but pass through typological phases. The importance of dynamic shifts can be best seen in *kimbanguisme*. This movement was, as we have said, in origin strongly messianic. The appearance of Kimbangu as a visionary was accompanied by a rush of expressive behaviour and adherence to the apocalyptic promise implicit in his visions – the purification of the earth and the banishment of the whites. The Belgian administration, however, dealt swiftly with Kimbangu and prevented him from stabilizing the movement personally. Balandier (1955, p. 431) makes it clear that *'nouveaux organisateurs'* came forward to establish the *'missions des noirs'* in Kimbangu's name. These successors were much more organizational and nationalistic in intention, even though they kept alive the millenarian vision. The Eglise Jesus Christ Sur Terre Simon Kimbangu (E.J.C.S.K.) and Ngunzism, the surviving forms of the Kimbanguist movement, display likewise a much more instrumental and hence separatist character, since the orientation towards acculturated symbolism has been maintained. This shift towards instrumentalism is no doubt responsible for the movement's growth and political significance in the Congo (Léopoldville).[12]

Three more examples of these kinds of shifts are Matswaism and Mpadism in the Lower Congo, and Bwiti in Gabon. The original intentions and the programme of André Matswa and his followers were instrumental and almost wholly secular in nature. He was very clearly assessing the nature of the colonial situation, and seeking to deal with the existing abuses and deprivations as realistically as possible. Neither Matswa's movement nor that of Mpadi – whose Ngunza, a Khaki cult, was a reworking of latter-day Kimbanguist enthusiasm (Andersson, 1958, pp. 139–40) – began with a visionary experience and apocalyptic promise. Matswa's original intention, in the Paris founding of *l'Association Amicale des Originaires de l'AEF*, was that of creating an economic union to improve the situation of Africans. Though he acquired early a religious symbolism, it was mainly acculturated; for he constantly endeavoured to obtain, and at first succeeded in obtaining, administrative approval for his activities. But what began as a totally instrumental movement in Paris, rapidly

12. Balandier points to reformative tendencies; see (1955, pp. 434–5).

acquired messianic overtones, when carried forth in the Congo. Salvation from white oppression and rapid restoration of dignity were in the minds of many who responded to Matswa's call. Even features of nativism became apparent, and the *Association Amicale* became known as *Amicale Balali*, after a subgroup of the Bakongo. The messianic-cum-nativistic characteristics became so marked that the movement was soon suppressed and Matswa himself, at first deported, was later imprisoned.

From very early days it appears that Matswa and his followers permitted, if they did not actually encourage, syncreticisms and reinterpretations of Christianity, and the traditional ancestor worship (Andersson, 1958, pp. 124–5); though very probably the founder intended the movement to maintain an instrumental orientation moving from separatist to reformative. But his followers, particularly after his death, identified Matswa with Christ and shifted the movement into a messianic configuration, bringing both passive and active detachment from the colonial situation and considerable unrest (Balandier, 1955, p. 398). One surviving form of Matswaism, Nzambi ya Minda (God of the Candle) plays down the messianic element and is more reformative, combining Christian elements with traditional forms of ancestor worship. The history of Matswaism, in sum, shows us the subversion of an intended shift from separatist to reformative subverted by an exaggerated swing to messianism which was suppressed. Due to the exigencies of the Second World War, the colonial authorities also imprisoned Simon Mpadi. But his movement did not make the broad shifts of Matswaism. His original Salvation Army-oriented movement has simply shifted to a later and rather inactive reformative stance (Andersson, 1958, p. 146).

It may be pointed out, incidentally, that the shift made by Matswaism from a modern instrumental orientation towards the expressive pole is also seen in the Chilembwe movement in Nyasaland in 1915, and in Harry Thuku's Young Kikuyu Association and its immediate successors in Kenya in the 1920s. Both of these latter movements began with pragmatic attempts to deal with the colonial situation. A series of frustrations led Chilembwe to the abortive revolt in 1915 and Thuku's successors through a series of transformations to Mau Mau in the 1950s.

Bwiti, in Gabon and Rio Muni, is the oldest movement in western equatorial Africa, extending its roots back into the last century. But, like practically all the African religious movements, it was given great impetus by the European moral débâcle of the First World War. Bwiti was, from the first, a reformative-type cult of nativistic inclinations. It represented in the early years of the century the attempt by a minority of Fang to rework their own ancestral cult, Bieri, by adding elements from the more elaborate rituals and cosmologies of neighbouring Bantu peoples, with whom the Fang had been brought into contact by their conquest of Northern Gabon. The ancestral cult that most impressed the Fang was that of the Mitsogo Massango peoples called Boeti. The shift towards Christian symbolism occurred much later. For a surprising length of time Bwiti resisted the authority of Christian evangelization. After the Second World War, however, an increasing number of Christian elements found their way into most branches of the cult, so that at the present time there is a Christian dimension to most cult symbolism.

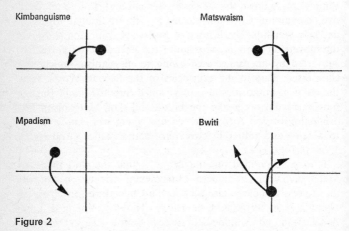

Figure 2

As we have already noted, fission has produced a diversity of forms in Bwiti, and the various subcults differ in their acculturation and their instrumental orientation. Under the impetus of

Christianity and colonial development in the late forties and fifties we even find, for the first time, the charismatic authority of leaders expressing itself in messianic fashion. In general we may say of the dynamism of Bwiti that it has shifted from nativism–reformative through reformative to the present tendency to become separatist. One branch of Bwiti, however, rapidly moved through a separatist stage into messianism. Those that led this shift were dissident Catholic catechists or seminarians.

We may illustrate the dynamics of the movements we have just discussed in another simple diagram, based on the first (see p. 398).

III

Having offered a simple set of characteristics by which African religious movements may be typed, and their dynamics assessed, we return to a larger perspective. The questions which most frequently arise in relation to these movements are of a social and political nature. This, in fact, has been such a preoccupation that C. G. Baëta feels obliged to emphasize the religious thrust in the movements he studied, taking to task Schlösser's (1949, p. 401) emphasis on economic and political motivations. He points out:

If the prophets whose preponderant interest was religious appear to have been few it must be remembered that those who have assembled the data at present available have been for the most part persons primarily interested in and on the look-out for any happening which might have political import (Baëta, 1962, p. 5).

Banton, in a more recent article, has also voiced caution against a social–economic–political bias in assessing these cults. Though they may 'serve political functions these are not so immediate as some writers have implied'. Banton (1963) also points out, as we have above, that the distinction between politics and religion is by no means as relevant to Africans as to post-reformation westerners.

These cautions are no doubt well taken; but the scheme we have presented is not encumbered by this bias (though the classifications we have tentatively made may very well be, by reason of the data on which we are forced to rely). Since it cannot overlook expressive elements, it is sensitive to the most characteristic features of religion. In its awareness of instrumental actions it recognizes the political intentions of these cults. Reference to it is thus an aid in all the major questions asked of these movements, whether of a religious or political nature.

For example, it is frequently argued that African religious movements offer to their members a sense of competence and creativity in face of the colonial denigration of these qualities. Indeed, it is more than a sense or feeling of these qualities. The church organization that was required of the South African separatists, for example, or the need for a more comprehensive and more African elaboration of dogma and ritual that resulted in the aesthetic creativity of the Shembe movement or Bwiti, actually produced these qualities. But this argument cannot be adequately pursued without assessing the instrumental or expressive nature of the groups involved. In the colonial period, when Africans were largely excluded from wielding the substantial tools of progress, life within movements of an instrumental kind offered them possibilities of developing competence in the ways of a more complex world, thereby acting to secularize the membership. For movements of expressive type, a transitory substitution of autonomy for dependence was achieved.

Again, anyone who has experienced present-day village life in Africa, and the comparative deprivation that progress has brought upon it, cannot ignore the entertainment value in the social and ritual life of these movements. They almost all act to replace the village boredom and deprivation with the satisfaction of sociability and religious adventure: a social invitation to an enthusiastic in-group: a ritual invitation to a spiritual universe, apprehended but not fully grasped, full of possible surprises, but always exhilarating. The more expressive the orientation of the cult, of course, the more satisfying and the more involving is this ritually created spiritual universe – the more instrumental, the more are the satisfactions of a purely social and political nature.

The major question remains as to the present and future place of these movements in an independent Africa. Where autonomy was not politically possible it is understandable that Africans should have sought for it in other realms. But now it may be asked, as Welbourn (1961, p. 161) asks concerning the Kikuyu, whether 'the desire for independence is likely to express itself in manifestly religious symbols'. For it is now possible to achieve autonomy by manipulating political symbols. While this question ignores the host of other satisfactions, from aesthetic to psychosomatic, achieved by these movements, as well as the extent to which Africans have identified political with religious symbols, and may continue to do so, it remains of foremost importance (cf. Evans-Pritchard and Fortes, 1940, pp. 16–23).

To put it in another way, the viability of these movements is said to hinge on the organizational rationality that is produced in African societies in the processes of modernization. Greater rationality, it is supposed will militate against them. But it may be argued that some of these movements, despite their minority status, might be rationally employed as religious vehicles of national integration. This would be particularly likely with those that have attained pan-tribal distribution, such as Bwiti in Gabon, Aladura in West Africa and Kitawala in Central Africa. In the late 1950s there seemed to be this possibility with the Lumpa church. Otherwise, whatever organizational rationality is achieved, if colonial domination in Africa is replaced by a sense of ethnic domination, the situation of subordination and deprivation will persist and continue to produce religious movements of a compensatory character.

As for the movements themselves, it remains true that their survival depends upon their powers of organization, in terms of long-term goals and a correlated sensitivity to the larger situations of which they are a part.[13] If we return to our scheme we re-

13. This is not to deny the importance of the attitude taken by the main forces in the superordinate, that is, outside situation. An expressive, tradition-oriented movement can survive for a very long time if the administration takes a permissive view, and if the world-view implied by the cult's symbolism does not too strongly imply their elimination. However, the administration, whether colonial or independent, is invariably goal-minded and instrumental, and therefore in fundamental tension with the more expressive and traditional movements. Thus with Bwiti in Gabon, despite its modest instrumentalism, it is nevertheless the constant complaint of the present administration that 'dancing all night and eating *eboka* does not much contribute to the building of modern Gabon'. 'Think how much energy is going into that which could be going into road building', said one administrator.

cognize that those movements which have persisted longest are those which have stayed within or passed into the instrumental hemisphere. Similarly Voget (1956, p. 259), in his study of American Indian movements, notes 'a progression towards more secular, pragmatic and accommodative adjustment'.

The survival capacity of religious movements is thus roughly predictable by reference to the rapidity of their shift away from expressive and totally traditional orientation. Prolonged inertia as a messianic or nativist movement seriously diminishes its viability.

What seems to be implied in a broader frame of reference by our scheme is a movement from religion to politics. This is surely the tendency though not an inevitable one, and we cannot exclude, for reasons which we have exposed, the possibility of moves from politics to religion.[14] Nor should this tendency be taken to imply that politics is in every way a functional alternative to religion, or that religion is inert as an instrument of politics. In fact, the scheme we employ suggests, without specific reference to politics or religion, that there are varying proportions of instrumental and expressive tendencies in all acts and institutions. In fact, every viable institution must strike an appropriate balance for its circumstances between the instrumental and the expressive. There must therefore be numbers of African religious movements which combine a 'right' proportion of the expressive and the instrumental for the times, both adapting the group to the larger situation while at the same time providing adjustment for the individuals involved by expressive techniques.

What this optimum proportion may be in the changing African situation remains to be ascertained. That it will be primarily instrumental seems clear. That it will be exclusively instrumental seems doubtful. These movements, in short, embody many cultural imperatives, primarily expressive techniques which can and will facilitate African adjustments to modernization, just as they provided adjustment to the colonial situation. In other

14. Worsley in his New Guinea study is led to distinguish between activist and passivist movements. All the former movements ultimately result in the emergence of secular political organization, or failing this, are eventually themselves led, much in the manner of the South African separatists, to a state of passive resignation. See Worsley (1957), p. 236.

words, African politics, should its instrumentalism lead it to abolish African religious movements as irrational and intractable enclaves, must still provide some of the gratifications previously offered in these movements.

References

ANDERSSON, E. (1958), *Messianic Popular Movements in the Lower Congo*, Almquist och Wiksell.

BAËTA, C. G. (1962), *Prophetism in Ghana*, S.C.M. Press.

BALANDIER, G. (1955), *Sociologie actuelle d'Afrique noire*, Presses Universitaires.

BALANDIER, G. (1957), *Afrique Ambiguë*, Plon.

BANTON, M. (1963), 'African prophets', *Race*, vol. 5.

CUNNISON, I. (1951), 'A Watchtower assembly in Central Africa', *Int. Rev. Miss.*, vol. 40.

EVANS-PRITCHARD, E. E., and FORTES, M. (1940), *African Political Systems*, Oxford University Press.

FERNANDEZ, J. W. (1964), 'The idea and symbol of the saviour in a Gabon syncretist cult', *Int. Rev. Miss.*, vol. 53, pp. 281–91.

FIELD, M. J. (1960), *Search for Security*, Faber.

FISHER, H. J. (1963), *Ahmadiyyah – A Study in Contemporary Islam on the West African Coast*, Oxford University Press.

HERSKOVITS, M. J. (1962), *The Human Factor in Changing Africa*, Knopf.

JAMIL, A.-N. (1963), 'The Salifiiya movement in Morocco – the religious bases of the Moroccan Nationalist Movement', *Mid. East. Affairs*, no. 3, pp. 90–105.

KOPYTOFF, I. (1963), African religious movements: indigenous versus acculturative factors, unpublished manuscript.

LINTON, R. (1943), 'Nativistic movements', *Amer. Anthrop.*, vol. 65, pp. 230–40.

MARWICK, M. (1950), 'Another modern anti-witchcraft movement in East Central Africa', *Africa*, vol. 20, pp. 100–12.

MITCHELL, R. L. (1963), The Aladura movement among the Yoruba in Nigeria, unpublished manuscript.

PARRINDER, G. (1953), *Religion in an African City*, Oxford University Press.

PARSONS, T. (1951), *The Social System*, Free Press of Glencoe.

PAULME, D. (1962), 'Une religion syncrétique en Côte d'Ivoire', *Cahiers d'études Africaines*, vol. 3, pp. 5–90.

RICHARDS, A. I. (1935), 'A modern movement in witch-finders', *Africa*, vol. 8, pp. 448–61.

ROTBERG, R. (1961), 'The Lenshina movement of Northern Rhodesia', *The Rhodes–Livingstone Inst. J.*, vol. 29, pp. 63–70.

SCHLÖSSER, K. (1949), *Propheten in Afrika*, Braunschweig.

SHEPPERSON, G. (1962), 'Nyasaland and the millennium', in S. L. Thrupp, ed., *Millennial Dreams in Action*, Mouton.

SHEPPERSON, G., and PRICE, T. (1958), *Independent African John Chilembwe and the Nyasaland Native Rising of 1915*, Mouton.

SPIRO, H. J. (1962), 'Comparative politics – a comprehensive approach', *Amer. polit. Scien. Rev.*, vol. 41, pp. 577–95.

SUNDKLER, B. (1961), *Bantu Prophets in South Africa*, Butterworth.

TAYLOR, J. V., and LEHMANN, D. (1961), *Christians of the Copperbelt*, S.C.M. Press.

TURNER, H. W. (1962), 'The Church of the Lord', *J. Afr. Hist.*, vol. 3, pp. 91–110.

VOGET, F. W. (1956), 'The American Indian in transition reformation and accommodation', *Amer. Anthrop.*, vol. 58, pp. 249–63.

WELBOURN, F. B. (1961), *East African Rebels – a Study of some Independent Churches*, S.C.M. Press.

WORSLEY, P. (1957), *The Trumpet Shall Sound*, McGibbon & Kee.

ZESSNER, W. (1961), 'Co-operation and competition in geometric vectorial symbolism', in M. Mead, ed., *Co-operation and Competition among Primitive Peoples*, McGraw-Hill.

V. Religious Authority and Specialization

Religious beliefs, values and symbols depend for their survival and transmission on some form of social organization. Not all religious culture is, however, sustained in organizations as we understand that term in industrial societies. In primitive societies such formal organization is typically absent. Nevertheless, even in primitive societies there has to be at least some degree of specialization in religious roles, even if religious belief and practice are not sustained in any formally organized and differentiated manner. We may, in fact, indicate two main social 'vehicles' which sustain religion. One of these, the religious collectivity, we have already dealt with in the previous section. The other is that of the *religious role*. In nearly all societies there have been religious practitioners who occupy a special position which entails specific duties, according to the established expectations of their congregations. In some societies these roles are located in bounded organizations or movements; in others, like the primitive society, they are not. Reading 22 by Max Weber contrasts the roles of the priest and the magician with reference to what in many ways is the ultimate source of religious authority, the god. The selection from Lienhardt's *Divinity and Experience* (Reading 23) focuses on the role of the diviner among a primitive people, the Dinka. (It should be noted that in addition to these 'free diviners' the Dinka also have a form of hereditary priesthood.) The extract from Harrison's book on the American Baptist Convention (Reading 24) is concerned with the way in which a religious tradition emphasizing the virtues of individual access to religious knowledge and values has, nevertheless, to cope with the problems of social organization and distribution of authority within the organization. Finally, Towler's article (Reading 25) deals with the problem of the degree to which the English clergyman has lost social prestige and status during the twentieth century.

22 M. Weber

Gods, Magicians and Priests

M. Weber, *The Sociology of Religion*, Beacon Press, 1963, chapter 2.
(First published 1920.)

Just as the forms of the gods vary, depending on natural and
social conditions, so too there are variations in the potential of a
god to achieve primacy in the pantheon, or to monopolize divinity.
Only Judaism and Islam are strictly monotheistic in their essence.
The Hindu and Christian forms of the sole or supreme deity are
theological concealments of the fact that an important and unique
religious interest, namely in salvation through the incarnation of
a divinity, stands in the way of strict monotheism. The path to
monotheism has been traversed with varying degrees of consistency, but nowhere was the existence of spirits and demons permanently eliminated. Even in the Reformation spirits and demons
were simply subordinated unconditionally to the one god, at least
in theory.

The decisive consideration was and remains: who is deemed
to exert the stronger influence on the individual in his everyday
life, the theoretically supreme god or the lower spirits and demons?
If the spirits, then the religion of everyday life is decisively determined by them, regardless of the official god-concept of the ostensibly rationalized religion. Where a political god of a locality
developed, it was natural enough that he frequently achieved
primacy. Whenever a plurality of settled communities with established local gods expanded the area of their political association
through conquest, the usual result was that various local gods of
the newly amalgamated communities were thereupon welded into
a religious totality. Within this amalgamated totality, the
empirical and functional specializations of the gods, whether
original or subsequently determined by new experiences concerning the special spheres of the gods' influences, would reappear in
a division of labor, with varying degrees of clarity.

The local deities of the most important political and religious centers (and hence of the rulers and priests in these centers), e.g. Marduk of Babel or Amon of Thebes, advanced to the rank of the highest gods, only to disappear again with the eventual destruction or removal of the residence, as happened in the case of Assur after the fall of the Assyrian empire. Once a political association as such has come to be regarded as a society under the tutelage of a particular deity, it would seem to be unprotected until the gods of the individual members were also incorporated, amalgamated and even adopted locally in a sort of synoecism. This practice, so common in antiquity, was re-enacted when the great sacred relics of the provincial cathedrals were transferred to the capital of the unified Russian empire.

The possible combinations of the various principles involved in the construction of a pantheon or in the achievement of a position of primacy by one or another god are almost infinite in number. Indeed, the jurisdictions of the divine figures are as fluid as those of the officials of patrimonial regimes. Moreover, the differentiation between jurisdictions of the various gods is intersected by the practice of religious attachment or courtesy to a particular god who is especially cultivated or directly invoked and who is treated as functionally universal. Thus all possible functions are attributed to the universal god, even functions which have been assigned previously to other deities. This is the 'henotheism' which Max Müller erroneously assumed to constitute a special stage of evolution. In the attainment of primacy by a particular god, purely rational factors have often played an important concomitant role. Wherever a considerable measure of constancy in regard to certain prescriptions became clearly evident – most often in the case of stereotyped and fixed religious rites – and where this was recognized by rationalized religious thought, then those deities that evinced the greatest regularity in their behavior, namely the gods of heaven and the stars, had a chance to achieve primacy.

Yet in the routinized religion of everyday life (*Alltagsreligiosität*), only a comparatively minor role was played by those gods who, because they exerted a major influence upon universal natural phenomena, were interpreted by metaphysical speculation as very important and occasionally even as world creators. The reason for this is that these natural phenomena vary but little in their course, and hence it is not necessary to resort in everyday religious practice to the devices of sorcerers and priests in order to influence them. A particular god might be of decisive importance for the entire religion of a people (e.g. Osiris in Egypt) if he met a pressing religious need, in this case a soteriological one; but even so, he might not achieve primacy in the pantheon. The process of rationalization (*ratio*) favored the primacy of universal gods; and every consistent crystallization of a pantheon followed systematic rational principles to some degree, since it was always influenced by professional sacerdotal rationalism or by the rational striving for order on the part of secular individuals. Above all, it is the aforementioned relationship of the rational regularity of the stars in their heavenly courses, as regulated by divine order, to the inviolable sacred social order in terrestrial affairs, that makes the universal gods the responsible guardians of both these phenomena. Upon these gods depend both rational economic practice and the secure, regulated hegemony of sacred norms in the social community. The priests are the primary protagonists and representatives of these sacred norms. Hence the competition of the stellar deities Varuna and Mithra, the guardians of the sacred order, with the storm god Indra, a formidable warrior and the slayer of the dragon, was a reflection of the conflict between the priesthood, striving for a firm regulation and control of life, and the powerful warlike nobility. Among this warrior class, the appropriate reaction to supernatural powers was to believe in a heroic god avid for martial exploits as well as in the disorderly irrationality of fate and adventuresomeness. We shall find this same contrast significant in many other contexts.

The ascension of celestial or astral gods in the pantheon is advanced by a priesthood's propagation of systematized sacred ordinances, as in India, Iran or Babylonia, and is assisted by a rationalized system of regulated subordination of subjects to their overlords, such as we find in the bureaucratic states of China and Babylonia. In Babylonia, religion plainly evolved toward a belief in the dominion of the stars, particularly the planets, over all things, from the days of the week to the fate of the individual in the afterworld. Development in this direction culminates in astrological fatalism. But this development is actually a product of later sacerdotal lore, and it is still unknown to the national religion of the politically independent state. A god may dominate a pantheon without being an international or universal deity, a transnational god of the entire world. But his dominance of a pantheon usually suggests that he is on his way to becoming that.

As reflection concerning the gods deepened, it was increasingly felt that the existence and nature of the deity must be established unequivocally and that the god should be 'universal' in this sense of unequivocal. Among the Greeks, philosophers interpreted whatever gods were found elsewhere as equivalent to and so identical with the deities of the moderately organized Greek pantheon. This tendency toward universalization grew with the increasing predominance of the primary god of the pantheon, that is, as he assumed more of a 'monotheistic' character. The growth of a world empire in China, the extension of the power of the Brahman caste throughout all the varied political formations in India, and the development of the Persian and Roman empires favored the rise of both universalism and monotheism, though not always in the same measure and with quite different degrees of success.

The growth of empire (or other comparable social processes that tend in the same direction) has by no means been the sole or indispensable lever for the accomplishment of this development. In the Yahweh cult, a case of fundamental importance in the history of religion, there evolved at least an approach to universalistic monotheism, namely monolatry, as a result of a concrete historic event – the formation of a confederacy. In this case, universalism was a product of international politics, of which the pragmatic interpreters were the prophetic protagonists of the cult of Yahweh and the ethics enjoined by him. As a consequence of their preaching, the deeds of other nations that were profoundly affecting Israel's vital interests also came to be regarded as wrought by Yahweh. At this point one can see clearly the distinctively and eminently *historical* character of the theorizing of the Hebrew prophets, which stands in sharp contrast to the speculations concerning nature characteristic of the priesthoods of India and Babylonia. Equally striking is the ineluctable obligation resulting from Yahweh's promises: the necessity of interpreting the entire history of the Hebrew nation as consisting of the deeds of Yahweh and hence as constituting a pattern of world history. In view of the many dire threats to the people's survival, its history appeared contradictory to the divine promises, as well as inextricably intertwined with the destinies of other nations. Thus, the ancient warrior god of the confederacy, who had become the local god of the city of Jerusalem, took on the prophetic and universalistic traits of transcendently sacred omnipotence and inscrutability.

In Egypt, the monotheistic, and hence necessarily universalistic, transition of Amenhotep IV (Ikhnaton) to the solar cult resulted from an entirely different situation. One factor was again the extensive rationalism of the priesthood, and in all likelihood of the laity as well, which was of a purely naturalistic character, in marked contrast to Israelite prophecy. Another factor was the practical need of a monarch at the head of a bureaucratic totalitarian state to break the power of the priests by eliminating the multiplicity of sacerdotal gods, and to restore the ancient power of the deified Pharaoh by elevating the monarch to the position of supreme solar priest. On the other hand, the universalistic monotheism of Christianity and Islam must be regarded as derivative of Judaism, while the relative monotheism of Zoroastrianism was in all likelihood determined at least in part by Near Eastern rather than intra-Iranian influences. All of these monotheisms were critically influenced by the distinctive character of 'ethical' prophecy, rather than by the 'exemplary' type.[1] All other relatively monotheistic and universalistic developments are the products of the philosophical speculations of priests and laymen. They achieved practical religious importance only when they became associated with the quest for salvation.

Almost everywhere a beginning was made toward some form of consistent monotheism, but practical impediments thwarted this development in the workaday mass religion (*Alltagsreligion*), with the exceptions of Judaism, Islam and Protestant Christianity. There are different reasons for the failure of a consistent monotheism to develop in different cultures, but the main reason was generally the pressure of the powerful material and ideological

1. For Weber's account of these types see above, p. 39. – *Ed.*

interests vested in the priests, who resided in the cultic centers and regulated the cults of the particular gods. Still another impediment to the development of monotheism was the religious need of the laity for an accessible and tangible familiar religious object which could be brought into relationship with concrete life situations or with definite groups of people to the exclusion of outsiders, an object which would above all be accessible to magical influences. The security provided by a tested magical manipulation is far more reassuring than the experience of worshipping a god who – precisely because he is omnipotent – is not subject to magical influence. The crystallization of developed conceptions of supernatural forces as gods, even as a single transcendent god, by no means automatically eliminated the ancient magical notions, not even in Christianity. It did produce, however, the possibility of a dual relationship between men and the supernatural. This must now be discussed.

A power conceived by analogy to living persons may be coerced into the service of man, just as the naturalistic power of a spirit could be coerced. Whoever possesses the requisite charisma for employing the proper means is stronger even than the god, whom he can compel to do his will. In these cases, religious behavior is not worship of the god but rather coercian of the god, and invocation is not prayer but rather the exercise of magical formula Such is one ineradicable basis of popular religion, particularly in India. Indeed, such coercive religion is universally diffused, and even the Catholic priest continues to practice something of this magical power in executing the miracle of the mass and in exercising the power of the keys. By and large this is the original, though not exclusive, origin of the orgiastic and mimetic components of the religious cult – especially of song, dance, drama and the typical fixed formulae of prayer.

The process of anthropomorphization may take the form of attributing to the gods the human behavior patterns appropriate to a mighty terrestrial potentate, whose freely disposed favor can be obtained by entreaty, gifts, service, tributes, cajolery and bribes. On the other hand, his favor may be earned as a consequence of the devotee's own faithfulness and good conduct in conformity with the divine will. In these ways, the gods are conceived by analogy to earthly rulers: mighty beings whose power differs only in degree, at least at first. As gods of this type evolve, worship of divinity comes to be regarded as a necessity.

The two characteristic elements of 'divine worship', prayer and sacrifice, have their origin in magic. In prayer, the boundary between magical formula and supplication remains fluid. The technically rationalized enterprise of prayer (in the form of prayer wheels and similar devices, or of prayer strips hung in the wind or attached to icons of gods or saints, or of carefully measured wreaths of roses – virtually all of which are products of the methodical compulsion of the gods by the Hindus) everywhere stands far closer to magic than to entreaty. Individual prayer as real supplication is found in religions that are otherwise undifferentiated, but in most cases such prayer has a purely business-like, rationalized form that sets forth the achievements of the supplicant on behalf of the god and then claims adequate recompense therefor.

Sacrifice, at its first appearance, is a magical instrumentality that in part stands at the immediate service of the coercion of the gods. For the gods also need the soma juice of the sorcerer-priests, the substance which engenders their ecstasy and enables them to perform their deeds. This is the ancient notion of the Aryans as to why it is possible to coerce the gods by sacrifice. It may even be held that a pact can be concluded with the gods which imposes obligations on both parties; this was the fateful conception of the Israelites in particular. Still another view of sacrifice holds that it is a means of deflecting, through magical media, the wrath of the god upon another object, a scapegoat or above all a human sacrifice.

But another motive for sacrifice may be of greater importance, and it is probably older too: the sacrifice, especially of animals, is intended as a *communio*, a ceremony of eating together which serves to produce a fraternal community between the sacrificers and the god. This represents a transformation in the significance of the even older notion that to rend and consume a strong (and later a sacred) animal enables the eaters to absorb its potencies. Some such older magical meaning – and there are various other possibilities – may still provide the act of sacrifice with its essential form, even after genuine cultic views have come to exert considerable influence. Indeed, such a magical significance may even

413

regain dominance over the cultic meaning. The sacrificial rituals of the Brahmans, and even of the Atharva Veda, were almost purely sorcery, in contrast to the cultic sacrifices of the ancient Nordics. On the other hand, there are many departures from magic, as when sacrifices are interpreted as tribute. First fruits may be sacrificed in order that the god may not deprive man of the enjoyment of the remaining fruits; and sacrifice is often interpreted as a self-imposed punishment or sacrificial sin-offering that averts the wrath of the gods before it falls upon the sacrificer. To be sure, this does not yet involve any awareness of sin, and it initially takes place in a mood of cool and calculated trading, as for example in India.

An increasing predominance of non-magical motives is later brought about by the growing recognition of the power of a god and of his character as a personal overlord. The god becomes a great lord who may fail on occasion, and whom one cannot approach with devices of magical compulsion, but only with entreaties and gifts. But if these motives add anything new to mere wizardry, it is initially something as sober and rational as the motivation of magic itself. The pervasive and central theme is: *do ut des*. This aspect clings to the routine and the mass religious behavior of all peoples at all times and in all religions. The normal situation is that the burden of all prayers, even in the most other-worldly religions, is the aversion of the external evils of this world and the inducement of the external advantages of this world.

Every aspect of religious phenomena that points beyond evils and advantages in this world is the work of a special evolutionary process, one characterized by distinctively dual aspects. On the one hand, there is an ever-broadening rational systematization of the god concept and of the thinking concerning the possible relationships of man to the divine. On the other hand, there ensues a characteristic recession of the original, practical and calculating rationalism. As such primitive rationalism recedes, the significance of distinctively religious behavior is sought less and less in the purely external advantages of everyday economic success. Thus, the goal of religious behavior is successively 'irrationalized' until finally otherworldly non-economic goals come to represent what is distinctive in religious behavior. But the extra-economic evolution just described requires as one of its prerequisites the existence of specific personal carriers of the otherworldly goals.

The relationships of men to supernatural forces which take the forms of prayer, sacrifice and worship may be termed 'cult' and 'religion', as distinguished from 'sorcery', which is magical coercion. Correspondingly, those beings that are worshipped and entreated religiously may be termed 'gods', in contrast to 'demons', which are magically coerced and charmed. There may be no instance in which it is possible to apply this differentiation absolutely, since the cults we have just called 'religious' practically everywhere contain numerous magical components. The historical development of the aforementioned differentiation frequently came about in a very simple fashion when a secular or priestly power suppressed a cult in favor of a new religion, with the older gods continuing to live on as demons.

The sociological aspect of this differentiation is the rise of the 'priesthood' as something distinct from 'practitioners of magic'. Applied to reality, this contrast is fluid, as are all sociological phenomena. Even the theoretical differentiae of these types are not unequivocally determinable. Following the distinction between 'cult' and 'sorcery', one may contrast those professional functionaries who influence the gods by means of worship with those magicians who coerce demons by magical means; but in many great religions, including Christianity, the concept of the priest includes such a magical qualification.

Or the term 'priest' may be applied to the functionaries of a regularly organized and permanent enterprise concerned with influencing the gods, in contrast with the individual and occasional efforts of magicians. Even this contrast is bridged over by a sliding scale of transitions, but as a pure type the priesthood is unequivocal and can be said to be characterized by the presence of certain fixed cultic centers associated with some actual cultic apparatus.

Or it may be thought that what is decisive for the concept of priesthood is that the functionaries, regardless of whether their office is hereditary or personal, be actively associated with some type of social organization, of which they are employees or organs operating in the interests of the organization's members, in contrast with magicians, who are self-employed. Yet even this distinction, which is clear enough conceptually, is fluid in actuality. The sorcerer is not infrequently a member of an organized guild, and is occasionally the member of a hereditary caste which may hold a monopoly of magic within the particular community. Even the Catholic priest is not always the occupant of an official post. In Rome he is occasionally a poor mendicant who lives a hand-to-mouth existence from the proceeds of single masses, the acquisition of which he solicits.

Yet another distinguishing quality of the priest, it is asserted, is his professional equipment of special knowledge, fixed doctrine and vocational qualifications, which brings him into contrast with sorcerers, prophets and other types of religious functionaries who exert their influence by virtue of personal gifts (charisma) made manifest in miracle and revelation. But this again is no simple and absolute distinction, since the sorcerer may sometimes be very learned, while deep learning need not always characterize working priests. Rather, the distinction between priest and magician must be established qualitatively with reference to the different nature of the learning in the two cases. As a matter of fact we must later, in our exposition of the forms of domination, distinguish the rational training and discipline of priests from the different preparation of charismatic magicians. The latter preparation proceeds in part as an 'awakening education' using irrational means and aiming at rebirth, and proceeds in part as a training in purely empirical lore. But in this case also, the two contrasted types flow into one another.

'Doctrine' has already been advanced as one of the fundamental traits of the priesthood. We may assume that the outstanding marks of doctrine are the development of a rational system of religious concepts and (what is of the utmost importance for us here) the development of a systematic and distinctively religious ethic based upon a consistent and stable doctrine which purports to be a 'revelation'. An example is found in Islam, which contrasted its scriptural religion with simple paganism. But this description of priesthood and this assumption about the nature of doctrine would exclude from the concept of priesthood the Japanese Shinto priests and such functionaries as the mighty hierocrats of the Phoenicians. The adoption of such an assumption would have the effect of making the decisive characteristic of the priesthood a function which, while admittedly important, is not universal.

It is more correct for our purpose, in order to do justice to the diverse and mixed manifestations of this phenomenon, to set up as the crucial feature of the priesthood the specialization of a particular group of persons in the continuous operation of a cultic enterprise, permanently associated with particular norms, places and times, and related to specific social groups. There can be no priesthood without a cult, although there may well be a cult without a specialized priesthood. The latter was the case in China, where state officials and the heads of households exclusively conducted the services of the official gods and the ancestral spirits. On the other hand, both novitiate and doctrine are to be found among typical, pure magicians, as in the brotherhood of the Hametze among the Indians, and elsewhere in the world. These magicians may wield considerable power, and their essentially magical celebrations may play a central role in the life of their people. Yet they lack a continuously operative cult, and so the term 'priests' cannot be applied to them.

A rationalization of metaphysical views and a specifically religious ethic are usually missing in the case of a cult without priests, as in the case of a magician without a cult. The full development of both a metaphysical rationalization and a religious ethic requires an independent and professionally trained priesthood, permanently occupied with the cult and with the practical problems involved in the cure of souls. Consequently, ethics developed into something quite different from a metaphysically rationalized religion in classic Chinese thought, which lacked an independent priesthood; and this also happened with the ethics of ancient Buddhism, which lacked both cult and priesthood.

Moreover, the rationalization of religious life was fragmentary or entirely missing wherever the priesthood failed to achieve independent class status, as in classical antiquity. Wherever a class of primitive magicians and sacred musicians did rationalize magic, but failed to develop a genuinely sacerdotal occupational pattern (as was the case with the Brahmans in India), the priesthood developed in a rather strange way. Not every genuine priesthood developed the distinguishing features of a rational

417

metaphysic and a religious ethic. Such developments generally (though there were exceptions) presupposed the operation of one or both of two forces outside the priesthood: prophets, the bearers of metaphysical or religious-ethical revelation, and the laity, the non-priestly devotees of the cult.

23 G. Lienhardt

Diviners in Dinkaland

Excerpts from chapter 2 of G. Lienhardt, *Divinity and Experience*, Clarendon Press, 1961, pp. 56-7, 64-74.

All Dinka assert that divinity is one, *nhialic ee tok*. The implications of this affirmation are that their *nhialic* is the same divinity as that which different peoples know under different names, the divinity the Nuer call '*kwoth*', the Muslims 'Allah', the Christians 'God' and so on. Yet *nhialic* is also a comprehensive term for a number of conceptions which differ considerably from each other. Powers, of which the most important religiously are those I have called free divinities and clan divinities, are distinct from each other, though of most of them the Dinka may say simply *ee nhialic*, 'it is Divinity'. This unity and multiplicity of Divinity causes no difficulty in the context of Dinka language and life, but it is impossible entirely to avoid the logical and semantic problems which arise when Dinka statements bearing upon it are translated, together, into English.

The most important and active of the free divinities known in western Dinkaland are *Deng*, *Garang*, *Macardit* and *Abuk*. Deng, Garang and Macar are common personal names for men and Abuk is probably the commonest name for women, so here the names of the free divinities appear in italic letters to distinguish them from human personal names. Among the Agar and Cic Dinka, another free divinity called *Loi* is also important, but knowledge of this divinity had not spread farther westwards during my visits to Dinkaland, ending in 1950.[1] Elsewhere in Dinkaland there are others, which are unknown in the west, or

1. As will appear, it is characteristic of these free divinities that they should extend the range of their activities, and it would not be surprising if *Loi* were now more widespread.

have been forgotten in all but name because they are thought no longer to be active there.[2]

None of the free divinities, with the possible exception of *Macardit*, also sometimes called *Colwic*, is thought to exist independently of the particular name by which the Dinka know it. That is, unlike Divinity, who is thought to be universal and known by various names to different peoples, the free divinities are active only where their specific names are known and where effects in human life can be attributed to them.

Free divinities make their presence known by causing illness, by possessing human beings and announcing through their mouths their names and demands, and sometimes by speaking in dreams. They do not, strictly speaking, *appear*, for in themselves they are held to be formless, though each has a set of colour and other associations. [. . .]

There are several categories of 'religious' specialist (I here use the term widely) in Dinka society and the boundaries between some of them are not very clearly defined. The permanent hereditary priesthood of masters of the fishing-spear is described elsewhere.[3] Here we consider those seers, diviners and prophets whose powers, unlike those of the priests, are not necessarily hereditary.

I first consider and then dismiss as marginal a number of magical practitioners whose powers reside in their possession of fetish bundles, which they may have bought or inherited. A man who possesses such fetishes is called *ran* (*lo*) *wal*, 'a person with medicine'. *Wal* is the term for grass and vegetable life generally, and hence for medicine, in the dual sense of herbal remedies and magical medicines. Among the Western Dinka the most famous of such magical medicines is one called *mathiang gok*, though the varieties of *wal* may be as numerous as the private superstitions of which individuals are capable. *Mathiang gok*, however, is the very type of potent medicine possessed by medicine men, and a

2. Such are *Adim*, a free divinity said to have originated in Agar country, and connected with hyaena and the protection of stock against hyaena; *Ayak*, the mother perhaps of *Abuk*, known among the Bor Dinka; and *Dayim*, also known among the Bor Dinka and the subject of a hymn translated by Archdeacon Shaw (1915), p. 20.

3. Lienhardt discusses the masters of the fishing-spear at a later point in the book from which this excerpt is taken. – *Ed.*

brief account of it will be enough to suggest the nature of all; as I have said, they are not to be regarded as of great *religious* importance, and the Dinka themselves are quick to point out the difference between the characters and abilities of such earthly medicines and their owners, and those of priests and prophets, in their roles as such.[4] I say 'in their roles', because anyone may possess and use such medicines; they serve individual human ends and, as individual human beings, priests and prophets may acquire them like anyone else. I think, however, that they are less likely to do so, as although they fear them they pretend to despise them.

Mathiang gok, like other medicines of a magical nature, is in the general category of powers, *jok*. It resides in the physical fetish bundle and can be bought with it; but its action is of a spiritual nature, and is attributed to a power informing the fetish bundle but which also moves outside it, to affect the consciences and fortunes of men against whom it is directed. *Mathiang gok* is called a 'black power' (*jong col*), or sometimes an 'earth power' (*jong piny*), to distinguish it and other medicines of its kind from the higher powers, the divinities.

I do not know what the physical constituents of a *mathiang gok* bundle are; the one I saw consisted of bits of unidentifiable wood and withered roots, and I think that roots of some kind are always included. The connexion of the medicine with the earth is thus perhaps reinforced, for I do not think that among the various material things associated with the higher powers, the divinities, there are any which come from under the ground. The name, *mathiang gok*, is not given any consistent etymology by the Dinka. *Mathiang* indisputably means 'dark brown', but it might also be a man's name, as is supposed by Captain Fergusson.[5] *Gok* similarly may be a man's name, or the name of a tribal area. I have also been told by a Dinka that the name means 'brown dove', since, he said, the name of the medicine

4. Fetishes are thought by the Dinka to be particularly characteristic of the Sudanic-speaking peoples to the south of their country.

5. V. H. Fergusson (1923, p. 112) calculates that in about 1902 an Agar Dinka called Mattiang went to settle near the Gell river. There he found the root, which a 'jur' (non-Dinka) of Tonj told him to call 'Mattiang Goh', since Goh was his father's name. Fergusson says that the root protects its owner against theft.

may really be *mathiang guk*, and *guk* is a dove. Yet I cannot think that this is more than a piece of *ad hoc* etymology, since in Dinka the adjective follows the noun and 'brown dove' would correctly be *guk mathiang*.

The circumstances in which *mathiang gok* is thought to operate, and its mode of operation, are consistently described by all Dinka. Its main function is to obtain for its possessor an influence over those whom he thinks to have wronged him, particularly to enforce the payment of cattle debts. Its mode of operation is said to be as follows. A man has enemies, or he has a grudge against others for keeping from him what is rightfully his own. He does not feel strong enough to obtain his rights without the assistance of a power which will work for him individually. Perhaps invocation of divinity has been of no avail. He therefore buys *mathiang gok*, a purchase which will normally involve a trip to another part of the country, or into the land of the non-Dinka peoples to the south. People may suspect what this trip is for; they will not be quite sure, as a Dinka does not usually publicly admit to the possession of *mathiang gok* and it is not lightly spoken about. This may be partly because the Government has imposed heavy penalties on those who are found with it, though I doubt if it is these alone which surround the transaction with secrecy. The Dinka themselves tolerate, but do not really approve, dealings which involve the manipulation of amoral medicines for purely individual ends. Members of any particular group of Dinka are convinced that *mathiang gok* is a foreign importation, some say from the Agar Dinka, who say it comes from the non-Dinka ('Jur' Beli and Sofi) to the south, and some even say it comes from the Nuer, who also know it, but trace it to the Dinka.

The man returns and hides the bundle of roots somewhere in his cattle byre. From time to time he speaks to it and tells it his desires, and will also make it small offerings. It, in its turn, will demand sacrifices, which may be covertly carried out, or which may be secretly included by the man in the intention of other sacrifices made to powers which are not in the same way publicly disapproved. In return for these attentions, *mathiang gok* will go out after a man who owes its owner cattle. The Dinka say that it will come to such a man when he is walking alone, and will speak to him and threaten to injure him or his family unless the debt is paid. It may go further, and actually kill an enemy of its owner by causing swellings, most commonly in the throat and head or in the belly. A man intimidated by *mathiang gok* will often pay his debts, though a man who feels himself to have been wrongly injured by the *mathiang gok* of another will perhaps retort with physical violence if he is sure of the source of his suffering.

I have found that Dinka are never prepared to admit that they are *quite* sure that a man possesses or is using *mathiang gok* until a further stage is reached, that is until a man, having by recourse to *mathiang gok* obtained what he desires, is many years later taken seriously ill himself. He may then either announce himself that he has in the past bought *mathiang gok* to which he has for long failed to pay appropriate attentions, or a diviner will attribute his sickness or death openly to this cause. Then the possession of *mathiang gok* by the man is openly admitted, and sacrifice is made to the power to try to divert its wrath from the neglectful owner. By this time, of course, the original disputes and enmities for which the *mathiang gok* was obtained are probably no longer live issues, though the Dinka are less sympathetic towards its owner and victim than they are to those who suffer through the unsought intervention of a higher power, which they have not themselves attempted to harness to their own individual advantage.

Anyone may be a *ran* (*lo*) *wal*, one who possesses medicines. More specifically, however, a *ran wal*, 'medicine-man', is one who is suspected of trafficking in medicines, and though he may not himself admit to possessing them knows their qualities and knows where to get them. A medicine-man is the lowest form of specialist in control and knowledge of powers, just as medicine bundles are informed with the lowest, if yet dangerous and fearful, powers. A *ran wal* is usually, I think, in any part of Dinkaland, a visitor, perhaps an itinerant Nuer or Dinka. Such people may purvey roots and charms as no permanent member of a Dinka village could, for by selling medicines or admitting to their possession within his own community a man would also be suspected of causing the sicknesses of his neighbours. The line between *ran wal* and *apeth*, the possessor of the evil eye, is often not very clearly drawn; both injure others for their own advantage, whatever their justification may be thought to be.

Though 'medicines' like *mathiang gok* are thought to inhere sufficiently in particular bundles of roots to make it possible to transfer them with the roots, and to regard them as residing in the roots, they are yet not totally bound to their material homes. Their influence or virtue – their power – emanates from them, and its action is upon the mind and hearts of men as well as upon their physical health. So even these lower powers transcend any material form with which they are associated. There is no question, for example, of simple 'contagious magic' in the use of fetish bundles. They 'speak' to men – or as we might say, to men's consciences, for we cannot fail to notice how like the workings of our 'conscience' is the action attributed to them; and when they speak to men, they are not necessarily visually imaged. I have heard it said that *mathiang gok* may speak, when conjured by a diviner, from the walls of a cattle byre, and that it has on occasions appeared to people in the form of a small brown dog. When functioning as a power it does not seem to appear to others in the form of a bundle of roots, though this is known by all to be its physical basis and vehicle, as far as transmission from hand to hand is concerned. The active principle even of this lowly power is capable of being detached, in thought, from any specific material form in which it may be supposed at times to inhere, and this is true of the relation between any power and its emblem. It is never, among the Dinka, simply material things in themselves which are of central religious importance, but something formless, immaterial, invisible, associated with them.

Much higher in esteem than men who possess *only* such fetish bundles are people called *tyet* (pl. *tiit*), a class of specialists that comprises individuals of widely differing reputations for occult knowledge and powers. I begin with a brief description of one of the least of them, one of those who may also be called *acoor*. *Acoor* is related to the word *car*, meaning to divine, and is also I think connected with the word *coor*, blind. Blind people may often be thought to have special insight. It would be unlikely that any *tyet* with a high reputation would be spoken of as *acoor*, though an *acoor* would also be referred to as *tyet* by those who thought highly of him. Diviners of lower and higher reputation stand in a relationship similar to that between minor fortune-tellers and well-known clairvoyants in our own society.

When we were all a long way from home, my companions who were worried about what might be happening to their families announced that they wished to consult an itinerant *tyet*, diviner, who had arrived in the village. The man had had some schooling. He was asking 10 piastres (about 2s.) to tell fortunes. His mode of procedure was first to set a ring – the gift, he said, of a missionary – in the dust in front of him. We sat around him, and after a few moments of apparently deep concentration he began to trace tracks in the dust between himself and the ring. As though reading these tracks as a hunter follows spoor, he would pause and consider for a while now and then, and then put forward tentative statements about matters which he could easily have picked up in the course of a few hours of ordinary village gossip. For his clients, he referred to their kinsmen's minor illnesses that would pass, cattle cases that would eventually be settled, and other generalities such as he might rightly suppose any Dinka away from his home to be troubled about. It was clear that he was following up leads given to him by the conspicuous heightening of interest shown by the audience where he was on the right lines, and he would hazard guesses, again in generalized and tentative form, until the manner of his audience convinced him that he should continue in a particular direction. When he divined for me, I deliberately misled him by showing interest in suggestions which could not possibly be true – such as, for example, that my father had had four wives, and that I was worried about half-sisters, who did not exist, and he reassured me about these matters. The Dinka, who then knew what was happening, lost faith in his statements about them, saying that after all there were many fraudulent *tiit*, diviners, or people who 'are not real *tiit*'; but of course the experience of one false diviner, far from calling into doubt the abilities of all, reminded them of many others who really had the insight which this man claimed.

The following text from the Twij Dinka illustrates something of the thought of the Dinka in this matter, and the ambivalent attitudes they may adopt towards diviners:

A young man was very ill, and his father called in a diviner who lied and said that Divinity (*nhialic*) wanted a very big fat ox. And the father of the man said 'Good', and fetched an ox from the herd and killed it. But the young man was still on the point of death.

And a lion used to come to the homestead and watch the man from a hiding-place near by, so that some day when he found him alone he could eat him. And the father of the sick man had walked and walked until he was tired out [because he was searching for more beasts to sacrifice from the herds of his relatives and friends]. And everything was finished [in sacrifices]. And that lion knew what was injuring the man.

One day a man went into the woods to get honey. He lit a fire under a tree (to smoke out the bees) and climbed the tree to cut more wood. The lion heard the axe and made for the foot of the tree. The man heard him coming and put out his fire and sat in the tree.

Two lions met at the foot of the tree, and greeted each other and asked about each other's affairs. The lion called Mangar Dit said 'I ate two men – one was thin but the other was fat.' And the other lion said, 'They have sent for you from your home, for your father and mother say "If you see Mangar Dit, and he has eaten a man, tell him that his sister has menstruated, and will he please bring the man's puddings[6] for her to eat."'

Mangar Dit said: 'Good. I have found a sick man in the village here, but I can't get hold of him because his people sleep by him day and night. And I will tell you that the Power which injures him is not a big Power at all, it is merely a little one.' And the other lion asked 'What sort of a Power is it?' And the first said 'It is a tiny Power which is in the pool in the village. If they bring a small *mangok* ox and kill it in the pool the man will get better at once.' Then the lions picked up their spears and went off to the cattle-camp. And that man in the tree heard all they said.

So the man went off to the home of the sick young man, and said, 'You people of the sick man, give me a little *mangok* ox and I will see what I can do.' The father of the sick man brought a little ox, and the ox was taken along to the pool with the sick man. And the ox was prayed over; and the sick man was possessed. Then they killed the ox.

And the sick man arose at once and ate the meat of the sacrificed ox. The next morning he went to the cattle-camp, and people were astonished by his recovery.

And that man who had climbed the tree had no Power in his body (was not a diviner); they wanted to reward him with a cow in calf, but the man refused and said, 'Just reward me with a single goat.'

6. In Dinka *abyar*, an euphemism for the anus, frequently a topic of jocular impropriety.

Minor practitioners of divination may use mussel-shells, like the Nuer, or scatter grain and interpret its fall, or, more commonly, draw in the sand as a *mise-en-scène* for their display of insight. Their reputation naturally varies according to their luck in hitting upon something which their clients are prepared to recognize as true and perceptive; but their standing is never unambiguously respectable for, as in the above story, they can be thought to defraud while still being called *tiit*,[7] diviners.

A higher type of diviner is one who is thought to have an important power, a free divinity, in his body. This may come about in several ways. He may have become sick and been told by another diviner that he has been possessed by a power of such and such a name. This power then becomes his divinity – it becomes related to him, that is, and he sacrifices to it. When he recovers from the illness he may come to regard himself as inspired by this divinity and gain a reputation for diagnosis of other people's illnesses and misfortunes by displaying an insight which he attributes to his divinity. Many people whose illnesses are attributed to particular divinities are content merely to offer sacrifice to them and return to their normal way of living; but a few (and, from those I have seen, I should say a few who are nervously very highly organized) become practising diviners. They continue to hoe and tend their cattle like other Dinka, but are called in to diagnose illnesses and causes of misfortune. The divinity may pass from a diviner to any, or none, of his children. Once the divinity has seized a man, he may learn more of the technique of divining from an established diviner.

The least regarded of these are also consulted about suspected witchcraft, and they may extract from the patient's body bits of wood or sand which have been shot into the body by witches, *apeth*. Such people again may also be suspected of being also prone to bewitch people. More highly regarded are those whom the Dinka sometimes assimilate to the yet higher category of inspired person, later described, by calling them also *ran nhialic*,

7. The word *tyet* is sometimes confused by non-Dinka with the word *atet*, which means simply 'someone who has a special skill or facility'. It is applied to bonesetters and masseurs, and more widely to anyone clever with his hands. Some diviners also have these skills but many who are not diviners also have them.

a 'person of Divinity', or *aciek*, prophet or 'creator'. The categories shade into each other, but a famous 'person of Divinity' and prophet would be demeaned by being called only *tyet*, a mere diviner.

All Dinka give consistent accounts of the way in which established diviners operate. The diviner is invited to the home of a sick man, whose kinsmen sit around him. They place on the ground spears and money as an initial payment, and an earnest of their intention to give a larger present, perhaps even a calf, if the seance is successful. The people of the sick man will then ask the diviner the name of the divinity through whom he divines, and he will tell them. The free divinities earlier mentioned – *Garang*, *Deng*, *Macardit or Colwic* – are the commonest and most widely recognized in Rek country. In Western Twij country there are also several others – *Atem*, *Aiwel*, *Yath* and *Biar Yath*. It is interesting to note that possession by divinities is thought both by Western Twij and Rek Dinka to be more common among the Twij than among the Rek, and that some divinities known in Rek-land are said to have entered from the land of the Twij, to the north and east, in the direction of Kordofan. This was a point of contact in the nineteenth century with the great Arab prophet, the Mahdi, a matter the significance of which we later discuss.

When the diviner has announced the name of the divinity through which he divines, the people ask him if he wants them to sing to it. It is considered usual for the diviner to ask that they should, and they then sing hymns, in some of which his particular divinity may be mentioned. After a period of singing the diviner begins to shake himself and to appear to feel pains in his neck and his back. He then begins to quiver and tremble and make curious squeaking noises (these I have heard from possessed people) and to breathe heavily. It is then thought that the divinity has begun (as the Dinka say) to 'rise', or to 'wake up' (*pac*) in his body, or to 'warm' his body. He is then progressively 'seized' by the divinity, which speaks in an unknown tongue through his mouth. He translates the sounds, usually twittering and groaning sounds, into partly intelligible Dinka. He thus announces, guided by his divinity, the grounds of the trouble which he has been asked to treat. The commonest and expected diagnoses are that the sick man or his father or mother or grandfather committed some hidden sin, or disposed lightly of a cow dedicated to a divinity. In one case I heard of, but did not see treated, a diviner called in to cure the paralysis of a girl of marriageable age attributed the illness to an act of her grandfather, who had cut off the arm of an enemy to take his ivory armlet, and had thereby offended the ghost (*atiep*) of the dead man. In this case the ghost required satisfaction in the form of an expiatory sacrifice. I had seen the girl before the sacrifice, and supposed that she was suffering from sleeping-sickness. She could not stand and appeared to be permanently dazed. A few weeks after the sacrifice this girl who had appeared to be incurable was walking about cheerfully with the help of a stick. I mention this to suggest that cures are sometimes conspicuously effected, though the Dinka are prepared to find that their sacrifice may be ineffective. They then simply resign themselves to the refusal of divinity to help in a particular case, or suppose that the real grounds of the trouble have not been diagnosed by the diviner.

The diviner's usual suggestion for treatment is that a sacrifice, or dedication of a beast for later sacrifice, should be made. He may kill the beast himself, or he may leave it to the senior man of the homestead or someone asked by him to officiate. A master of the fishing-spear may be asked to carry out a diviner's instruction on behalf of the sufferer, adding his own prayers, to divinity and the clan divinity of his clan, to those of the diviner and the people. They pray to divinity and to the clan divinities of those descent-groups most concerned in the case, and to such free divinities or other powers as are indicated by the diviner. These acitivies are left for fuller description and illustration later.

As I have said, diviners vary very much in reputation. There are minor personalities, of no great importance, whom many may suspect of practising fraud, or witchcraft, or even sorcery. In the middle ranks are respectable and reputable men whom the Dinka always compare to Arab or European doctors. Sometimes those who know a little Arabic try to distinguish between the lower class of diviners, who shade into practitioners with magic roots, by referring to the latter as *kujur*, a general Sudani, and, I think, originally Nuba term, which might be translated roughly as 'magician', and to the former as *zara*,[8] diviners or soothsayers. At the higher level of reputation, the *tyet* shades into a figure ideally of a quite different type, the *ran nhialic*, man of divinity, or *aciek*, 'creator', which we here call the 'prophet'.[9]

Prophets of outstanding reputation are not, and have not been, numerous in Dinkaland. In the area I knew best there had been only two whose names were widely known. One, Cyer Dit, may be still alive at the time of writing. The other Arianhdit, died in about 1948 after a long period of exile, following a patrol carried out against him by the Government in 1922. I failed to reach Arianhdit before he died and Cyer Dit showed no disposition to receive me, so I thought it better not to force my company upon him. Both men, however, represent an ideal type of religious leader, a type in which the Dinka include also the prophets of other peoples, in particular the outstanding Nuer prophet Ngundeng (Deng Kur) and also, where they have heard of him, the inspired Arab who, as the Mahdi, led his people against the British.

It is said of the great Dinka 'men of divinity' that they unite two 'things' – two principles – in their bodies. They are overtly inspired, more than others of their clans, by their clan divinities, and it is said that the really great prophets are always also hereditary masters of the fishing-spear, or members of spear-master clans, whose clan divinities are in any case thought to be more powerful than those of other clans. The special strength of their clan divinities in them is one of the principles of their effectiveness. The other is that they are in addition vehicles, and representatives on earth, of divinity. Unlike ordinary diviners, therefore, they necessarily have a place in the priestly organization of Dinkaland, but by special inspiration they are able to show powers which are denied to ordinary masters of the fishing-spear. Their genius is thought to show itself less in the states of possession which the ordinary diviner induces in himself than in the direct insight they have into the truth of situations, and their ability to help or injure others by a mere word or gesture. They are universally acknowledged by the

8 This probably refers to the Arabic *zar*, spirits which possess people.

9. Following Professor Evans-Pritchard's usage in his writings on the Nuer.

Dinka as true prophets, while many diviners may be thought, by some who have consulted them, to be capable of falsehood or error. Further, the Dinka think of them as being essentially men of peace, who, nevertheless, may be forced by external circumstances into uniting their numerous followers against a common enemy.

References

FERGUSSON, V. H. (1923), '"Mattiang Goh" witchcraft', *S.N. and R.*, vol. 6.

SHAW, ARCHDEACON (1915), 'Dinka songs', *Man*, vol. 15.

24 P. M. Harrison

Authority and Power in the American Baptist Convention

Excerpt from chapter 4 of P. M. Harrison, *Authority and Power in the Free Church Tradition*, Princeton University Press, 1959, pp. 53–64.

Emerging as they did from the neo-Calvinist Free church movement of the seventeenth century, the Baptists have always regarded the problem of authority and power as a fundamental concern. The attitude of the left-wing Protestant churches was expressed by John Cotton when he cautioned all the world to 'learn to give mortal man no greater power than they are content they shall use, for use it they will. . . . It is necessary . . . that all power that is on earth be limited, church-power or other' (cf. Hudson, 1953, p. 53).

While it is true that the radical ideals of the Puritan left-wing were stimulated within an environment of religious persecution, they were 'derived in the first instance from the two theological doctrines of the sovereignty of God and of human bondage to sin' (Hudson, 1953, p. 49). Because concentrations of power lead to rebellion against God, the churches must be independent of government, voluntary in membership, and limited in authority. No official could be trusted to wield the administrative instruments of both church and civil government. Thus the Baptists insisted upon the separation of church and state, and for the same reason they were of the opinion that church officials should not exercise authority over more than a single congregation.[1] No church leader could legitimately claim special access to the divine power, and since God is the only absolute sovereign it follows that all religious authority must be penultimate and limited. The church 'executive must always be subject to correc-

1. Some modern Baptists insist that the minister has no special authority even in his own congregation. 'The pastor of a Baptist church is simply the preaching member of that church. In a congregational meeting he has one vote . . . and the vote of the most insignificant member of the church counts for just as much as the vote of the pastor' (Pruden, 1951, p. 56).

tion by the will of Christ, for which a partial criterion was at hand in the Scriptures' (Nichols, 1951, p. 268).

But difficulties arose when these doctrinal ideas were expressed through the polity of the churches. The Baptists believed it was sufficient to point to the Scriptures, the personal experience of the Holy Spirit, or to the gathered congregation of believers as the principal mediators of divine authority. But emphasis upon the autonomy of the local churches ignored the sinful potentialities within these religious groups. The divine presence among the people was sometimes interpreted to signify the possession of God by the community, so that the will of the congregation was equated with the will of God. When God is possessed by the local church, external direction from ecclesiastical officials is obviously superfluous.[2]

One of the primary problems in every religious community is the discovery of a method for historical expression of the divine sovereignty. In any case, the sovereignty of God must be historically mediated, whether it be through 'spontaneous inspiration' of special individuals or by means of an official priestly class which preserves and transmits the oral or written tradition. However, every form of polity contains possibilities of corruption. The genius of the Free Church polity lies in the conception of the limitation and balance of power; but this form of church government tends to break down when an effort is made to eliminate the effective authority of those leaders who have been given ecclesiastical responsibilities.

The Authority of the American Baptist Convention

The crux of the problem of authority was recognized by many of the leaders who participated in the formation of the Con-

2. This phenomenon is neither new nor is it confined to the left-wing Protestant tradition. Martin Buber shows that primitive religious societies undermined the authority of the chief priests 'by establishing, within the tribe but external to the official tribal life, a secret society in which the actual, the true, the "holy" communal life is lived, free from the bonds of the "law" . . . but in holy action.' The problem always arises, that if the authority of the priests 'is disputed and extended to all, then the actual dominion is taken away from God; for without law, that is, without any clear-cut and transmissible line of demarcation between that which is pleasing to God and that which is displeasing to Him, there can be no historical continuity of divine rule upon earth' (Buber, 1946, pp. 186 ff.).

vention. Some believed the Convention itself would provide the answer:

So far as organization is concerned, these problems center in the task of getting efficiency without dependence upon external authority.

We are our own spiritual masters. Of course there is difficulty in having so many masters, and the process of getting cooperative efficiency with us has been one of long development. We have taken step after step, and at last we have evolved the Convention (Mathews, 1916, p. 22).

The need for some form of social mediation of God's sovereignty led the Baptists to locate ultimate historical authority in the Holy Scriptures. But even the authority of the Bible must gain social expression in the religious community. The Bible may be the normative referent to which the various personal authorities turn, but in every case its meaning must be interpreted and the problem remains: who are the interpreters and what is their authority? The Baptist answer is ambiguous.[3]

On the one hand, the authority of Scripture 'was to be exercised under the guidance of the Spirit of Christ operative in the Christian community' (Harrelson, 1954, pp. 3–4). Therefore, under the gospel, the local church was the ultimate authority. But the Baptist effort to scatter authority throughout the land does not cease with the positing of authority in the local communion. On the foundation of the doctrine of the priesthood of all believers, the same people who affirm the authority of the community hold that 'once saved, any person has free and direct access to the Father through the one and only High Priest, Jesus' (Pruden, 1951, p. 2). In Baptist thought there often seems to be more involved than an effort to sustain a tradition of prophetic criticism of the community by means of an inspired individual. McNutt (1935, p. 9) affirms that the true church 'will be a fellowship of the religiously competent, with every man a priest, a spiritual democracy, with every man in God a king'. With such royal opportunities offered every individual in the Baptist denomination it is not difficult to discover one of the primary sources of a constantly threatening disorder.

3. The Baptists are not alone. With the possible exception of the fundamentalists, the entire Protestant view of authority is ambiguous. (Cf. Davies, 1946, pp. 10, 154.)

However, there are many spokesmen who deplore the individualism inherent within the Baptist doctrine of the church. 'Individualistic voluntarism has no place in the New Testament,' says one Baptist who was writing a report for a committee of the Convention. 'The fellowship,' he continues, 'is the mother which gives birth to each new child' (Skoglund, 1954, p. 18). In the contemporary situation some of the basic issues have been discerned. For example, the contradiction of positing two ultimate authorities – the individual and the community to which he belongs – has been recognized. Nonetheless, the tension still exists between the kings – 'each man on his throne' holding 'absolute sway over his own realm' (McNutt, 1935, p. 24) – and those who believe that 'private interpretation of the Bible must always be subjected to the testing of the Spirit, and this testing takes place in the regenerate Christian community . . . (Harrelson, 1954, p. 19).

It is clear that the Baptists are faced with a more critical problem than the autonomy of the local church.[4] The intramural tensions inherent in this principle may be superseded by the anarchic potentialities of a radical individualism. The problem of authority of the regional or associational group in relation to the local church would be considerably simplified if the locus of authority at the congregational level were a settled issue.

But Baptists have a genius for obscuring the problem of authority by means of a labyrinth of theological doctrines. There is no effective way of predicting what a given document will pronounce on this vital issue. According to one source there may be no possibility of a mediated authority beyond the New Testament: 'Christ is the only Head over, and Law-giver to, His churches. Consequently, the churches cannot make laws, but only execute those which He has given. Nor can any man, or body of men, legislate for the churches. The New Testament alone is their

4. Lesslie Newbigin simplifies the problem of congregationally ordered churches when he asserts that there is no 'intelligible reason why we should be asked to acknowledge the spiritual authority of the local fellowship over the individual but to deny the spiritual authority of the regional or ecumenical fellowship over the local'. It is evident that many Baptists do not acknowledge the spiritual authority of the local churches over the individual except in a very limited way. See Newbigin (1954), p. 120.

statute book, by which, without change, the body of Christ is to govern itself' (Hiscox, 1890, p. 14).

Or, the local church may be the primary locus of authority:

We Baptists are the recognized democrats of the Protestant world. The local church is our depository of ecclesiastical authority. The Association has no authority over the local church; the State Convention has no authority over the Association; and the Northern Baptist Convention has no authority over the State Convention. All these are voluntary cooperative associations created for the sake of greater effectiveness in the business of the kingdom (Montgomery, 1922, p. 38).

A third possibility is that the individual under God may be the supreme authority. A fourth variation, of more recent origin, may be expressed in many ways. This final perspective represents a more realistic effort to account for the existing power of the associational groups and to discover a biblical rationale for the support of this power.

In 1954 a committee of the American Baptist Theological Conference observed that authority extends beyond the limits of congregational membership. If missionary work is an 'integral part of the responsibility and authority given to the church by its Lord,' then Baptists must agree that in working through a national society or its board, the local church 'has virtually delegated parts of its authority to that board' (Pruden, 1951, p. 19). But this unanticipated shift of power and confirming of authority is not to be treated lightly by the national leadership. They receive a warning from the same committee which indicates that final ecclesiastical authority remains with the local church. The authority given to the national executives is provisional and the position they enjoy is precarious, depending, as it does, upon proper rendition of the Baptist tune composed by the local churches:

At the same time it must be clear that such delegation of authority can remain justified only in so far as the board retains the confidence of the church and can be regarded as a fit repository for the authority involved. Unless the church has the right to terminate the delegation of authority when the necessary confidence has been shattered, then it could have had no right to delegate the authority in the first place. Under the Baptist system the Boards and their officials are necessarily the servants of the churches, not their masters. To give up authority once for all would be, not a justifiable limitation, but a violation of the autonomy of the church (Pruden, 1951, p. 20).

This quotation seems to indicate that God may work through the national boards only if the local churches permit Him to do so. Since He had nothing to do with the creation of these boards, except in an indirect way, He can guide them only through the medium of the local churches. If for some reason communication between the local churches and the national boards is seriously impaired, then, according to the Baptist theology of the church, these boards inevitably would become secularized because God's only means of communication with them had been destroyed. On the other hand, if the local churches become corrupted the national boards possess no legitimate authority to criticize or correct them. According to Baptist polity, in such a situation the national boards would be servants of God but only by means of the diseased churches.

It is beyond argument that the boards should serve the local churches and in some sense should be responsible to them. In a strict historical sense they were brought into being by the churches, but from a theological perspective a distinction must be made between the desires of the churches – which may be corrupted – and the needs of the churches. Since it is possible that God conceived the national boards as a corrective for the sins of the churches, it is dangerous on principle to preclude the possibility of conferring official authority upon the ecclesiastical officers of the boards. This authority need not be unlimited, and according to Baptist principles it should not be. But it seems no less a violation of the freedom of God and of the original intention of the Baptist fathers to deposit ultimate authority under God with any historical individual, whether it be the local church, the state association, the national boards, the General Secretary of the Convention or a prophetic layman in the local congregation. 'The recognized democrats of the Protestant world' seem to have forgotten the first principles of democracy as developed by the Independents: the separation of powers and the freedom of God to speak through the most unlikely of historical individuals.

This is not surprising, since with regard to the authority of leadership Baptists have been preoccupied with control and restriction rather than with the element of freedom which is no less necessary for leaders than for the constituency. Baptists attended to the limitation of the leader's authority and power, but they have largely ignored the problem of the fulfilment of his duties. From the Baptist point of view the chief responsibility of a leader is to avoid seeking enough power to meet his responsibilities. But without authority and freedom the ecclesiastical leader cannot be held accountable for failing to achieve goals to which he has been assigned. Baptist voluntarism has resulted in an effort to pulverize ecclesiastical authority and power. Realizing that concentrations of power contain great demonic potentialities, the Baptists have placed a higher value on the minimization of power than on establishing effective means to attain other goals. If the Baptists had enjoyed substantial success in achieving the primary goal of their polity there would be considerably less ground for criticism. But the Baptist denomination has been no more successful in establishing a 'democratic polity' than many other Protestant denominations which do not place primary emphasis upon this goal.

According to Pruden's (1951, p. 20) committee on church government, 'our system is based upon the assumption that churches of regenerate believers will be sensitive to the promptings of the Spirit and will do their proper share voluntarily'. This places an unbearable pressure upon the motivations of the regenerate soul and reveals a faith in the power and goodness of the individual which is unsupported by traditional Christian doctrine. 'Moral and spiritual suasion,' the committee reports, 'are the means at our disposal. If they fail us it is because we have failed' (Pruden, 1951, p. 21).

The Problem of Authority in the Present Situation

Notwithstanding the ambiguities and restrictions on their authority, the executive officials of the American Baptist Convention have managed to gain enough power to meet their responsibilities with reasonable effectiveness. Since they have no official ecclesiastical authority they seek to secure their position by other means, and they have been remarkably successful in their efforts. It has often been observed that the American

Baptist Convention 'has no authority, but has very great influence'.[5] In order to analyse the character of this influence as well as the problems which surround the executives of the Convention, it is best to draw a clear distinction between power and authority. Power signifies the ability to carry out one's own will despite the inertia or resistance of others (Weber, 1947, p. 152); it is the ability to influence or control the actions of others even though there is no institutional sanction for this control. However, 'power may be, and generally is, used to acquire legitimized status and symbols of recognition' (Parsons, 1949, p. 172). Therefore, power is a more comprehensive term than authority; in fact, authority is a specialized function of power.[6]

Authority is defined as formalized or institutionally recognized power. 'Authority is thus the expected and legitimate possession of power.'[7] Since authority is the more specialized concept it will be used whenever the intent is to indicate that kind of power which is officially legitimated and voluntarily accepted by the group. This does not signify that those who wield authority always satisfy every member of the constituency, but that despite particular dissatisfactions the constituency recognizes the right of the leader to lead. However, when a leader exercises power, which, within this analytical framework could be called 'illegitimate authority', he is controlling the actions of others despite their wishes, or he is controlling them without their knowledge. The latter often occurs in the Baptist situation because the Baptists are unwilling to confer authority upon their leaders and are equally unwilling to recognize that they have attained power apart from authority. Thus they do not

5. 'Baptists', *Encyclopaedia Britannica*, vol. 3, 1953 edn.

6. Marion Levy defines power as 'the ability to exercise authority and control over the actions of others'. More accurately, it should be 'authority and/or control'. Power can exist apart from institutional sanction. See Levy (1952), p. 333.

7. Lasswell and Kaplan (1950), p. 133. This definition is in agreement with Parsons, who describes authority as the 'institutionally recognized right to influence the actions of others, regardless of their immediate personal attitudes to the direction of influence'. It is also in agreement with Weber's definition of authority or imperative control which 'is the probability that certain specific commands (or all commands) from a given source will be obeyed by a given group of persons'.

possess adequate analytical instruments to discern the existence of 'illegitimate authority'.

Those Baptists who do recognize the existence of power either ignore the situation because they enjoy its fruits and recognize it as a functional necessity of every social system, or they deplore it because they enjoy no benefits and engage in an effort to eliminate it as an 'un-Baptist' phenomenon. But power is required for achievement in any field whatsoever (Heiman, 1947, p. 119). Even though it contains the seeds of corruption,[8] power in itself is not an evil thing. It is necessary for life, which is capable of both good and evil.

Those leaders in a social group who are given responsibilities and goals to achieve will strive for legitimate authority from their constituency in order to gain the necessary support for the achievement of the group's goals. Those who hold power will seek to legitimate it; that is, they will seek authority (Lasswell and Kaplan, 1950, p. 137). If, as in the case of the Baptists, the ideology of the group does not permit the granting of legitimate authority to the leaders, any struggle for power will probably be increasingly complicated. Each group will strive to establish itself as the legitimate authority.

The Baptist denominational executives are given responsibility and limited power, but no legitimate authority. In order to overcome the lack of official status, they seek more power and when they are successful in this enterprise they seek authority. Relatively speaking, it has not been difficult for them to acquire the power necessary for the achievement of their assigned tasks. This has been accomplished by means of an unanticipated formation of an informal system of interpersonal and intergroup relations which bypasses the formal rules of order. The distinction between the formal and informal systems of action is a category of interpretation which enables the observer to answer crucial questions concerning the Convention. Why do the national leaders possess considerable power when the Convention itself does not have

8. Never 'absolute corruption'. Acton's dictum is in error because absolute corruption presupposes absolute power, which is a historical impossibility. Power and authority are both relational concepts. Even in the limiting case of slavery the leaders must exercise caution because of the constant threat of a revolutionary uprising (Weber, 1947, pp. 62 f., 276 ff.).

any 'legislative power' or legal authority? What is the actual –
as distinguished from the official – locus of authority in the
Convention? Is the informal power of the executives gradually
becoming legitimated on a formal basis? Or, to reformulate
the last question: are there any signs that the Baptist interpretation of the nature of the church is changing in order to adjust to
changes in the environment?

According to sociological theory, authority is generally
associated with the formal system of action, i.e. the officially
sanctioned relations of the group. Power is associated with
the informal system.[9] Even before the Convention came into
being the national executives of the missionary societies discovered that their duties extended far beyond the specific
functions of the organizations. Whether they wanted it or not[10]
their positions enabled them to exercise tremendous influence
in the life of the denomination. They made decisions about the
content of the denomination's educational and pamphleteering
enterprises, the fund-raising activities, the development of
seminaries and colleges, in addition to determining the policies
of the missionary boards (Hudson, 1958, pp. 14 ff.).

Hudson notes that fifty years before the Convention was formed
a large number of important posts were held by a small group
of influential men. Francis Wayland, President of Brown University, was active in the affairs of the Triennial Convention from its
inception until the middle of the century. During those years he
held the following posts: recording secretary of the Triennial
Convention, secretary of the Baptist Convention of Massachusetts,
secretary of the Boston Baptist Foreign Missionary Society, member of the Board of Trustees of Newton Seminary, board member

9. Recall that Lasswell and Kaplan defined authority as formal power.
Conversely, power could be called informal authority (1950, p. 133).

10. Indications are that most executives desired all the power they could
acquire. Hudson notes that a power struggle was in progress among the
denominational leaders shortly after the creation of the Triennial Convention (predecessor of the Foreign Mission Society) in 1814. At one of the
annual meetings a movement to create a General Convention was set aside.
'Apparently, Luther Rice had feared that some maneuver to seize control
of the Convention was afoot because he pointed out that the ... arrangement could easily be abused by an "active and intriguing man"' (Hudson,
1958, pp. 5 ff.).

of the Baptist Missionary Society of Massachusetts, board member of the Baptist Education Society of Massachusetts, board member of the Evangelical Tract Society, member of the Boston Standing Committee for the Triennial Convention and editor of the *American Baptist Magazine*. 'Wayland was not a unique figure in this respect. Actually, all the offices of the various societies and boards in Massachusetts were held by a dozen men. In New York and elsewhere the situation was the same' (Hudson, 1958, p. 20).

The by-laws and resolutions of the Convention prevent a single individual from holding so many posts today, but the situation has changed only in degree. This circumstance, however, should not necessarily be interpreted as an undesirable appropriation of power by men of evil intent, but rather as an inevitable emergence of leadership which occurs in any social system.

References

BUBER, M. (1946), *Moses*, East and West Library.

DAVIES, R. E. (1946), *The Problem of Authority in the Continental Reformers*, Epworth Press.

HARRELSON, W. J. (1954), 'The biblical basis of the Gospel', *Basic Papers Prepared for the American Baptist Theological Conference* (mimeographed).

HEIMAN, E. (1947), *Freedom and Order*, Scribner.

HISCOX, E. T. (1890), *The Standard Manual for Baptist Churches*, The American Baptist Publication Society.

HUDSON, W. S. (1953), *The Great Tradition of the American Churches*, Harper.

HUDSON, W. S. (1958), 'Stumbling into disorder', *Foundations*, vol. 1.

LASSWELL, H. D., and KAPLAN, A. (1950), *Power and Society*, Yale University Press.

LEVY, M. J. (1952), *The Structure of Society*, Princeton University Press.

MCNUTT, W. R. (1935), *Policy and Practice in Baptist Churches*, Judson Press.

MATHEWS, S. (1916), 'President's Address to the Convention', *Annual*.

MONTGOMERY, W. A. (1922), 'President's Address to the Convention', *Annual*.

NEWBIGIN, L. (1954), *The Household of God*, Friendship Press.

NICHOLS, J. H. (1951), *Democracy and the Churches*, Westminster Press.

PARSONS, T. (1949), *Essays in Sociological Theory Pure and Applied*, Free Press.

PRUDEN, E. H. (1951), *Interpreters Needed*, Judson Press.

SKOGLUND, J. E. (1954), 'The nature of the Church', *Basic Papers Prepared for the American Baptist Theological Conference* (mimeographed).

WEBER, M. (1947), *The Theory of Social and Economic Organisation*, Oxford University Press.

25 R. Towler

The Social Status of the Anglican Minister

R. Towler, 'The changing status of the ministry?', *Crucible*, May (1968),
pp. 73–8. [With slight alterations by the author.]

One of the most significant differences between the denominations
of the Christian Church has always been the variation in forms
of full-time leadership. The Ministry of each denomination is
unique, and ministers occupy quite different statuses both with
respect to the members of their own denomination and also
with respect to the wider society. This is a situation with which
all are familiar. At the present time, however, a less familiar
situation has arisen, where the Ministry of each denomination
seems to be changing from its established form, and moving
towards something new. An attempt will be made here to clarify,
in sociological terms, the changes which appear to be taking
place in the ordained Ministry of the Anglican Church. Such
changes are not limited to the Church of England, but are felt
alike in the Roman Catholic and Free Churches in varying
degrees. It seems best to limit the discussion to the Anglican
situation for the sake of simplicity, but it should be possible to
see how the same points apply to other religious organizations
without spelling out the details.

It can be maintained that the problems of the Ministry, in
common with all problems of organized religion, are due to the
anachronistic relationship of religion to a secular society and
culture. Dr Bryan Wilson (1966) has referred to the 'alienation
of the clergy', and the resemblance of sections of the clergy to
'the charcoal-burners or alchemists in an age when the processes
in which they were engaged had been rendered obsolete, technically or intellectually'. This may be so, but secularization has
been much written about recently, and it seems best to try to find
the roots of the problem within a more limited context, if that is
possible.

A Threefold Problem

Crisis is an over-worked expression, but the Ministry does face something of a crisis at the moment. This is not to suggest that the dilemma is insoluble, but there are a number of problems which require some radical changes from what has been a traditional pattern, in order to reach a new pattern of Ministry which will prove viable under our changed social circumstances. There are those who maintain that the established pattern, with modifications in personnel deployment such as are suggested in the report *Partners in Ministry*, is still perfectly satisfactory. However, the problems go deeper than that, and they come under three broad headings. It is hoped that the sociological statement of the problems, if accurate, may go a little way towards finding a solution.

The first general problem to be faced is the shrinkage of the Ministry. This shrinkage itself has four separate aspects. The absolute numerical strength of the Ministry has declined by some 20 per cent since the turn of the century. The decline is even greater when compared with a 40 per cent rise in the total population. A third aspect of the shrinkage is seen in the age profile of the clergy as a whole, which has become progressively more biased towards older men. This is accounted for by an increasing proportion of older men entering the Ministry, as well as by the drop in recruitment. This shift in the age profile results in an effective reduction in the number of years of work available from personnel, even when numbers are held constant. Yet a fourth aspect is to be found in the number of clergy leaving the parochial Ministry, and this loss is made the more serious by the high proportion of younger men involved, thus biasing the age profile even more.

The second problem is the loss in social status which the Ministry has suffered. Of course it is possible to dismiss this, and claim it as an advantage rather than a hindrance in the discharge of their office by men who have been classically defined as *servi servorum Dei*. But it remains a radical break from tradition, even if readily accepted, and as such demands a readjustment on the part of the clergy, which they have yet to make. Although the factual basis of this contemporary problem is rarely questioned, it is nonetheless difficult to substantiate empirically. Perhaps the nearest we can come to a demonstration of this loss of social prestige is the relative drop in clerical incomes. Although the phenomenon of the 'poor clergyman' has been with us for a long time, it is a trend of this century that clergy incomes have come to be on a level with, and often below, those of manual workers. But the relationship of prestige to remuneration is neither simple nor direct. The results of most investigations show that clergy are held in great respect. Thus in one study (Richards, 1962) clergy were ranked as the fourth most prestigious occupation, after surgeons, G.P.s and solicitors; and a recent study conducted by Gallup Poll (1965, para. 285) found that clergy were thought to be 'influential in the community, devoted to public service, useful in the parish, sincere, overworked and underpaid . . .' Dr Wilson (1966, p. 82) suggests, perceptively, that the reason for these findings might be that there are 'spiritual affinities of the occupation which induce respondents to give relatively high ratings to clerics, since people with any religious dispositions at all cannot but pay some attention to the traditional claim of all religious professionals to have the highest calling of all'. Perhaps an effective measure of the social status of the clergy has yet to be devised, but for the moment a real loss in prestige must be granted, of a sort well described by a recent speaker (Furlong, 1966):

The clergyman has suffered throughout this century (and it still continues) a decline in status. This is indicated, as well as accentuated, by the fact that his income is less than that of the majority of his parishioners. In some cases he earns about the same as an unskilled worker and this is perhaps how an un-churched society is coming to think of him – as someone who is not qualified as the twentieth century understands qualification. In an age which is not particularly interested in faith it is difficult for people to understand what the clergyman is up to, and so they are apt to suggest that he isn't up to anything in particular. He is thrust on one side where serious issues are being discussed – he isn't a social worker, he isn't a psychiatrist, he isn't a doctor, he isn't a probation officer, or a teacher or a welfare worker. He is granted a little elbow room in hospitals or prisons – after all it is well known that when people are unhappy, ill or dying they like a bit of religion, and the clergyman can at least talk about God without getting uncomfortable. But I believe there is a growing feeling in the community as a whole that the Church is played out and the clergy with it, and this is perhaps as obvious in the exaggerated respect – an almost superstitious awe – which is sometimes shown to the clergy and which indicates how little religion is a part of people's ordinary, everyday lives . . . .

The third problem may be termed the 'role uncertainty' of the clergy, mentioned in the preceding quotation. By this is meant the uncertainty on the part of the clergy themselves as to precisely what they are there to do. The full impact of this problem is yet to be felt, but it is perhaps the biggest single problem. In the established pattern of the ordained Ministry, a parochial clergyman has had a number of different roles which he has exercised. He has been the teacher of the Christian faith, the organizer of his Church activities, the preacher of the Word of God, the administrator of Church affairs, the pastor of his flock and the priest of the parish in his sacramental duties.[1] In the present trends of Church affairs, almost all of these roles are affected. As Dr Trevor Ling (1967) has pointed out, the drop in the proportion of clergymen who have had a university education in theology has been accompanied by an increase in the number of lay people, especially in the teaching profession, who have got theological degrees. In the next few years an increasing proportion of parishes will have among the laity persons admirably trained to teach the Christian faith; better trained in fact than their clergy, who have had less theological education and no training whatever in teaching methods. The clergy have been trying to persuade members of their congregations to assume more responsibility in the spheres of organization and administration for some time now, and in many places the clergy have already been relieved of most of this work. Where this is not yet so, it may be expected to become so in the foreseeable future. Lay readers have for many years assisted in the Ministry of the Word, and there is no reason why the number of readers should not increase, to ease the work of the declining number of clergy, and utilize the theological knowledge which is becoming more current among the laity. Action arising from the 'People Next Door' campaign and trends in Church organization are increas-

1. Work on the clergy role components has been done notably by Professor Samuel Blizzard.

ing in a most dramatic way the share of pastoral responsibility taken by the non-ordained members of the local Church.

In short, the professional activities of the clergy, other than their duties in the administration of the sacraments, are coming to be shared more and more by the laity. As this change becomes more widespread it is increasingly difficult to define the extra-liturgical role of the parochial clergyman as anything other than a full-time Christian. This trend, when seen in conjunction with the lowering prestige of the Ministry as an occupation, and its rapid shrinkage, leads to a conclusion, stated in its boldest terms by Dr Ling (1967, pp. 142–3), that:

There are no clear or compelling reasons for supposing that this process of decline will be other than temporarily halted; and it is possible that what we are witnessing, therefore, is the gradual dis-appearance of a once familiar figure, the full-time parochial clergy-man ... Whether the complete disappearance of a paid (or more accurately half-paid) professional caste of clergyman is a tragedy for the Churches or not is still something of a matter of controversy.

The Ministry as a Profession

Dr Ling's use of the term 'caste' when speaking of the parochial clergy has something more than a derogatory implication. It raises the question of the nature of the social group we call the ordained Ministry. It is assumed almost universally that the clergy constitute an occupation – albeit a rather special occupa-tion – which takes its rightful place among the other professional occupational groups. Thus Professor Gordon Dunstan (1967), considering the relationship of the Ministry to groups such as doctors, social workers and psychiatrists, says it is the duty of the clergy, 'as a condition of proper co-operation with men and women of *other professions*, to search out the ground, meaning, opportunity, disciplines, of *our own*' (author's italics).

Space does not permit a discussion of Professor Dunstan's argument, but it is not in any case central to this paper. What is open to serious question is the assumption, not that the Ministry is a profession, but that it is an occupation at all. Any definition of an occupation, and especially a sociological definition, is based on an understanding of what activities and goals characterize it.

447

The prerequisite of an occupation is that it should be possible to make a definite statement of what its members *do* in their work.

We have seen three major problem areas which emphasize the dilemma of the Ministry in contemporary society, and it should be noted that none of the problems arises as a result of a change in the Ministry itself. In each case the problem arises as a result of changes in Western industrial society. Hence the [original] title of this article – 'The changing status of the ministry?' – with an emphasis on the query. The sociological nature of the Ministry has not changed to a significant extent since the Middle Ages and the period of 'Christian imperialism.' But society has changed fundamentally.

Seen in an historical perspective (see Carr-Saunders and Wilson, 1933), the 'learned professions' grew out of the social group of the clergy. This was perfectly natural, since the first, second and third Estates were in broad terms the social groups in which were located respectively leadership, learning and labour. So it is not surprising that the professions bear many marked similarities to the Ministry in terms of their organization and behaviour. But the clergy, as such, have never constituted an occupation, let alone a profession. Even the post-Reformation parson's position in society was more akin to that of the squire than that of the physician; parson and baron alike were social positions highly relevant to the structure of medieval society, and each is now alike in having none but honorific consequences in contemporary social structure.

Of the many ways in which our society has changed, the way most relevant here is its shift from a structure in which social status was based on ascription, to one in which social status is based on achievement. In technical terms, we live in an achievement-oriented society. But clergymen are made, not qualified; clerical status is ascribed, not achieved. Membership of occupational groups (and pre-eminently of the professions) is achieved. To be a barrister or a sheet-metal worker is to occupy a position in society which is defined by what the member of the occupation *does*. Skill, competence and legitimation in these characterizing activities is achieved and it is achievement of occupational status which forms the fundamental basis of contemporary social structure. The clergyman is an odd-man-out in any sociological analysis of his position. He has a social position, but it is ascribed; it is comparable to that of a Knight of the Bath, or Earl or Doctor of Letters, each of which was relevant to the structure of an ascription-oriented society, but fundamentally irrelevant to contemporary social structure.

For these reasons, which cannot be expanded here, the Ministry cannot be considered as an occupation, as we currently understand that concept. I am arguing that this change in the character of the ordained Ministry relative to Western society as it has evolved is at the root of the three major problem areas which at present face the Church's Ministry.

Possible Innovation

The particular problems which face the Ministry will demand some form of solution before the end of this century. Solutions are not to be found in relatively minor modifications in deployment and payment of clergy. Nor will any structure of Ministry prove viable for future generations if the Church continues to ignore the basic fact that the Ministry, as we have it, is not an occupation.

There seem to be roughly three lines of development which could lead to a stable and viable form for the Ministry. Each seems equally feasible sociologically, though recent trends in theological writing seem to suggest that all would not prove theologically acceptable. It goes without saying that any change in the structure of the Ministry would imply a prior change in church organization as a whole.

1. One line of development would be for clergy increasingly to become efficient, full-time religious organizers, co-ordinating and administrating Church affairs. This change would presuppose a change in local churches in developing more clearly and exclusively as social units, and their becoming gradually more sect-like. In a de-Christianized, or secular, society this would make sociological sense. In the U.S.A. this is the trend, as it is also in some of the best-attended Anglican churches in English suburbs.[2]

2. Recent research on clergy in the London area (Daniel, 1967), shows, interestingly, that the degree to which the crisis in the Ministry is felt by clergy is in inverse proportion to the size of their congregations.

2. Another possible development, which is really no development at all, would be the acceptance of shrinkage and loss of prestige, and the conscious acceptance by the clergy of their anomalous social status. They would have to accept that they have not only a social role different to other members of the 'helping professions', but a quite unique position in society. While this is a possibility it is improbable, in sociological terms, that any substantial number of men and their families would find this impecunious and anomic mode of existence commending itself to them. It is rather more likely that the first line of development would spontaneously set in.

3. The other possible development would be the gradual decline of service of the full-time clergy, and their replacement by lay leadership in the church. Liturgical functions would be exercised by members of the church in lay occupations, who had been ordained. As Dr Ling points out, in the article quoted above, there could still be full-time religious functionaries such as members of the religious orders and teams of evangelists.

Before the end of this century there will be sociological changes in the nature of the Church and its group of full-time employees. Of that there can be no doubt. What direction the changes take depends on a large number of factors, most of which have yet to be discussed. Prediction and the possibility of control must rest, however, on an accurate analysis of the present position. This paper is simply an attempt to clarify some of the facts about the social position in which the Church finds itself at present.

References

CARR-SAUNDERS, A. M., and WILSON, P. A. (1933), 'The professions before the industrial revolution', *The Professions*, Clarendon Press.

DANIEL, M. (1967), *unpublished M. Phil. thesis, University of London.*

DUNSTAN, G. R. (1967), 'The sacred ministry as a learned profession', *Theology*, vol. 10, pp. 142–51.

FURLONG, M. (1966), *Address to a Conference of Clergy in the Diocese of Wakefield.*

GALLUP POLL (1965), *The Television Audience and Religion*, Social Surveys Ltd.

LING, T. A. (1967), 'Religion, society and the teacher', *The Modern Churchman*, vol. 10, pp. 142–51.

RICHARDS, N. D. (1962), *unpublished M.A. thesis, University of Nottingham.*

WILSON, B. R. (1966), *Religion in Secular Society*, Watts.

Further Reading

General

Textbooks

W. A. LESSA and E. VOGT (eds.), *A Reader in Comparative Religion*, Row, Peterson, 1968, 2nd edn. A good selection of essays in the anthropology of religion.

L. SCHNEIDER (ed.), *Religion, Culture and Society*, Wiley, 1964.

Discussions of classical problems

R. BENDIX, *Max Weber: An Intellectual Portrait*, Doubleday, 1960; Heinemann, 1961. Part 2 contains an excellent overview of Weber's sociology of religion.

E. DURKHEIM, *The Elementary Forms of the Religious Life* (trans. by J. Swain), Collier Books, 1961.

E. E. EVANS-PRITCHARD, *Theories of Primitive Religion*, Clarendon Press, 1965. A brief and lucid analysis of theories of primitive religion current in the late nineteenth century and early twentieth century, with a useful bibliography.

B. MALINOWSKI, 'Magic, science, and religion', in J. Needham (ed.), *Science, Religion and Reality*, Macmillan, 1926, pp. 19–84.

G. OBEYESEKERE, 'Theodicy, sin and salvation in a sociology of Buddhism', in E. R. Leach (ed.), *Dialectic in Practical Religion*, Cambridge University Press, 1968, pp. 7–40. An excellent critique of a central theme of Weber's studies.

I. SEGER, *Durkheim and his Critics on the Sociology of Religion*, Bureau of Applied Social Research, Columbia University, 1957.

M. WEBER, *The Sociology of Religion* (trans. by Ephraim Fischoff), Beacon Press, 1963. The richest and most wide ranging selection of Weber's writings in the sociology of religion. The introduction by Talcott Parsons is invaluable.

Discussions and surveys of current problems

M. ARGYLE, *Religious Behaviour*, Routledge & Kegan Paul, 1958. A social psychological analysis, which includes a lot of useful empirical data.

M. BANTON (ed.), *Anthropological Approaches to the Study of Religion* (A.S.A. monograph), Tavistock Publications, 1966. A volume containing excellent essays by Geertz and Spiro.

P. BERGER, *The Sacred Canopy*, Doubleday, 1967. An important essay which is highly sensitive to the relationship between sociology and religious belief.

Further Reading

C. Y. GLOCK and R. STARK, *Religion and Society in Tension*, Rand McNally, 1968. Contains some important empirical, as well as purely theoretical, studies.

R. ROBERTSON, *The Sociological Interpretation of Religion*, Blackwell and Schocken Books, 1970. An analytical treatment of the major themes in the sociology of religion.

L. SCHNEIDER, 'Problems in the sociology of religion', in R. E. L. Faris (ed.), *Handbook of Modern Sociology*, Rand McNally, 1964, pp. 770–807.

Major Societal Patterns of Religion

Primitive societies

M. DOUGLAS, *Purity and Danger*, Routledge & Kegan Paul, 1966.

R. FIRTH, *Tikopia Ritual and Belief*, Allen & Unwin, and Beacon Press 1967. Contains particularly good essays on magic and mana.

J. GOODY, 'Religion and ritual: the definitional problem', *Brit. J. Sociol.*, vol. 12 (1961), pp. 142–64.

E. R. LEACH (ed.), *The Structural Study of Myth and Totemism* (A.S.A. Monograph), Tavistock Publications, 1967. A good collection of appraisals of the work of Lévi-Strauss.

C. LÉVI-STRAUSS, *Totemism* (trans. by J. Needham), Merlin Press, 1964; Beacon Press, 1963.

G. LIENHARDT, *Divinity and Experience*, Clarendon Press, 1961.

S. F. NADEL, *Nupe Religion*, Routledge & Kegan Paul, 1954.

G. E. SWANSON, *The Birth of the Gods*, University of Michigan Press, 1960. A controversial attempt to account for a variety of religious beliefs and a book of great theoretical significance.

World religions

R. N. BELLAH, *Tokugawa Religion*, Free Press, 1957.

P. BERGER, 'Charisma and religious innovation: the social location of Israelite prophecy', *Amer. sociol. Rev.*, vol. 28 (1963), pp. 940–50.

S. N. EISENSTADT, 'Religious organizations and political process in centralized empires', *J. Asian Stud.*, vol. 21 (1961–2), pp. 271–94.

M. E. SPIRO, *Burmese Supernaturalism*, Prentice-Hall, 1967.

E. TROELTSCH, *The Social Teaching of the Christian Churches* (trans. by O. Wyon), Macmillan, 1950, 2 vols.

J. WACH, *The Sociology of Religion*, University of Chicago Press, 1944. First published in Germany in 1931, this book is still extremely useful as a rich survey of the variety of religious phenomena.

M. WEBER, *Ancient Judaism* (trans. by H. H. Gerth and D. Martindale), Free Press, 1952.

M. WEBER, *The Religion of India* (trans. by H. H. Gerth and D. Martindale), Free Press, 1958.

M. WEBER, *The Religion of China* (trans. by H. H. Gerth), Free Press, 1964 (new edition).

C. K. YANG, *Religion in Chinese Society*, University of California Press, 1961.

J. M. YINGER, *Religion in the Struggle for Power*, Duke University Press, 1946.

Some of the above items are geared to Weber's thesis about the vital function of religion in the development of industrial societies. The following are even more specific in this respect, dealing mainly with Christianity. These are also highly relevant to the whole problem of religion and social, cultural and societal change.

S. N. EISENSTADT (ed.), *The Protestant Ethic and Modernization*, Basic Books, 1968. An extremely important collection of recent essays on many aspects of the Weber theses; includes an excellent bibliography.

R. W. GREEN (ed.), *Protestantism and Capitalism*, Heath, 1959. A useful collection of older appraisals of Weber's thesis.

R. K. MERTON, *Social Theory and Social Structure*, Free Press, 1957, revised edn. Chapter 18 deals with the relationship between Puritanism and scientific development.

G. E. SWANSON, *Religion and Regime*, University of Michigan Press, 1967.

M. WEBER, *The Protestant Ethic and the Spirit of Capitalism* (trans. by T. Parsons). Allen & Unwin, 1931; Scribners, 1958. Weber's most famous, if not his best, contribution to the sociology of religion.

Religion in modern industrial societies

W. HERBERG, *Protestant, Catholic, Jew*, Doubleday, 1955. A pathbreaking analysis of religion in America.

T. LUCKMANN, 'Religion in modern society', *J. sci. Stud. Rel.*, vol. 2 (1963), pp. 147–62.

D. A. MARTIN, *A Sociology of English Religion*, Heinemann, 1967.

W. McLOUGHLIN and R. N. BELLAH (eds.), *Religion in America*, Beacon Press, 1968.

D. O. MOBERG, *The Church as a Social Institution*, Prentice-Hall, 1962. Mainly concerned with America.

T. PARSONS, 'Christianity and modern industrial society', in E. Tiryakian (ed.), *Sociological Theory, Values and Sociocultural Change*, Free Press 1963, pp. 33–70. A highly abstract essay dealing with the evolution of Christianity from the Roman Empire to contemporary America.

R. STARK and C. Y. GLOCK, *American Piety: The Nature of Religious Commitment*, University of Berkeley Press, 1968. The first in a series of major analyses of religious life in America.

B. R. WILSON, *Religion in Secular Society*, Watts, 1967; Penguin Books, 1969. Deals mainly with England and the U.S.A.

Mixed forms of religion in the contemporary world

Some of the references listed under world religions are relevant here, as are those dealing with millennial movements. (See under religious organizations and movements, next page.)

Further Reading

M. M. AMES, 'Magical-animism and Buddhism: a structural analysis of the Sinhalese religious system', *J. Asian Stud.*, vol. 23 (1964), pp. 21–52.

C. GEERTZ, *The Religion of Java*, Free Press, 1960.

Religion and Social and Cultural Differentiation

The references which follow mainly refer to modern industrial societies or to societies affected by modern industrialism. The reader is referred to the special section above for historical aspects of the relationship between religion and politics and between religion and economic factors.

Religious commitment and political, economic and other preferences

R. R. ALFORD, *Party and Society*, Rand McNally, 1963.

D. E. APTER, 'Political religion in the new nations', in C. Geertz (ed.), *Old Societies and New States*, Free Press, 1963, pp. 57–104.

A. M. GREELEY, *Religion and Career*, Sheed & Ward, 1963. Largely intended as a refutation of Lenski's findings on the low achievement motivations of American Catholics.

G. B. JOHNSON, 'Ascetic protestantism and political preference', *Pub. Opin. Quart.*, vol. 26 (1962), pp. 35–46.

G. LENSKI, *The Religious Factor*, Doubleday, 1961. An important book, which has aroused a lot of controversy.

S. M. LIPSET, 'Religion and politics', in R. Lee and M. E. Marty (eds.), *Religion and Social Conflict*, Oxford University Press, 1964.

Religion and social stratification

N. J. DEMERATH, III, *Social Class in American Protestantism*, Rand McNally, 1963. An important new perspective on class and religious involvement.

L. POPE, *Millhands and Preachers*, Yale University Press, 1942. A minor classic.

M. N. SRINIVAS, *Caste in Modern India*, Asia Publishing House, 1962.

R. STARK, 'Class, Radicalism and religious involvement in Great Britain', *Amer. sociol. Rev.*, vol. 29 (1964), pp. 698–706.

Religious organizations and movements

P. BERGER, 'A market model for the analysis of ecumenicity', *Soc. Res.*, vol. 30 (1963), pp. 77–94.

N. EHRENSTROM and W. G. MUELDER, *Institutionalism and Church Unity*, Association Press, 1963.

G. B. JOHNSON, 'On church and sect', *Amer. sociol. Rev.*, vol. 28 (1963), pp. 539–49.

J. LOFLAND and R. STARK, 'Becoming a world saver: a theory of conversion to a deviant perspective', *Amer. sociol. Rev.*, vol. 30 (1965), pp. 862–75.

D. A. MARTIN, 'The denomination', *Brit. J. Sociol.*, vol. 13 (1962), pp. 1–14.

T. O'DEA, 'Five dilemmas in the institutionalization of religion', *J. sci. Stud. Rel.*, vol. 1 (1961), pp. 30–39.

C. H. PAGE, 'Bureaucracy and the liberal church', *R. Rel.*, vol. 16 (1952), pp. 137–50.

Y. TALMON, 'Pursuit of the millennium: the relation between religious and social change', *Eur. J. Sociol.*, vol. 3 (1962), pp. 125–48.

Y. TALMON, 'Millenarian movements', *Eur. J. Sociol.*, vol. 7 (1966), pp. 159–200.

B. R. WILSON, 'An analysis of sect development', *Amer. sociol. Rev.*, vol. 24 (1959), pp. 3–15. An excellent discussion of sects in modern societies.

B. R. WILSON, 'Millennialism in comparative perspective', *Comp. Stud. Soc., Hist.*, vol. 6 (1963), pp. 93–114.

B. R. WILSON (ed.), *Patterns of Sectarianism*, Heinemann, 1967. A valuable collection of essays, containing a wealth of references.

Religious authority and roles

S. W. BLIZZARD, 'Role conflicts of the urban protestant parish minister', *City Church*, vol. 7 (1956), pp. 13–15.

E. Q. CAMPBELL and T. P. PETTIGREW, 'Racial and moral crisis: the role of the Little Rock Ministers', *Amer. J. Sociol.*, vol. 64 (1959), pp. 509–16.

J. H. FICHTER, *Religion as an Occupation*, University of Notre Dame, 1961.

E. GELLNER, 'Sanctity, puritanism, secularization, and nationalism in North Africa', *Archiv. sociol. Rel.*, vol. 8 (1963), pp. 71–86.

J. F. MACLEAR, 'The making of the lay tradition', *J. Rel.*, vol. 33 (1953), pp. 113–36.

K. D. NAEGELE, 'Clergymen, teachers and psychiatrists', *Canad. J. Econ. polit. Sci.*, vol. 22 (1956), pp. 46–62.

L. M. SMITH, 'The Clergy: authority structure, ideology and migration', *Amer. sociol. Rev.*, vol. 18 (1953), pp. 242–8.

B. R. WILSON, 'The pentecostal minister: role conflicts and status contradictions', *Amer. J. Sociol.*, vol. 64 (1959), pp. 494–504.

Journals

Journal for the Scientific Study of Religion
Social Compass
Review of Religious Research
Archives de Sociologie des Religions

Yearbooks

International Yearbook for the Sociology of Religion
The Religious Situation (edited by D. R. Cutler, published by Beacon Press)

Acknowledgements

We are grateful to the following for permission to reproduce the material in this selection of Readings:

Reading 1 Oxford University Press Inc.
Reading 2 Collier-Macmillan
Reading 3 Free Press
Reading 4 *Sociology and Social Research*
Reading 5 Routledge & Kegan Paul Ltd and Frederick A. Praeger Inc.
Reading 6 Clarendon Press
Reading 7 Harper & Row
Reading 8 Institut de Sociologie, Rabat
Reading 9 Collier-Macmillan
Reading 10 C. A. Watts & Co. Ltd and B. R. Wilson
Reading 11 Free Press
Reading 12 Westdeutscher Verlag and E. Willems
Reading 13 MacGibbon & Kee and Schocken Books Inc.
Reading 14 University of Michigan Press
Reading 15 University of California Press
Reading 16 American Sociological Association and R. N. Bellah
Reading 17 Basic Books Inc. and S. N. Eisenstadt
Reading 18 Rand McNally & Co.
Reading 19 Rand McNally & Co.
Reading 20 Centre National de la Recherche Scientifique and B. R. Wilson
Reading 21 Cambridge University Press
Reading 22 Associated Book Publishers Ltd and Beacon Press
Reading 23 Clarendon Press
Reading 24 Princeton University Press
Reading 25 The Church Assembly

Author Index

Subject Index

Adventists
 in Brazil and Chile, 216
 and missionary work, 378
Africa
 religious movements in, 384
 early imperial enterprise of, 385
 Christian orthodoxy in, 392
 cults in, 393–402
Ancestors, 228
Anglicanism
 and low-level participation, 144
 and clergy, 156
 attitudes to life among, 225–6
 the Ministry of, 443
 problems in the Ministry of, 444–7
Asceticism
 and civil strata, 39
 and Javanese religion, 185
Azande
 and poison oracle and magic, 91–2
 and intellectual consistency, 94–5
 and situational belief, 224

Baptism
 in Brazil, 214–15
 the proletarian background of, 334
 and separation of Church and State, 432
 and authority in the Church, 433–8 *passim*
 the Convention of, 438
 authority of the Convention of, 439–42
Blackfoot Indians, 237
Brazil, 196, 197, 201
 and growth of Protestantism, 203
 and power centralization, 209
 class basis of, 212

Buddhism, 19
 and Nirvana, 31
 propaganda of, 39
 and the sacred objects of, 42
 lack of primitivism in, 97
 as a social movement, 239
 and the image of Buddha, 264
 and human greed, 277
 and the lack of priesthood, 417
Bureaucracy
 and the contemporary Church, 63
 structural, 147–8
 in China, 409
 in the Anglican Ministry, 447–50
  passim

Calvanism
 and predestination, 41
 the cognitive patterns of, 58
 ethic of, 159
 the commonwealths and, 282–4
 and economic ethics, 298–9
 impetus of, 300–303 *passim*
 and the rise of capitalism, 303–13
  passim
Capitalism
 development of, 298
 and Protestantism, 303–13 *passim*
Categories of thought
 fundamental levels of, 47
Catholicism
 and sacraments, 38
 and intellectual regeneration, 61
 literature of, 62
 social ideals of, 119
 social doctrine and, 126
 levels of participation, 144, 146
 differences from Protestantism and Judaism, 147
 ideology and, 148
 and Established Churches, 153

Subject Index

Established Churches, 153
Ethics
  rational religious, 29
  imperatives, 30
  codes of, 236
Europe
  and localization and
    privitization of worship, 67–72
  and history and ecclesiasticism,
    97
  and religiosity in the countryside,
    142
  Church orientation in, 145
  as ruling class in Java, 175
  and Christian culture, 312

Family
  as social group, 243–4
Fascism
  as social movement, 239
Fetish, 43
France
  and religious sociology, 62
Functional analysis
  and goals and values, 60
  and cross-cultures, 67
  mode of analysis, 224
  schemata of, 230

Gnosticism
  propaganda of, 39
  and the European experience,
    226
God
  and the Virgin Mary, 31
  conceptions of, 40
  and the Nuer, 100–110 *passim*
  blessings of, 159
  man's relation to, 222–3
  and ultimate reality, 257
  the evolution of, 263
  complexes of, 273
  and sects, 362
  as Saviour, 369
  forms of, 407
  and community, 433

Grace, 37
  and Catholicism, 38
  and Christianity, 59

Heresy, 230
Hinduism, 19
  and hereditary caste, 21
  and Bhakti, 31
  and Karma, 59
  and lack of primitivism in, 97
  arrival in Java, 166
  mysticism and, 168
  commitment to, 255–6
  and status markings, 345
  and supreme deity, 407
Holy Orders, 112–13
Homeric myth, 87–8
Huguenots, 299, 303

Ideology
  and religion, 61, 280
  and familism, 72
  and inter-religious differences,
    148
  and conflicts in Java, 169–73
India
  religiosity in, 40
  religio-social patterns in, 58
  world rejection in, 264
  sacred ordinances in, 409
  political formations in, 410
Industrialism
  and Churches, 150
Intellectualism
  and Judaism, 21
  and class, 33
  quest for, 35
  and civilization, 48
  tradition of, 58
  of 'primitive' peoples, 80
  of Java leadership, 185
  and mass religiosity, 287
Islamism, 19
  as world conquering religion, 21,
    128
  prophecy of, 39
  sociology of, 127

Subject Index

Missionary prophecy
  and devout experience, 39
  and conversionalist religious sects,
    378
  in Africa, 385
Monasticism
  and exclusiveness, 45
Monotheism, 129–30
  and historic religions, 276
  in Islam and Judaism, 407
  in Egypt, 411
Morals, 4
  and duties, 159
Mormons, 97
  in Brazil and Chile, 216
  proletarian background of, 334
Morocco
  and Islam, 133
Mysticism
  and contemplation, 39
  and Javanese religion, 185
  and anthropology, 223
Mythology
  primitive, 26
  contemplation and, 40
  contrary forces in, 50–51
  in primitive religion, 270–72

Nationalism
  growing importance in Java, 169,
    182–4
  in Brazil, 211
  incipient forms of, 377
Natural sciences
  and disbelief, 29
  religious basis of, 48
  and secularization, 69–70
Naturalism
  and Tillich's 'ecstatic' theory,
    286
Nature
  reliance on, 121
  and structuralism, 229
Negroes
  in U.S. proletariat, 147
Neo-Pythagorism
  propaganda of, 39

Nobility
  and Zoroaster, 39
Norms
  and moral sanctions, 56–7
  and functional analysis, 60
  and attitudes to life, 225
Nuer religions, 100–111 *passim*,
    422

Orgies, 31–2

Papal authority, 116
Peasants
  and magic, 37–8
  and Zoroaster, 39
Penance
  and repentance, 27
Pentacostalism
  in Chile, 202–5 *passim*
  sects and, 206–8
  and self-description, 209
  in Brazil and Chile, 214–16
Phenomenology
  and Schutz's 'world-taken-for-
    granted', 66
Pilgrims, 119
  in Latin America, 202
Pluralism, 153
  in Java, 188–90
  and Protestantism, 312
Plymouth Brethren
  and communism and anarchism,
    362
Polytheism, 129–30
Positivism
  in religious studies, 57
  and sociological research, 65
Prayer, 413
Predestination
  and Calvinism, 41
Presbyterianism
  and the mass market, 71
  in Brazil, 213–15
  as bourgeois reaction to
    Catholicism, 345
Priests, and confession, 25
  in archaic religion, 273

Penguin Modern Sociology Readings

Industrial Man
Edited by Tom Burns

'Industry', writes Professor Burns, 'is the characteristic institution
of modern advanced societies . . . it is seen as the prime mover of
economic, political and social change in Europe and America during
the past two centuries and, because of this, is in large measure the
"substructure" of the present social and cultural order.'

Professor Burns has selected Readings which examine the whole range
of influences of industrialization on social systems. They look at the
critical importance of industrialism as an agent of social change, at
the emergence of groupings peculiar to industry – management, the
labour force – and, above all, at the way our personal relationships,
careers and identities are defined by the industrial setting in which
they are worked out.

Tom Burns is Professor of Sociology at the University of Edinburgh,
and is General Editor of Penguin Modern Sociology.

Peasants and Peasant Societies
Edited by Teodor Shanin

This volume of Readings looks at five aspects of the subject: first, the units of peasant social organization – family farm, village community, etc.; second, the typical forms of production and exchange; third, the peasantry as a class; fourth, peasant cultural patterns, including customs, religions and aesthetics; and finally, some of the prevailing attitudes towards peasant societies, and the shape of government policies.

Teodor Shanin is Lecturer in Sociology at the University of Sheffield.

Social Inequality
Edited by André Béteille

Social inequality has always been one of the major preoccupations of sociology – largely, perhaps, because of the strong moral commitment which many sociologists bring their work.

Professor Béteille has tried to steer his selection between, on the one hand, philosophical speculation on the moral basis of equality, and on the other, an over-concern with the technique of analysis of stratification.

The result is a fascinating blend of sociology and social anthropology that looks at stratification along class, caste and racial lines in a wide range of different societies.

André Béteille is a Jawaharlal fellow, and Reader in Sociology at the University of Delhi.

Sociology of the Family
Edited by Michael Anderson

Michael Anderson's volume of Readings, which concentrates on the family in Western industrial society, is especially concerned to show the diversity of family types. But, he argues, the study of the family has too often gone no further than this sort of description – partly, perhaps, because the sociologist himself is inevitably emotionally involved with the subject. We need to develop new theoretical and methodological approaches to explain the enormous variety of relationships found inside the Western family.

Michael Anderson is Lecturer in the Department of Sociology at the University of Edinburgh.

Sociology of Law

Edited by Vilhelm Aubert

There are many superficial similarities between the disciplines of law and sociology: they both deal with concepts like rights and sanctions, and often have as the raw material of their analyses the same social phenomena.

But, as Professor Aubert points out, doctrinal legal research is concerned with how the law *ought* to operate, the sociology of law with *why* it operates in the way it does. Clearly the findings of the latter process are highly relevant to the proper functioning of the former.

In his five-part collection Professor Aubert looks at law as a product of a social system, and as an instrument of social change; at conflict resolution and decision making in the courts; and finally at the legal profession itself.

Vilhelm Aubert is Professor of the Sociology of Law at the University of Oslo, and also Research Director of the Oslo Institute for Social Research.

Witchcraft and Sorcery
Edited by Max Marwick

There are still many societies in existence for whom witchcraft, sorcery and other magical systems are tangible and threatening realities. Nor is our own emancipation from a belief in magic very far advanced, as is demonstrated by our continuing observance of superstitions.

Professor Marwick's collection of Readings paints a fascinating picture of the current worldwide status of witchcraft. Part One looks at the different approaches to the topic, and includes an extract from Evans-Pritchard's classic study of the Azande. Part Two samples the rich ethnography of witchcraft and contains papers on the European and Salem witch-hunts. Part Three looks at theories of witchcraft, and particularly at how witchcraft and cultist movements are often indicators of social strain. Part Four examines how a study of witchcraft can throw light on other sociological problems; on, for instance, the differences between 'primitive' and 'scientific' thought.

Max Marwick is Professor of Sociology at the University of Stirling, Scotland.